A HISTORY

OF THE

PEOPLE OF THE UNITED STATES,

FROM THE REVOLUTION TO THE CIVIL WAR.

BY

JOHN BACH McMASTER,
UNIVERSITY OF PENNSYLVANIA.

IN EIGHT VOLUMES.

VOLUME V.

1821-1830.

NEW YORK AND LONDON

D. APPLETON AND COMPANY

1914

Printed in the United States of America

To the Memory of
my Mother.

CONTENTS OF VOLUME V.

CHAPTER XL.

CHAPTER XLI.

CHAPTER XLII.

CHAPTER XLIII.

CHAPTER XLVI.

CHAPTER XLVII.

CHAPTER XLVIII.

CHAPTER XLIX.

CHAPTER L.

CHAPTER LI.

CHAPTER LIII.

MAPS.

HISTORY

OF THE

PEOPLE OF THE UNITED STATES.

CHAPTER XL.

TEXAS, OREGON, AND THE SLAVE-TRADE.

MARCH fourth, 1821, the day whereon, according to law, Monroe should a second time have taken the oath of office, fell on a Sunday. Never in our history had such an event happened on such a day, and, considering the peculiar character which the Christian world has given to the first day of the week, Monroe was uncertain what to do. Regard for the Sabbath prompted him to put off the oath till the morrow. Regard for his duty prompted him to take it the moment his first term expired. In the end his religious feelings triumphed, and he was sworn into office at noon on March fifth, thereby establishing a precedent which has twice been followed since his death.

The first important act of his second term was the appointment of Andrew Jackson to the Governorship of Florida. After two years of delay, due to the state of affairs in Spain, the Florida treaty of 1819 had at last been ratified by Ferdinand and reratified by the Senate of the United States on Washington's birthday, 1821. Time did not serve to organize the new territory; hence, beyond spreading over it the revenue laws and the law against the slave-trade, and authorizing the President to invest the powers of the existing Government in a proper person, no legislation had been attempted when the session closed. Whoever was sent as Governor would be invested, therefore, with all the immense powers of the old Captain-General of Cuba and the old Governors of Spanish Florida, save that he could neither levy taxes nor grant land. For this post a man of the utmost prudence was needed. But it pleased Monroe to select Jackson, because, in his opinion, some amends were due for the attack made upon the general in the House of Representatives two years before; because the victory at New Orleans had given him a popularity such as was not enjoyed by any other American then living; and because, by a recent act of Congress, he was about to be turned out of the military service of the United States.

The law provided that after June first, 1821, there should be but one major-general, and, as Jackson was the youngest in commission, he must go. That the nation might be spared the odium of discarding the most distinguished soldier then in her service, Monroe at once appointed him Governor of Florida, and commissioner to receive the territory from the Spaniards. He promptly accepted the office, and, while James Grant Forbes was despatched in the sloop of war Hornet to carry the order of the King of Spain to the Captain-General of Cuba for the delivery of the province, and bring back the necessary orders for the surrender of Florida, its forts, and its archives to the American commissioner, Jackson travelled slowly southward to Pensacola. At that city, in July, amid the tears and sobs of the people, the province was formally delivered to the Americans.

Had the weeping Spaniards at Pensacola looked over the world on that memorable July day, they could have found no spot on earth so blessed as the United States, no people so prosperous and happy as those with whom their lot was cast. Abroad, near by, around them on every hand, were nations struggling desperately for a little of that kind of liberty of which henceforth it was to be their privilege to enjoy so much. With all the details of the revolutions and counter-revolutions of Mexico and Colombia, Guatemala, Chili, Buenos Ayres, Naples, Greece, Portugal, and Spain we are most happily not concerned. Yet the story of them must be told with some fulness if we are to understand two memorable events of Monroe's second administration—the announcement of the doctrine that bears his name, and the early settlement of Texas.

The uprising of the Spaniards against Joseph Bonaparte, in June, 1808, had been followed by a struggle between the new King and the revolutionary juntas that sprang up in every Spanish city and struggled for control of the American colonies. Chief among these dependencies of the Crown was Mexico. There the natives of Spain and the Mexicans in office, influenced by the emissaries of Bonaparte, would gladly have obeyed the order of the Council of the Indies and declared for King Joseph. The Viceroy Iturigaroy and the Mexican people, led by the agents of the junta of Seville, were for adhering to Ferdinand Seventh; but, when agents of other juntas appeared and claimed to govern the country, the people in their distraction appealed to the viceroy to establish a revolutionary government for Mexico. As he was about to comply, the Spaniards holding office under the Crown seized and committed him to the prison of the Inquisition. When the junta of Seville heard of this, it approved the act, and appointed the Archbishop of Mexico viceroy. He was soon removed, however, and the government intrusted to the Court of Audience, which held it when the victories of Napoleon in Spain scattered the junta of Saville for the time being. It reassembled, however, at Cadiz, and sent out Don José Venegas as viceroy.

The dispersion of the junta had been the signal for a revolt of the native Mexicans under the lead of Don Miguel Hidalgo, a curate of Dolores, in the province of Guanaxuato. Half-breeds and creoles, Indians and mestizos, even royal troops, hurried to his standard, and, with an army growing as it marched, he set off for and took the city of Guanaxuato. The revolt now became general, and Hidalgo, after providing abundance of munitions with the money found in the city treasury, started for Mexico. His troops were many and enthusiastic; his supplies were plentiful; all opposition melted away as he approached, and there seemed to be nothing to stop his triumphant progress. But, though the viceroy had few troops, he had a weapon which to the ignorant and superstitious rabble that followed Hidalgo was far more terrible than guns and soldiers—the spiritual arms of Rome. This he used, and Hidalgo and his followers were excommunicated. To weapons of this sort the revolted priest paid no heed, and made his way to the outskirts of the city of Mexico. But his people had deserted him in such numbers that he was forced to retreat, was pursued, betrayed, taken, and executed in the usual Mexican way. One of his followers, Bernardo Gutierres, made good his escape, and, after a long flight across Texas, found refuge at Natchitoches, where he made the acquaintance of Lieutenant Augustus W. Magee.

Magee was a graduate of West Point, had caught the spirit of the Wilkinson school of soldiers on the frontier, and was quickly persuaded by Gutierres to join in an attempt to conquer Texas. To get followers was an easy matter, for the neutral strip which lay between the Sabine and the Arroyo Hondo had long been inhabited by a lawless, desperate set of freebooters, who lived by plundering the overland trade between Mexico and New Orleans, and were ready for any enterprise however reckless. A call to them to join the " Republican Army of the North " and receive forty dollars a month and a league of land in the Republic of Texas was promptly responded to, and in June, 1812, one hundred and fifty, under Gutierres, began their march for Spanish Bluffs, on the Trinity river. With the history of that army—how it captured Nacogdoches and the fort at Spanish Bluffs; how it crossed the Colorado and was besieged by Don Manuel de Salcedo, Governor of Texas, at La Bahia; how it drove him to San Antonio; how it captured the town, and treacherously put to death Salcedo, Simon de Herrera, Governor of New Leon, and a host of officers—need not be related. With the capture of San Antonio success left the Republicans. They deposed Gutierres, placed Don José Alvarez Toledo in command, were defeated, and in two months' time the few that remained were back on the west bank of the Sabine.

After establishing a camp at Gaines's Ferry, Toledo returned to the United States, collected arms, ammunition, and a few men, whom he led to El Puente del Rey, a place between Vera Cruz and Jalapa, fortified it, and waited for the troops of the Mexican republic to join him.

The fall of Hidalgo had not ended the struggle for independence. Another priest, Morelos by name, had rebelled, had raised an army in the southwestern provinces, had won a great battle at Tixtla, and had summoned a congress to meet at Chilpanzingo, which in 1812 published a declaration of independence, and sent Don José Manuel Herrera to represent the Mexican republic in the United States. But with the death of Morelos, while on his way to join Toledo at El Puente del Rey, the cause of the Republicans languished, and the duty of reviving it fell on Herrera.

For three years his efforts were fruitless; but in December, 1815, Don Luis Aury, with three small vessels, broke through the Spanish fleet which then besieged Cartagena and escaped. Gathering about him, as commodore of the joint fleet of Mexico, Venezuela, La Plata, and New Granada, some fifteen vessels, Aury was about to scour the gulf when Herrera persuaded him to co-operate in another attempt to conquer Texas. Learning from the former pirates of Barataria of the splendid harbor afforded by Galveston Bay, the commodore and the Minister decided to occupy it, and in September, 1816, landed on its beach, raised the flag of the republic, established a government, and chose Aury civil and military Governor of Texas and Galveston Island, which were declared part of the Republic of Mexico.

Success now seemed near. Men joined him from the United States. The pirates of Barataria, glad of a place of refuge, took service under his flag. A great slave-trade which he opened with New Orleans brought money, and, what was equally important, his army was increased by the unexpected arrival of Xavier Mina, a gallant soldier of Navarre, with arms, ammunition, military stores, and two hundred well-officered troops. By the spring of 1817 there were thus gathered at Galveston some six hundred fighting men under three commanders—Aury, Xavier Mina, and Colonel Perry—all ready and eager to act. Just at this time some letters taken by a privateer from a Spanish ship made known the defenceless state of the town of Soto la Marina—sixty miles up the Santander river—and against this, in April, the three commanders set out. It fell without opposition, and with its fall the expedition ended and the leaders parted. Aury, in a fit of jealousy, went back to Galveston. Mina, eager for more conquests, announced his determination to march farther inland. Perry, protesting that such a march was madness, led his troops toward the United States. Ill fortune attended them all. Mina was captured by the royal troops and put to death; Perry, after a desperate fight at La Bahia, in which every man who followed him was slain, blew out his brains on the field of battle; Aury, on his return to Galveston, found the place in the hands of the pirates, with Lafitte in command, and, after a vain effort to establish himself at Matagorda, he sailed away to join McGregor at Amelia Island, whence the United States drove him out.

With 1819 came the Spanish treaty, the adoption of the Sabine as part of the boundary, and the relinquishment of the claims of the United States to Texas. All over the southwest that treaty awakened profound indignation, but nowhere did it rise so high as in the town of Natchez. From it had gone out each of the expeditions which since the days of Philip Nolan had invaded Texas. To it had come for refuge every leader who, after his discomfiture, had escaped death. In it as a great river town enjoying a fine trade with the interior of Tennessee was gathered the most reckless, lawless, enterprising population—flatboatmen, steamboatmen, frontiersmen—to be found on the river. To them an appeal was made by the leaders of the new attempt, and at a public meeting a company of seventy-five volunteers was raised for the invasion of Texas. Dr. James Long, who, after serving as a surgeon at the battle of New Orleans, had settled at Natchez, was chosen to command, and early in June the little band set out for Nacogdoches. As they passed across Louisiana and crossed the Sabine and entered the old neutral ground, every survivor of former bands hurried to join them, so that when Nacogdoches was reached Long had with him some three hundred men. Among them was Bernardo Gutierres.

At Nacogdoches the "patriots"—so they called themselves—established a provisional government, appointed a supreme council of nine, and issued a proclamation declaring Texas to be a free and independent republic. The citizens of Texas, so the document reads, have long indulged the hope that when the boundaries of the Spanish possessions in America were drawn, Texas would be brought within the United States. An expectation so flattering has prevented any serious effort to throw off the yoke of Spain. But the recent treaty has dispelled the illusion so long and so fondly cherished, and roused the citizens of Texas from the torpor into which a fancied security lulled them. Spurning the fetters of colonial vassalage, scorning to submit to an atrocious despotism, they have therefore resolved, under the blessing of God, to be free, and are prepared unshrinkingly to meet and firmly to sustain any conflict in which this declaration may involve them.*

The supreme council then proceeded to make laws for raising revenue and disposing of the public lands, established a printing office, and despatched Colonel Gaines to Galveston to ask aid of Lafitte. The old pirate chief assured the officer that Long had his best wishes for success, but told him that the fate of Perry, Mina, and a host of others ought to show how idle it was to wage war by land with a small force of men. Long, however, would not profit by the advice, and, thinking that a personal visit to Lafitte might bring success, he set off for Galveston, and got back to find the Royalist army close at hand, his own forces scattered, and with difficulty made his escape to the United States.

Scarcely had Long and his troops been scattered when Moses and Stephen Austin, the final conquerors of Texas, made their appearance. Moses Austin was a native of Durham, in Connecticut, but, after a series of migrations, had taken up his abode about 1800 at the lead mines of Missouri, then a part of Spanish Louisiana. Whether it was the restless spirit which had driven him half across a continent, or the treaty of 1819, or the rapid settlement of Missouri, that turned his attention to Texas is uncertain, but it is known that in that year he began to make inquiries as to the best way of bringing a plan for the settlement of Texas before the au-

---

* Issued at Nacogdoches, June 23, 1819. Printed in full in Nile's Register, vol. xvii, p. 31.

thorities of Old Spain. He was advised to apply to the authorities of New Spain, and in 1820 set out for Bexar to do so. The story is related that Governor Martinez, to whom he applied, treated him as an intruder, bade him quit the province, and that he was actually on his way out when he fell in with the Baron de Bastrop, whose name is forever associated with that of Aaron Burr. Bastrop, it is certain, took up his cause, explained his purposes to the Governor, and obtained leave to draw up a memorial asking permission to colonize three hundred American families in the northeastern inland provinces. While the paper was on its way to the Commandant-General Don Joaquin Arredondo at Monterey, Austin started back to the United States. But between Bexar and the Sabine he was robbed and left to find his way as best he could to the Louisiana settlements. The exposure and suffering were too much for him, and in June, 1821, he died, laying a solemn injunction on his son, Stephen F. Austin, to go on with the scheme.

The injunction, it is needless to say, was obeyed; indeed, no sooner was the father buried than the son hastened to San Antonio, conferred with the Governor, selected his tract, and drew up the plan for distribution of the land among the settlers. The tract selected stretched along the coast from Galveston Bay to Matagorda Bay, and ran inland to the great highway connecting Nacogdoches and Bexar.

The terms of the grant required four things. Three hundred families must be brought in from Louisiana; each settler must be a Roman Catholic or become so before he put foot on the soil of Texas; must give evidence of good character and good habits; must take the oath of allegiance to the King of Spain, and swear to uphold the government and constitution of the Spanish monarchy. All who came on those conditions were to be assigned tracts of lands proportionate to the size of the family, and were to pay twelve and a half cents an acre.*

To find settlers ready to go on such terms was an easy

---

* Each man, 640 acres; a wife, 320 acres; each child, 160 acres; for each slave the owner was to have 80 acres.

matter, and in November, 1821, the schooner Lively, with eighteen emigrants, sailed for Matagorda Bay, while Austin with fourteen more went on by land to the Brazos, down which he hurried to the coast to meet the Lively. But of the schooner and her company no tidings of any kind ever reached him. For three months he waited and searched the coast, and then in despair went on to San Antonio to report his loss to the Governor.

It was March, 1822, when Austin reached the city and heard with amazement that Mexico was in rebellion against Spain. In 1816, when Apodaca succeeded Calleja as Viceroy of Mexico, he found the Republicans dispersed but far from conquered, and, in the hope of winning them back, adopted a mild policy of forgiveness. This proved successful. Leader after leader threw down his arms, till between Mexico city and Acapulco there was but one band of Republicans under arms. Their stronghold was a mountain on the road between the two cities, and was most difficult of access; their leaders were Guerrero, Asensio, and Bradburn, a native of Virginia, who had gone to Mexico with Mina, and their number about fifteen hundred.

In the hope of overcoming this last remnant of the Republicans, the viceroy appointed Augustine Iturbide to the command of the Department of the South, gave him some three thousand troops, sent him to Iguala, on the road to Acapulco, and bade him disperse the rebels. But before Iturbide had time to act news came of the revolution in Old Spain, of the re-establishment of the constitution, and of the introduction of reforms which aroused and alarmed the clergy. A cry for independence of the mother country was immediately raised, which Iturbide was not slow to turn to his own profit, and from his camp at Iguala he issued his pronunciamento in February, 1821. This famous plan proposed that Mexico should be turned into a limited constitutional monarchy; that the Crown should be offered to each member (if necessary) of the Bourbon family, beginning with Ferdinand Seventh; and that, if all refused it, the Mexican Cortes should select the king. A field-marshal with an army was at once sent against Iturbide. But the clergy, the soldiers, the whole people were behind him, and in four months' time Mexico was in their hands and Apodaca in prison. Hardly had these events happened when Lieutenant-General Don Juan O'Donojú, sent out by the reformed government of Spain, landed at Vera Cruz, approved what Iturbide had done, requested an interview, met him, and, on August twenty-fourth, signed and published the treaty of Cordova. Till Spain could act, a regency of six persons, with Iturbide president, was to administer government; and until a congress could assemble a junta of five persons was to act as a legislature. As Spain refused to ratify the treaty of Cordova, Mexico became free and independent.

The first Congress under the new order of things assembled on February twenty-fourth, 1822, and was already well on in a quarrel with Iturbide when Austin arrived at San Antonio and was told by the Governor that he must obtain a confirmation of his grant by the Congress. The prospect of success was poor; but he proceeded to Mexico, where he found Hayden Edwards, Robert Lefwitch, Green Dewitt, three Cherokee chiefs—Bolles, Fuldo, and Nicollet—and General James Wilkinson, each seeking a contract or a grant of land in Texas. So many applicants gave the matter much importance, and it was referred by the Congress to a committee who brought in a general colonization law, which was about to pass when, one morning in October, Iturbide perpetrated a political crime worthy of Charles and Cromwell.

Iturbide had long been quarrelling with the Congress and with the regency, and one night in May, when all was in readiness, the soldiers and the rabble, excited by his agents and headed by corporals and sergeants, filled the streets of Mexico and proclaimed him Emperor. It was a night of violence, of uproar, and of terror. The seven hundred bells of the city pealed from every convent, church, and monastery. Musketry and cannon were fired from the barracks, while the shouts of the mob announced to the startled people that the fate of Mexico was settled. When morning came the man thus proclaimed in darkness and in tumult by a rabble was duly decreed Emperor of Mexico by the Congress sitting in its hall surrounded by bayonets. Iturbide, who thenceforth called himself Augustine the First, having no further use for the Congress, determined to dismiss it, and accordingly, just after the members had assembled on the morning of October the thirtieth, General Cortazar entered the hall, read the imperial order dissolving Congress, and announced that if the members did not leave within ten minutes he would be compelled, in obedience to orders, to drive them from the building. The president directed the order to be spread on the journal, called on Cortazar to sign it, and, when the general had done so, the members retired.* The Emperor Augustine at once organized a Junta of thirty-five members named by himself, and by this body was enacted, in January, 1823, the first law for the colonization of Texas. It began with a repeal of the royal order of Philip Second for the extermination of foreigners; guaranteed them liberty, security of property and civil rights, provided they professed the Roman Catholic religion; promised each farmer not less than one labor,† and each stock-raiser not less than one league ‡ of land; and freed them for six years from the payment of all taxes, duties, and tithes. Settlers could come individually or as members of an empresario, or contractor's company.

Under this law the contract of Austin was formally approved in February, 1823, and he was about to return to his colony when another revolution swept the Emperor from his throne and restored the republic.

During all these many revolts, uprisings, and revolutions the castle of San Juan d'Ulloa had remained in the hands of Spain. Iturbide had attempted to secure the surrender of the castle by treaty, and had gone to Jalapa for this purpose, when a quarrel arose between Santa Anna, who commanded the city of Vera Cruz, and General Echavani, who commanded both the city and the southern division of the empire in which it lay. Santa Anna repaired to Jalapa to exculpate himself, but was rudely received and removed from command. Hurrying to Vera Cruz before the news of his dismissal was known, he paraded the troops, renounced allegiance to the Emperor,

---

* Poinsett's Notes on Mexico, p. 63.   ‡ A league was equal to 4,428 acres.
† A labor equalled 177 acres.

raised the standard of revolt, gathered an army about him under Guadalupe Victoria, Guerrero, and Bravo, and prepared for war. Iturbide in terror fled to Mexico, called together such members of the old Congress as were near, and tendered his resignation.* But, as a quorum was not present, they refused to act. A few days later,† when a quorum had assembled, his letter of abdication was again sent in. To accept it would be to legalize the acts by which he had established the empire. The Congress therefore would not consider his request, but allowed him to leave Mexico, promised him an annual pension of twenty-five thousand dollars, and he was soon on his way to Lisbon with his family.

The moment Iturbide was gone the old Congress appointed an executive of three men, summoned a new Congress, which promptly declared every act of the late Emperor void, and among them the colonization law of 1823 and the confirmation of Austin's contract. A new confirmation, however, was obtained from the executive, and in the early summer of 1823 Austin returned to Texas, laid off the town of Colorado, and marked out the foundation of San Felipe de Austin.

The new Congress—the Constituent Congress, as it was called—after a labor of five months framed and adopted the Constitution of the United States of Mexico, which created eighteen States and three Territories, and assigned to each the duty of establishing a government of its own.‡ Until this time the province of Texas had never been connected with that of Coahuila, which adjoined it; but by an act of the Cortes both were now joined and made the State of Coahuila and Texas.

The first Congress of this new State began its sitting in August, and in the following March passed a decree intended, "to increase the population of its territory, promote the cultivation of its fertile lands, the raising and multiplication of stock, and the progress of the arts and commerce." *

---

* March 8, 1823.   † March 19, 1823.

‡ The Constitution was adopted by the Congress on January 31, 1824, and proclaimed October 4, 1824.

* Leyes y Decretos del Estados de Coahuila y Texas Decreto No. 16, 24 de Marzo de 1825.

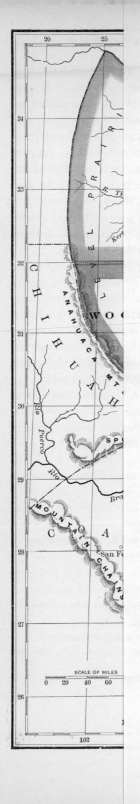

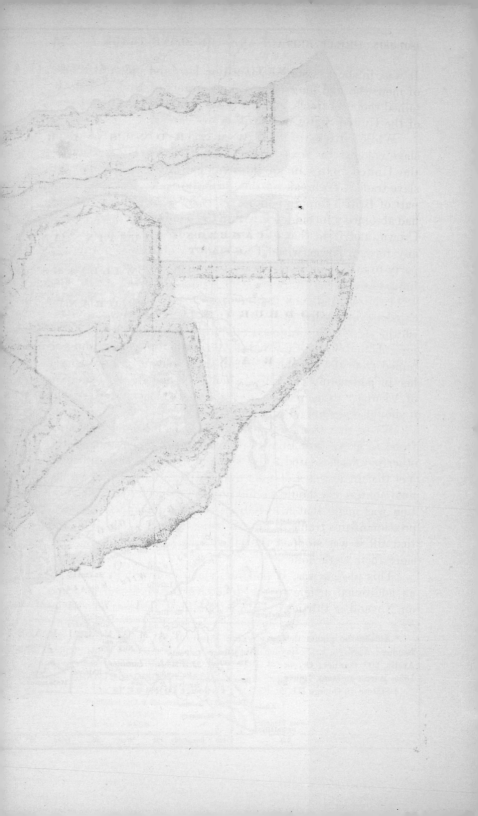

It was, in short, a state colonization law, and under it a host of men who had long been seeking grants of land at last obtained their contracts, and the settlement of Texas by citizens of the United States began in serious earnest. *

While citizens of the United States were thus planting slave colonies in Texas, Great Britain was striving to enlist the United States in an international effort to destroy the slave-trade. To break up this shameful traffic had long been part of British foreign policy. As early as 1807 † Parliament had absolutely forbidden it within the dominions of the British Crown, and from that day forward no treaty was made with any foreign power without an effort to bind the contracting party to take some steps toward the suppression or at least the limitation of the African slave-trade. Between 1810 and 1814 she secured such treaties from Portugal, Denmark, and Sweden; persuaded the Netherlands by royal decree to abolish the slave-trade; induced Spain to limit it to her own colonies; bound France to abolish it within five years; and obtained from the French Government a solemn promise to aid her in persuading the allies when they met in the Congress of Vienna "to decree the abolition of the slave-trade so that it should cease universally and forever."

When that Congress met in 1814, France and Spain refused to go further than they had already gone, and, as the other powers hesitated to press them, little was accomplished. Yet that little was a distinct gain. It was agreed that an annual conference should be held on the subject, and a declaration was made that all civilized nations demanded the suppression of this traffic in human beings as soon as possible, and that till it was stopped the allied sovereigns would not consider their work done.

This pledge was, if possible, made more binding still by an additional article to the definitive treaty signed at Paris on November thirtieth, 1815. The high contracting parties

---

* Among the grants then made were: April 15, 1825, Robert Leftwich, 200 families; April 18, 1825, Hayden Edwards, 800 families; June 4, 1825, Stephen Austin, 500 families; October 6, 1825, Green Dewitt, 300 families; October 6, 1825, Martin de Leon, 150 families.

† Statute 46 George III, ch. 52, 119; 47 George III, sess. I, ch. 36.

then declared that they had in their respective dominions prohibited their colonies and their subjects from taking any part in the slave-trave, and agreed to concert by their ministers at the court of London the most effective measures for the entire abolition of " the traffic so odious and so highly reproved by the laws of religion and Nature."

To neither of these solemn engagements would Spain or Portugal consent to be a party. Their flags, therefore, at once became the cover for a trade more cruel, more extensive, and more defiant than ever before. Slavers now came in brigs and swift-sailing schooners, well armed, well manned, and flying the flags of Portugal and Spain, and scoured the coast from Sherbro and the Gallinas to Cape Appolonia. Many of them were American privateers of the late war, and in more than one encounter beat off the Princess Charlotte, one of the armed vessels Great Britain kept on the coast. Another sent an insolent challenge to the Prince Regent to meet her. Others were not taken till a desperate engagement had been fought. Others, by sailing in company, were enabled to defy any force that could be brought against them. The Governor of Sierra Leone declared, in 1817, that the slave-trade was raging dreadfully. All commerce was stopped, as no vessel with negro sailors dared venture to sea.

In this state of affairs Great Britain, in 1817, under the treaty of Paris, invited the Ministers of Russia, Prussia, Austria, and France to a conference, and concluded conventions with Portugal and Spain. Each agreed to the abolition of the slave-trade north of the equator at once, and south of the line at a time in the near future. Just when, Portugal would not say; but Spain fixed the time as May thirtieth, 1820.

In December, 1817, the ministers met at London. Castlereagh reminded them that since the treaty of 1815 the slave-trade had greatly revived; that it had been attended with new horrors caused by the dreadful crowding of slaves into ships not intended for the transportation of human beings, but for escape from armed cruisers; and that Great Britain had made earnest effort to crush the growing evil, but had found the difficulties almost irrepressible. In the first place, the right of search, which was a belligerent right, had ceased with the war, and it had been found that unless the right was renewed and exercised in visiting ships engaged in this illicit trade, the trade would go on more prosperously than ever. In the second place, fraudulent papers were obtained so easily and real ownership hidden so adroitly that it was possible for the subject of any State to carry on the slave-trade while it remained legal for the subjects of any State. He proposed, therefore, that the five powers represented should frame a convention and agree to prohibit the importation of slaves into their dominion; to make the trafficking in slaves by their subjects a criminal offence; and to allow to their war ships the right to visit vessels suspected to be slavers; and that Portugal and Brazil should be urged to abolish the trade after May twentieth, 1820.

These propositions were at once sent off by the plenipotentiaries to their courts; but no answer was made till the second annual conference of the powers at Aix-la-Chapelle in October, 1818.

Meantime Castlereagh turned to the United States, and in June, 1818, transmitted to Richard Rush, our Minister in London, copies of treaties for the suppression of the slave-trade which Great Britain had concluded with Spain, Portugal, and the Netherlands, and formally invited the United States to join in like arrangements. But the thing was not to be thought of. The convention into which she would have us enter provided for mixed courts to be established in the colonial possessions of one of the parties. The United States had no colonies, nor was it clear that under the Constitution Congress could set up a court to execute its penal laws beyond its territorial limits—a court too whose judges were partly foreigners, who could not be removed by impeachment for corruption, and from whose decisions, even under the laws of the United States, there was no appeal. The convention would have provided again for a reciprocal right of search by such armed vessels of the two powers as might have especial authority and instructions. The admission of the right of search in time of peace for any purpose whatever would have raised a storm of indignation which no President and no party could then have withstood. For these reasons, there-

signed by the King.   In it was a provision for a limited
right of search by officers appointed by the two Governments
to cruise " on the coasts of Africa, America, and the West
Indies for the suppression of the slave-trade."

To come to an agreement with Great Britain on any matter was quite impossible.   An act of Russia had suddenly
brought up for discussion the question of the ownership of
Oregon.

In the autumn of 1818, as Mr. J. B. Prevost, the American commissioner sent out by the President to receive the
formal delivery of Astoria, was on his way home, he stopped
at the port of Monterey, in California.   While there he wrote
a long report of his mission, described the Columbia river,
the climate, soil, and physical features of Oregon, and closed
his narrative with an account of an incident which he thought
most serious.   Until 1816 the Russians, he said, had no settlement south of fifty-five degrees.   But in that year, excited
very probably by the glowing descriptions of Humboldt,
they had established two colonies of an important character.
One was at Atooi, in the Sandwich Islands.   The other was
on the California coast, a few leagues from San Francisco,
the northern limit of Spanish occupation.   Only two days before he reached Monterey two vessels had left that town for
the Russian settlement, carrying to it implements of husbandry and mechanics of every sort.   So plain an intention
to acquire a site on the shore of the Pacific by a race but
just emerging from savagery, and ruled by a chief who sought
not to emancipate but to inthrall, ought surely, Mr. Prevost
thought, to excite the serious apprehensions of the United
States.*

But it did not excite the apprehensions of the United
States, and neither the President nor Congress cared what
went on in Oregon.

In December, 1820, attention was for a moment drawn
to the country by a motion for a committee to inquire into
the situation of the settlements on the Pacific Ocean and the
expediency of occupying the mouth of the Columbia river.

---

* J. B. Prevost to the Secretary of State, November 11, 1818.

The committee were diligent, and soon made a long report and presented a bill to authorize the occupation of the Columbia and regulate trade with the Indian tribes.

The report began with a careful review of our title to the country, told of the discovery of the river; of its exploration by Lewis and Clarke; of the building of Fort Clatsop at its mouth; of the founding of Astoria; of the establishment by Astor's men of five sub-stations between the mountains and the sea; and dwelt at length on the value of the fur trade. It told of the wonderful energy displayed by the Hudson Bay and Northwest Fur Companies in their search for furs; how they carried the supplies intended for the Indians and the traders across the continent from Montreal to the Rocky Mountains, and brought back the furs by a route three thousand miles long, paddling their birch canoes through innumerable rivers, across more than sixty lakes, and carrying them over one hundred and thirty portages from a few yards to thirteen miles in length. Many of the establishments of the Northwest Company were within the limits of the United States. To bring to the people of the United States all the profits of this fur trade it was only necessary, therefore, to put a few troops on the upper waters of the Missouri, and confine the British to their own domain. If the Canadians could carry on their trade in spite of such natural obstacles, how much more easily and profitably could the citizens of the United States conduct theirs along the deep and smooth Missouri, running through a soil of boundless fertility, and separated by a portage of less than two hundred miles from another great river flowing into the Pacific! This portage was not a matter of doubt. In several places the Rocky Mountains were so smooth and open that ten men in twenty days could take a wagon loaded with furs from the navigable waters of the Missouri to those of the Columbia. All that was needed to develop Oregon was a small and permanent post at the mouth of the Columbia, and this was provided for in the bill.

To the majority of Congressmen who listened to the report, Oregon and the upper waters of the Missouri seemed farther away and less accessible than Africa. That the United States could ever want a foothold on the Pacific seemed preposterous, and, having heard the visionary report of the committee, their bill was laid on the table.

There it lay when, one day in February, 1822, the Chevalier Pierre de Politica, the Russian Minister, placed a most alarming document in the hands of the Secretary of State. It was an edict of the Emperor Alexander, and set forth that the pursuits of commerce, whaling, and fishing, and, indeed, of all other industries, whether on the islands or in the ports and gulfs of the northwest coast of America from Behring Strait to fifty-one degrees, were exclusively granted to Russian subjects. Foreign vessels were therefore forbidden not only to land on the coast and islands, but even to come within one hundred Italian miles of them.

So unexpected an attempt to define the boundary of the two countries aroused the President, who demanded of the Russian Minister the grounds on which it was based. Why had not the boundary been arranged by treaty? Why were vessels of the United States excluded beyond the limit to which territorial jurisdiction extended? He answered that the Russians had long maintained a settlement at Novo Archangelsk, in latitude fifty-seven, and that fifty-one degrees was about midway between Novo Archangelsk and the mouth of the Columbia. The restriction forbidding an approach to the coast was laid in order to keep out foreign adventurers who, not content with carrying on an illicit trade injurious to the interests of the Russian American Fur Company, had supplied arms and ammunition to the natives of the Russian possessions in America and incited them to revolt.* Against these doctrines Adams protested; † but Politica cut short the discussion by the statement that he had no authority to continue it.‡

This curt answer gave a new aspect to the matter, and Monroe, in his annual message to Congress in December, 1822, suggested that the time had come to think seriously of occupying Oregon. The House at once called up the old bill of 1821,

---

* Politica to Adams, February 28, 1822.
† Adams to Politica, March 30, 1822.
‡ Politica to Adams, April 2, 1822.

and listened again to speeches in which the manifest intention of Great Britain to seize and hold the country, the great value of the fur trade of the upper Missouri and Columbia valleys, and the many advantages to be derived from a settlement on the Pacific coast were once more set forth with argument and statistics, all to no purpose. The House flatly refused to consider it.

Failure in the House did not discourage the friends of the idea in the Senate, and a couple of weeks later Benton moved that the Committee on Foreign Relations be instructed to inquire into the expediency of making an appropriation to enable the President to take and hold possession of our Territories on the northwest coast. To this the Senate agreed. But the session soon ended, and no report was made.

Two months after the members had gone to their homes Adams received a note from the Baron de Tuyl, who had succeeded the Chevalier de Politica, asking that the American Minister at St. Petersburg be given power to settle the differences by negotiation.* The invitation was accepted, and instructions were duly drawn and despatched.†

While Adams was busy preparing them, the baron called one morning at the Department of State, and, in the course of conversation, was told that Russia's claim to a right to colonize on the Pacific coast could not be listened to, because both North and South America, in consequence of the independent position the nations of this hemisphere had assumed and maintained, were closed to colonization by European powers. From this doctrine the baron dissented most heartily; but it seems to have impressed Mr. Adams so strongly that it was reasserted by him in a letter to our Minister at St. Petersburg.

Mr. Middleton was to admit no part of the Russian claims, and rest those of the United States on the Spanish treaty of 1819, which secured all the rights and pretensions of Spain to the coast north of forty-two degrees; on the discovery of the Columbia by Gray, on the exploration of the country by

---

* Baron de Tuyl to Adams, April 24, 1823.
† Adams to Mr. Middleton, July 22, 1823.

Lewis and Clark, and on the settlement at Astoria. He might, however, agree that no citizen of the United States should land at any Russian settlement without permission of the Russian commander, that no subjects of the Emperor should land at any American settlements without consent of the American authorities, and that no American settlements should be made north and no Russian settlements should be established south of fifty-five degrees north latitude.

Meantime Great Britain had protested against the imperial ukase, and had in like manner been invited to an amicable negotiation for the adjustment of her claims. It was supposed that, as England and America held the country in joint occupation, the two nations would carry on a joint negotiation with Russia. But when it was found that the British envoy had power to discuss but not to conclude anything, and that authority to act jointly was not likely to be given him, Henry Middleton began the negotiation on behalf of the United States alone by offering fifty-five degrees as a boundary or line of demarcation. Russia then offered fifty-four degrees forty minutes, which was accepted and incorporated in the convention signed in April, 1824.

The discussion thus raised by Russia made it most fitting that the United States and England should come to an understanding as to their respective pretensions. Adams therefore instructed Richard Rush to bring up the matter and to state definitely the grounds on which the United States took her stand. The Russian application of the colonial principle of exclusion was not to be admitted as lawful on any part of the northwest coast of America. Indeed, it was to be denied that such a principle could be applied by any European nation. It was true that, by the Nootka Sound Convention of 1790, England had agreed that, so far as Spanish settlements extended in North and South America, Spain possessed the exclusive rights territorial, and of navigation and fishery, to a distance of ten miles from the coasts so actually occupied. But the independence of the South American nations and of Mexico had extinguished, said Adams, the exclusive colonial rights of Spain in North and South America, and " the American continents henceforth will no longer be subjects of colonization. Occupied by civilized independent nations, they will be accessible to Europeans on that footing alone, and the Pacific Ocean and every part of it will remain open to the navigation of all nations, in like manner with the Atlantic."

As to the boundary, Rush was to offer to stipulate that no settlements be made in future by the Russians south of fifty-five degrees, by citizens of the United States north of fifty-one degrees, or by British subjects either south of fifty-one or north of fifty-five degrees. He might, however, if England insisted on it, accept forty-nine degrees as the boundary from the Rocky Mountains to the sea. These two propositions were accordingly made by Rush, and were met, the one with a declination and the other with a flat denial. Great Britain, it was answered, considered the whole of the unoccupied parts of America open to her for settlement in the future just as they had been in the past, and would make no exception of the northwest coast, whether north of forty-two degrees or south of fifty-one. Yet she would from pure goodness, from a desire to close sources of disagreement which the future might multiply and aggravate, waive her rights and suggest a line of demarcation. This line was the parallel of forty-nine degrees from the summit of the Rocky Mountains to the northeasternmost branch of the Columbia river, and thence down the Columbia to the Pacific Ocean. Rush rejected it as promptly as England had rejected that of the United States, and tendered forty-nine degrees from the mountains to the sea. Again England declined the offer, and the negotiation came to naught.*

So the matter stood when Monroe, in December, 1824, met Congress for the last time. In his message he once more called attention to our interests on the Pacific coast, once more urged the establishment of a military post at the mouth of the Columbia river, and the House once more went back to the matter. The old bill was taken up, and, when the objections had been made and answered, it was passed. In the Senate, however, it encountered strong opposition from men

---

* Negotiations ended in July, 1824.

whose ideas were best expressed by a senator from New Jersey. He objected because the ten years of joint occupation under the convention of 1818 had not yet expired; because till it had expired, to take possession by military force would be highly improper; because we had never yet spread our laws over a territory but with the intention of sooner or later making it a State, and a State Oregon never could be. Our union, said Mr. Dickerson, is already too extensive. The distance from the mouth of the Columbia to the mouth of the Missouri is 3,555 miles. But the mouth of the Missouri is 1,148 miles from Washington, which city is therefore 4,703 miles from the mouth of the Columbia. Suppose now that Oregon is a State in the Union, and that a member of Congress from the far western confines of our country sets out from his home to make the journey of 4,700, or say 4,650 miles to Washington. At the rate members of Congress travel, according to law—that is, twenty miles a day—he would require, to come to the seat of government and go home again, four hundred and sixty-five days. If he should lie by on Sundays—say sixty-six of them—he would spend five hundred and thirty-one days on the way. But suppose he made haste, and travelled thirty miles each day and rested every Sunday, he would then consume three hundred and fifty days. This would enable a young and energetic traveller to leave his home, come to Washington, spend two weeks attending to his duties in the House, and get back home again in the course of just one year to a day. For this long and perilous journey he would receive $3,720 dollars as mileage. He might come by water around Cape Horn, or by Behring Strait around the north coast of our continent to Baffin's Bay, and so to Washington. True, this northwest passage had not been discovered except on the maps. But it would be before Oregon became a State.

Benton answered him. Ignoring what he was pleased to consider Mr. Dickerson's wit, the senator from Missouri reviewed at great length the claims of the two countries to Oregon, declared ours to be incontestable, and to rest on the discovery of the Columbia by Captain Gray in 1790; on the purchase of Louisiana in 1803; on the exploration or discovery of the Columbia from its head to its mouth by Lewis and Clark in 1805; on the settlement at Astoria in 1811; and on the Spanish treaty of 1819.

The question of title disposed of, Benton turned to that of occupation. On this he took four positions: That the United States had the right of possession; that Great Britain had actual possession; that she resisted occupation by the United States; and that after 1828 the party *in* possession would have the right of possession till ownership was settled by negotiation or by arms. After touching briefly on the first point, Benton passed to the second, and reminded the Senate that the delivery of Astoria to the United States was a pretence and a shame. Mr. Prevost, said Benton, was carried on a British sloop of war from Lima to Astoria where he stayed just five days. During this time he signed a receipt for the delivery of the post, and accepted a remonstrance from the British, protesting against the delivery till the question who owns Oregon had once and for all been decided. This was all he did. The actual control of the fort was not changed for an hour. The British flag was hauled down and the Stars and Stripes were run up to satisfy the words of the Treaty of Ghent. But Mr. Prevost could not man the fort himself. He brought no sailors and no soldiers to do so for him, and on the day he sailed away it was as much under the crown of Great Britain as on the day he came. Over it at this moment the British flag is flying. It still bears the name of Fort George, and at it the medals of George the Fourth are still distributed to the chiefs of the surrounding Indian tribes. And more than this: Five other posts have since been built along the banks of the Columbia from the sea to the mountains, as part of a great cordon three thousand miles in length stretching along our frontier for a purpose which every citizen and every Indian of the West well understands, and which the United States makes no effort to counteract.

In evidence of his third point, Benton cited the public documents. He recalled to the Senate how, in 1815, the British *chargé d'affaires*, Mr. Baker, had refused to give an order for the delivery of Astoria; how in 1817 Mr. Bagot, the Minister, had remonstrated against the occupation of the country by the United States; how in 1821 Mr. Canning, then Minister, when the question of occupation was before Congress, had twice attempted to arrest discussion; and how, inspired by British agents, the National Intelligencer had published essay after essay ridiculing the claim of the United States to any part of the northwest coast of America. " With a fleet on the coast, with a fort at the mouth of the Columbia, with batteries along its banks, with a line of posts to Canada and 140,000 Indians at her command, does any man suppose that when 1828 comes Great Britain will give up possession of the country she is doing so much to secure?

" But gentlemen ask, What are the advantages to be derived from occupation? I answer, The advantages will be securing of the fur trade of the Columbia, the Rocky Mountains, and the upper Missouri; preventing the Russians and the British getting control of the Indians on the Columbia; a naval station for us on the Pacific; communication between the valley of the Mississippi and the Pacific; and, chief of all, the exclusion of foreign powers from Oregon.

" Gentlemen ask again, What effect will a new territory or a new State have on the Union? I answer, It will be the nucleus of a new and independent power. This Republic should have limits. Where they should be on the north or the south is not now for me to say. But westward they are fixed by the hand of Nature, and the ridge of the Rocky Mountains may be named as offering a convenient, natural, and everlasting boundary. In planting the seed of a new power on the western coast, it should be well understood that when strong enough to take care of itself the new Government should separate from the mother empire as the child separates from the parent. You think this is looking far into the future. It is not. Within a century from this day a population greater than that of the present United States will exist on the west side of the Rocky Mountains.

" But the question now before us is, Shall we execute the Treaty of Ghent, expel the British from the Columbia, perfect our title, and take possession of the country? What use shall then be made of it is to be settled later. But on one point there should be no doubt—the people of the United

States will neither be tricked nor bullied out of this territory, nor suffer a monarchical power to grow upon it."

The manly speech of Benton fell on dull ears. The report of Major Long had done its work.* That magnificent stretch of rolling prairie which lies between Missouri and Iowa on the east and the Rocky Mountains on the west, and extends from Texas to our northern frontier—a region now cut up into eight States, supporting a population of more than five millions, dotted with towns and cities, five of which may each boast of more inhabitants than any city in the Union in 1825; a land of wheat fields and cornfields and mines and ranches— was condemned as a wilderness, over which buffaloes and Indians might roam, but on which civilized man could find no habitation. With such a desert barrier between the States and Oregon, it seemed idle to the senators to give any heed to the Pacific coast, and the bill for the occupation of the mouth of the Columbia river was laid upon the table by a vote of twenty-five to fourteen.

---

* " The vast region commencing near the sources of the Sabine, Trinity, Brazos, and Colorado, and extending northwardly to the forty-ninth degree of north latitude, by which the United States territory is limited in that direction, is, throughout, of a similar character. The whole of this region seems peculiarly adapted as a range for buffaloes, wild goats, and other wild game, incalculable multitudes of which find ample pasturage and subsistence upon it.

" This region, however, viewed as a frontier, may prove of infinite importance to the United States, inasmuch as it is calculated to serve as a barrier to prevent too great an extension of our population westward."—Long's Expedition, vol. ii, p. 361.

sion of Pinckney from France, the insult to the X. Y. Z. commissioners, the naval war with France, served but to prove the wisdom of Washington's policy and the soundness of his reasons, and drew from Jefferson on two occasions indorsements both vigorous and precise. On the day he was inaugurated the first time he took occasion to remind his countrymen of the happiness of their lot, of the fact that much of that happiness was due to separation from Europe, and told them that the essential principles of our Government—the principles which should shape his administration—were " peace, commerce, and honest friendship with all nations—entangling alliances with none." *

When Jefferson spoke these words Europe was fast being pacified by Napoleon. But when he met Congress in December, 1803, peace had been broken, the Napoleonic wars had opened, our country was again called on to declare her position toward Europe, and for the second time he asserted his policy of " peace, commerce, and friendship with all—entangling alliances with none." +

Thus, before the days of the Long Embargo and our

---

* *Jefferson's Inaugural Address, March 4, 1801.*—Kindly separated by Nature and a wide ocean from the exterminating havoc of one quarter of the globe; too high-minded to endure the degradations of the others; possessing a chosen country, with room enough for our descendants to the hundredth and thousandth generation; entertaining a due sense of our equal right to the use of our own faculties, to the acquisitions of our industry, to honor and confidence from our fellow-citizens, resulting not from birth but from our actions and their sense of them; enlightened by a benign religion, professed, indeed, and practised in various forms, yet all of them including honesty, truth, temperance, gratitude, and the love of man; acknowledging and adoring an overruling Providence, which by all its dispensations proves that it delights in the happiness of man here and his greater happiness hereafter; with all these blessings, what more is necessary to make us a happy and prosperous people? . . . It is proper that you should understand what I deem the essential principles of our Government, and consequently those which ought to shape its administration . . . peace, commerce, and honest friendship with all nations—entangling alliances with none.

† *Jefferson's Annual Message, October 17, 1803.*—Separated by a wide ocean from the nations of Europe, and from the political interests which entangle them, together with productions and wants which render our commerce and friendship useful to them, and theirs to us, it cannot be the interest of any to assail us, nor ours to disturb them.

struggle for commercial independence, the principle had been announced over and over again that we would not meddle in European affairs. The counterpart of this—the principle that the Old World must not meddle in the affairs of the New—was called forth by the attempt of Spain to get back her lost colonies in South America.

As all the world knows, the overthrow of the French at Waterloo was followed by a second abdication of Napoleon, by a second lifting of the wretched Louis Eighteenth to the throne of France, and by a second meeting of the allied Kings or their representatives at Paris in the autumn of 1815. To the mind of Alexander of Russia, this new triumph over the " Man of Destiny " was but another signal instance of the mysterious workings of Providence; but another demonstration of the great truth that God in his own good time will confound the policy of the wicked and will raise up those who put their trust in him. So deeply was Alexander convinced of this that he determined then and there to rule henceforth, and, if possible, persuade his fellow-monarchs to rule in strict accordance with the principles of the Christian religion. To accomplish this end the more easily, he persuaded Frederick William, King of Prussia, and Francis, Emperor of Austria, to join with him in a league which he called the Holy Alliance, and to sign a treaty which is commonly supposed to have bound the allies to pull down constitutional government and stamp out liberal ideas. It did nothing of the sort.

It was, in truth, a meaningless pledge, framed in a moment of religious excitement, and well described in its own words, which assert " that the present act has no other aim than to manifest to the world their unchangeable determination to adopt no other rule of conduct either in the government of their respective countries or in their political relations with other governments than the precepts of that holy religion, the precepts of justice, charity, and peace."

Considering themselves members of one great Christian family whose real and only sovereign was Almighty God, these three kings announced that they looked on themselves " as delegates of Providence " sent " to govern so many branches of the same family," and would make the Word of

flung into prison. Great Britain protested and urged the King to stop; but priests, confessors, and palace favorites ruled him, and the work went steadily on. May twenty-third he re-established the monasteries and gave them their old lands; June twenty-fourth he exempted the clergy from taxation; July twenty-first he once more put in operation the most diabolical of all the inventions of man—the Spanish Inquisition. But it mattered little, for of what consequence is it how people are governed in Spain?

That France must sooner or later have experienced a like reaction was inevitable. Signs of the coming storm were already apparent when, on March first, 1815, Napoleon landed with his guards in the bay of Juan, and the Hundred Days commenced. When they had ended, when the news of Waterloo spread over France, the storm broke with fury. A Royalist mob at Marseilles sacked the quarters of the Mamelukes, drove out the garrison, and murdered the citizens. Nismes was pillaged. Avignon disgraced herself by the foul murder of Marshal Brune, and Toulouse by the assassination and savage mutilation of General Ramel. When the Chamber of Deputies, chosen in the midst of this excitement, assembled, a new proscription, a new emigration, a new reign of terror began. Labédoyère was executed. Ney was shot. Royalist committees, in imitation of the Jacobin clubs, sprang up in every department, overawed the officials, and forced them to drive thousands of Liberalists from the army, from the navy, from the courts of law, and from the schools and colleges.

In Germany, in 1815, it seemed as if Liberalism would win. At the very moment when Ferdinand of Spain was about to issue his manifesto establishing the monasteries, Frederick William (May twenty-second, 1815) sent forth his promise that Germany should have a constitution and representative assembly, and that the work of framing the Constitution should begin in September. But delays arose, and two years sped by before even the first step was taken. Then it was too late. The middle classes cared not. The nobility were eager for a restoration of their old privileges. The sole defenders of the Constitution were the professors in the universities, the students, and the journalists, who conducted their cause with so much more zeal than wisdom that after the famous Warburg Festival took place in 1817 Frederick William justly and seriously doubted the expediency of granting the promised liberty.

Amid all this reaction, one ruler, and one alone, stood out as the earnest friend of liberal ideas. Alexander of Russia, too, had made promises. But, unlike Frederick William, he had kept them, had restored the Duchy of Warsaw to independence as the Kingdom of Poland, had given it a constitution and representative assembly, and in the spring of 1818 summoned the Diet. The speech which he addressed to it marked him out as one of the most advanced of Liberals. Yet before the Diet ended its session a great change came over him. What caused it no man knows; but when, in October, 1818, he met the sovereigns and ministers at the Conference of the Powers, Alexander was the despot he ever after lived and died.

By the Quadruple Treaty, signed at Paris in 1815, England, Prussia, Russia, and Austria bound themselves to maintain the government they had just set up in France, and to hold a Congress of the Powers in 1818. They met, accordingly, in September, at Aix-la-Chapelle, and with that conference a new era opens in the constitutional history of Europe. Then and there was formed the real "Conspiracy of Kings." The reactionary movement of three years had extinguished in the hearts of the best of them the last trace of liberalism, and they all stood together on a common ground of hatred of popular liberty. It was the conference at Aix-la-Chapelle, not the Holy Alliance, that united the sovereigns in the project of a joint regulation of European affairs, and turned the Holy Allies into a mutual association for the insurance of monarchy.

Scarcely had this new purpose been formed when the alliance was called upon to act. For ten years past the Spanish colonies in America had been in a state of revolt, first against the rule of Joseph Bonaparte, and then against the tyranny of Ferdinand Seventh. Every resource of the restored King was used against them and used in vain. The struggle went on till, the last fleet having been fitted out, the last regiment having been sent to perish of yellow fever, and the last dollar having been drawn from the treasury, Ferdinand turned to the sovereigns of Europe for aid. They had restored to him his throne. It is not surprising, therefore, that he should ask them to restore his colonies; but it is amusing to note the impudence with which he intimated that the work of subjugation should be done by Great Britain. She might have acted as mediator. More she would not do, and as subjugation, not mediation, was wanted, Alexander came to the relief of Ferdinand and sold him a fleet of war. When it reached Cadiz it was found that this Emperor, who in 1815 was so eager to see all Europe ruled in accordance with the teachings of Christ, had sold his friend ships so rotten and unseaworthy that not one of them was fit to cross the Atlantic.

The expedition was put off, and the condition of Spanish America was laid before the sovereigns when they met at Aix-la-Chapelle. The dangers which threatened Europe if a federation of republics was allowed to grow up in America were discussed; a proposition was made that a conference between Spain and the powers should be held at Madrid, and that Wellington should preside; but Spain wanted troops, not advice, and the proposition was not accepted.

That our countrymen could look on with indifference while so gallant a struggle for liberty was at their very doors was impossible. They were deeply concerned, and, as time passed, the belief gained ground among them that something more than the independence of a few colonies was at stake; that Spain was less eager to put down rebellion than to stamp out liberal ideas; that rather than see her fail, all European nations would aid her; and that, if they succeeded, it was just possible that the United States, whose example was the cause of so much political unrest, might be the next to feel their vengeance. Monroe therefore said no more than many of his countrymen were thinking when he told them in his first inaugural speech that dangers from abroad were threatening, and that the day might come when, in spite of the wide ocean and our policy of non-intervention, we might be attacked and the attempt made to demolish us as a nation.*

Till that day came, however, our policy was to be strict neutrality, and year after year in his annual messages Monroe insisted on it.† Even when it was known that the powers were to meet at Aix-la-Chapelle and that Spain would surely ask the Holy Allies to help her, the President, unwilling to believe that force would be used, still held to non-intervention.‡

The failure of the Holy Allies to interfere left Spain to deal with her colonies in her own way. Her way was to gather a rabble at Cadiz in the summer of 1819, call it an

---

* Dangers from abroad are not less deserving of attention. Experiencing the fortune of other nations, the United States may again be involved in war, and it may, in that event, be the object of the adverse party to overset our government, to break our union, and demolish us as a nation. Our distance from Europe, and the just, moderate, and pacific policy of our Government, may form some security against these dangers, but they ought to be anticipated and guarded against.— Monroe's Inaugural Speech, March 4, 1817.

† *Monroe's First Annual Message, December 2, 1817.*—It was anticipated, at an early stage, that the contest between Spain and the colonies would become highly interesting to the United States. It was natural that our citizens should sympathize in events which affected their neighbors. It seemed probable, also, that the prosecution of the conflict, along our coasts and in contiguous countries, would occasionally interrupt our commerce and otherwise affect the persons and property of our citizens. These anticipations have been realized. Such injuries have been received from persons acting under the authority of both the parties, and for which redress has in most instances been withheld. Through every stage of the conflict, the United States have maintained an impartial neutrality, giving aid to neither of the parties in men, money, ships, or munitions of war. They have regarded the contest not in the light of an ordinary insurrection or rebellion, but as a civil war between parties nearly equal, having, as to neutral powers, equal rights.

‡ It appears that the allies have undertaken to mediate between Spain and the South American provinces, and that the manner and extent of their interposition would be settled by a congress which was to have met at Aix-la-Chapelle in September last. From the general policy and course of proceedings observed by the allied powers in regard to this contest, it is inferred that they will confine their interposition to the expression of their sentiments, abstaining from the application of force. . . . From the view taken of this subject, founded on all the information that we have been able to obtain, there is good cause to be satisfied with the course heretofore pursued by the United States with regard to this contest, and to conclude that it is proper to adhere to it, especially in the present state of affairs.—Monroe's Annual Message, November 17, 1818.

army, and send it off to America. Before it could sail, yellow fever broke out, the troops went into camp, and while there were won over to the cause of constitutional government by the agents of a great conspiracy which had long been growing under the tyranny of the King. On January first, 1820, the day fixed for the outbreak, the troops, under Colonels Quiroga and Riego, rose and declared for the Constitution of 1812. The rebellion of the soldiers was a small affair in itself, but it set an example; it stirred up others, and on February twentieth the garrison and people of Corunna in their turn proclaimed the Constitution.

And now rebellion spread fast. Town after town followed Corunna. The whole country was up, and Ferdinand in great alarm announced his willingness to assemble the Cortes. His people had long since learned that his word was of no value, and, filling the great squares in Madrid, they clamored all day long for the Constitution. Then he gave way, and agreed to take the oath to support the Constitution. The next day—the famous eighth of March, 1820—was one of wild rejoicing. The prison of the Inquisition was sacked; the instruments of torture were broken in pieces; political prisoners were set free, and the Constitution carried in procession through the streets. March ninth a mob entered the palace, forced the King to make good his promise, and constitutional government once more existed in Spain.

As tidings of the collapse of absolute government in Spain spread over Europe, all the members of the Holy Alliance save Alexander seemed uncertain what to do. He alone acted with decision, and at once insisted that the great powers should require the Cortes to disavow the revolution of the eighth of March—the revolution to which it owed its existence—and give a pledge of obedience to the King. In such a demand England flatly refused to join, and the first proposed attack on Spanish liberty by the Holy Alliance was postponed.

Meantime absolute monarchy fell at Naples. The success of the Liberalists in Spain aroused the Carbonari, a great secret society with lodges in every city and hamlet, and a membership numbering at least one quarter of the male inhabitants of the Kingdom of Naples. They had long been plotting and secretly waiting for the hour of deliverance which now seemed at hand. Ferdinand of Sicily was the uncle of Ferdinand of Spain, and, as he might some day be called to the Spanish throne, he too had signed and sworn to support the Constitution of 1812 that his claims to the Crown might not be endangered. If he were willing to have a Constitution in a country which he might some day rule, why not force him to give the same Constitution to the kingdoms over which he was already ruler? The Carbonari could see no reason, and, rising in armed rebellion, they compelled Ferdinand to proclaim the Constitution of Spain to be the law of the Kingdom of the Two Sicilies, and on July thirteenth, 1820, he took the oath to maintain it.

The men of Portugal were next to awake, and in September, 1820, they deposed the Regency which ruled in the name of the absent King, set up a junta, and elected a Cortes to frame a constitution. For a moment it seemed not unlikely that France might be the next nation to throw off the yoke of absolutism. But Louis cried out for another meeting of the powers, and in October, 1820, the Emperor of Austria met the Czar and the King of Prussia in the little town of Troppau, in Moravia. England sent an ambassador, but he was instructed to look on and do nothing. France sent two envoys, but they took opposite sides, and her influence counted for nothing. The three founders of the Holy Alliance were thus free to do as they pleased, and very quickly decided what course to take. Ferdinand was to be invited to meet them at Laybach; a summons was to be sent, through him, to the Neapolitans to abandon their Constitution or fight; and a circular explaining and defending the new doctrine of armed intervention was to be issued, in the name of the three powers, to all the Courts of Europe. The events of March eighth in Spain, and those of July second in Naples, have produced, said the circular, a deep feeling of inquietude and alarm, and a desire to unite and save Europe from the evils ready to burst upon her. That this desire should be most keen with governments which not long ago conquered the revolution, and now see it once more appearing triumphant, is natural. The allied powers have therefore availed themselves of an incontestable right, and have decided to take common measures of precaution and restrain such states as, having revolted against legitimate governments and institutions, are seeking by their agents to introduce like disorders and insurrections into other states. As the revolution at Naples strikes deeper root every day, and sensibly menaces the tranquillity of the neighboring powers, it is necessary to immediately apply to her the principles agreed on.

Before resorting to force, however, it was thought best, the circular went on to say, to make one effort of a peaceful character and summon the King of Naples to meet the Allied Powers at Laybach.

Thither in January, 1821, with the consent of the Neapolitan Parliament, the old King accordingly went, leaving his son to act as regent, only to be told that if the order of things existing since July, 1820, was not at once abolished an Austrian army would occupy Neapolitan soil. The same ultimatum was made known to the prince regent at Naples, who stoutly refused to consider it, and summoned the Parliament, which declared that it considered the old King as under restraint at Laybach, bade the Grand Duke of Calabria continue to exercise the regency, and ordered measures to be taken for the safety of the state. A rush to arms followed. The Prince put himself at the head of most of the troops. The King appealed to the others; but they answered that they would not serve against their fellow-countrymen, and cried out for the Constitution. Ferdinand, now reduced to impotence, abdicated and went back to Sicily, and one hundred thousand Austrians entered Italy and crushed the republican uprisings in Naples, in Piedmont, in all Italy, and Ferdinand, in spite of his abdication, was restored to the throne of Naples.

A new declaration and a new circular were then issued by the Holy Allies, about to separate at Laybach, and in this circular was announced a principle which was to guide them in their future dealings with nations struggling for liberty. Having, in the language of the time, " taken the people of Europe into their holy keeping," the three autocrats declared that henceforth all " useful or necessary changes in the legislation and administration of states must emanate alone from the free will, the reflecting and enlightened impulse of those whom God has rendered responsible for power! "

Tidings of the collapse of absolute government in Spain reached the United States in March, 1820, and were welcomed with unconcealed delight. The cause of the republics of South America became more than ever the cause of liberty and constitutional government, and found no warmer champion in all the land than Henry Clay. The time to be neutral had, in his opinion, long passed, and determined to force the administration from its position of neutrality, he demanded a speedy recognition of the independence of the young republics. Toward this end the House, over which he presided as Speaker, could do little, but that little he easily persuaded it to do, and in May secured the passage of a resolution that it was expedient to provide a suitable outfit and salary for such Ministers as the President might send to any of the governments of South America which had established and were maintaining their independence of Spain.*

Monroe saw fit to send none. He was anxiously awaiting the ratification of the treaty of 1819 by Spain, and was determined to do nothing likely to give Ferdinand an excuse for withholding his signature. He was sure, he told Congress, that the powers of Europe would take no part in the struggle; he was confident that an adjustment of the dispute would soon be reached; and he was ready by friendly counsels with Spain or other powers to promote that result in every way. But Clay was not to be turned from his purpose, and with the words of the President still ringing in his ears moved an appropriation for sending a Minister or Ministers to South America. When this was lost by a small majority, he promptly brought in a resolution that the House of Representatives shared with the people of the United

---

* *Resolved*, That it is expedient to provide by law a suitable outfit and salary for such Minister or Ministers as the President, by and with the advice and consent of the Senate, may send to any of the governments of South America which have established and are maintaining their independence of Spain. Moved April 3, 1820; carried May 9; yeas 80, nays 75.

States in the deep interest they felt for the Spanish provinces of South America struggling for liberty and independence, and that whenever the President deemed it proper to recognize the sovereignty and independence of any of them the House would give him its constitutional support. The long-deferred Spanish treaty had now been ratified, and, as the passage of the resolution, which was a mere expression of a wish, could do no harm, the House passed it by fine majorities,* and sent Clay at the head of a committee to deliver it to the President. But Monroe was not to be driven by Clay. He took his own time, and allowed a year to go by before, on the eighth of March, 1822, he recommended recognition. Late in January the House, weary with the dilatoriness of the President, undertook to spur him on to action by a call for information concerning the political condition of the South American provinces of Spain and the state of the war between them and the mother country. In transmitting the report of Adams, the President reviewed at great length the history of the revolts and declarations of independence by Mexico, Chili, Peru, Buenos Ayres, and Colombia, and gave it as his opinion that, as Spain after so many years of trial had failed to reduce them to obedience, they were actually in a state of independence which ought to be recognized. The message ended with a suggestion that an appropriation should be made to enable him to send ministers. In this the House gladly concurred † with but one dissenting vote, and then unanimously appropriated one hundred thousand dollars. The Senate agreed to the bill some weeks later, and on May fourth, 1822, Monroe signed it.

No act of that session was so popular. Members of the House who were absent when the first vote was taken hastened to have their names entered among the yeas. Clay

---

* The resolution was divided. On the first part, expression of sympathy, the yeas were 134, the nays 12. On the second part, tendering constitutional support, the yeas were 87, the nays 68.

† *Resolved,* That the House of Representatives concurs in the opinion expressed by the President in his message of March 8, 1822, that the American provinces of Spain which have declared their independence and are in the enjoyment of it ought to be recognized by the United States as independent States.

was the hero of the hour.   The people everywhere sanctioned the recognition, and began to believe that necessity might drive the republics of the New World into an alliance for the preservation in America of the liberal ideas and democratic institutions the Holy Allies were so successfully stamping out in Europe.

When the Congress at Laybach adjourned in 1821, it did so with the understanding that it should meet again in 1822.   That the question of intervention in the affairs of Spain would then come up, and that when it did, Great Britain would have much to say, was well known to the powers.   What they would do might be doubtful, but the course she should pursue was to her certain.   She would leave the revolution in Spain to run its course; she would urge the European powers to do the same, and, following her own interests, would acknowledge the independence of the Spanish South American colonies.   A trade so great had sprung up with them that it was impossible to put off the day when she must have in each, if not a minister, at least a diplomatic agent.   Such a policy ran so directly counter to the wishes of the Holy Alliance that it was felt to be necessary that her position should be upheld by her foremost diplomat.   The Foreign Secretary, Lord Castlereagh, was accordingly chosen to represent her.   In the instructions which he drew up for himself, and which the Cabinet and the King approved, he was commanded to inform the Congress that it was the intention of England to send accredited agents to some of the South American Republics, which meant a steady opposition on England's part to any intervention by the Holy Alliance.   Unhappily, when the Congress met at Vienna, in September, Castlereagh was dead, Canning was Foreign Secretary, and the Duke of Wellington was England's representative.

After a short session at Vienna, the Congress adjourned to Verona, where, in October, 1822, the affairs of Spain were carefully considered.   No declaration was made in the name of the Alliance, but an agreement was entered into that certain changes should be demanded in the Spanish Constitution, and, if not granted, the French army, supported, if

of these meetings that John Quincy Adams, then Secretary of State, bearing in mind his conversations with the Russian Minister regarding Oregon, suggested a declaration relating to colonization, and urged it so successfully that Monroe gave it a place in his memorable message to Congress on December second, 1823.

As then set forth, the Monroe Doctrine consisted of three great principles:

The first, called forth by the claims of Russia to the northwest coast, and by her attempt to found a colony in California, asserted that the two continents of America are no longer open to colonization by European powers, because of the free and independent character the nations living in North and South America have assumed.*

The second related to the conduct of the Holy Allies, and was a formal notice to them and to all nations that if any European power should ever attempt to extend its political system to any part of the New World, whether " for the purpose of oppressing " the nations or " controlling in any other manner their destiny," the United States would interfere. †

The third had to do with our policy toward Europe, was the reassertion of a principle as old as the Constitution—

* " In the discussion to which this interest (the rights of the United States on the northwest coast of America) has given rise, and in the arrangements by which they may terminate, the occasion has been judged proper for asserting, as a principle in which the rights and interests of the United States are involved, that the American continents, by the free and independent condition which they have assumed and maintained, are henceforth not to be considered as subjects for future colonization of any European powers."

† " We owe it, therefore, to candor, and to the amicable relations existing between the United States and those powers, to declare that we should consider any attempt on their part to extend their system to any portion of this hemisphere as dangerous to our peace and safety. With the existing colonies or dependencies of any European power we have not interfered, and shall not interfere. . . . But with the governments who have declared their independence, and maintained it, and whose independence we have, on great consideration and on just principles, acknowledged, we could not view any interposition for the purpose of oppressing them, or controlling in any other manner their destiny, by any European power, in any other light than as the manifestation of an unfriendly disposition toward the United States."

" the United States will not interfere in the internal concerns of any European power." *

Stated more briefly, the doctrine was this:

1. No more European colonies on either of the American continents.

2. The United States will " not interfere in the internal concerns " of any European power.

3. " But in regard to these continents (North and South America) circumstances are eminently and conspicuously different," and if any European power attempts at any future time to extend its political system to any part of this hemisphere " for the purpose of oppressing " the nations or " controlling in any other manner their destiny," the United States will interfere.

Monroe might have informed the Holy Allies of his doctrine under cover of an official note. But he preferred to announce it before the world, and in his message warned them that any attempt on their part to violate the doctrine would be " dangerous to our peace and safety " and a " manifestation of an unfriendly disposition toward the United States."

In England the words of the President were hailed with extravagant delight. The English people, the English statesmen, the English press were loud in their praise of the firm stand Monroe had taken against the allies.

" The question," said Mr. Brougham, " with regard to South America is now disposed of, or nearly so, for an event

---

* " Our policy in regard to Europe, which was adopted at an early stage of the wars which have so long agitated that quarter of the globe, nevertheless remains the same, which is not to interfere in the internal concerns of any of its powers; to consider the Government *de facto* as the legitimate Government for us; to cultivate friendly relations with it, and to preserve those relations by a frank, firm, and manly policy; meeting in all instances the just claims of every power, submitting to injuries from none. But, in regard to these continents, circumstances are eminently and conspicuously different. It is impossible that the allied powers should extend their political system to any portion of either continent without endangering our peace and happiness; nor can any one believe that our Southern brethren, if left to themselves, would adopt it of their own accord. It is equally impossible, therefore, that we should behold such interposition, in any form, with indifference."

At home the message was read with enthusiasm and pride.* There were many, it is true, who condemned Monroe, accused him of saying things likely to bring on the country the

will greatly tend to lessen the evils of national contention. It is proposed to do away altogether with the system of privateering in so far as it is countenanced by governments.

It is also suggested, as a means of effectually suppressing the slave-trade, that vessels found by the ships of any nation to be engaged in this traffic shall be treated on the same footing with vessels caught in piracy.

While in her power and resources, as they are illustrated in this speech, the nation of the United States exhibits the vigor of ripe years, she, in those sentiments of active humanity, seems to our thought to preserve the fresh feeling of youth, and not to be wholly engrossed as older States are, in the pursuit or support of purely selfish interests. And we have thus a pleasure from contemplating her less as that metaphysical insentient thing, a State, than as an actual human and feeling being.

From Bell's Weekly Messenger of December 17th.—The main object of any interest during the week now passed is the arrival of the speech of the President of the United States. It is a document of the first interest and importance. It is interesting because it is a brief, simple, and direct *exposé* of Republican government; always true, plain dealing, and sincere. It is important because, fearing nothing, it conceals nothing, and is totally divested of all trick, artifice, and commonplace jargon, which renders the diplomacy of Europe so much more than merely nugatory.

Long, very long, have we wished that Canada might be sold or exchanged with the United States. Exchanged for what? it may be demanded. Why, for such an annuity for a term of years as would redeem what remains of the English assessed taxes, and redeem them forever.

If America would give us enough for this purpose for five or seven years, the natural progress of our revenue would do what would be required after that time. Add to this that we should save upward of half a million yearly in the expense of the Canada Government, and nearly as much more in the reduction of the army which it would allow. This has long been our own view, and we are persuaded that half, at least, of our best statesmen unite with us in it. As to the right of doing so, there can be no doubt that the Canadians would agree, and for that reason—because it is their decided interest to do so, and because (if we were Canadians) we should not hesitate one moment.

* *J. Madison to Monroe.*

MONTPELLIER, *Dec. 6, 1823.*

DEAR SIR : I received by yesterday's mail your favor of the 4th, covering a copy of the message and another copy under a blank cover. It presents a most interesting view of the topics selected for it. The observations on the foreign ones are well moulded for the occasion, which is rendered the more delicate and serious by the equivocal indications from the British Cabinet. The reserve of Canning after his frank and earnest conversations with Mr. Rush is mysterious

wrath of the Holy Allies, and asserted that, as the powers were sure to pay no heed to the message, Monroe must back down or fight. Happily, these men were in the minority, and in all parts of the country the approval was general. Encouraged by this, some admirers of Monroe came forward with the proposition to elect him to a third term. It is plain, they argued, that a few months—nay, a few weeks—will see at least five candidates in the field. Not one of them is strong enough to secure the two hundred and sixty-one electoral votes necessary to a choice. There will be no choice by the electors, and that even the House, when the matter comes before it, will agree on any one of them is very doubtful. Monroe at the last election was entitled to have received the unanimous vote of the electors. During his second term he has done nothing to forfeit this confidence of the people, but has done much to maintain it. If now he is succeeded by another, the rulers of Europe, who do not understand our system, will construe this to mean that the people have repudiated the fine stand he has taken in his message against the allies, and may go on with the infamous work of destroying the republics of South America.

Even Clay was so far carried away by the enthusiasm of the moment that he laid before the House of Representatives a resolution that the people of the United States would not see without serious alarm any forcible intervention of the allied powers of Europe in behalf of Spain in the war then going on between her and her late colonies.* The influence

and ominous. Could he have stepped in advance of his superiors? Or have they deserted their first object? Or have the allies shrank from theirs? Or is anything taking place in Spain which the adroitness of the British Government can turn against the allies and in favor of South America? Whatever may be the explanation, Canning ought in candor, after what had passed with Mr. Rush, not to have withheld it, and his doing so enjoins a circumspect reliance on our own councils and energies. One thing is certain: that the contents of the message will receive a very close attention everywhere, and that it can do nothing but good everywhere.

(Indorsed)   MONROE, JS.
    Decr. 6, 1823.

    MSS. in the Department of State, Washington.

    * "Resolved, by the Senate and House of Representatives of the United States of America in Congress assembled, That the people of these States would not see,

of Clay was great. He was a favorite. He was Speaker of the House. He was an avowed presidential candidate; but he forgot that because he was a candidate the resolution if pressed would ruin him. He forgot that ten years before, a great section of the country whose votes he needed had denounced him as a " war hawk " because of the vigorous support he gave to the war for " free-trade and sailors' rights " ; he forgot that in the same section he would again be accused of seeking to provoke a war; and he forgot, what was far more important still, that no Southern State could be carried by any man who was actively interested in the welfare of the anti-slavery republics of South America.

But Clay remembered all this before the session closed, and one day in May, when the House was in Committee of the Whole, he rose and asked for a moment's attention while he said a word regarding his resolution. He had introduced it, he declared, because of information disclosed in the President's message, and under the belief that the Holy Allies meditated an attack on Spanish America. It was now clear that, if such a purpose had been seriously meditated, it was abandoned, and to pass the resolution after all that had occurred might be construed by them as unfriendly, if not offensive. Under the full conviction, therefore, that they did not entertain any purpose as diabolical as reducing South America to its ancient subjection, he would not press the resolution, " but would allow it to sleep where it now reposes— on the table."

For this Clay has been accused of abandoning the Monroe Doctrine. It seems more reasonable to believe that he acted from political necessity; for when that necessity passed away, when Adams was President and he was Secretary of State, he recovered the courage of his convictions, and in his instructions to Joel R. Poinsett, Minister to Mexico, thought proper to clearly define the meaning of the new doctrine, and,

without serious inquietude, any forcible intervention of the other powers of Europe in behalf of Spain, to reduce to their former subjection those parts of the continent, of America which have proclaimed and established for themselves, respectively, independent Governments, and which have been solemnly recognized by the United States."

having done so, bade Mr. Poinsett " urge upon the Government of Mexico the utility and expediency of asserting the same principles on all proper occasions." *

Thus instructed, the Minister set out, and had not been long at his post when the appearance of a great French fleet on our coast gave the republics of South America just cause to believe that the French, having stamped out constitutional government in Spain, was about to invade and seize Cuba and Porto Rico. Such an event was so much to be dreaded that Mexico called on the United States " to fulfil," in the

---

* " Whatever foundation may have existed three centuries ago, or even at a later period, when all this continent was under European subjection, for the establishment of a rule, founded on priority of discovery and occupation, for apportioning among the powers of Europe parts of this continent, none can be now admitted as applicable to its present condition. There is no disposition to disturb the colonial possessions, as they may now exist, of any of the European powers; but it is against the establishment of new European colonies upon this continent that the principle is directed. The countries in which any such new establishments might be attempted are now open to the enterprise and commerce of all Americans. And the justice or propriety cannot be recognized of arbitrarily limiting and circumscribing that enterprise and commerce, by the act of voluntarily planting a new colony, without the consent of America, under the auspices of foreign powers belonging to another and a distant continent. Europe would be indignant at any American attempt to plant a colony on any part of her shores, and her justice must perceive, in the rule contended for, only perfect reciprocity.

" The other principle asserted in the message is that while we do not desire to interfere in Europe with the political system of the allied powers, we should regard as dangerous to our peace and safety any attempt on their part to extend their system to any portion of this hemisphere. The political systems of the two continents are essentially different. Each has an exclusive right to judge for itself what is best suited to its own condition and most likely to promote its happiness, but neither has a right to enforce upon the other the establishment of its peculiar system. This principle was declared in the face of the world, at a moment when there was reason to apprehend that the allied powers were entertaining designs inimical to the freedom, if not the independence, of the new Governments. There is a ground for believing that the declaration of it had considerable effect in preventing the maturity, if not in producing the abandonment of all such designs. Both principles were laid down after much and anxious deliberation on the part of the late administration. The President, who then formed a part of it, continues entirely to coincide in both. And you will urge upon the Government of Mexico the utility and expediency of asserting the same principles on all proper occasions."—Clay to Joel R. Poinsett, March 26, 1825. Register of Debates, 1825–'26, Part ii, App., p. 84.

words of Mr. Clay, " the memorable pledge of the President of the United States in his message to Congress of December, 1823." Clay, with as little delay as possible, acceded to the request, applied the Monroe Doctrine, instructed our Minister at Paris to notify France " that we would not consent to the occupation of those islands by any other European power than Spain under any circumstances whatever," and bade Mr. Poinsett inform Mexico what had been done.*

---

* *Clay to Poinsett, November 9, 1825.*—"No longer than about three months ago, when an invasion by France of the island of Cuba was believed in Mexico, the United Mexican Government promptly called upon the Government of the United States, through you, to fulfil the memorable pledge of the President of the United States in his message to Congress of December, 1823. What they would have done had the contingency happened may be inferred from a despatch to the American Minister at Paris, a copy of which is herewith sent, which you are at liberty to read to the plenipotentiaries of the United Mexican States."

CHAPTER XLII.

BREAKING UP OF THE REPUBLICAN PARTY.

THE campaign which sent John Quincy Adams to the White House and put Henry Clay at the head of the Department of State began in 1821. Many things combined to give it a peculiar character and a lasting interest. A great national party, the sole one then in existence—a party which but a few months before presented the most singular illustration of harmony and unity afforded by our political annals —was, on a sudden, split into fragments. A piece of political machinery in use for four-and-twenty years was utterly destroyed and never resorted to again. Then for the first time was heard the cry that the President should be " a man of the people." Then for the first time the people made themselves felt not only in the election, but in the selection of a President. Then for the first time in its history the Republican party had no leader pre-eminent over a dozen others.

The generation which fought the war for independence, which furnished the men who signed the Declaration of Independence, who constituted the Continental Congress, who created the confederation, who framed the Constitution, was practically extinct. The generation of men then in control of affairs had been born since Bunker Hill and Yorktown, and possessed no leader who, having hazarded life and fortune in the struggle for the rights of man, had peculiar claims on the gratitude of his countrymen. The development of the country in the course of forty years had produced yet greater changes. The rush of population into the Mississippi Valley, the rise there of nine new States with democratic constitutions of the modern type, the rapid extension of the franchise, the introduction of new methods of locomotion, not only created a new constituency, but surrounded the voters with industrial, social, and political conditions utterly unlike those of the days of Washington. New issues, new questions, new points of view followed, and new leaders, sprung in every case from the honest, hard-working masses, rose to guide the people in their efforts to settle the problems of self-government—Federal, State, and municipal—forced on them by the changed state of society. Had these questions and issues been national in their character, it might have been possible for some statesman of that day to have so towered above his fellows as to have won the support of the whole country. But they were not national; they were sectional, and, hampered by them, no leader could expect to become the candidate of any section save that whose peculiar views and interests he represented. The uncontested and unanimous election of Monroe in 1820 meant nothing. It was a graceful compliment to the last representative of the statesmen of the Revolution. Precedent entitled him to another term, and he received it; but no sooner was he a second time sworn into office than the four quarters of the Union hastened to put forward men to succeed him.

Late in the autumn of 1821, while the Legislature of South Carolina was holding session, a majority of the Republican members met in caucus and nominated or, as they expressed it, recommended William Lowndes for the Presidency. Lowndes had not the smallest chance of success, yet the action of his friends so alarmed the supporters of the Secretary of War that in December, as soon as possible after Congress assembled, a delegation of Northern and Southern members waited on Calhoun and invited him to become a candidate. Meanwhile there suddenly loomed up in the far Southwest the most serious contestant of all.

Broken in health and wearied by a thousand petty annoyances, Andrew Jackson had resigned the governorship of Florida in 1821 and had gone back to Tennessee, fully determined to pass the remainder of his days in peace and quiet at the Hermitage. But he had not been long on his plantation when devoted admirers began to talk of him as a possible presidential candidate. We are told that he laughed at the idea, and declared he was too old and too broken in health to think of such a thing. But, in the opinion of his friends, he was just the man for the place and the hour. His name was familiar to every voter in the land. His services to the public had been many and great; yet he held no public office, and had not, as had Adams, Crawford, Calhoun, and Clay, drawn immense sums of money from the public treasury as the result of a life spent in office-holding. He did not belong to " the dynasty of the Secretaries," and was not an aristocrat, but a plain man of the people, who knew their needs and would respect their will. The subject of Jackson's candidacy was therefore broached to the public one day in January, 1822, in the Nashville Gazette, and found such a hearty indorsement in every part of Tennessee that nothing remained but to make the nomination, which the General Assembly did in August, 1822.* The friends of the Speaker now rallied, and in November a caucus of Kentucky legislators nominated Clay, and pledged themselves to support no other man.

No higher compliment could have been paid to Jackson, for nothing but his immense popularity enabled his managers to overcome the prejudice which long usage and party allegiance had built up in favor of a nomination by congressional caucus. Lest even this popularity might not

---

* " The members of the General Assembly of the State of Tennessee, taking into view the great importance of the selection of a suitable person to fill the presidential chair at the approaching election for the chief magistracy of the United States, and seeing that those who achieved our independence and laid the foundations of the American republic have nearly passed away, and believing that moral worth, political requirements, and decision of character should unite in the individual who may be called to preside over the people of the United States, have turned their eyes to Andrew Jackson, late major-general in the armies of the United States.

" In him they behold the soldier, the statesman, and the honest man ; he deliberates, he decides, and he acts ; he is calm in deliberation, cautious in decision, efficient in action. Such a man we are willing to aid in electing to the highest office in the gift of a free people. . . . Therefore,

" Resolved, As the opinion of the members composing the General Assembly of the State of Tennessee, that the name of Major-General Andrew Jackson be submitted to the consideration of the people of the United States at the approaching election for the chief magistracy."

in the end triumph over the scruples of the voters, two judges of note were assigned the task of preparing for publication in the Nashville newspapers a series of articles attacking King Caucus, and justifying the propriety of legislative nomination. But precautions did not stop here. That the electoral colleges would fail to elect a President, and that the duty of providing a Chief Magistrate would fall on the House of Representatives, seemed almost certain. In such an event it was but natural to suppose that the members of the House would be more inclined to vote for a man they knew personally than for a man of whom they had merely heard, for the Secretary of War, or the Secretary of State, or the Secretary of the Treasury, or the Speaker, rather than for Andrew Jackson, who had neither place, patronage, nor power. An opportunity was therefore gladly seized to put Jackson in the company of congressmen, and in December, 1823, he took his seat as senator from the State of Tennessee.

As news of the nomination of Jackson by Tennessee spread over the Western States the people became enthusiastic. At last the Virginia dynasty was broken. At last the West was to have a candidate—no secretary, no diplomat, but a man of the people, devoted to their interests and knowing their wants. During the autumn and winter of 1822 and 1823 it was not possible for a dozen men to be assembled for any purpose without somebody making a canvass of Jackson's strength. On the steamboats as they went up and down the Mississippi, in the stage coaches, at the taverns, during military parades, wherever a court was sitting, the sense of those assembled was sure to be taken. At a meeting of citizens at Cincinnati early in January, 1823, De Witt Clinton was nominated and recommended to the people of Ohio and of the Union as a man worthy to be intrusted with the duties of the President. Almost at the same time the members of the Ohio Legislature recommended Clay. When spring came and it was easier to go about, meetings were held to give public expression to the sentiments of the people.

One night in April a crowd gathered, pursuant to notice, at the Court-House at Louisville. The object of the meeting was to indorse the nomination of Jackson, and after a struggle in which the friends of Clay came within seven votes of defeating this purpose, a long address was adopted. Voters were reminded that the strength of the several candidates was so equal that it was idle to expect a choice by the electoral colleges, and that an election by Congress was the greatest evil the country had to dread. To prevent this, said the addressers, we have searched among the candidates for the integrity, the patriotism, the well-tried public service which ought to distinguish each, and have found them in Jackson. The popularity of others is sectional or partisan, and their public service richly repaid by long years of office-holding; but the popularity of Jackson rests on the gratitude and confidence of the whole people. He is not an office-seeker, he is not a party man, and if elected will owe it to no congressional caucus nor to any legislative cabal, and will have no hungry office-seekers to reward.* At Nashville a popular meeting resolved that at the coming election the people ought to select the candidate; that he ought to be a citizen whose Republican principles had been tried by long experience, and whose political integrity, public virtue, and energy of character gave assurance that the Government would be administered with purity, and that Andrew Jackson was such a man.† Still later in the year the citizens of Alleghany County, in Pennsylvania, met at Pittsburg and took a vote as to which of the five candidates they should indorse. Adams received sixty votes, Clay fifty, and Clinton a few more; but when Jackson's name was presented the resolution indorsing him was carried by acclamation. It was then resolved as the sense of the meeting that the decisive character, acknowledged ability, and public services of Jackson gave him the best-earned claims to the Presidency, and that his friends in every county in the State ought to come forward and say so.‡ During the summer of 1823 the people in Tennessee pledged the candidates for Congress to vote for Jackson just as the people in Kentucky pledged theirs to vote for Clay, and in South Carolina to vote for Calhoun.

---

* Western Monitor, May 2, 1823.   ‡ Richmond Enquirer, August 22, 1823.
† Ibid., May 16, 1823.

country was threatened with internal schisms which could not
fail to engender angry feelings in different parts of the Union.
In the face of such a condition the committee could not see any
ground for the hope that, in the absence of unity of action, a
President could possibly be elected by the people.   In times
past the struggle for political supremacy had been carried on
between two great parties.   But no geographical line was
drawn.   No local feeling was aroused.   Members of both
parties were found in every State.   Now all had changed, and
the country was threatened with sectionalism, with an array
of State against State, of the East against the West, of the
North against the South.   Should this happen, the election
would surely go into the House of Representatives, than which
nothing could be less desirable.   Once there, it was in the
power of a small minority to impose on the United States
a man objectionable to the majority.   In the House sat two
hundred and thirteen members representing twenty-four
States.   As the election would be by States, thirteen would
make a majority.   Now there were thirteen States so small
and sparsely settled that, all told, they sent but forty-five
representatives to Congress.   The population of ten of them
when added together was less than that of New York alone.
In one of them—Mississippi—there were at most 55,211
human beings.   Yet her influence in the choice of a President, should that choice be made by the House, would be equal
to that of New York with a population of 1,372,812, and a
delegation of thirty-four representatives.   Worse than all, it
was in the power of a mere handful of men to control the
election.   A majority of each delegation would determine the
vote of that delegation, and the combined majorities of the
thirteen States in question added up to thirty-two.   These
thirty-two men might therefore, if they supported one man,
overcome the votes of one hundred and eighty-one representatives concentrated on some other man.   They might even prevent an election, for, as three names would come before the
House, they could so arrange it that no candidate should receive a majority.

Deeply impressed by these dangers, there seemed to be
no reason, the report went on to say, why Virginia, in con-

cert with other States, should not strive to prevent the occurrence of conditions so much to be feared. It was then recommended that a resolution be adopted declaring that a caucus nomination was " both politic and expedient to preserve harmony and secure union," and pledging Virginia to support the candidate. But, in spite of the efforts of Tyler, the motion was voted down by one majority.

Though defeated, the friends of Crawford in the Legislature were not discouraged, and a few days later * one hundred and fifty-seven of them met and adopted resolutions asking the Republican members of Congress from Virginia to endeavor to secure a caucus nomination.†

Almost at the same moment ‡ the Republican members in Congress from Pennsylvania issued an anti-caucus address to their constituents. They reminded them that ever since 1804 the presidential nominations of their party had been made by congressmen, that there had always been some opposition to this method, and that the events which happened in 1816 had aroused a firm belief in the minds of Republicans in many States that the wish of the people had not been heeded. The justness of this belief need not be discussed. It was enough to know that the people held it, and, knowing this, they had carefully considered what to do, and had decided that, owing to the pressure of public feeling in a majority of the States, many members would not go into caucus; that it would therefore be partial, and that a partial caucus they would not attend. The address ended with a recommendation that a convention of delegates be held at Harrisburg in March and select an electoral ticket pledged to none of the candidates.

So greatly were the members of Congress puzzled that a committee of twenty-four, representing fourteen States, was appointed to canvass the matter, find out how many congressmen thought a caucus inexpedient, and then publish the result for the information of the people. This committee ascertained that out of the two hundred and sixty-one members of the House and Senate one hundred and eighty-one deemed it

---

* January 5, 1824.   ‡ January 6, 1824.
† Western Monitor, January 27, 1824.

Connecticut to resort to a general ticket of electors, now stirred the people of Massachusetts to revise their election law, to abandon the old system of appointment by the Legislature, and to adopt a choice by the people. Of her fifteen electors, one was to reside in each of the thirteen congressional districts, while two were to be electors at large. As soon as the act was approved, a caucus of the Legislature named fifteen Adams electors. The old Federalists then met, and, after twice failing to make a ticket, left the matter to be taken up by the people in the congressional districts, in each of which an elector was nominated. The central committee added two more to be electors at large, and called the product the " Unpledged Electoral Ticket." In New Jersey a State convention, attended by delegates from twelve of the thirteen counties, assembled at Trenton, and before proceeding to business adopted a rule that no delegate pledged to support any candidate should have a seat. This shut out the Adams men, who organized by themselves and framed an Adams ticket. The rest of the delegates chose seven Jackson men and one friendly to Crawford. In Ohio a caucus of members of the Legislature, after resolving to support a candidate opposed to slave-holding, put John Quincy Adams in nomination, and made a State ticket of " Free Federal Electors." *

Some Clay Republicans meantime, after correspondence and conference with friends of his all over Ohio, prepared a list of names and gave it to the editor of the Columbus Gazette to publish, which he did with the remark, " We have thought proper to publish the following electoral ticket in favor of Clay." The Adams men thereupon dubbed it " The We Ticket." But Adams and Clay were not the only favorites. At a meeting of citizens of Steubenville, in December, 1823, De Witt Clinton had been nominated for President and Andrew Jackson for Vice-President. The nomination of Clinton was so severely ridiculed that a second meeting was held at Cincinnati, where a motion was made to strike out his name from the Steubenville resolutions. The church

---

* Ohio Monitor, April 24, 1824.

in which the people met was so crowded that to divide was impossible, so those present adjourned to a field near by, where they divided and were tolled off. Four hundred and fifty were for Clinton and three hundred and thirty opposed to him.

In Pennsylvania Adams had no following. Acting on the advice of their members of Congress, the people in every county save one had chosen delegates to attend a convention at Harrisburg, where, on the fourth of March, Jackson was nominated with but one dissenting voice. Calhoun was selected for the Vice-Presidency.*

Never before had the people shown so deep an interest in the choice of a President. In Philadelphia " Hickory Clubs " were formed, and each member required to wear a black silk vest stamped with portraits of Jackson. Public meetings were held; resolutions were passed; pamphlets were written and scattered broadcast. The substance of such documents was that the people were heartily in favor of Jackson. His services in the late war, in the Indian campaign of 1813, in the Seminole War, were glowingly described. Who among his rivals, it was asked, could show a like record? Were Crawford, like Jackson, in private life, would he be a candidate? Did not everybody know that the Secretary of the Treasury was the favorite of the caucus because the patronage of his office was lucrative and great? Adams, it was admitted, had served his country well. But to elect him would be to indorse and continue a custom dangerous to republican institutions—the custom of making the Secretary of State the successor of the President whom he served. Madison had been Secretary to Jefferson, Monroe to Madison, and if Adams followed Monroe, the dynasty of the Secretaries would be well established, and the Presidents would practically select their successors. What this meant the people well knew.

In Virginia some members of the Legislature nominated Clay, and urged his election on the ground that he was a Virginian born and bred.

In Sevier County, East Tennessee, the people showed their preference by means of a novel device. Five banners

---

* United States Gazette, March 8, 1824.

were hoisted in a line, and at suitable distances apart. On each was the name of one of the five candidates—Adams, Jackson, Clay, Crawford, and Calhoun. When the meeting had been called to order, those present were asked to fall into line and march past the banners, each stopping at that of his favorite. After this was done, six hundred and sixteen men were counted under the Jackson banner, seven under the Adams, one under the Crawford, and three under the Clay. Calhoun had not one friend present.

In many places throughout the South a favorite ticket was Adams and Jackson, or, in the language of one of the newspapers—

> John Quincy Adams,
> Who can write,
> And Andrew Jackson,
> Who can fight.

In Maryland the people of Cecil Council gathered at Elkton, and, after denouncing the caucus nomination, declared for an Adams and Jackson ticket. In North Carolina a caucus of the Legislature indorsed Crawford. But a " People's Ticket," composed of the friends of Adams and Jackson, was at once put in the field. In Mississippi a convention of members of the Legislature and private citizens met and balloted for a candidate. When the vote was taken on the question, Shall he be Adams or Calhoun? Adams had all the votes save two that went to his rival. Adams was next pitted against Crawford, and then against Clay, with a like result. But when he was put up against Jackson, the vote was a tie. The chair then gave a casting vote in favor of Adams, whereupon the convention nominated both. Alabama was strong for Jackson. Indeed, the Legislature in formal session went so far as to indorse his candidacy in a set of resolutions, copies of which it requested the Governor to transmit to the Governors of the sister States. This he refused to do, not because he disliked Jackson, but because, in his opinion, the Legislature had no right to meddle in the matter of the selection of a presidential candidate.

As the summer of 1824 wore away the people in States where electors were to be chosen in districts or by a general ticket became more active than ever, and nomination followed nomination in quick succession. The friends of Jackson in Ohio called so vigorously for a State convention that one was held, and men pledged to Jackson and Calhoun were formally chosen.* This action made a popular nomination of Adams necessary, and it was accomplished during a session of the United States Circuit Court. The judges, the bar, the jury-men, the witnesses, the suitors, all who were in attendance on the court, men from every part of the State, were called together one evening, and before they dispersed Adams was indorsed and an address in his behalf was issued. The same thing took place in Alabama, where, during a sitting of the Supreme Court of the State, the judges, lawyers, and citizens from all parts of Alabama met and formed an Adams and Calhoun electoral ticket.† In Virginia delegates from each congressional district assembled at Fredericksburg and made a Jackson electoral ticket. That Jackson would carry Penn-sylvania was by this time certain. Nevertheless, delegates from Philadelphia and ten counties gathered at Harrisburg, approved of the congressional caucus and its nominees, and made a " Democratic Republican Electoral Ticket " pledged to Crawford and Gallatin.‡

The campaign had now gone far enough to prove beyond a doubt that at least two candidates had no chance whatever of election. Not a State save Virginia, and no public body save the few delegates from ten counties of Pennsylvania, had declared for Gallatin. No State save South Carolina wanted to see Calhoun President. For the office of Vice-President, however, his indorsement by Jackson men and Adams men was so general all over the South and West that before autumn came he had ceased to be regarded as a presi-dential candidate, and had become the choice of Republicans for the Vice-Presidency.

The appearance of the name of the Secretary of War on the Jackson and Adams tickets suggested to the friends of Crawford the idea of attempting a like fusion of the support-

---

* Ohio Monitor, July 17, 1824.

† Ibid., August 7, 1824.

‡ American Daily Advertiser, August 13, 1824.

ers of Crawford and Clay, and in September, accordingly, the offer of second place was made to the Speaker and firmly declined.* But the Republican leaders would not give up hope of such a coalition, and, in order to remove every possible obstacle in the way, they now forced Gallatin to withdraw. The letter requesting his resignation was written late in September, and informed him that in North Carolina, Virginia, Maryland, Delaware, New Jersey, and New York the belief was strong that Calhoun would be chosen Vice-President by the electors; that his warmest friends advised him to retire, as such action would perhaps make it possible to come to an understanding with Clay which would do much to secure the election of Crawford.† Gallatin complied at once, and copies of his resignation were soon on their way to Martin Van Buren at Albany, and to the committee of correspondence in Virginia,‡ and were published in the newspapers.

He might as well have never written it, for, when the Legislature of New York attempted to choose electors, a quarrel broke out between the supporters of Crawford and Clay.

The people of New York made a new Constitution in 1821, and seized the occasion to abolish the Council of Appointment and extend the suffrage by removing the property qualification until that time required of voters. Two consequences followed. In the first place a new party machine —a group of able politicians then in office—was organized by Van Buren and his friends, to take the place of the Council of Appointment, and by controlling the Governor control the patronage of the State. The new machine was the " Albany Regency." # In the second place, the absolute certainty that this little group of able men if left to themselves would capture

---

* Clay to J. S. Johnston, September 3, 1824. J. S. Johnston to Clay, September 4, 1824. Clay to J. S. Johnston, September 10, 1824. Cotton's Life and Works of Henry Clay, vol. iv, pp. 100–103.

† Walter Lowrie to Gallatin, September 25, 1824. Adams's Life of Gallatin, pp. 602, 603.

‡ Gallatin to Walter Lowrie, October 2, 1824. Adams's Life of Gallatin, pp. 604–606.

Chief among them were the Controller (W. L. Marcy); the District Attorney of Albany County (Benjamin F. Butler); the Attorney-General; the State printer; the United States district judge; the State treasurer.

the Legislature in 1824 and secure electors pledged to Crawford aroused their opponents to found a " People's Party " and demand that in 1824 the choice of the electors of President should be by vote of the people. On this demand the election of 1823 turned, and, many seats in the Legislature having been obtained by candidates of the People's Party, a bill providing for the popular choice of electors was laid before the Assembly in January, 1824. By that body, after a long and bitter struggle, it was passed; but the Senate defeated it by a majority of three votes.

Had the Albany Regency been content to stop with this, all might have gone well. But they went out of their way to aid the People's Party, and a few hours before the session closed rushed through both Houses a resolution removing De Witt Clinton from the office of Canal Commissioner. This was too much. Everywhere the people cried out in indignation. Public meetings were held all over the State, addresses of thanks poured in upon Mr. Clinton, and threats of vengeance grew so fierce that the Governor in alarm called a special session of the Legislature to begin on August second, and urged the passage of the electoral law. As the day of meeting drew near the interest shown by the public was intense. Men who were not politicians came from all parts of the State, for the feeling was general that the contest was not so much one between the friends of Adams and Clay as between the people and the Albany Regency. Long before the hour of noon on the day the Legislature was to meet the members were in their seats, and the lobbies, the galleries, even the space within the bar, were crowded with visitors. In the Assembly room, says one report, there was a solid mass of heads from the Speaker's chair to the topmost seat in the gallery.

When the Speaker had rapped for order and the chaplain, as the report states, had " offered one of the most fervent and appropriate prayers ever delivered within the walls of the Capitol," the Governor's proclamation summoning the members was read, and a committee sent to inform his Excellency that the House was ready to receive his message. The message came at once, and was no sooner read than a violent contest began. The friends of Crawford took the stand that nothing had occurred of such importance as to make an extra session necessary; that the proclamation of the Governor was therefore unconstitutional; that any proceedings of a Legislature so convened would be illegal; and that, the Senate concurring, it was the duty of the Assembly to immediately adjourn. The friends of Adams insisted that the message should go to a committee, and brought in resolutions declaring that a bill giving the choice of electors to the people ought to pass; and when a concurrent resolution to adjourn came down from the Senate, laid it on the table by a handsome majority amid shouts from the gallery and the lobbies. Next day a joint resolution was passed for the enactment of an electoral law, and sent to the Senate. But the Senate took no action, and when the Assembly asked why, the answer was returned that the session was illegal, and, being illegal, it was improper to legislate. This ended the matter, and both branches adjourned till the regular time of meeting, November second.

Before that day, however, the people had made good their threats, and had nominated and elected De Witt Clinton Governor of New York. The State rang with the cries, " No more congressional caucuses!" "No more Legislative nominations!" " The people must be heard! " The names of the seventeen senators who voted against the electoral law were printed, in glaring letters surrounded by a broad black border, on a poster, which was hung up in bar-rooms and country taverns, was nailed on trees by the roadside, was fastened on court-house doors, and was displayed in the windows of city shops and cross-road grocery stores all over the State. But one of the seventeen dared to run for re-election, and he was beaten. In a total vote of 190,000, Clinton had a majority of 16,000.

In this condition of the public mind the old Legislature reassembled on November second.

The day for the joint meeting of the Houses to choose thirty-six electors was Wednesday, the tenth of November, and as the members took their seats on the morning of the ninth each found on his desk three printed slips of paper, which proved to be an Adams, a Clay, and a Crawford ticket. As the law then stood, the two Houses must ballot separately, and when each had chosen electors they must meet in joint session and declare the results. The senators found no difficulty in making up a ticket on which were seven Clay and twenty-nine Crawford men. But in the House, on the first ballot, Adams had fifty votes, Crawford forty-three, Clay thirty-two, and Jackson one. After three days of balloting, with no change in the result, it became so apparent that a compromise must be effected that one was attempted. First, the Clay ticket was offered and rejected. Next, the Jackson ticket was moved, and received twenty-eight votes. A compromise ticket of twenty-one Crawford and fifteen Clay electors was then submitted. When this failed, the Adams ticket was offered and adopted by a vote of sixty-two to fifty-five. It was in no sense the choice of the Assembly, but was accepted in order that there might be a joint session with the Senate. The difficulty being removed, the two Houses met and proceeded to vote on the Adams ticket offered by the Assembly and the Crawford-Clay ticket offered by the Senate. One hundred and fifty-seven ballots were cast, so that seventy-nine were necessary to a choice. Seven men on the Crawford ticket— men who were supporters of Clay—received each ninety-five votes, and were declared by the President of the Senate elected. But three of the ballots were blank, and, it was held, ought not to be counted. If they were not, then seventy-eight would be a majority, and twenty-five of the Adams ticket would be elected. A stormy debate now sprang up and continued till late in the afternoon, when the President suddenly left the chair and hurried from the room, calling on the Senate to follow him. Next day in its own chamber the Senate voted that the seven Clay men who had ninety-five, and the twenty-five Adams men who had seventy-eight, were elected. The Assembly then adopted a like resolution, and once more met the Senate in joint session and chose four more electors, who were open advocates of Crawford. The college then stood twenty-five for Adams, seven for Clay, and four for Crawford.

It was not then the custom, as it is at present, to choose electors all over the country on the same day. Each State fixed such time as best suited the convenience of the people, if they voted, or of the Legislature, if that body made the appointment. An election was therefore a slow process, made slower still by the absence of the telegraph, the railroad, the modern newspaper—of all the agents, in short, which we now possess for the gathering and spreading of information. By the middle of November, however, returns had come in from eleven of the seaboard States north of Virginia. In Rhode Island the election had not yet taken place. In New York the struggle in the Legislature was still raging. In Delaware a fine foundation had been laid for what promised to be a contest. The thirty members of the Legislature, according to law, assembled at Dover and balloted for three electors. Ten men were put in nomination, of whom one received twenty-one votes and two others each fifteen, or exactly half the whole number cast. Now, the law provided " that if an equal division of ballots shall appear for two or more persons not being elected by a majority of the votes, the Speaker of the Senate shall have an additional casting vote." Construing this to meet the case before him, the Speaker voted for the two who received fifteen votes apiece, and then declared them elected. The Adams men in the Legislature were furious, protested, and threatened to dispute the legality of the act. By Thanksgiving Day returns had arrived from all the Southern States, except South Carolina, where no election had been held, and from the nearby Western States. The poll then stood, Adams 80, Jackson 58, Crawford 40, Clay 7, and was made up on the supposition that every pledge would be kept and every elector would vote as he was expected to. But when the colleges began to meet and the results of their actions were known, it appeared that strange things had happened. In New York three of the seven Clay men deserted him and voted one each for Jackson, Adams, and Crawford. In North Carolina a fusion ticket had been arranged, which the friends of Adams and Jackson were to support. Each voter was to write across the ballot the name of his candidate, and the electoral votes were to be divided in proportion to the strength of the Adams party. From the returns it appeared that Adams had one third of all the ballots cast. He was therefore entitled to one third of the electors. But when the college assembled and proceeded to vote the pledge was utterly disregarded, and every elector voted for Andrew Jackson.

When the year drew to a close the poll stood, Jackson 99, Adams 84, Crawford 41, Clay 37, provided Louisiana, the one State to be heard from, voted as it was supposed she would.* All eyes now turned to her, for, should her electors support Clay, his name and not Crawford's would come before the House. About the middle of December this last hope was destroyed, when a vessel from New Orleans reached New York with news that the Legislature, after six ballots, had chosen three electors for Jackson and two for Adams. Clay was shut out of the contest, for the Constitution limits the number of contestants for the Presidency that can appear before the House of Representatives to three. Had the three New York electors who deserted Clay been faithful, he would have

* STATES.	Jackson.	Adams.	Crawford.	Clay.	Choice made by
Maine..............	.....	10,289	2,336*	.....	Districts and 2 at large.
New Hampshire....	643	4,107	.....	.....	General ticket.
Vermont..........	.....	....	.....	.....	Legislature.
Massachusetts......	.....	30,687	6,616*	.....	13 districts, 2 at large.
Rhode Island	.....	2,145	200*	.....	General ticket.
Connecticut........	.....	7,587	1,978*	.....	General ticket.
New York..........	.....	......	.....	.....	Legislature.
New Jersey........	10,985	9,110	1,196†	.....	General ticket.
Pennsylvania.......	36,100	5,440	4,206	1,609	General ticket.
Delaware..........	.....	.....	.....	.....	Legislature.
Maryland....	14,523	14,632	3,646	695	Districts.
Virginia...........	2,861	3,189	8,489	416	General ticket.
North Carolina.....	20,415‡	.....	15,621	.....	General ticket.
South Carolina.....	.....	.....	.....	.....	Legislature.
Georgia...........	.....	.....	.....	.....	Legislature.
Alabama..........	9,443	2,416	1,680	67	General ticket.
Mississippi	3,234	1,694	119	. ..	General ticket.
Louisiana	.....	.....	.....	.....	Legislature.
Kentucky..........	6,455	.....	.....	17,321	3 districts.
Tennessee..........	20,197	216	312	.....	Districts.
Missouri...........	987	311	.....	1,401	Districts.
Ohio..............	18,457	12,280	.....	19,255	General ticket.
Indiana.	7,343	3,095	.....	5,315	General ticket.
Illinois............	1,901	1,542	219	1,047	Districts.
Totals	153,544	108,740	46,618	47,136	

* " Opposition " ticket.　　　　　　　　　　‡ " People's " ticket.
† " Convention " ticket.

could neither be persuaded nor frightened, an attempt was made to ruin him politically. That he was greatly disappointed when Monroe did not make him Secretary of State was well known. That if Adams were elected, Clay would in all likelihood be offered the place and would accept was almost certain. On this certainty a scheme was concocted which, it was hoped, would force him to support Jackson if he wanted to be Secretary, or if he gave his influence to Adams would compel him to decline the portfolio of State.

A member of Congress was persuaded to write an anonymous letter to a newspaper published in Philadelphia and called the Columbian Observer. He declared that an attempt had been made to corrupt the friends of Jackson; that when it failed the Clay men had applied to followers of Adams; that a most " unholy coalition " had been made, and that, in return for the office of Secretary of State, Clay had promised to use his influence in the House of Representatives to secure the election of Adams to the Presidency.

Lest Clay should not see the letter, the editor of the Columbian Observer sent him a marked copy. He ought to have flung it in the fire. But, stung to the quick, he snatched his pen, dashed off a card to the National Intelligencer—a newspaper published in Washington—and gave to the libel publicity and importance. In his card Clay denied the coalition, denounced the unknown writer as " a base and infamous calumniator, a dastard, and a liar," who, if he would disclose his name, should be held responsible " to all the laws which govern men of honor." In plain words, he should be summoned to the duelling grounds at Bladensburg. The writer thus challenged did discover himself, and, in a note to the National Intelligencer, informed the " Hon. H. Clay " that George Kremer of the House of Representatives was ready to prove to the satisfaction of unprejudiced minds that a bargain had really been made. Kremer was a bustling member of the House from Pennsylvania, whose chief claims to notoriety were a leopard-skin overcoat and eccentric manners. The thought of the great Mr. Clay—of " Harry of the West "—Speaker of the House for twelve sessions, hurrying off to Bladensburg in the dusk of a winter morning to take aim at

one of the spots on Kremer's coat now made the whole affair
ridiculous.

But Clay was angry, and, having forced from cover the
member who had stated things which, if true, were as dis-
graceful to the House as to its Speaker, he took occasion one
morning, as soon as the House was organized, to lay the matter
before it, and asked an investigation. " The respectability,"
said he, " of the station which the member holds who prefers
the charges, and that of the people he represents, entitle his
accusation to grave consideration. It may well be worthy of
consideration whether the character and dignity of the House
itself does not require a full investigation; for if they are true,
if I am base enough to betray the solemn trust which the
Constitution has confided to me, the House would be scandal-
ized by my continuing to occupy the chair with which it has
so long honored me, and I ought to be instantly expelled. I
earnestly hope, therefore, that the House will be pleased to
direct an inquiry to be made into the truth of the charges."

The House was amazed. Not half the members had seen
the cards in the newspapers or knew that one of their fellows
had made so serious an attack on the Speaker and themselves.
Indignant at such behavior, the appeal of Clay was ordered
to be spread on the journal, and a committee was appointed
to investigate. Kremer, standing in his place and in the presence of the House, now solemnly promised to appear before
the committee, and if he did not make good the charge he
hoped he might receive the reprobation he should in that case
deserve. But when the committee had been chosen and called
on Kremer to submit proof, he refused to come, and sent instead a long letter denying the right of the House to take any
action in the matter.

When the House had listened to the reading of Kremer's
letter, the document was laid on the table, and, the day being
the second Wednesday in February, a messenger was sent to
inform the Senate that the House was ready to witness the
counting of the electoral votes.

Precisely at noon the Senate, preceded by its sergeant-
at-arms and its President, entered the hall and took seats
on the right of the Speaker's desk. The representatives on

CHAPTER XLIII.

SOCIALISTIC AND LABOR REFORMS.

FIFTY years had now gone by since the farmers of Massachusetts made the first appeal to arms in the struggle for independence, and forty-nine since the thirteen colonies threw off allegiance to Great Britain and founded the Republic of the United States. Our country when independence was obtained was a very little one. It nowhere touched the Gulf of Mexico. It just touched the Mississippi. Its population numbered scarcely three million and a half of souls, and nowhere within its bounds was a city of forty thousand people. Since that time its domain had been extended across the continent; the waves of the Pacific now beat upon its western confines; the waters of the gulf now washed the shores of three great States and one Territory; while on the soil of the Republic dwelt six million of the happiest people on earth. The States had multiplied from thirteen to four-and-twenty. Four * cities boasted of more than forty thousand inhabitants each, and two † of more than one hundred thousand. Fourteen had each more than ten thousand, while scores of towns which in 1825 contained a thousand and more population did not exist in 1776.

Quite as marvellous was the social betterment. No man, whatever his station in life, whatever his business, trade, or occupation, was without its influence. Life along the seaboard was getting easier. Much of the old hardship of earlier times was gone. Increase in population and in wealth, joined with improved means of communication, had greatly expanded

---

* New York, Philadelphia, Boston, and Baltimore.
† New York (1820), 123,706. Philadelphia (1820), 112,772.

business opportunities. New industries, new trades, new occupations had arisen, and now afforded ways of gaining a livelihood unknown in the time of Washington. Manufactures
had grown up since 1807, and had dotted the Eastern and
Middle States with a thousand mills and factories. Steamboats were now on lake and river. Canals now joined great
waterways, while a network of turnpikes spread out in every
direction from the chief cities. These civilizers had so
abridged distance that in 1825 the frontier and the seaboard
almost touched. Boston was but two days from New York,
New York but eleven hours from Philadelphia, and Philadelphia but five days from Pittsburg and fifteen hours from
Washington. Freight could now be moved from New York
to Buffalo through the Erie Canal for four cents a ton per
mile, tolls included. These rates revolutionized business. The
field a merchant or a manufacturer could cover by his enterprise seemed boundless. The whole West, as well as the East,
became his market, and transportation companies for the hand-
ling of freight had been established in order to enable him
to reach that market. Banks were multiplying. Insurance
companies, steamboat, turnpike, and canal companies, mills,
and factories were springing up on every hand. Simple as
these things seem, they changed the whole course of life.

Tens of thousands of men who under the old conditions
would have been doomed to eke out a scanty livelihood by
farming, or by cobbling, or by toiling in the crowded ranks
of unskilled labor, now found new occupations opening before
them. They became mill hands and operatives; they turned
machinists and mechanics; they served as engineers and fire-
men on the steamboats, as clerks and book-keepers in banks
and insurance companies; they handled freight, tended
the gates on the turnpikes or the bridges on the canals; drove
the horses that dragged the canal boats, or found employment
in some of the older industries which, such as tailoring and
printing, shoemaking, stage-driving, hatmaking, and carpen-
try, had been greatly expanded since the war.

The rise of new industries and the development of old
caused an immense increase in the number of working-men
and working-women. The growth of this class brought up

questions of reform, and with 1825 the labor movement began. Less hours of labor, higher wages, better treatment, payment in honest money and not in depreciated bank paper, became the demands of the time. Some of these were as old as the Republic. Journeymen shoemakers, journeyman tailors and carpenters over and over again had struck, or " turned out," during the past forty years. Now the grievance was the employment of non-union men; now it was low wages; again, it was giving out work to women. Twice the purpose of the strike was to secure a shorter working-day. The first of these movements occurred in 1791, when the members of the Union Society of Carpenters at Philadelphia ordered a turnout. They complained that in summer they were forced to toil from sunrise to sunset for five shillings a day, and in winter were put on piecework, and demanded that the year through a working-day should be from six in the morning to six at night, with an hour for breakfast and another for dinner; or, what was the same thing, ten hours of labor. Nothing came of the movement, they were forced to yield, and in all likelihood not one of them ever lived to see the time when the working-man did not labor thirteen hours out of the twenty-four. During the summer, when the sun rose early, every cobbler, every carpenter, mason, stone-cutter, every laboring man, was hard at work at four o'clock in the morning. At ten an hour was taken for lunch, and at three another for dinner, after which work went on till, according to the almanac, the sun had set.

The second protest against so long a working-day was made in 1822 by the journeymen millwrights and machine workers of Philadelphia. They met at a tavern, and passed resolutions that ten hours of labor were enough for one day, and that work ought to begin at 6 A. M. and end at 6 P. M., with an hour for breakfast and one for dinner. Their action went no further, and led to no immediate result. But the fact that the men who formed the meeting were machinists was one of many signs of the expansion of labor. Yet another was afforded in 1824 in New York city. A tariff bill was then before Congress, and the people all over the seaboard States were supporting or opposing it in memorials and petitions. New York, as a great commercial city, was full of anti-tariff men, and by them a meeting was called and held in the City Hall. But a band of weavers from Paterson, from Westchester, and from the mills in the city marched to the Hall, took possession, interrupted the proceedings with cries of " No British goods! " " Tariff, tariff! " " American manufactures ! " " Protection to domestic industries ! " smashed some chairs, tore up some benches, broke lamps and windows, and went away. The rioters, it was said in explanation, were aliens, weavers imported from Great Britain, men who had not been long enough in the United States to acquire citizenship. The statement was true, and, trifling as was the affair, it showed that the time had come when the ranks of labor were being recruited abroad; that the importation of foreign operatives had begun; and that a new element was introduced to still more complicate the industrial questions pressing for settlement.

The condition of the working-man stood in need of betterment. In the general advance made by society in fifty years he had shared but little. Many old grievances no longer troubled him, but new ones, more numerous and galling than the old, were pressing him sorely. Wages had risen within ten years, but not in proportion to the increase in the cost of living. In some States he was no longer liable to imprisonment for debt, unless the amount was larger than fifteen dollars, and in others than twenty-five. If he was so fortunate as to save a few cents out of the pittance he earned, and lived in either of the four great cities, there were savings banks in which he might with reasonable safety deposit the fruits of his economy and receive interest thereon. These were decided gains. Nevertheless, his lot was hard. The hours of labor were still from sunrise to sunset. Wages were not always paid weekly or monthly, but often at long and irregular intervals, and frequently in bad money. His ignorance of finance and of the tricks of business men made him the recipient of counterfeit notes and bills of broken banks, or of institutions of such doubtful soundness that the paper he was forced to receive at its face value would not pass with the butcher or the baker save at a heavy discount. When his employer failed, no lien law gave him a claim on the product of his labor. In many States he was still disfranchised. In all, he was liable under the common law of England to be punished for conspiracy if by strikes, by lockouts, or by combination with others he sought to better his condition or raise his pay. One thing he did not lack—he now had friends ready and willing to help on his cause.

The pleas they put forth in his behalf dwell at great length on the awful misery of drunkenness; declare that the poverty of the working-classes is the real cause of intemperance; call for legislation to " prevent the rich from swallowing up the inheritance of the poor "; hold up as a warning the " injurious consequences to the community of individuals amassing large landed property "; point out the dangers to which factory operatives are daily and hourly exposed; and ask for cleaner shops and healthier mills and lodgings.

Such pleas had small effect on the public, but much on the working-man and woman, who, after 1825, began to organize in earnest. Social unions of various crafts were formed in all the seaboard cities and manufacturing centres north of Baltimore. In New England the women weavers and cotton operatives led the way. In New York city the ship carpenters and calkers, following the example of the machinists of Philadelphia, in their turn began to agitate for a ten-hour day. So energetic was the labor movement that in 1828 an attempt was made in the New York Legislature to secure a mechanics' lien law, and a report strongly favoring such a measure of relief was presented. In Philadelphia the workingmen, breaking old ties, entered politics on their own behalf and formed a labor party. At a public meeting in August it was formally resolved to urge the working-men to support no candidate for a seat in the Legislature or in the city councils who would not pledge himself to further the interests and demands of " the working-classes," and a call was issued for organization.* The city and county were marked off into four districts, from each of which delegates were sent to a general

---

* United States Gazette, August 14, 1828.

convention which nominated assemblymen, common council-
men, and auditor.*

The tickets were defeated; but the organization continued,
and ere another year went by made two demands for reform—
one that the managers of the House of Refuge, who had just
introduced mechanical occupations into their institution,
should see to it that the mechanics and working-men of Philadelphia suffered no injury; and another that the State of
Pennsylvania should establish a system of free republican
schools, open to the children of the rich and of the poor without distinction.

Judged by the standard of public instruction as now maintained in Pennsylvania, the demand of the working-men was
reasonable and just. The constitution of the commonwealth,
framed a generation before, required that the children of the
poor should be educated at the public cost. The injunction
was mandatory; the meaning was plain. Yet no steps were
taken to carry it out till 1809, when a law was enacted requiring the assessors of taxes to make a census of the children
whose parents were too poor to educate them, send the boys
and girls to the nearest school, and assess the cost on the tax-
payers. Even this wise provision was neglected. Some districts had no schools of any kind; in others the funds were
embezzled, misapplied, perverted, or the law but partly executed, for the people refused to accept the benefit conferred
lest their children should be looked on and treated as paupers.
Meanwhile the cities increased in population, and the number
of children growing up in absolute ignorance became so large
that in 1818 a second step forward was taken, and the city and
county of Philadelphia, the city and borough of Lancaster,
and the city of Pittsburg were formed into three districts,
with free schools in which children whose parents were too
poor to educate them were taught reading, writing, arithmetic,
and geography. No child whose parents could pay his schooling was admitted, and this in the eyes of the working-men was
an offensive class distinction. It separated the children of
the rich from those of the poor, and said to the latter, " You

* United States Gazette, August 21 and October 1, 1828.

are paupers." That some men should be rich and others poor was inevitable, but to build up class hatred was not necessary, and no surer way of preventing it could be devised than a system of equal republican education, with free schools open to the children of all citizens alike.

The efforts which working-men were thus making to secure great social reforms, and especially their demands for free public schools, now warmly enlisted in their cause another body of reformers, known as the Free Enquirers, who were regarded at that day by conservative people with the same horror and detestation that anarchists and socialists are regarded in ours. The origin of this movement for free inquiry goes back to a little community of men and women who gathered in 1825 at New Harmony, near the Wabash river, in Indiana. The founder of the community, Robert Owen, was a native of Wales, where he was born in 1771. Forced to earn his living while still a lad, he became a clerk in a draper shop near London at ten, went to Manchester at fourteen, was made manager of a cotton mill at eighteen, and at twenty-seven bought the mills at New Lanark, in Scotland, from David Dale, whose daughter he married.

From the day when as a mere lad he entered the Manchester mills his mind seems to have been full of schemes for the social betterment of the laboring classes, held down by ignorance, by squalid poverty, and by lack of character. Once in control at New Lanark, Owen put his plans in operation, and after long opposition built and opened what he called an Institution for the Formation of Character, but what was, in fact, a great school for the instruction of children from the time they were infants till they were boys and girls of twelve. He shortened the hours of daily labor in the mills, introduced rules to enforce morality and promote cleanliness and good habits; he added to the comfort and happiness of all, and little by little established co-operation on the community system of living. The fame and the success of the New Lanark experiment spread far and wide. Co-operation, "unrestrained co-operation on the part of all the members for every purpose of social life," became the reform hobby of the hour, and Owen the great teacher of a new economy. Co-operative economical societies sprang up all over England and Scotland, and attracted the attention of men in the New World.

Among those whose attention was so attracted was an agent for the sale of a village built in the far West by one of the many religious communities which then flourished in the United States. The founder of this sect was George Rapp, the son of a small farmer and vine-dresser of Würtemberg, in Germany, where he was born in 1757. He was a man far more inclined to read and think than to plough and reap, and having no books save the Bible, he read it constantly, with the result so common in the case of bright men with little education. He began to see new meanings and to catch new ideas. Religious doubts tormented him; then firm convictions took their place, and a sense of duty arose which drove him to make known the new truths he had discerned for the good of mankind. He was moved to preach first in his own house, and then in public. But when he began to preach the clergy began to persecute, and as persecution continued, his followers increased in number and in earnestness. At last, wearied with the perpetual struggle for the rights of conscience, Rapp turned to the one land where men were free to worship as they pleased, and prepared to lead his followers to the United States of America. In 1804, with his son and a few friends, Rapp came to Baltimore, travelled over Maryland, Pennsylvania, and Ohio, and finally chose a tract of land in the valley of the Conoquenessing, twenty-five miles northwest of Pittsburg, in Pennsylvania, and on it in 1805 seven hundred Rappites built the village of Harmony. Hitherto they had formed a religious body. Now they became a community, put all property into a common fund, adopted a simple style of dress, plain houses and plain living, and agreed that each should labor for the good of all.

As time passed the site of Harmony proved to be ill-chosen, for the soil and climate were unsuited for vine-growing, the only industry in which the people were skilful, and the town had no water communication with the outside world. A new home was therefore sought in the far West, and found in the valley of the Wabash, whither, in 1815, the society migrated and built a second Harmony. Once more the site proved far from satisfactory. The wild rush of population westward brought them neighbors of a most unpleasant sort; malaria, or " the shakes," was worse than the neighbors, and so disheartened the people that in 1824 an Englishman named Richard Flower was offered five thousand dollars to find a purchaser for the land and houses. Flower went straight to Great Britain, sought out Owen, and sold him the town of Harmony, with all its mills, houses, factories, and thirty thousand acres of land, for one hundred and fifty thousand dollars. Three thousand acres were under cultivation, eighteen were covered by full-bearing vines and flourishing orchards, while the village itself was well built and well laid out, with broad streets and a public square, around which were brick buildings used by the Rappites for schools, churches, and community purposes.

The purchase concluded, Owen, in December, 1824, came over to the United States, and, while the Rappites were on their way to a new home, which they built in Beaver County, Pennsylvania, and named Economy, he began preparations for the founding of the first Owenite community in our country. That his scheme and his views might be as widely known as possible, he went to Washington, secured the use of the Hall of Representatives, and in it, on two evenings,[*] delivered long addresses to most distinguished audiences. In making such appeals, it was his custom to begin by attempting to show that the construction of modern society was all wrong; that the prevalence of error, prejudice, vice, and crime was due to the practice of bringing up the young in a system of society which he called the individual, or selfish; and that there were two sets of circumstances which entirely regulated the formation of a man's character. The one was his religious belief, and the other was his education. Every child was possessed of a body and a mind over which he had no control; whether that mind was moulded for good or for ill depended on the circumstances with which the parents sur-

---

[*] Two Discourses on a System of Society as delivered in the Hall of Representatives of the United States on the 25th of February and the 7th of March, 1825, etc. By Robert Owen, of New Lanark. The plan for a community is given on pages 42–52.

rounded the child.* " Had you," he would say, " on my right hand been brought up under the influence of such circumstances as are to be found at the foot of the Rocky Mountains, you would all have been Indians, save as to the color of your skins. Had you on my left hand been exposed from infancy to the circumstances which prevail in China, you would all have been Chinese, except in form and figure." Any social system, then, which ignored the power of circumstances was wrong. That system which was based on " the science of circumstances " was right. As to religion, it should be a rational one, founded on matter of fact and the evidences of the senses —in short, the revealed word of God. Any events recorded in books professing to be of divine origin which were in opposition to this principle were false. The Scriptures were not divine nor written by men under divine influence, nor did they more than any other writings contain the revealed word or will of God. All religions, the Christian included, were founded in error, and, so far from being fitted to promote happiness and virtue among mankind, they had the opposite tendency. If the human race, then, was to be made virtuous and happy, the old system must be done away with, for its institutions and its prejudices could not exist together with the principles of the new.†

It was for this reason, therefore, that he urged the formation of communities in which should be associated persons in sympathy with his views. The number in any community should never be less than five hundred nor more than two thousand, and they should begin by purchasing a tract of twenty thousand acres of good land. In the centre should be four buildings, each a thousand feet long, so placed as to form the four sides of a hollow square. From the middle of each side a building should project into the square, and in it should be the dining-hall, the kitchen, the laundry, the storerooms—in short, all the domestic appliances needed for the comfort and convenience of those living in the dormitory to which it was attached. The school-rooms, lecture-rooms, lab-

---

* National Advocate (N. Y. C.), November, 1825. American Daily Advertiser, November 22, 1825.

† American Daily Advertiser, November 30, 1825.

new constitution was made. The principles now laid down for the guidance of the Community of Equality were, for those days, socialistic in the extreme. There was to be the utmost freedom of speech, absolute equality of rights and equality of duties, common ownership of property, co-operation to the fullest extent, and a rigid practice of economy. That these ends might be secured, the pursuits of daily life were classified, and six departments created and named—agriculture, manufacture, and mechanics; literature, science, and education; domestic economy; general economy; commerce.*

Under the watchful eye and fostering care of Owen the community now for the first time showed signs of prosperity. Idleness and waste gave place to industry and thrift such as had not been seen since the Rappites left New Harmony. Every man, every woman was busy in some chosen occupation. The streets were no longer full of groups of idle talkers. The meetings at Harmony Hall were held for business, and not for the vain display of oratory. To the community, moreover, had come men of marked ability. There were now gathered Charles Alexander Le Seur, a naturalist of note, an authority on turtles and fishes, and one of the company on the Péron during her voyage around the world; George Francis Vigo, the painter; Gerard Troost, the Dutch geologist; Thomas Say, the conchologist, who had been with Long across the plains; Robert Dale Owen; and William Maclure, of Philadelphia, a man of means, a geologist of distinction, and a firm believer in co-operation and the Pestalozzian system of education. He was often heard to assert that the community system must prevail; that the cities of the East had seen their best days; that houses and lots in them would no longer rise in value; that they would soon be literally deserted; and that, as he expressed it, men then living would see the day when foxes would stare from the windows of the crumbling buildings of Philadelphia. His mission was to conduct a school of industry in which " the arts that conquer the forces of Nature " should be taught.

The new constitution and the establishment of the six

---

* United States Gazette, March 21, 1826.

departments had been cheerfully accepted by the people. But the next reforms to be introduced bred trouble. First came a decree prescribing uniformity of dress. For men, the outer garments were to be a collarless jacket, drawn on over the head, pantaloons buttoned to the jacket, and a belt around the waist. The women were to wear pantalets, and a sleeveless frock that came down to the knees. Against this many of them openly rebelled, refused to wear the costume, and would have nothing to do with those who did. Still, the great projector did not lose heart. Such things were but the fruit of the irrational system in which the human race had been trained since the first man set foot on earth. They were painful and hard to endure, yet they must be borne with the patience of a reformer.

As such Owen took up his burden, and on the fourth of July, 1826, went one step further, and made a Declaration of Mental Independence which shocked and horrified far more people than it ever converted. Man, he said, up to that hour, all the world over, had been a slave to a trinity of the most monstrous evils that could possibly be combined to inflict mental and physical evils on the whole race. One was private or individual ownership of property; another was absurd and irrational systems of religion; the third was the marriage tie, which, he declared, ought to be made without any ceremony and terminated at the pleasure of those concerned. This was too much. His theories about property and co-operation, the arrangements of buildings, and the education of children were matters of opinion. In a land of toleration he might hold any religious belief or none. But the moment he touched the marriage rite he touched public morality, and his views were denounced from one end of the country to the other. Newspaper after newspaper attacked him. People whose friends, sisters, daughters had gone to New Harmony were shocked and alarmed. One anxious mother, whose three daughters were members of the Community, wrote to Maclure in great stress of mind to know what this declaration meant. He assured her that he had been six months in New Harmony, yet had seen no immorality, no vice; that he knew of no place where the married were so faithful and the young so chaste, " and for the best of reasons, for the bribe to abuse

purchase of his freedom and that of his children, who meantime were to be trained in a " school of industry." *

That an example of such a community might be set, Miss Wright, in the autumn of 1825, purchased a tract of twenty-four hundred acres on the Wolf river, thirteen miles from Memphis, and there planted a town which she called Nashoba. Her purpose was threefold: She wished to found a community in which the negro slave should be educated, trained, and made fit for freedom; she wished to emancipate him when educated, and so set an example which, if followed, would in the end abolish slavery in the South; and she wished to bring together in one village men and women of all nationalities who were eager to devote their lives to the search for truth and rational happiness. Money was freely given, and the experiment was tried. But Nashoba shared the fate of New Harmony, and in 1829 Miss Wright took her negroes off to Hayti, whither another abolitionist, Benjamin Lundy, was entreating his countrymen to send their manumitted slaves.

After the failure at Nashoba, Miss Wright went to New Harmony, and with Robert Dale Owen edited the Nashoba and New Harmony Gazette. But in the autumn of 1828 she entered the lecture field and made a tour of the chief cities, delivered courses of free lectures on education, manners, morals, and religion, and shocked her auditors by the boldness of her projects and the immorality of her teachings. Some were horrified at the appearance of a woman on the lecture platform; some thought her opinions on free education and the wisdom of co-operation little better than the vagaries of a lively imagination; but when she urged the abolition of the marriage rite, told her audiences that incompatibility of temper was good ground for divorce, and that no distinction ought to be made between legitimate and natural children, the cry for her suppression grew so fierce that it soon became almost impossible to secure a lecture hall, a church, a court-house, or a school in which to deliver her lectures. Yet she

---

* Genius of Universal Emancipation. United States Gazette, December 16, 28, 1825.

was not without followers.   " Fanny Wright Societies " were formed in many towns and cities, the reforms she advocated were seriously undertaken, and New York city made the centre of the new movement.   There an old wooden church was purchased, and, under the name of Hall of Science, it became the headquarters of the sect.   To it in 1829 the New Harmony Gazette was removed and issued as the Free Enquirer.   It claimed to be a weekly newspaper under the influence of no religious sect, controlled by no political party, and muzzled by no fear of lack of patronage.   It was to be free to inquire into every social abuse; free to express any opinion it pleased on any subject social, moral, religious, or political; and was to be the friend of the working-man in his efforts to secure his rights.

Scarcely was the Free Enquirer established when the campaign opened and the working-men were summoned to meet and organize for defence of their rights.   Hundreds responded, and before adjournment a committee of fifty was appointed to prepare a plan of organization and an address.   At another meeting a month later an Assembly ticket was put in the field, and resolutions, which did duty as the platform of the Working-man's party, were adopted.*   On this occasion Robert Dale Owen was present, acted as secretary, and was accused later with having had much to do with drafting the platform.   This he denied, but the anti-religious, the communistic, the agrarian doctrines it contained leave no doubt that the Free Enquirers were in control, and had used the name of the working-man to make popular a social system which concerned him but little.

In the opinion of the reformers, the first appropriation of the soil of New York to private possession was " barbarously unjust."   It was feudal in character, for those who were given enormous grants were in reality lords, and those who received little or nothing were no better than vassals.   The hereditary transmission of wealth on the one hand, and of poverty on the other, thus provided for, had brought down to the generation then living all the ills of feudalism, and these were the

---

* The meeting was held October 19, 1829.

causes of present calamities. Banks and bankers were next denounced. A hundred broken banks, a thousand kinds of counterfeit notes, an army of bankers, " the greatest knaves, impostors, and paupers of the age," who had promised to redeem thirty-five million of papers with four million of specie, admonished the people to destroy banks altogether. A third form of privilege which ought to be destroyed was the exemption from taxation of churches, church property, and the property of priests under fifteen hundred dollars, for it was nothing short of a direct and positive robbery of the people. Auctions ought also to be regulated. As then conducted, they were a source of immense and unjust revenue to the auctioneers, who, without any return to the public beyond a small tax, divided two and even three millions of dollars among them each year. When the resolutions were adopted, an " Association for the Protection of Industry and for the Promotion of National Education " was formed, and every member pledged to support no man at the polls who would not support the cause of the people in the Legislature.

The seriousness of this movement, and the eagerness with which laborers, mechanics, clerks, men who belonged to every class of the great body of toilers, hastened to give it encouragement and support now brought into existence a new journal, and in October, 1829, the first number of The Workingman's Advocate made its appearance. The editors were two young mechanics who had caught the spirit of the age and were eager for the reform of society. "We think," said they in the prospectus of the Advocate, " we see in the existing state of society around us something radically wrong. We see one portion living in luxury and idleness. We see another engaged in employments which are useless or worse than useless. We see a third part—and it is the most numerous—groaning under the oppressions and miseries inflicted on it by the other two, and we see all suffering from the effects of vice produced by luxury and indolence, and of ignorance caused by poverty. We are therefore opposed to monopolies, exemptions, exclusive privileges. We consider it an exclusive privilege for one part of the community to have the means of education in college while another is restricted to the common schools, or forced by dire poverty to have no education at all. We are therefore in favor of a system of education equally open to all men." On the same principle the Advocate was opposed to banks in general, and to the Bank of the United States in particular, was against imprisonment for debt, against the ownership of land in large quantities by private individuals, and in favor of a lien law.

Shocking as these demands seemed to the clergy, the men of property, and the conservative part of the community, they were regarded as mild by a half-crazy Quaker named Russell Comstock, who now came forward as the agitator of reforms still more sweeping and radical. As described by himself in his handbills and advertisements, he was a "Ciderist," a steady friend to the downtrodden and oppressed, the enemy of monopolists, and a firm believer in equal rights for men and women. No man, he thought, was fit to be an assembly-man or a State senator who did not believe in the establishment of national schools, where children should be taught trades and morality, but not religion; who was not willing to see the wife put on a par with her husband; who did not advocate a lien law for working-men, the abolition of imprisonment for debt, a bankrupt law for the benefit of honest debtors, and the gradual abolition of all laws for the collection of debts. These were the principles of what he called "pure republicanism"; and that they might be tested he issued a call for a public meeting one day in October, and asked that all who came should be prepared to pledge themselves to give his pure republicanism a hearty support.

On the appointed day and hour quite a crowd gathered about the City Hall, from the steps of which Comstock made a long speech in explanation of his views. His hearers were so delighted that they nominated him for President, for State senator, for member of the Assembly, and would probably have gone on down the list of officers had not the constable arrested Comstock for disturbing the peace and carried him before a magistrate.* But he was not to be suppressed, and up to the day of election scattered handbills broadcast over the city.

---

* New York American, November 6, 1829.

Though his efforts did him little good—he received but one hundred and thirty-seven votes for member of the Assembly—they went far to arouse the working-men to support the ticket the committee of fifty had placed in the field. It was then the custom in New York to open the polls on three consecutive days. At the close of the first day it seemed so likely that the Working-men's Ticket would triumph that the journals which upheld the Republican cause called loudly on the friends of good order to rally. The general impression prevails, said one newspaper, that the ticket for Assembly got up by the disciples of Fanny Wright, and wrongfully called the Mechanics' Ticket, has received a large proportion of the votes given yesterday. Some have declared that it is far ahead of every other. Be this as it may, it becomes the friends of good order in this community, of whatever party, to go to the polls and by their votes prevent so shameful a result. Shameful it would be if even a moderate support were given to tickets prepared by persons who scoff at morality and demand a system of public robbery.* " We understand," said another, " with astonishment and alarm that the ' Infidel Ticket,' miscalled ' the Working-men's Ticket,' is far ahead of every other Assembly ticket in the city. What a state of things have we reached! A ticket got up openly and avowedly in opposition to all banks, in opposition to social order, in opposition to the rights of property, running ahead of every other! Is not this sufficient to startle men who have regard for the fundamental laws of society?" † On the second and third days the friends of religion and order thus appealed to did rally, and but one candidate on the Mechanics' Ticket, Ebenezer Ford, was elected.‡

The great vote cast for Ford—6,166—alarmed the community. All the horrors of anarchy seemed at hand. The " Fanny Wright Ticket," the " Infidel Ticket," was denounced, and the Legislature called on to unseat Mr. Ford. The leaders of this miscalled Mechanics' party, the people

---

* New York American, November 6, 1829; New York Evening Post, November 3, 1829.

† Courier and Enquirer, November 3, 1829.

‡ New York Evening Post, November 9, 1829.

were told, held that everything was wrong in the present state
of society, and that the whole system must be changed.
Their object was represented to be to turn the State into an
Owenite Community, confiscate all land and hold it for the
general use of the people, strike down religion, and abolish
marriage.

So horrid a picture of socialism disturbed the mechanics,
who now made haste to publicly disavow all connection with
Owen, with Fanny Wright and the Free Enquirers, and at a
ward meeting passed resolutions denying all sympathy with
the "Infidel Party"; repelling with scorn the charge that
they were hostile to the civil, moral, and religious institutions
of the country; and declaring agrarian laws to be debasing,
wicked, and dishonest. The New York Typographical Society
went further yet. Some time before the election the newly
formed Association for the Protection of Industry and the
Promotion of National Education sent to every organized
trade in the city a copy of the plan of the association, a pamphlet on National Education, by Robert Dale Owen, and a
request that the society would join in the effort to secure the
needed reforms. It was high time, the accompanying letter
said, that the friends of equal rights made a firm stand against
the unrepublican influences of the day. Labor was not only
unprotected, but was oppressed, despised, and stripped of its
just reward. There was no system of education affording
instruction to the children of the rich and poor alike; none
free from clerical and sectarian influences and class distinc-
tions; none suited to induce in the rising generation habits
of industry, plant principles of morality, or awaken feelings
of brotherly love. Yet it was possible to obtain a better system
of education and proper protection to industry if those most
concerned would bestir themselves. Let tracts be written
and scattered among the working-classes; let associations be
formed all over the land, and a regular correspondence carried
on between them; let the clergy be watched, and the needed
legislation would soon be obtained.

The Typographical Society, in common with the other
trade associations, having received these documents, proceeded
to consider them, and noticing that the pamphlet was written

by Owen, and the letter signed by Owen as secretary of the association, supposed he was also the author of the plan, and appointed a committee to report as to who he was and in what his scheme consisted. The committee assured the typesetters that Robert Dale Owen was a Scotchman, that he probably had never been naturalized, and that he had been assisted in his labors " by one Fanny Wright, also an exotic of some notoriety."

It does seem unaccountably strange, said the report, that a native of that part of the world where thousands are every day groaning under oppression should leave these unfortunates, come over to the New World, and in the midst of a people enjoying the fullest liberty proclaim himself the apostle of equal rights and tender them the hand of friendship against their oppressors. Such insolence might well be treated with contempt were it not for the fact that a band of choice spirits of foreign origin have united and, taking advantage of our mild laws, are sowing the seeds of discontent and rebellion. It is true that there is some distress among laboring people. It is true that labor is not as well paid as in times past; that a man working with his hands is now unable to earn as much as he once could. But in our country, at least, the distress is caused not by anything Owen would reform, but by the introduction of labor-saving machinery during the last thirty years. Has Owen any remedy to propose? Far from it. He calls on the working-men to associate for defence of their rights when no rights are endangered. The report ended with a repudiation of his plan and a denial of all sympathy with his purposes.* The Painters' Society, on the other hand, took a different view, admitted that much Mr. Owen said was true, and was disposed to favor his plan for free education. At Philadelphia, where the working-men supported a ticket at the October election for city and county officers, they too denied the charge of sympathy with Miss Wright as warmly as their fellow-laborers in New York. " We view," so ran a resolution adopted at a public meeting after the election, " the re-

---

* New York Evening Post, December 8, 1829.   Free Enquirer, December 19 1829.

port charging us with being disciples of Miss Wright, and connecting religious points with our contention, as a base fabrication propagated by our enemies; we disclaim all adherence to Miss Wright's principles, and hold them foreign to our views, and appeal to the fact of the existence of the Working-men's party on the principles it now professes for nearly a year before she appeared among us."

But it mattered little whether the working-men avowed or disavowed sympathy with the Free Enquirers. The fact remained that a serious reform movement was well under way, and was spreading and gaining in importance daily. All over the country journals were appearing to advocate it, and societies were forming to labor in its behalf. In New York city the Telescope was busy exposing the designs of the clergy, and holding up to public view the dangers of ecclesiastical encroachment. At Rochester the Spirit of the Age was denouncing imprisonment for debt and capital punishment, and calling loudly for a mechanics' lien law. At Canton, in Ohio, the Farmers' and Mechanics' Society of Stark County had been founded to spread the new doctrines and agitate for co-operation and reform. At St. Louis there was a Society of Free Enquirers. In Alabama " The Ladies Bill," to give women the right to hold after marriage property which belonged to them before, was warmly debated in the Legislature, and in Tuscaloosa another Spirit of the Age upheld the cause of the people as vigorously as its Rochester contemporary. The Southern Free Press, of Charleston, South Carolina, announced its principles to be " No sect, no creed, open to all," and declared that it would collect such information as was useful to mechanics and working-men, and would look to them for support. " Our great object," said the editor in his prospectus, " will be to urge you to break down the barrier which separates your children from those of lordly aristocrats by the establishment of national schools." At New Castle, in Delaware, an Association of Working People was formed with a membership open to any person twenty-one years of age who was engaged in any branch of productive labor. How is it, said the preamble to their constitution, that all classes save the laboring are heard in the Legislature? The commercial, the agricultural, the manufacturing ask for protection, and it is granted. But what is accorded the working-man? Nothing. Yet who needs protection more? The price of labor is hourly going down because of the numbers thrown out of employment by labor-saving machinery. The cost of every article of consumption meantime is increased by taxation. " Does not the present system under such circumstances tend to increase the poverty of the poor and add to the riches of the rich? " Let us then be represented in the Legislature. Let us unite at the polls and give our votes to no candidate who is not pledged to support a rational system of education to be paid for out of the public funds, and to further a rightful protection of the laborer. At Wilmington, Delaware, was another Free Press likewise pledged " to be open to all for the free, chaste, and temperate discussion of subjects connected with the welfare of the human family." Its mission was " to arouse the attention of working-men to the importance of co-operation in order to attain the rank and station in society to which they are justly entitled by virtue of industry, but from which they are excluded by want of a system of equal republican education." In New York city two new journals of a strongly agrarian sort began their career early in 1830. The one, The Friend of Equal Rights, demanded the equal division of property among the adults of a family at the age of maturity. The other, the Daily Sentinel, was devoted " to the interests of mechanics and other working-men," and at once became a political power. Indeed, it was started for the sole purpose of becoming such a power.

The late election in the city made it clear that the working-men had, in the language of our time, bolted their party, had supported a ticket which was not put forward by any political faction, and had done so because they were discontented, and because they did not believe that their grievances would ever be removed by the men then in power. Six thousand votes cast solidly for or against any of the three parties then struggling for control in the city and State was too serious a matter to be treated lightly, and each of the three began to strive eagerly for the support of the working-man.

These three parties were the friends of Adams and Clay,

who called themselves the Administration party; the friends of Jackson and Van Buren, who were known as the regular Republicans, and the Antimasons. The Republicans, with a show of public virtue to which they could lay small claim, sought to destroy the union of Working-men and Free Enquirers, and, in the hope of doing so, raised the cry of Infidel party, and called on the priests and ministers of every sect to stop the new movement. They expressed horror at the communistic and agrarian doctrine of the so-called Mechanics' party and its organ, the Daily Sentinel, and summoned manufacturers, business men, land-owners, farmers, " bank gentlemen," and friends of law and order to rally to the support of popular government; they held ward meetings and county conventions, and under the name of mechanics and working-men protested against the doctrines of Frances Wright and Robert Dale Owen. But all in vain.

From the city the movement spread to the State, where it was taken up by the leaders of every one of the innumerable knots of anti-regency, anti-Van Buren, Antimasonic and Clay Republicans. At the charter election in Albany, in the spring of 1830, the working-men united on a ticket and carried four wards out of five. In Troy the same course was pursued, and " not one regency man," it was boastfully said, was elected. For this they were ridiculed by the Republican or Jackson press as " workies," and were held up as Federalists, as " the old enemy in a new disguise," as men bent on the destruction of society. When the autumn came and the time approached for the election of State officials, a convention was called to meet at Salina and name working-men's candidates for Governor and Lieutenant-Governor. Seventy delegates from thirteen counties responded, and put Erastus Root and Nathaniel Pitcher in the field, but neither would accept. To this convention New York city sent two delegations, one of which was rejected; whereupon it met and nominated a rival working-men's ticket, on which were the names Smith and Hertlett. Neither of these men were serious candidates. The strength and the weakness of the party was in New York city, where, in September, a meeting was held in the North American Hotel. All who were in favor of a republican sys-

As reports of the intended publication passed from mouth to mouth the respectable part of the community gave them no heed, or regarded the forthcoming book as a catchpenny for hawkers and pedlers. But there were among the Masons a few hot-heads, who took alarm, and, having made up their minds that the book should never appear, went on to carry out their decision, and began with intimidation. Many patrons of Miller's newspaper suddenly withdrew their subscriptions; suits were commenced against him to enforce the payment of small debts; and threats were made which led him to believe that an attack on his office was meditated. Even Morgan did not escape, and one day in August an abusive " notice and caution " was published in a Canandaigua newspaper called the Ontario Messenger, and was reprinted in the Batavia Spirit of the Times and the People's Press.

The publicity thus given to the matter now attracted the attention of a man of some means, who believed that, rightly managed, the book would prove to be a source of great profit. He came to Batavia accordingly, took lodgings at the tavern, represented himself as a Canadian, gave his name as Daniel Johns, and soon offered to join Miller in the publication of Morgan's book. The offer was gladly accepted. Johns was admitted to the partnership, advanced forty dollars, and obtained possession of some of the manuscript. The little he saw was enough to convince him that the book would never succeed, and a demand was at once made on Miller for a return of the money. Failing in this, Johns sued out a warrant before a magistrate of Le Roy. On the night of that same day some fifty men, under the lead of a resident of Canandaigua, met at a tavern in Stafford and marched thence to Batavia for the purpose of breaking into the printing office and destroying the manuscript and printed sheets of the book; but something deterred them, and no attack was made till the night of Sunday, September tenth, when the two buildings used by Miller as printing offices were discovered to be on fire. The flames were extinguished, and on examination it was found that an incendiary had been at work. The sides of the buildings were smeared with turpentine. A brush used for the purpose was

picked up near by, and balls of cotton and whisps of straw
soaked with turpentine were found under the stairways.
Meantime early in the morning of this same Sunday Nicholas
G. Chesebro, of Canandaigua, a hatter by trade, and one of
the coroners of Ontario County, obtained from Jeffrey Chip-
man, justice of the peace, a warrant for the arrest of Morgan
on a charge of stealing a shirt and cravat from an innkeeper
named Kingsley. Armed with this, and attended by the constable and a small posse, Chesebro repaired to Batavia, and on
Monday, September eleventh, Morgan was apprehended. The
prisoner had been arrested for debt in July, was at that time on
the limits of the jail, and could not lawfully be taken without
them. But it mattered not, and in utter defiance of law he
was carried to Canandaigua, and there discharged by the justice when it was proved that the shirt and cravat were borrowed and not stolen. The next minute he was rearrested
for an old debt of two dollars and sixty-five cents due an innkeeper, confessed judgment, and, stripping off his coat, asked
the constable to levy on it. The request was refused, and
Morgan was sent to the common jail. There he remained till
about nine o'clock on the night of September twelfth, when
a man named Loton Lawson appeared at the jail, paid the debt,
persuaded the jailer's wife, who was in charge in her husband's
absence, to liberate the prisoner, and came out of the jail with
Morgan on his arm. When a few yards from the door, Morgan
was seized by a number of men, and, despite his struggles and
cries of murder, was hurried into a carriage. Many persons
living near heard his cries, and one man, hurrying from his
house to ascertain the cause, met Edward Sawyer and Nicholas
G. Chesebro, who were standing by quiet spectators of the
scene, and asked what was the matter. Chesebro answered,
" Nothing, only a man has been let out of jail and has been
taken on a warrant and is going to be tried." Thus assured,
he did not interfere, and the carriage was driven to Rochester.
Just beyond the town a change of carriage, horses, and driver
was made, after which Morgan was taken westward along the
ridge road toward Lewiston. As the journey proceeded the
utmost secrecy is said to have been observed. Public houses
were avoided as much as possible, the blinds of the carriage

imprisonment in the common jail of Ontario County. Sheldon stood trial, was found guilty, and was confined in the jail for three months. Had the men been acquitted, the disgust and indignation of that part of the community which owed no allegiance to masonry could not have been greater. In its opinion the whole masonic fraternity was now in league to shield the murderers of Morgan. The sentence of the court was described as an insult to an enlightened people; the newspapers were accused of suppressing facts, of holding back information, and of taking no notice of any public proceeding concerning Morgan. At Seneca the people, in mass meeting assembled, resolved that all secret societies were dangerous to freedom; that masonry was especially so, as Masons had now shown themselves ready to murder their fellow-men in the interests of their order; that no Mason should be supported for any public office; and that every newspaper which did not publish full accounts of Morgan meetings must be proscribed. The committees appointed by the towns, convinced that the trial had been a farce, that the pleas of guilty were to stop investigation, and that the affidavits of Chesebro, Sawyer, and Lawson did not begin to disclose all they knew, called for a convention at Lewiston for the purpose of determining what steps should be taken to restore Morgan to his country, his freedom, and his family; to discover and punish those who had by violence and fraud deprived him of his liberty and perhaps of his life; to disclose the extent of the conspiracy; and to make known to the public the motives which prompted the conspirators to acts ruinous to our free institutions.

While the Lewiston committee was gathering information, all manner of guesses as to the fate of Morgan were made. One newspaper asserted that he was kept at Fort Niagara a few days and then put to death. Another maintained that three men took him into Canada; that Captain Brant, a son of the Mohawk chief whose name is forever joined with the massacres in Wyoming and Cherry Valley, was asked to send him to the northwest coast; that when Brant refused, some British officers were urged to take him down the St. Lawrence, and that when they declined Morgan was killed and his body flung into the river. Yet another version represents him as led, bound and blindfolded, to Newark, Upper Canada, only to be brought back to the fort and executed.

So firm was the belief that Morgan had at one time at least been taken over the border, that the Lieutenant Governor of Upper Canada offered a reward of fifty pounds for information as to his whereabouts,* and Brant publicly denied that he had ever been asked to dispose of Morgan.† At the request of the Lewiston committee, Governor Clinton now issued a third proclamation, offering one thousand dollars for the discovery of Morgan if alive, and, if dead, two thousand dollars for the discovery of the murderers.‡

When the spring local elections came on, the excitement against the Masons took on a political form. It was now not uncommon to find five, six, even seven columns of a newspaper filled with accounts of Morgan meetings, and the assertions and counter-assertions of private citizens. The people of one town resolved not to support a Mason for any office, State, county, or town; those of a second declared that they deemed " Freemasons unfit for any office of confidence "; those of a third dismissed their minister because he belonged to the fraternity; the resolution adopted at Poultney reads: " We will not hear any person preach unless the said preacher should refuse to meet with any lodge of Freemasons, and openly declare that masonry is bad "; at Middlebury a town meeting was warned " for the purpose of taking into consideration the late masonic outrages and to make nominations to fill the different offices in this town."

To such a height had the popular feeling been raised that the county committees, finding that sometimes, as in the case of Niagara County, the grand juries were packed and would not indict, and at others, as in Monroe County, the grand juries could secure no direct testimony, though much circumstantial evidence, and so failed to return a bill, appealed by petitions to the Legislature. These early in March were laid before the Assembly, and sent to the Committee on Courts of Justice. But finding that a majority of the members were

---

* American Daily Advertiser, February 19, 1827.
† York Observer, February 26, 1827.   ‡ March 19, 1827.

Masons, it asked to be discharged, and the papers went to another. The report when made closed with a statement that, having failed to devise a tribunal for the investigation of the outrage, a tribunal with jurisdiction over the whole extent of country covered by the conspiracy, with power to enforce the attendance of witnesses, with right to imprison such as refused to obey, and with authority to arrest and hold for trial, yet not infringe the chartered privileges of the humblest citizen, nothing was left but to recommend a joint committee of investigation and a reward of five thousand dollars for the discovery of Morgan if living, and a like sum for the apprehension of his murderers if he were dead. Resolutions embodying these suggestions were, however, voted down by a great majority of nearly three to one.*

The refusal of the Legislature to act, the continued failure of grand juries to indict, the silence of the masonic newspapers, or, what was worse, the imperfect reports of Morgan meetings, and even positive assertions that Morgan was not dead, served but to increase the excitement. The whole population of Ontario, Monroe, Livingston, Genesee, Erie, Niagara, and Orleans Counties seemed arrayed as Masons and Antimasons. In Genesee, where the feeling was especially strong, a great meeting of citizens of the county was held at Batavia, and every voter pledged to support none but Antimasons. Three thousand people, men and women, were estimated to have been present. This was followed by a call from the " Morgan Committee " for a convention at Warsaw to nominate a candidate for the State Senate.

Without the limits of New York, Antimasonry excited little or no interest. In many places it was regarded as a shrewd electioneering movement. At others it was believed that the commotion had been stirred up in order to sell a new edition of an old book, and that Morgan had been abducted by his friends.

To disprove these rumors and, if possible, confirm the belief that he had been murdered, the Lewiston committee

---

* Albany Argus, April 12, 1827. The report of the committee is in Niles's Register, April 14, 1827, vol. xxxii, pp. 120, 121.

kept boats and vessels busy for months dredging the Niagara river and the shore of Lake Ontario. But no body was found till one day in October, when a hunting party discovered a corpse stranded on the lake shore some forty miles from Fort Niagara. A coroner was at once sent for, an inquest was held, and, as the body was in such an advanced stage of decomposition as not to be recognizable, a verdict of drowning was rendered and the remains buried on the beach. In ordinary times an event so common would have passed unnoticed. But these were no ordinary times, and the report of the coroner was no sooner published than the Lewiston committee began to suspect that the dead man had been Morgan. Hurrying to the spot, the grave was opened, and what seemed a strong resemblance to Morgan was recognized. The coroner thereupon assembled a new jury, examined Mrs. Morgan and a host of men who knew her husband, and, influenced by the testimony so collected, a verdict was rendered by the jury that the body was that of Morgan. The corpse was then removed with great ceremony to Batavia, where it was interred in the presence of an immense crowd.

The account of these proceedings soon reached Canada and came before the eyes of the friends of a man named Timothy Monro, who in September was drowned by the upsetting of his boat in the Niagara river. The description of the body, and especially of the clothing and the bundle of tracts in the pockets, convinced them that the corpse found on the beach was not that of Morgan, but of Monro. So sure were they that they came to Batavia, persuaded the coroner to hold a third inquest, and presented evidence so overwhelming that a third verdict was obtained, and the unknown dead declared to have been Timothy Monro. The fate of Morgan then remained as impenetrable a mystery as before.

By this time Miller had published the now famous " Illustrations of Masonry by One of the Fraternity who has devoted Thirty Years to the Subject "; the Lewiston committee had given to the world a long " Narrative of the Facts and Circumstances relating to the Kidnapping and Presumed Murder of William Morgan," and in the local elections some seventeen thousand votes had been cast for Antimasons. To secede from the fraternity and make a public declaration of the fact became the most popular act an aspiring politician, a doctor with small practice, or a tradesman with little business could perform. So great was the defection that in February, 1828, a convention of seceding Masons was held at Le Roy. Morgan's "Illustrations of Masonry" was there declared to be a fair and full exposition of the first three degrees; a committee was appointed to prepare and publish all degrees above that of master; a memorial was ordered to be sent to Congress complaining of the use of Fort Niagara for the imprisonment of Morgan, and a second convention called to meet July fourth. Shortly after the delegates had gone home yet another body, representing the Antimasons of the twelve western counties of New York, assembled in the same town. The address which it issued to the people of the State set forth that the existence in such a country as ours of any society whose purpose, principles, and measures are secret is hostile to the spirit and dangerous to the existence of free institutions; that masonry was such a society, and had showed itself ready to subvert law and defy justice in furthering its own ends; that the entire subjection all over the Union of the press to masonry was an evil which called for correction; that it was necessary for the people to establish free presses with editors ready and willing to uphold the rights of citizens and the laws of the land; and that a convention of Antimasons ought to meet at Utica and take measures to destroy masonry as an institution, to establish free presses, assert the supremacy of the law, and protect the rights of citizens against the vindictive persecutions of masonic bodies.*

This was a serious movement. A presidential election was at hand; congressmen, a Governor, a State Legislature were to be chosen, and the political results of the convention were quickly apparent. When the memorial from Le Roy reached Congress, no committee wanted to receive it, and a good excuse was found for sending the paper to the President.

When Pitcher, who by the death of De Witt Clinton in

---

* Proceedings of a Convention of Delegates opposed to Freemasonry, which met at Le Roy, Genesee County, N. Y., March 6, 1828.

February had become Governor of New York, heard of the proceedings at Le Roy, he lost no time in urging the Legislature to act, and easily obtained authority to appoint a special commissioner to investigate the Morgan affair. When the memorial from the convention was laid before the Legislature, it was found to contain a request that, as the masonic oaths were profane and impious, no oaths should be allowed unless administered by a public officer. This was not granted, though an act to do so was passed by the Assembly.

Much stress was now laid on the character of the masonic oaths, and no pains were spared to excite the animosity of the churches and array them against masonry. Its oaths were depicted as shockingly unchristian, its ceremonies as sacrilegious, and the whole institution as antireligious in that it profaned Holy Scripture by using it for unholy purposes, made religion a performance of outward duties, confounded knight-errantry with Christianity, and was regarded by its members as a saving institution.*

To the American proud of his country and her free institutions, to the firm believer in democracy, the appeal was made from the standpoint of politics. He was assured by men who had once been Masons that the very design and purpose of freemasonry were hostile to the principles of our Government and the welfare of society. He was told that it exercised an absolute jurisdiction over the lives and persons of its members, and, with the recollection of the Morgan case in mind, he believed the statement. He was assured that it arrogated to itself the right to administer oaths and to punish for offences unknown to the law; that it hid crime and protected the guilty; assumed titles and dignities not compatible with republican institutions; and created an aristocracy odious in the sight of a free people. †

---

* Two oaths were cited as especially offensive: "Furthermore do I promise and swear that I will aid and assist a companion royal arch Mason wherever I shall see him engaged in any difficulty, so far as to extricate him from the same, whether he be right or wrong." "I swear to advance my brother's best interests by always supporting his military fame and political preferment in opposition to another."

† Proceedings of the Convention of Seceding Masons, held at Le Roy, July 4, 1828.

The effect of such charges was lasting. Gradually a firm conviction took possession of the public mind that masonry was all it was said to be; that it did exercise a too powerful influence on the press; that it did control the acts of tribunals of justice in civil as well as in criminal cases; and that judges, juries, justices of the peace, and even referees had been forced to do its will.

In this state of the public mind the antimasonic convention assembled at Utica in August to take measures, so the call said, to destroy masonry as an institution, and, fully satisfied that no help would be given by either the friends of Adams or of Jackson for such a purpose, it disregarded both parties, nominated candidates of its own for Governor and Lieutenant-Governor of New York, and appointed a general committee to call future conventions if necessary. The candidates selected were Francis Granger and John Crary. Granger, who had already been nominated for Lieutenant-Governor by the Adams party, declined, and at a second convention of Antimasons at Le Roy, Solomon Southwick was chosen in his stead, and polled more than thirty thousand votes.

Meanwhile the excitement had spread to Vermont, where, in the congressional election of 1829, seven thousand votes were cast by the Antimasons. The whole New England belt from Boston to Buffalo fairly teemed with antimasonic newspapers.* A new political party had arisen to complicate still more the political situation in New York, and, indeed, in all the States from New England to Ohio.

---

* There were thirty-two in New York State.

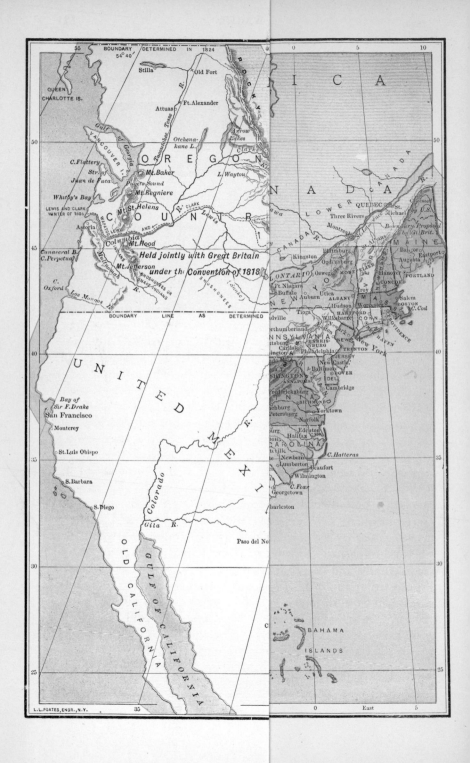

CHAPTER XLIV.

STATE OF THE COUNTRY FROM 1825 TO 1829.

THE social and economic conditions of the working people in the cities—conditions out of which the early labor movements grew—did indeed call loudly for reform. Ten years of rapid industrial development had brought into prominence problems of urban life and municipal government familiar enough to us, but new and quite beyond solution in 1825. The influx of paupers to partake of the benefits of the many charitable societies; the overcrowded labor market; the steadily increasing number of unemployed; the housing of the poor; the rise of the tenement house; the congestion of population in limited areas, with all its attendant vice and crime; and the destitution produced by low wages and lack of constant employment, had already become matters for serious consideration. An unskilled laborer, a hod-carrier, a wood-sawyer, a wood-piler in a city was fortunate if he received seventy-five cents for twelve hours of work and found employment for three hundred days in a year. Hundreds were glad to work for thirty-seven and even twenty-five cents a day in winter who in spring and summer could earn sixty-two and a half or perhaps eighty-seven and a half cents by toiling fourteen hours. On the canals and turnpikes fifteen dollars a month and found in summer and one third that sum in winter were considered good pay. In truth, it was not uncommon during the winter for men to work for their board. Nothing but perfect health, steady work, sobriety, the strictest economy, and the help of his wife could enable a married man to live on such wages. But the earnings of women were lower yet. Many trades and occupations now open to them either had no existence or were then confined to men. They might bind shoes, sew rags, fold and stitch books, become spoolers, or make coarse shirts and duck pantaloons at eight or ten cents a piece. Shirt-making was eagerly sought after, because the garments could be made in the lodgings of the seamstress, who was commonly the mother of a little family, and often a widow. Yet the most expert could not finish more than nine shirts a week, for which she would receive seventy-two or ninety cents. Fifty cents seems to have been the average.

To the desperate poverty produced by such wages many evils were attributed. Intemperance was encouraged, children were sent into the streets to beg and pilfer, and young girls were driven to lives of shame to an extent which but for the report of the Magdalene Society in New York and the action of the people * elsewhere would be incredible. The cities, in short, were growing with great rapidity, and were exhibiting every phase of life.

At New York, now the metropolis of the country, the growth of the city was astonishing to its own citizens. The population numbered one hundred and sixty-two thousand, an increase of forty thousand in five years. To keep pace with such an inpouring of strangers was hardly possible. More than three thousand buildings were under way in 1825; † yet such was the press that not an unoccupied dwelling house existed in the entire city, and it was quite common to see families living in houses with unfinished floors, with windows destitute of sashes, and in which the carpenters had not hung a single door. Nor was this an accident. Year after year the same thing occurred, and on one first of May—the great " moving day "—three hundred homeless people gathered in the park with their household goods and were lodged in the jail till the houses they had rented were finished and made habitable.

---

* At Portland the people on three occasions gathered and pulled down houses of ill fame. Portland Argus, November 11 and 14, 1825. A similar riot occurred in Boston. New York Evening Post, August 1, 1825.

† Most of these houses were built by speculators, and were erected so cheaply and hastily that several fell down while in course of construction; others were torn down by order of the authorities.

In the upper wards entire blocks of fine brick buildings had arisen on sites which in 1820 were covered with marshes or occupied with straggling frame huts of little value. In the neighborhood of Canal Street a new city stood on what a few years before was the shore of a stagnant pool. In Greenwich new streets had been opened, and all along the Bowery new houses had been put up. Never in the history of the city had its commerce been greater. Ten million dollars had been collected in duties in one year, a sum larger by eighty thousand than in the same time had been gathered at the customhouses of Boston, Philadelphia, Baltimore, Norfolk, and Savannah combined. Sixteen packets plied regularly between the city and Liverpool. Four more were engaged in trade with Havre. Seven were in the Savannah line, ten in the Charleston line, and four in the New Orleans, while innumerable brigs, sloops, schooners, and steamboats made stated trips to every seaport of importance on the coast. The city, it was said boastfully, was visited by merchants of every clime and from every part of the United States, so that New York might truly be called the mart of nations. Nor was this an idle boast. Five hundred new mercantile houses were said to have been established in the city in the early months of 1825, a statement well borne out by the crowded condition of the mercantile newspapers. The Gazette in seven days contained 1,115 new advertisements,* and in one issue, a week later, printed 213, and stated that 23 others were left out for want of space.†

There were now twelve banks in the city, with an aggregate capital of thirteen millions of dollars, paying dividends of from five to eight per cent., and ten marine insurance companies with a capital of ten million dollars. Yet even these were not enough to transact the volume of business, and when the Legislature met applications were made for charters for twenty-seven more banks with a combined capital of twenty-two and a half millions, and for thirty-one corporations of all sorts with a total capital of fifteen millions.

Thirteen hundred sailing vessels entered the port yearly.

---

* New York Gazette, April 14 to 21, 1825.
† New York Gazette, April 26, 1825.

nor wade a horse into the waters of either river; nor deliver milk between nine in the morning and five in the afternoon; nor buy nor sell; nor bring anything into nor take anything out of the city.

Restrictions of this sort were by no means peculiar. Indeed, there was little in the city government of New York that could not be paralleled in that of Philadelphia. There, too, were a mayor, a recorder, fifteen aldermen, and select and common council. The people elected councils. But the Governor of Pennsylvania appointed the recorder and the aldermen to hold office during good behavior, and the councils each year elected one of the aldermen to serve as mayor. Even in the selection of so important an officer as the constable the people had little to say. Annually the voters of each ward were required to elect two persons fit to be constables, and one of them must be appointed to the office by the mayor.

In Philadelphia, as in New York, occupants of houses must have the pavement before their premises swept to the middle of the street every Friday or pay a fine of five shillings. These sweepings the city would remove; but ashes, mud, shavings, or refuse not arising " from common housekeeping " must be removed at the cost of the housekeeper. There, too, each tenant must have fire buckets and a canvas bag hanging in his hall, and must lend a hand in the extinguishment of fires. There, too, on Sundays the streets were chained in the neighborhood of churches and houses of public worship. There, too, the constables preserved the peace during the day and the superintendent of the night watch and his men guarded the city by night.

To the watch belonged the care of the oil, wicks, lamps, and utensils used in illuminating the streets, and the duty of lighting the lamps each night at sundown and keeping them burning till dawn.

As far back as 1816 an effort was made to introduce gas, and the manufacture of what was called carbonated hydrogen was begun by a Dr. Kugler. Peale promptly put the apparatus in his museum, and informed the public that on certain nights the hall would be illuminated with " gas-lights which will burn without wick or oil." The managers of the new theatre next introduced it into their building as an attraction. Finally, a citizen put one of Kugler's gas machines in his dwelling house, and invited councils to come and see the new light. A committee was accordingly sent, and, after visiting Peale's Museum, the theatre, and Mr. Henry's residence, recommended that a standing committee on gas-light should be appointed to watch the progress of the new invention and report from time to time.

The public having satisfied its curiosity, the new light shared the fate of the velocipede just then exhibited in the museum, and was forgotten. In 1820, however, attention was again drawn to gas by the Masons, who, when they built their new hall, lighted it with Kugler's carbonated hydrogen. The whole neighborhood complained of the stench, and voted the Lodge Gas Works a nuisance. But the experiment proved so successful that in 1822 the Masons applied to councils for leave to lay pipes in the streets and furnish gas to such as were willing to burn it. The petition was rejected. Councils had no desire to encourage an innovation so dangerous, so offensive, and one likely to injure the business of candle makers and oil-dealers.

In other cities the friends of the new light fared better. Gas as a means of street lighting was adopted by Boston in 1822, and by New York in 1823, when the New York Gas-Light Company was incorporated. The work of actual introduction was slow, for there was not a foundry in the country where long iron pipes were cast, and every foot of the street main was brought from England.

An exhibition of Kugler's gas at Peale's Museum in Baltimore in 1816 led to the formation of a gas-light company in that city in 1817. There also the process of pipe-laying was slow, so that 1820 came before the company began business with three customers.

Now that Philadelphia had fallen behind her sister cities in enterprise, another attempt was made to introduce gas, and in 1825 a bill to incorporate the Philadelphia Gas-Light Company and give it power to lay pipes in the streets and furnish gas was reported in the Legislature. But again public prejudice defeated the scheme. Gas was denounced as an unsafe,

company thereupon gave grates to such consumers as were willing to be beholden to it, and then, the economy of coal having been proved, the sale was rapid, and the demand so great that at one time four thousand tons were stored in the city, and made, it was boastfully said, the largest coal heap in the United States.

To New Yorkers the new fuel was most welcome, for the price of wood was rising because of the quantity consumed by the steamboats. Thirteen that plied on the Hudson burned sixteen hundred cords a week. The ferry-boats used fourteen hundred more, making a total of three thousand cords per week, or one hundred thousand for the eight months the river was open. Each steamer on the Sound consumed sixty cords a trip, and, though all the immense quantity required for the purposes of transportation on river, bay, and Sound was not furnished by New York city, so much came from it that fuel had grown to be a heavy item in household expenses.

Now that the Supreme Court had destroyed the monopoly so long held by the Fulton-Livingston Company, and had opened the waters around New York to all vessels moved by steam no matter to whom they belonged, a sharp competition had resulted, and a fuel more economical than wood was needed by the steamboat companies. Already the effect of competition was visible. The fare to Providence had fallen to three dollars, and to Albany to a dollar, and on one line to seventy-five cents, provided no meals were furnished. The old Fulton Company met this by placing on their route a " safety barge," which was hailed as one of the remarkable improvements of the day. The Lady Clinton, as the barge was named, was a vessel of two hundred tons, with neither sails nor steam nor any means of propulsion, and was used exclusively for the transportation of passengers. Within was a spacious dining room ninety feet long, a deck cabin for ladies, state-rooms, a reading-room, and over all a promenade deck one hundred feet long shaded by an awning and provided with comfortable settees. As the barge had no means of locomotion, it was towed by the Commerce, one of the regular steamers of the line, and made the trip to Albany twice a week in sixteen hours. Passengers, said the advertisement, on the safety barge will not be exposed in the least to any accident which may happen by reason of fire or steam on board the steamboat. The noise of the machinery, the trembling of the vessel, the heat from the boilers, the furnace, and the kitchen—in short, everything which may be considered unpleasant or dangerous on a steamboat are wholly wanting on the barge.* Success attended the venture from the start, and as quickly as possible a companion, the Lady Van Rensselaer, was put on the route.

A journey northward by daylight on such a vessel was indeed a pleasure, for along no other river in all the land could be found scenery so magnificent and places of such historic interest. These—as the Commerce, pouring forth great clouds of smoke and cinders from its tall stack, crept northward at a speed which would now be thought insufferably slow, with the Lady Clinton tugging at the long hawser in the stern— some self-appointed cicerone was sure to point out to the traveller. Now it was the spot on the west bank, where Hamilton fell in the ever-memorable duel with Burr; now Harlem Heights; now Fort Lee, on the summit of the Palisades, or Fort Washington, on the east bank, places famous as the scenes of gallant fights in the war for independence; now the beauty of the Palisades, rising hundreds of feet above the river and stretching away northward for twenty miles a solid wall of rock to Tappan Bay, where near the little village of Tappan had once been the grave of Major André. As the boats sped on across Tappan Bay and Haverstraw Bay to Stony Point and West Point, the story of Arnold and André and the great conspiracy was retold in all its detail. At Catskill village a landing was always made for the accommodation in summer of passengers bound for Pine Orchard, a " resort of fashion " on the mountain side, where the Catskill Mountain Association had built a fine hotel overlooking the valley of the Hudson for sixty miles around. Long before Catskill village was reached night had come on, and the first streaks of dawn were visible when the Lady Clinton made fast to the dock at Albany, where the travellers scattered, and took passage on

---

* Albany Argus, August 9, 1825.

some of the thirteen stage lines which ran out of the city in as many directions.

Albany was now a city of sixteen thousand inhabitants, and in commercial and industrial importance was second to no other in the State save New York. Her streets were crowded with emigrants gathered from every part of the East and bound for the growing towns of the West. Now that the Erie Canal was open and in use, the canal boats, steamboats, sloops, and schooners that clustered around her wharves made an array of water craft which in number and tonnage could not be equalled by any seaport in the Union. No event in the history of the State surpassed in lasting importance the completion of the canal. After eight years of persistent labor, " the big ditch," so constantly the subject of ridicule, was finished, and in June the gates at Black Rock were opened and the waters of Lake Erie for the first time were admitted into the western division. Later in the month the capstone of that splendid chain of locks at Lockport was laid with masonic ceremonies, but it was not till October that the canal from end to end was thrown open to the public.

The celebration of the opening began at Buffalo, where, on the twenty-sixth of the month, a procession of citizens and militia escorted the orator and the invited guests to a gayly decorated fleet lying in wait on the canal. On the Seneca Chief, which headed the line, were two painted kegs full of water from Lake Erie. Behind it were the Superior, the Commodore Perry, the Buffalo, and the Lion of the West, a veritable Noah's ark, containing a bear, two eagles, two fawns, two Indian boys, birds, and fish—all typical of the products of the West before the advent of the white man. When the address had been made the signal was given, and the Seneca Chief, drawn by four gray horses, started eastward on a most memorable journey. As the fleet moved slowly along the canal, saluted by music, musketry, and the cheers of the crowd on the bank, the news was carried to the metropolis by the reports of a continuous line of cannon placed along the canal to Albany and down the Hudson to New York. When the last gun was fired at the Battery, the forts in the harbor returned the salute, and the news that New York had heard the tidings was sent back to Buffalo by a second cannonade. The progress of the little fleet was one continuous ovation, as town after town along the route vied with each other in manifestations of delight. From Albany an escort of gayly dressed steamboats accompanied the fleet down the river to New York, where the entire population, increased by thirty thousand strangers, turned out to receive it, and whence thousands, boarding every kind of craft, went down the bay to Sandy Hook. There Governor Clinton, lifting the kegs from the deck of the Seneca Chief, poured their contents into the sea, saying as he did so: " This solemnity at this place, on the first arrival of vessels from Lake Erie, is intended to indicate and commemorate the navigable communication which has been accomplished between our Mediterranean Seas and the Atlantic Ocean, in about eight years, to the extent of more than four hundred and twenty-five miles by the public spirit and energy of the people of the State of New York, and may the God of the heavens and the earth smile propitiously on this work and render it subservient to the best interests of the human race."

This ceremony over and a grand salute fired, the boats returned to the city, where a fine industrial parade, to which each trade society furnished a float with artisans at work, closed the day. At night there were balls, parties, dinners, and illuminations.

The canal thus opened to the world, which was, in truth, little more than a large ditch, for it was but four feet deep and forty feet wide, was connected with the Hudson by a basin made by inclosing a part of the river between the shore and a pier forty-three hundred feet long. From this basin the canal passes along the west bank of the Hudson nearly to the mouth of the Mohawk, which it follows to Schenectady. This part was used solely by freight boats. No canal packet, as the passenger boats were termed, ever came east of Schenectady, because of the many locks between it and the Hudson. Travellers bound west by water were carried by stage from Albany to Givens's Hotel, which stood a few rods from the canal in Schenectady. Shortly before eight in the morning and seven in the evening two blasts on a horn would give notice that the Buffalo packet was about to start, whereupon the west-bound travellers would hurry from the hotel and board a vessel not unlike a Noah's ark. The hull was eighty feet long by eleven feet wide, and carried on its deck a long, low house with a flat roof and sloping sides, which were pierced by a continuous row of windows provided with green blinds and red curtains. At the forward end was a room six feet long containing four berths, and called the "Ladies' Dressing Room." Behind it was a room thirty-six feet long, which was used as a cabin and dining-room by day and a bedroom by night. Precisely at nine o'clock the steward and his helpers would appear loaded down with adjustable berths, sheets, pillows, mattresses, curtains, and in a little time the cabin would resemble the interior of a modern sleeping car. Each berth was a narrow wooden frame with a strip of canvas nailed over it, and was held in place by two iron rods which projected from one side and fitted into two holes in the wall of the cabin, and by two ropes attached to the other side of the frame and made fast to rings in the ceiling. In this manner the berths were suspended in tiers of three, one over the other, along the two walls of the cabin, making thirty-six in all, with curtains hung before them. If more than four women were on board, and there usually were, one or two tiers in front of the "Ladies' Dressing Room" were cut off for their use by an opaque curtain. When the passengers outnumbered the berths, the men slept on the dining table or the floor.

Behind the cabin was the bar, and in the rear of this was the kitchen, always presided over by a negro cook.

When the weather was fine, the travellers gathered on the roof, reading, sewing, talking, and playing cards, till the helmsman would shout, "Bridge! bridge!" when the assembled company would rush headlong down the steps and into the cabin, to come forth once more when the bridge had been passed. To walk on the roof, if the packet was crowded, was not possible. It was the custom, therefore, to jump ashore as the boat rubbed along the bank, and walk on the towpath till a bridge was reached, and then jump on board as the boat glided from beneath.

Three horses, walking one before the other, dragged the boat four miles an hour, and by dint of relays every eight miles Utica was reached in just twenty-four hours. According to the inscription on the china plates of the packet boats, Utica, the site of which thirty years before was a wilderness, was then " inferior to none in the western section of the State in population, wealth, commercial enterprise, active industry, and civil improvements." At this thriving town other packets were taken to Lockport, whence passengers bound for Niagara went by stage to the Falls. At the end of the fourth day from Schenectady the jaded traveller reached Buffalo, three hundred and sixty-three miles by canal from Albany. The debt entailed on the State by this noble work, and by another joining Lake Champlain and the Hudson, was a trifle under eight millions of dollars, carrying an annual interest of four hundred and twenty-eight thousand, to meet which the State had pledged a duty on salt and sales at auction.* But, to the astonishment of the most eager advocates of inland navigation, before the canal was finished the tolls began to exceed the interest charges. In 1825 five hundred thousand, and in 1826 seven hundred and sixty-five thousand dollars, were paid in tolls. Fifty boats starting westward from Albany day after day was no uncommon sight. During 1826 nineteen thousand boats and rafts passed West Troy on the Erie and Champlain Canals. The new business created by this immense movement of freight cannot be estimated. Before the Champlain Canal was opened there were but twenty vessels on the lake. In 1826 there were two hundred and eighteen bringing timber, staves, shingles, boards, potashes, and giving employment to thousands of men in navigation, shipbuilding, and lumbering. Rochester became a flour-milling centre, and turned out one hundred and fifty thousand barrels a year. Even Ohio felt the impetus, and boats loaded with pig-iron

---

* Governor Clinton, in his message in 1826, stated that the debt created by the Erie and Champlain Canals was $7,944,770.90, on which the interest was $427,673.55, and that the fund available for the extinguishment of the debt was:

Tolls...	$771,780 10
Auction duties....................................	200,737 31
Salt duties.......................................	77,405 83
Other sources....................................	7,635 19
Total...	$1,057,558 43

from Madison County were seen in the basin at Albany. Orders for cherry boards and dressed lumber were received at Buffalo from Hartford and from dealers in Rhode Island. The warehouses along the canal bank at Buffalo were filled with the products of the East and the West; with wheat, grain, lumber, posts and rails, whiskey, fur and peltry bound for the markets of the Atlantic, and with salt, furniture, and merchandise bound for the West.

To the people of the West the opening of the canal was productive of vast benefit. Said a Columbus newspaper: " It takes thirty days and costs five dollars a hundred pounds to transport goods from Philadelphia to this city; but the same articles may be brought in twenty days from New York by the Hudson and the canal at a cost of two dollars and a half a hundred. Supposing our merchants to import on an average five tons twice a year; this means a saving to each of five hundred and sixty dollars." It meant, indeed, far more: it meant lower prices, more buyers, a wider-spread market, increased comfort for the settlers in the new States, and, what was of equal importance, an impetus to internal improvements which should open up regions into which even the frontiersman would not go.

As section after section of the Erie Canal was finished and opened to travel, and the day of its completion came nearer and nearer, a mania for internal improvements swept over the commercial States, and one by one many of the long-discussed projects began to take shape. On July fourth ground was broken in Ohio for a canal to join Lake Erie and the Ohio river. A fortnight later a goodly company from the counties of Ulster, Sullivan, and Orange in New York assembled at the summit level of the Delaware and Hudson Canal, and with music, prayers, and speeches beheld the beginning of that great work.* The Delaware and Chesapeake was well under way; the Chesapeake and Ohio was about to be commenced; while plans were on foot for canals to join New Haven and Northampton, Providence and Worcester, Boston with the Connecticut river, and Long Island Sound with Montreal by way of the

---

* Albany Argus, July 26, 1825.

valley of the Connecticut river, Vermont, and Lake Memphremagog. Indeed, early in 1826 a convention of delegates
from the towns of New Hampshire and Vermont met at Con-
cord to consider the expediency of such an enterprise.* Massachusetts, alarmed at the prospect of a diversion of her trade to
New York, had already appointed a commission to examine
into the possibility of cutting a canal from Boston harbor to the
Hudson, that she might tap the great western trade on its way
down to New York.† In a message on the subject, the Governor told the General Court that trade was passing from
Boston. The cheapness of transportation from Albany to New
York, and the abundant and variously supplied market at the
basin of the Erie Canal, had drawn west, he said, the produce
of the green hills of Berkshire and the rich valley of the
Housatonic. If the navigation of the Connecticut were improved as proposed, the produce of that valley would go to
enrich a seaport of Connecticut, while the Blackstone Canal,
joining Worcester and Providence, would open a new way
from the interior of Massachusetts to the coast of Rhode
Island, and all the trade of western and central Massachusetts
would be taken from Boston. Land transportation from Boston to Worcester or Providence then cost ten dollars a ton;
but by the canal a ton of freight could be hauled from Worcester to Providence for three dollars and thirty-three cents.

Philadelphia was in much the same condition as Boston.
Her western trade was seriously threatened. The day seemed
at hand when articles of her own manufacture would be sent
by sloop to Albany and by canal to the West, when she would
be outstripped by cities on the shore of Lake Erie, and would
find herself surpassed in trade and manufactures by Pittsburg.
If the great western carrying trade—an industry to which the
interior of the State owed no small part of its prosperity—was
not to be taken away by New York, a short and cheap route
to the Ohio river must be opened, and opened quickly.

Thus impelled by necessity, the community went seriously to work on the problem before it, and was soon engaged

---

* New England Palladium, January 13, 1826.
† Ibid., January 3, 1826.

in discussing the relative merits of railroads and canals. As far back as 1811, John Stevens, of Hoboken, a man who richly deserves to be called the father of the American railroad, applied to the Legislature of New Jersey for a railroad charter. None was granted, and the following year he turned to New York, where the Erie Canal Commissioners had just been appointed, and by means of a memoir, with plans and estimates, endeavored to persuade the commission to build a railroad and not a canal across the State to Buffalo.* Again he failed, but the events of the next few years greatly changed public opinion. War with Great Britain destroyed the coastwise commerce, and developed an enormous inland-carrying trade. The sight of thousands of wagons hurrying across New Jersey with military stores and ammunition; the sight of great fleets of " the ox-marine " † scudding along between New York and Trenton; the report that two million dollars had been paid during the war for the cartage of goods, wares, and produce between the Hudson and the Delaware, convinced Jerseymen that a highway of transportation was really needed across their State. When, therefore, Stevens again applied to the Legislature, he met with no difficulty in securing, in 1815, the first railroad charter ever granted in the New World.‡ His road was to join the Delaware and Raritan rivers, and serve to connect the steamboat lines from Philadelphia to Bordentown with those from New Brunswick to New York. But the project was far ahead of the times; the money wherewith to build it could not be secured, and Stevens was again doomed to disappointment. Nevertheless, the idea of moving vehicles by steam on a railway was taking root, and in 1819 another projector yet more advanced applied to Congress for aid with which to test the utility of his invention.# He had, he said, devised in theory a way of moving wheeled carriages by steam

---

* Documents Tending to Prove the Superior Advantages of Railway and Steam Carriages over Canal Navigation. New York, 1812.

† History of the People of the United States, vol. iv, pp. 220–221.

‡ Laws of New Jersey, Thirty-ninth Session, Second Sitting, Statute 68, 1815.

This man was Benjamin Dearborn, of Boston. His memorial was presented to the House of Representatives February 12, 1819. Journal of the House of Representatives, Fifteenth Congress, Second Session, p. 258.

on level railroads at the rate of a mile in three minutes, and of using vehicles so large that passengers might walk in them without stooping, and be furnished with accommodations for taking their meals and their rest during the passage, as in packets.* The boldness of his aims marked him out as a dreamer on whom practical congressmen were not disposed to waste either time and money, and, with the reference of the memorial to the proper committee, Dearborn and his railway were forgotten.

Stevens meanwhile had not lost heart. After failing in New York and New Jersey, he turned to Pennsylvania, and addressed a letter † on railroads to the Mayor of Philadelphia, who sent it to Councils, a body which manifested not the slightest interest in the matter. With business men, however, he fared better. To them the situation was serious. The New York canal was well under way. The appearance of the steamboat on the Mississippi put it within the power of the West to ignore the East, and trade directly with the world through New Orleans. If western trade was to be held against such competition, some cheap means of transportation to Pittsburg must be opened, and this the railroad seemed likely to furnish. It was not so costly as a turnpike; it would not freeze in winter, as did the water in the canals. Some men of means and prominence were persuaded to give the enterprise a trial, and in December, 1822, Stevens and his friends applied to the Legislature for a charter. To have attempted to build a railroad across the State of Pennsylvania from the Delaware to the Ohio would have been rash in the extreme. Half the distance was all they thought of covering, and, as there were good pikes from Philadelphia to Harrisburg and a canal almost completed from the Schuylkill to the Susquehanna, the proposed railroad was to begin at Harrisburg and end at Pittsburg. The House of Representatives, however, would not hear of this.

---

* "For obtaining these results, he relies on carriages propelled by steam, on level railroads, and contemplates that they be furnished with accommodation for passengers to take their meals and their rest during the passage, as in packets; that they be sufficiently high for persons to walk in without stooping, and so capacious as to accommodate twenty, thirty, or more passengers, with their baggage."   † January 5, 1821.

be opened to the foot of the mountains by canal and slack-water navigation, and that they should be joined by a canal passing through a tunnel four miles long under the Alleghanies. Lest the Legislature might not know what a tunnel was, the commissioners described it as " a passage like a well dug horizontally through a hill or mountain."

The utmost interest in the work of the commissioners was manifested all over the State. In January, 1824, a public meeting at Philadelphia * called for canals from the Susquehanna to Lake Erie and to the Ohio, and petitioned the Legislature not to delay the work.† In May another meeting issued a call for a Canal Convention to be held at Harrisburg in August. Fifty-six counties sent delegates, who declared that canals were needed; that the money appropriated for them would not be an expenditure, but an investment; that all local objects leading to a diffusive and unconnected use of public funds ought to give way for the present; and that public opinion would fully sustain the Legislature in all its efforts in behalf of internal improvements.‡ The Legislature had already established a regular board of canal commissioners,# and a year later ordered them to proceed at once to build " The Pennsylvania Canal " at State expense, and made a first appropriation of money. On July fourth, 1826, ground was broken at Harrisburg, and Pennsylvania, after a long struggle, began the construction of her highway to the West.

Now that the State was seriously at work, the old idea of the railroad revived, and in 1826 the charter granted to Stevens was repealed, and the Columbia, Lancaster, and Philadelphia Railroad was incorporated, only to share the fate of its predecessor. Then the State, convinced that private enterprise was not equal to the task of railroad-building on a great scale, took the work into her own hands, bade the canal commissioners make surveys for such a road ‖ and build ᴬ it from Philadelphia through Lancaster to Columbia, and, if possible, finish the work in two years. By the same act they were instructed to examine a route for a railroad over the Alleghany

---

* American Daily Advertiser, January 28, 1825. † Ibid., February 10, 1825.
‡ Ibid., August 9, 1825.   # April 11, 1825.
‖ 1827.   ᴬ 1828.

Mountains from Huntingdon on the east to Johnstown on the west side—a route which in time became celebrated as the Portage Railroad, and was long one of the engineering wonders of America.

Two years had wrought a marvellous change in the place which railroads held in public estimation. The scheme which in 1823 and 1826 seemed too visionary to be seriously thought of, and which failed because nobody was rash enough to advance the needed money, was high in favor in 1828 all over the seaboard States. New York had chartered the Mohawk and Hudson to join Albany and Schenectady, and had given the company authority to use " the power and force of steam, of animals, or of any mechanical or other power." * Massachusetts had incorporated the Granite Railway Company,† whose track was to extend from Quincy to tide-water,‡ had appointed a Board of Commissioners of Internal Improvements to survey one route for a railway from Boston to the boundary line of Rhode Island * and another from the same city to the boundary line of New York near Albany,|| and had listened to reports urging that each road when built should be operated by horse power.^ In New York city a railway up the Hudson was seriously meditated. The objectors protested that it would never pay; but the projectors declared that success was certain, because rails could be used in winter when ice made transportation by water impossible. At Hoboken John Stevens built a circular railway, and demonstrated be-

---

* Laws of New York, Chapter CCLIII, 1826.

† Laws of Massachusetts, Chapter CLXXXIII, 1826.

‡ In many treatises on the history of railways, the Quincy road is called the first railway in America. This is a mistake. As early as 1809 Thomas Leiper built a railway from his quarry to the Delaware, and used it for eighteen years. History of the People of the United States, vol. iii, pp. 494, 495. Later still, but before 1823, Conroe, of Philadelphia, had another from his ice-house to the Delaware. Railways had long been used on the bridges of Pennsylvania to reduce the jar of rolling loads, while many of the fire companies in Philadelphia had tracks across the sidewalks in front of their houses.

Resolves of the General Court of Massachusetts, Chapter LXXXVI, March 2, 1827.

|| Ibid., Chapter VII, June 14, 1827.

^ Ibid., Chapters XLVI and XLVIII.

yond dispute that a locomotive could drag a train round a curve.* Pennsylvania chartered five railroads.† The business men of Baltimore, fully aware that the activity of Pennsylvania threatened their western connections, called a public meeting,‡ at which it was resolved to form a company and seek a charter for a railway to the West. The charter was obtained,# and on the fourth of July, 1828, the corner-stone of what is now the Baltimore and Ohio Railroad was laid with imposing ceremonies at Baltimore.||

Meanwhile the merchants of Charleston, South Carolina, became enthusiastic, called a public meeting, and sent a memorial to the Legislature praying for State aid and a charter. The State was asked to bear the cost of the survey of a route from Charleston to Hamburg—a town on the Savannah river, opposite Augusta—grant an act of incorporation, and exempt the property of the company from taxation. After a brief contest the act was passed.ᐰ Almost at the same time the old idea of a railroad from Camden to some point on the rivers emptying into New York Bay was revived in earnest in New Jersey. There, too, a public meeting was held, at Mount Holly, and a memorial adopted. Situated as the State was, between two great centres of trade and commerce, and blessed with resources of her own waiting to be developed, it was a reproach to the enterprise of her citizens, the resolutions declared, that no line of interstate communication had been extended across her territory. Such a link in the chain of internal intercourse along the Atlantic coast was of the utmost importance to New Jersey. Therefore the meeting earnestly recommended the Legislature to grant a charter, and a liberal one, to a company for the construction of a railway from Camden to Amboy.◊ Like meetings were

---

* A model of the locomotive, together with the original tubular boiler and a drawing of the circular track, are in the National Museum at Washington. The date was 1826.

† Laws of Pennsylvania.

‡ February 12 and 19, 1827.

Laws of Maryland, Chapter CXXIII, February 28, 1827.

| Niles's Weekly Register, July 12, 1828, vol. xxxiv, pp. 316–328.

ᐰ Laws of South Carolina.   ◊ New Jersey Mirror, January 16, 1828.

now held at Burlington, Bordentown, Princeton, Trenton, and similar memorials sent up to the Legislature in behalf of four proposed railroads,* none of which were chartered. Virginia had already surveyed a route for a railroad from the coal pits of Chesterfield County to the banks of the James river opposite Richmond,† and had incorporated the Chesterfield Railroad Company.‡   In Delaware, the people of Wilmington and vicinity met and discussed the expediency of a railroad from Elkton to Wilmington.#

Though many were planned, the work of construction went slowly on. The period 1825 to 1830 was one of preparation, and closed with but thirty-six miles of railroad in the country. The mechanical difficulties were great. The supply of engineers, of instrument-makers, of iron, was out of all proportion to the demand. When the Pennsylvania commissioners began work the president of the board reported that he had " made most diligent search and anxious inquiry after an engineer," and had not succeeded. When the Baltimore and Ohio Railroad Company was about to begin the building of its road-bed, Congress was asked to grant it permission to import the strap iron for its rails free of duty, because the quantity wanted—some fifteen thousand tons—could not be had in the United States. The statement was flatly denied by the friends of American manufactures. Nevertheless, the Senate passed a bill remitting the duties.‖

The only roads on which the work of track-laying went steadily forward were the Hudson and Mohawk, the Philadelphia and Columbia, the Baltimore and Ohio, and the South Carolina, and about as much was built in a year as can now be laid with ease in one day. Everything was experimental. The best form of road-bed, the strongest and

---

* Camden to Amboy, Bordentown to South Amboy, Trenton to New Brunswick, Elizabethtown Point to Easton.

† Resolutions passed at a General Assembly of the Commonwealth of Virginia. Resolution No. 4, December 10, 1827.

‡ Laws of Virginia, Chapter XCIII, February 27, 1828.

January, 1828.

‖ Journal of the Senate, p. 328.

most durable kind of rail, the most economical sort of motive power, were problems yet to be solved. According to the ideas then prevalent, there must be no steep grades, as few curves as possible, and these of the sharpest and worst sort. At first the rails were long wooden stringers, protected on the upper surface from the wear of the wheels by strap iron nailed on.* Then they were great blocks of granite, resting on granite ties,† and plated on the upper inner surface with strap iron bolted or riveted on; and, finally, " edge rails " of rolled iron on stone blocks and stone sills, or edge rails on stone blocks and wooden sills.‡ Even when the rails were laid what was the best kind of motive power had not been determined. The astonishing success of Stephenson's locomotives on the Stockton and Darlington Railroad in England, and the signal triumph of his Rocket over all other competitors in the Liverpool and Manchester contest, convinced many that steam was the proper agent to use. But every experiment with a locomotive ended in failure. The Stourbridge Lion was imported from England and tried on the rails of the Delaware and Hudson Canal and Railroad Com-

---

* When the road had been graded, a series of trenches two feet long, two feet deep, and twenty inches wide was dug on either side of the road and filled with broken stone rammed down. These were joined in pairs by other trenches cut across the road-bed and also filled with broken stone, on which cross-ties were laid with the utmost care and accuracy. On top of the ties, and four feet apart, were the wooden rails, six inches square and from twelve to twenty feet long, plated on their upper surfaces with strap iron two and a half inches by five eighths of an inch by fifteen feet.

† A committee of the New York Legislature thus describes the Baltimore and Ohio track: " A line of road is first graded, free from short curves, as nearly level as possible. A small trench is formed for each track, and filled with rubble on which are laid granite blocks one foot square and as long as possible. The upper end and inner surface of each track are dressed smooth, as well as the ends of the blocks where they join. Bars or plates of wrought iron, half an inch thick, are laid on the granite blocks or rails in a line with the inner surface, and fastened with iron bolts or rivets entering four inches into the blocks, and eighteen inches apart."

‡ The " edge rails " were usually fifteen feet long, three and a half inches high, and weighed about forty-one pounds to the yard. The chairs into which the rail fitted weighed about fifteen pounds each, and rested either on stone blocks (12″ × 12″ × 20″), on stone stringers, twenty inches deep, or were made fast to wooden cross-ties or longitudinal sleepers.

pany, only to be thrown aside.* The Tom Thumb was built by Peter Cooper, and run on the Baltimore and Ohio Railroad to prove that a locomotive could pass around a sharp curve,† and was soon forgotten. A locomotive built by Stephenson was exhibited in New York city, but never drew a car. The early railroad managers were quite content to use the horse.

While the people on the seaboard were thus promoting communication between the States by every means in their power by public meetings, by conventions, by subscriptions to the stock of railroads and canals, and by appeals to their Legislatures to undertake at public expense internal improvements too costly to be carried on by private enterprise, the Federal Government was besought year after year to do its share toward opening cheap communication with the remote parts of the far West.

The veto of the Bonus Bill by Madison in the last hours of his administration checked but did not cool the ardor of the friends of internal improvement. A more liberal spirit, a less strict construction of the Constitution was hoped for from his successor—a hope somewhat deferred by a passage in the first annual message of Monroe.‡ Putting aside early impressions, I have given the subject, said he, all the deliberation required by its importance and a just sense of my duty; I am convinced that Congress does not possess the right; and suggest, therefore, that the States be asked to adopt such an amendment to the Constitution as will give Congress the right in question.

The response of the House to this suggestion was prompt. Before a week had elapsed the proposed amendment was moved,# and before a fortnight ended a long re-

---

* August 8, 1829. See History of the First Locomotives in America. W. H. Brown. Pp. 83, 87.

† The experiment is fully described in Brown's History of the First Locomotives in America, pp. 108–122.

‡ Messages and Papers of the Presidents. Richardson. Vol. ii, p. 18. See also History of the People of the United States, vol. iv, p. 423.

" Congress shall have power to pass laws appropriating money for constructing roads and canals and improving the navigation of watercourses. *Provided, however*, that no road or canal shall be constructed in any State, nor the navigation of its waters improved, without the consent of such State. *And provided, also,*

port was made in which the objections of Monroe were answered.*

Thus was the issue as to the constitutional power clearly drawn between the House and the President. It now remained to be determined whether or not the House would go further and make an appropriation, a step which it showed a readiness to take by adopting two resolutions calling for information. One asked the Secretary of War for a plan for the application " of such means as are within the power of Congress " for the construction of roads and canals that would be of use for military purposes in time of war. The other called on the Secretary of the Treasury for a similar report on roads and canals not especially designed for military purposes, and for a list of such public works then building or contemplated as might be deserving of congressional aid.

Calhoun responded with a long report,† which the House laid on the table, and two years passed before anything more was heard of a national system of internal improvements.‡ By that time the progress made in digging the Erie Canal, and the persistent demands of State after State for aid in the construction of some road or canal or the improvement of some watercourse or harbor,* once more forced the subject on the attention of the House, and a committee made bold to present a bill. Taking up the reports of Gallatin in 1808, and of Calhoun in 1819, it recommended a line of canals from Boston to Savannah; a great highway from Washington to New Orleans; a canal around the falls of the Ohio at Louisville, another from Lake Erie to the Ohio, and a third from

---

that whenever Congress shall appropriate money to these objects the amount thereof shall be distributed among the several States in the ratio of representation which each State shall have in the most numerous branch of the National Legislature."

* Report in part of the Committee of the House of Representatives of the United States on so much of the President's Message as relates to roads, canals, and seminaries of learning. House Documents, No. 11, Fifteenth Congress, First Session, vol. ii. See also History of the People of the United States, vol. iv, pp. 423–426.

† Report on Roads and Canals, January 7, 1819.

‡ January 10, 1821, a Committee of the House reported a bill.

May 4, 1822.

ROADS, CANALS, AND
STEAMBOAT ROUTES
IN THE UNITED STATES
IN 1825.

Compiled from maps of the time.

———— Canals
———— Roads
- - - - - - Steamboat Routes

Longitude   2   East   from   4   Washington   6   L. L. POATES, ENGR., N.Y.

the Potomac at Washington to the Potomac at Cumberland; and good means of communication of some sort between the Susquehanna and the rivers Seneca and Genesee; between the Tennessee and the Savannah, and the Tombigbee and Alabama. That so grand a system might be undertaken intelligibly, the bill provided for the appropriation of a sum of money " to procure the necessary surveys, plans, and estimates." To have passed it would have been idle, for ere the session closed Monroe sent back a bill far less radical in character with his veto.

The national road from Cumberland in Maryland to Wheeling on the bank of the Ohio in Virginia was fast going into decay for want of regular superintendence and repairs. The Postmaster-General, who rode over it from end to end, declared that in some places the bed was cut through by wheels; that in others it was covered with earth and rocks that had fallen down from the sides of the cuttings; and that here and there the embankment along deep fillings had so washed away that two wagons could not pass each other. A bill was therefore sent to the President providing for the establishment of toll-gates at regular intervals along the road for the collection of tolls, and setting apart the money so gathered as a fund with which to meet the cost of repairs. But, in the opinion of Monroe, a power to establish turnpikes with gates and tolls, and to enforce the collection of tolls, implied a power to adopt and execute a general system of internal improvement, and this he did not consider Congress possessed. That his views might not be misunderstood, the veto was followed by a long message reviewing the history and explaining the meaning of the Constitution.*

All hope of a national system of internal improvements during the rest of Monroe's term was now ended. Maryland, indeed, attempted to revive the project, and bade her senators and representative introduce a constitutional amendment,† pledge her to a hearty support of internal improvements,‡

* Views of the President of the United States on the Subject of Internal Improvements. Richardson. Messages and Papers of the Presidents, vol. ii, pp. 144–183. † Resolution of January 11, 1823.
‡ Resolution communicated January 3, 1823.

and urge an appropriation to repair the Cumberland Road.* But all to no purpose. The utmost that could be obtained was an act appropriating money for surveys, plans, and estimates for such canals and roads as the President might deem of national importance from a commercial or military point of view or necessary for the transmission of the public mails,† and in the last hours of his administration another extending the Cumberland Road from Canton to Zanesville, and providing for a survey for a further extension to the capital of Missouri.‡

The completion of the National Pike was, in its day and time, a matter of much importance. It began at Cumberland, on the banks of the Potomac, passed through Hagerstown in Maryland, and Uniontown, Brownsville, and Washington in Pennsylvania, and across Virginia to Wheeling on the Ohio. With the pike from Baltimore to Cumberland, it made a great through line of communication between the East and the West, and was already the favorite highway with travellers bound for the Ohio Valley.

Such a journey was usually begun by taking boat at Philadelphia, going down the Delaware to New Castle, crossing by stage to Frenchtown on the Elk river, a tributary of Chesapeake Bay, and then boarding another steamboat for Baltimore. Twenty years had seen a marvellous betterment in the means and speed and cost of travel. Steamboats, turnpike, ferryboats, bridges, and, above all, competition, had accomplished wonders on the routes between the great seaboard cities. But no corresponding improvement had taken place in the comforts and conveniences of the inns and taverns at which the traveller was forced to stop. We lodged, said one traveller, at the City Hotel, which is the principal inn at New York. The house is immense, and was full of company; but what a wretched place! The floors were without carpets, the beds without curtains. There was neither glass, nor mug, nor cup, and a miserable little rag was dignified with the name of towel. At another inn the same traveller was shown to a

---

* Resolution of December 18, 1822. † Approved April 30, 1824.
‡ March 3, 1825.

room with nine other men. " I secured a bed to myself," said
he, " the narrow dimensions of which precluded the possibility of participation, and plunged into it with all possible
haste, as there was not a moment to be lost." His companions " occupied by triplets the three other beds which the
room contained." * When you alight at a country tavern,
says another, it is ten to one that you stand holding your
horse, bawling for the hostler, while the landlord looks on.
Once inside the tavern, every man, woman, and child plies
you with questions. To get a dinner is the work of hours. At
night you are put with a dozen others into the same room,
and sleep two or three in a bed between sheets which have
covered twenty wayfarers since they last saw the tub. In
the morning you go out-of-doors to wash your face, and then
repair to the bar-room to behold your countenance in the only
looking-glass the tavern contains.† Much allowance must indeed be made for the tales of travellers. Yet the combined
testimony of them all is that a night in a wayside inn was
something to be dreaded, and to this the western highways
afforded no exception. Saving the inns and such discomfort
as came from rising at three o'clock in the morning and sitting for sixteen hours in a crowded coach, still made on the
pattern of twenty years before, a ride from Baltimore to
Wheeling was most enjoyable. The road-bed was hard, the
horses were fine, and the scenery as the road crossed the mountains was magnificent.

Beyond the mountains every year wrought wonderful
changes. In the river towns and on the farms bordering the
Ohio and its tributaries life had become much easier. The
steamboats supplied the large settlements already claiming to
be cities, while smaller craft carried goods, wares, and merchandise to every farmhouse and cluster of cabins. The Ohio was
now dotted with floating shops. At the sound of a horn the
inhabitants of the village or the settler and his family would
come to the river to find a dry-goods boat fitted with counters,
seats, and shelves piled with finery of every sort making fast

---

* Personal Narrative of Frederick Fitzgerald De Roos, 1826, pp. 5, 85, 86.
† Miner's Journal, November 28, 1825.

carried in a bag slung over the back of a horse to a mill maybe fifteen miles away, or was pounded in a wooden hominy mortar with a wooden pestle, or ground in a hand mill made by placing one flat stone on a tree stump and hanging another over it in such wise that the upper stone could be rubbed around and around on the lower. Few implements were of more importance to the frontiersman than a sharp axe; but to sharpen it he used a grindstone consisting of a thick wooden disk into the circumference of which when green he had driven particles of fine gravel and sand.

Cooking stoves were unknown. Game was roasted by hanging it with a leather string before an open fire. All baking was done in a " Dutch oven," on the hearth, or in an " out oven," built, as its name implies, out of doors. The Dutch oven was a huge iron pot with an iron lid turned up at the rims. When in use it was buried in ashes, and hot coals were piled on the lid. To build an " out oven," chips and little sticks were heaped up near the house in an oblong mound some three feet long, two feet wide by the same in height, and covered over with a thick layer of clay, which, by setting fire to the wood, was burned hard as a brick. The oven was then ready for use. When about to be used, it was first made very hot by filling it with chips and allowing them to burn to ashes. The ashes were then swept out, the bread or the pies to be baked were put in, and something placed over the door and smoke hole to keep the oven from cooling too quickly.*

---

* "I know of no scene in civilized life," says a Kentucky pioneer, "more primitive than such a cabin hearth as that of my mother. In the morning, a buckeye back-log, a hickory fore-stick, resting on stones and irons, with a johnny-cake on a clean ash board, set before the fire to bake; a frying-pan, with its long handle resting on a split-bottom turner's chair, sending out its peculiar music, and the tea-kettle swung from a wooden lug-pole, with myself setting the table, or turning the meat, or watching the johnny-cake, while she sat nursing the baby in the corner, telling the little ones to hold still and let their sister Lizzie dress them. Then came the blowing of the conch-shell for father in the field, the howling of old Lion, the gathering around the table, the blessing, the dull clatter of pewter spoons in pewter basins, the talk about the crops and stock, the inquiry whether Dan'l could be spared from the house, and the general arrangements for the day. Breakfast over, my function was to provide the sauce for dinner; in winter, to

The land about the cabin was cleared by grubbing the bushes and chopping down trees under a foot in diameter and burning them. Big trees were "deadened," or killed, by cutting a "girdle" around them two or three feet above the ground, deep enough to destroy the sap vessels and so prevent the growth of leaves. When the settler was a shiftless fellow, he would make no attempt to clear away the dead trunks, but would suffer them to stand till, in the course of years, they became so rotten that one by one they fell to pieces or were destroyed by the wind and storms.*

In the ground thus laid open to the sun were planted corn, potatoes, or wheat, which, when harvested, was threshed with a flail and fanned and cleaned with a sheet. At first the corn and wheat raised would be scarcely sufficient for home use. But as time passed there would be some to spare, and this would be wagoned to the nearest river town and sold or exchanged for "store goods." Many an early settler made the shoes his family wore from leather of his own tanning, clothed himself and children in jeans of his own manufacture, and in linen every fibre of which had been grown on his own land, and had been pulled, rotted, broken, hackled, spun, and bleached by the members of his household.

If the site selected by the emigrant were a good one, others would soon settle themselves near by, and when a cluster of cabins had been formed some enterprising speculator would appear, take up a quarter section, cut it into town lots, and call the place after himself, as Piketown, or Leesburg, or Wilson's Grove. A storekeeper with a case or two of goods would next arrive, then a tavern would be built, and possibly a blacksmith shop, a saw-mill, and a grist-mill, and Piketown or Wilson's Grove would be established. Many such ventures failed; but others succeeded, and are to-day prosperous villages.

It was in such far-away settlements that frontier life ap-

---

open the potato or turnip hole, and wash what I took out; in spring, to go into the field and collect the greens; in summer and fall, to explore the truck patch, or our little garden." Drake. Pioneer Life in Kentucky.

* For a delightful account of life in the West read Recollections of Life in Ohio by William C. Howells.

Yet his lot was the common lot of lawyers, not a few of whom had attained to some distinction in the older States long before they moved to Illinois. To such men the chance of political preferment was the great attraction. In a frontier community, where no industries had been established, where neither trade nor commerce consumed the thoughts and energies of the ambitious and aspiring, where newspapers were scarce and books were little known, politics was almost a daily vocation. Wherever a body of men were gathered together, at the log tavern, at the cross-roads, at the store in the settlement, at the horse-races, or at a " raising," measures and candidates were the all-absorbing theme of never-ending discussion. No party organization, no caucus, no machine existed, and in the absence of such appliances the personal element counted for much, and the successful politician was he who knew the people face to face, and who won their votes because his character compelled esteem. If he wished to be a governor or a judge, a member of the Legislature, a sheriff, or a senator, he said so plainly, published an address, made a personal canvass from house to house, asked for the votes he needed, and argued the matter with the refractory. He was the candidate of no party. He was the nominee of no convention, and looked on every vote cast against him as a personal affront. On one occasion the State treasurer, after a protracted struggle in the Legislature, failed of re-election. But the vote had scarcely been counted when he entered the chamber, took off his coat, and soundly thrashed, one by one, four men who voted against him. Both friends and opponents considered this as no more than the occasion required, and he was promptly made clerk of the Circuit Court.*

Violence of this sort was of too common occurrence to excite even comment. " Men," said a pioneer, speaking of the good old times, " would fight for the love of it, and then shake hands and be friends." There is no reason to doubt the statement, for almost everything which passed as pleasure and amusement was rude and boisterous, and often bordered on

---

* History of Illinois. Ford, p. 81.

the brutal. Whatever brought men together—a raising, a husking, a log-rolling, a horse-race, a wolf hunt, or a wedding—was sure to be the occasion of rough games and practical jokes. One who was himself a frontiersman, and who knew his class well, assures us that " these men could shave a horse's tail, paint, disfigure, and offer it for sale to the owner. They could hoop up in a hogshead a drunken man, they themselves being drunk, put in and nail fast the head, and roll the man down hill a hundred feet or more. They could run down a lean and hungry wild pig, catch it, heat a ten-plate stove furnace hot, and, putting in the pig, could cook it, they dancing the while a merry jig." * It would be a great mistake to suppose that the community which tolerated such misdeeds and the men who took part in them were depraved and vicious. Nowhere else was the standard of morality higher or more fully attained. Nowhere else did religion have a firmer hold. Churches, indeed, were few, but the circuit-rider was everywhere.

His vocation was rarely a matter of accident or choice. He had been called to it by the voice of the Lord God of Israel. Judged by his own estimate of himself, he was a brand snatched from the burning. He had committed no particular sin; he had broken no commandment; yet he had in his own eyes begun life a sinner, and had long refused to listen to the voice of the Lord pleading with him. But at last he had come to his senses, and after a spiritual experience as terrible as that of Bunyan, had passed safely through the Dark Valley and had reached the House Beautiful. Thenceforth he regarded himself as an instrument of God for saving the souls of men, and went to his work sustained by a faith that never wavered and animated by a zeal that never flagged.

For the work which lay before him he needed little other equipment. There were, he readily admitted, many paths to grace; but the safest and the surest was that pointed out by John Wesley, to whom he looked up as the greatest teacher the world had seen since the advent of Christ. For educa-

---

* Life of Lincoln. Nicholay and Hay, vol. i, pp. 53, 54.

Every man who could get security made haste to borrow his hundred, and every man with real estate mortgaged it for a thousand. Coin now disappeared, and dollar bills torn into pieces were used for small change. Depreciation began at once, and went on till the paper of the bank was not worth twenty-five cents on a dollar.

Across the Ohio in Kentucky the financial situation was worse. In truth, politically, financially, and industrially, that State was the most distressed member of the Union. Her State bank paper would rarely pass at fifty cents on the dollar; her people were bankrupt, her relief system was a failure, and, in a desperate effort to sustain it, the Legislature had used methods and gone lengths revolutionary and anarchical in the extreme.

The decision of Judge Clark, in 1822, that the replevin and stay laws were unconstitutional had been followed by an attempt to remove him by an address of the Legislature to the Governor. The effort failed; but when, in 1823, the Court of Appeals likewise declared the whole system of relief laws unconstitutional, the Assembly voted that the decision of the Court was erroneous, cut down the salary of each of the three judges to twenty-five cents a year, and made the question of removing them a political issue. The State from end to end was greatly excited; but when the election was over, the relief men, though they had a large majority, were still without the two-thirds vote necessary to carry an address for removal. Nevertheless, when the Legislature met in November, 1824, formal charges were again preferred against the Court.* To these complaints the judges were suffered to reply. They acknowledged their responsibility to the Legislature, but reminded that body that the constitution of Kentucky limited its control over the judiciary to impeachment, trial, conviction, and removal for misdemeanors, and to removal on address to the Governor, which must be carried by a two-thirds vote of each branch; they proved by a long argument the right of the judiciary to decide what was

---

* Preamble, Resolutions, and Addresses of a Joint Committee of the Senate and House of Representatives.

law; dwelt at length on the importance of an independent judiciary to a free people living under free institutions, and cited in defence of this position that passage in the Declaration of Independence which reads, " He has made judges dependent on his will alone for the tenure of their offices and the amount and payment of their salaries."

Able as was the reply, it produced no effect, but was referred to a select committee, which reported a resolution vindicating the constitutionality of the replevin laws and the right of the Legislature to remove judges for errors of opinion. Yet another attempt was then made to carry an address to the Governor, and when this failed a bill was passed repealing the law which established the Court of Appeals. This the Senate and the Governor promptly approved, and the old Court was said to have no existence. A new Court was then created, and on its bench the Governor and Senate placed three men known to be supporters of the relief system.

It was in December, 1824, that the repealing law was enacted, and on the fourth Monday in January, 1825, the old Court met pursuant to adjournment,* but met merely to inform the bar that no business would be transacted till the autumn term, lest by so doing they should increase the confusion and anarchy already existing.

In February the new Court—" The People's Court of Appeals," as the newspapers named it—met, took the furniture of the old Court from its room to the Senate Chamber, and there began business. As about one hundred suits were then pending, a demand was made on the clerk of the old Court for the papers, and when he refused to comply he was cited to answer for contempt, and the clerk of the new Court, F. P. Blair, the sergeant, the tipstaves, and the crier, were sent to procure the documents by force. They went, accordingly, to the clerk's house, broke into it, and wrested part of the papers from him, and, finding they did not have all, made a second entrance by force and secured the remainder.†

---

* The old Court adjourned just before the passage of the law. The Argus of Western America, January 5, 1825.

† The Argus, November 14, 1825.

The excitement aroused by these acts was intense. The relief party was overjoyed at its success, declared that the Legislature had merely repealed a law, denied that any constitutional right was invaded, and denounced the old Court judges as the usurpers, the triumvirate, the enemies of popular liberty. On the other hand, the old Court party described the repealing law as a dreadful deed, a high-handed outrage, a stroke at constitutional government, and called on the people to condemn it at the polls. Pamphlets were written; the newspapers teemed with essays and editorials and long articles; politicians stumped the State from the Mississippi to the mountains; grand juries sometimes presented the Governor and the Legislature,* and sometimes the old Court judges; county and town meetings held by both parties issued addresses and passed resolutions of great length. " We complain," said the citizens of Green County, " that after the Court of Appeals had decided that the establishment of a branch of the United States Bank in Kentucky was unconstitutional, the judges yielded their opinion on the mere intimation that the Supreme Court had decided otherwise. The Court of Appeals of Virginia boldly refused to receive a decree of the Supreme Federal Court, but our Court of Appeals gave up its opinion, and the dangerous influence and power of the banks has spread over Kentucky. We complain that the Court of Appeals has denied the right of the Legislature to pass laws to relieve the unfortunate citizens of the Commonwealth even in cases of general calamity; that it has denied the right of the Legislature to tax the United States Bank branches doing business in Kentucky, and as a consequence thousands and tens of thousands of dollars of stock yields not one cent toward the support of government, while the poor laborer who owns one hundred dollars' worth of property must pay his tax or lose his all. We complain that the judges have denied the right of the Legislature to call them to an account for an official act or judicial opinion; that they have thereby attempted to make themselves independent and beyond the

---

* Grand juries of Garrard, Franklin, Montgomery, and others presented the Governor.

reach of any power; that they have arrogated to themselves the right to interpret the constitution, and have insisted that their opinion shall rule the Legislature. We deny that the judges have any vested right of office. The investiture is made by the Legislature, which is enjoined to establish one Court of Appeals, and, having once done so by the enactment of a law, the act becomes subject to amendment or repeal just as any other." *

A Harrison County meeting declared that all power is inherent in the people; that all constitutions are divestments of power by the people; that all authority not expressly given is reserved; and that, as the constitution of Kentucky did not forbid the repeal of the law establishing the Court, the Legislature, as the representative of the people, had a right to reorganize the Court at its pleasure.† Never had a more exciting campaign been made in Kentucky. The appeal was to the honesty, the hard sense, and the deliberate judgment of the plain people, and, as has always been the case whenever such appeals have been made, the right triumphed. In the House of Representatives which swept away the old Court relief men were greatly in the majority; but in the House elected in the autumn of 1825 there were sixty-two in favor of the old Court and thirty-eight in favor of the new. This signal victory was construed to mean a vigorous condemnation of the reorganizing act. The old Court, therefore, began once more to hear arguments and decide cases, and the House when it met in November repealed the law which established the new Court; but the Senate, by a vote of twenty to eighteen, rejected it,‡ and two Courts of Appeals continued to struggle for supremacy. The Governor urged the old Court judges to resign, that he might fill their places with relief men, but they would not. The minority of the Senate issued a long address to the people,# and another campaign almost as exciting as

---

* Argus of Western America, April 20, 1825.   † Ibid., April 27, 1825.

‡ The Senate consisted of thirty-eight members, of whom nine were elected in 1825. After the defeat of the bill by the Senate sixteen senators issued an Address to the People.

Address of Sixteen Senators to the People of the Commonwealth of Kentucky. American Daily Advertiser, January 12, 1826.

the last followed in the autumn of 1826. When it ended, the Senate had been won, and at the next session the new Court was promptly abolished by the passage of the repealing act over the veto of the Governor.

With the triumph of what were called "correct principles" the former prosperity of Kentucky returned. Her citizens ceased to migrate in large numbers, law and order took the place of anarchy, and she once more joined in the march of progress with her sister States of the West. Never had that progress been more rapid. Thirteen years before, the people of New Orleans would rush to the levee to see a steamboat as one of the curiosities of the age. Now there were ninety-five such vessels on the Mississippi and its tributaries and five at Mobile, while many more had been lost by fire, by boiler explosions, and by running foul of snags and sawyers. In 1820 the shortest voyage up the river from New Orleans to Shippingport was two-and-twenty days, and the shortest down was twelve. Now it was a slow boat that could not come up against the current in twelve days and go down in six. Increase of speed had thus practically doubled the number of trips by shortening the time one half, had reduced freight rates and fares, had greatly facilitated the interchange of commodities, and had stimulated production. In 1809 a barge of sixty tons, with a crew of thirty-five men, was slowly forced up the Cumberland river by warping and bushwhacking to Nashville, to the amazement of the citizens. Barges had many a time gone down to New Orleans, but never before had the river been ascended by a vessel large enough to engage in trade with the city at the mouth of the Mississippi. The whole State rang with the news, and planters and farmers for miles around Nashville came to see the little craft at anchor off the town as a monument of enterprise. Thereafter Nashville was annually visited by at least two, which made the voyage from New Orleans in ninety days. Now sixteen steamboats could scarcely do the transportation required by the citizens.* Louisville gave employment to forty-two steamers, making a hundred and forty trips and carrying all

---

* Ohio Monitor, June 10, 1829.

told twenty-eight thousand tons of freight. As many as thirty, building and repairing, loading and unloading, might almost any day be counted within the bounds of Cincinnati.

Despite this increase of steamboat traffic, the movement of freight down the rivers by flat-boat and raft was greater than ever. New Madrid was like a seaport. In the spring it was no uncommon occurrence for one hundred boats to arrive day after day from every part of the great valley loaded with the products of the East and the West. There would be gathered in one indescribable mass planks and lumber from the forests of Pennsylvania and New York; Yankee notions from New England; pork and flour, whiskey and hemp, to-bacco, cotton bagging, and bale rope from Kentucky and Tennessee; corn and apples and potatoes from Ohio; cattle and horses from Illinois; lead and poultry from Missouri; cider and dried fruit and spirits of all sorts from the Ohio Valley; and barges carrying nothing but turkeys. As they lay side by side at the river bank, with the crews wandering from boat to boat making inquiries, forming acquaintances, seeking old friends, and filling the air with shouts of recognition and congratulation and boisterous gayety, they formed a moving picture of life peculiar to the Father of Waters. At dusk all hands would go on shore to " raise the wind," as they expressed it; but by midnight quiet would settle down, and at the first streaks of dawn, as bugle after bugle rang out, the boats would again be astir, and before the sun was fairly up would be on their way down the river. Now they no longer went singly, but, lashed together in little fleets of eight or ten, they floated on toward New Orleans, while the boatmen whiled away the time as best they could with music, dancing, singing, and playing cards.* At the Crescent City the lumber and produce met a ready sale, after which the flat-boatmen worked their passage up the Mississippi as deck hands on the steamboats.

West of the Mississippi the chief city was St. Louis, the centre of the fur trade of the Northwest and of a promising

---

* For these details I am indebted to a description of the scene at New Madrid by Timothy Flint.

commerce with Mexico. The pioneers in the Mexican trade seem to have been two parties, the one led by two men named McKnight and Beard, who went across the plains to Santa Fé in 1812, and the other by Choteau, who made the journey in 1817. But the hostility of the Indians along the route, the jealousy with which the Spanish Government beheld any intercourse of foreign nations with her American provinces, and the risk attending the introduction of American goods, rendered the expeditions so uncertain and unsafe that no move was undertaken till 1821, when Mexico had become an independent power, and gladly received the goods and wares of the United States.

Thenceforth little bands of adventurers, with small trains of pack-horses, mules, and wagons, annually wound across the great American desert to Santa Fé, taking with them cotton and woollen goods of the cheaper and coarser sorts, light articles of cutlery, silk shawls, and looking-glasses, to be exchanged for horses, mules, beaver furs, Spanish milled dollars, and gold and silver bullion. On one occasion the party numbered eighty-one men, with one hundred and fifty-six horses and mules, twenty-three four-wheeled vehicles, and a piece of field artillery, for the route led through the hunting grounds of the Pawnees, the Arapahoes, Comanches, Apaches, Snakes, and Osages.

The hostility of these Indians, who never failed to attack and rob every party that crossed their territory, induced the traders to petition Congress to establish a post on the Arkansas where the trail crossed the river, and secure for them, by treaties with the Indians, an unmolested passage to the interior provinces of Mexico. Benton warmly espoused their cause, and brought in a bill to authorize the marking out of a road from the western frontier of Missouri to the confines of New Mexico. No opposition was made by either Congress or the President, and in June, 1825, a party duly empowered to treat with the Indians and mark out the road left St. Louis.

South of Kentucky lay the cotton belt. Ten years before, at the close of the war with Great Britain, no section of our country could boast of so promising an industrial future. The return of peace had opened to British enterprise many markets

long closed, our own among them, and had created a demand
for cotton which it was almost impossible to supply. The
price, as a consequence, rose till, in 1816, upland cotton sold
at Liverpool for twenty pence halfpenny a pound, and at
twenty-two pence two years later. A wild speculation in
negroes, land, and cotton followed. Planters made haste to
expand their fields. Men who had never been planters bought
land and slaves on credit, and rushed into cotton-growing.
One hundred dollars an acre was willingly paid for land and
one thousand dollars a head for negro laborers. A golden
harvest seemed at hand, but, unhappily, it was not gathered.
Extravagant prices led the factors of Great Britain to seek
in the East Indies for cheaper cotton, and large quantities
were exported. During the six years 1811 to 1816 not
eighty-five thousand bales of East Indian cotton came to Great
Britain. But in 1817 one hundred and seventeen thousand
and in 1818 two hundred and forty-seven thousand bales were
imported. Not one half was consumed, for the staple was
ill-suited to the machinery then in use.

To the surplus thus created was added a yet greater surplus from the United States, and before 1818 ended the price
fell twenty per cent. at Liverpool. Early in January, 1819,
news of this shrinkage reached our country, and in one day
cotton dropped from thirty-three cents to twenty-six and a
half, and went steadily down till June, when it reached sixteen and a half cents, a decline of fifty per cent. in five
months. Experts estimated the loss thereby inflicted on the
merchants at over four million dollars, and the diminution in the income of the planters at seven millions more.
Failure of the East India crops in 1819 raised prices in Great
Britain for a short time; but the production in the South
went on increasing year by year with such rapidity that
the one hundred and seventy-three million pounds of cotton
exported to Great Britain in 1823 yielded six hundred thousand dollars less than the eighty-seven million pounds exported in 1819. Then came the day of reckoning. Speculators, cotton merchants, planters, men who were in any
way connected with the growing, selling, or shipping of
cotton, went down in bankruptcy. For weeks at a time not a

pound was sold at any price. Planters who in 1818 bought one thousand acres on credit now gladly offered to part with two thousand to pay the debt incurred. Land purchased on credit in 1818 at three hundred dollars an acre could not be sold in 1825 for twenty. Negroes worth one thousand dollars in the flush time seven years before were now unsalable at three hundred.

The effect on the South of the rise of cotton-growing was already apparent. In every State, from Louisiana to North Carolina, cotton was the great staple. Here, then, was a long belt of States wholly agricultural with identically the same sort of agriculture, carried on by identically the same kind of labor—that of negro slaves. The diversified industry already characteristic of the North was wanting in the South.

The questions of an economic kind which now deeply concerned the North were therefore treated with indifference or viewed as hostile issues by the South. The South had no manufactures; therefore a tariff for the protection of manufactures was unconstitutional. The South had no interstate trade of any consequence; no market to seek in the West; no goods, wares, or merchandise to transport from the seaboard to the Mississippi; therefore the construction of internal improvements, of turnpikes, canals, good roads, or the opening of watercourses by the Federal Government was an exercise of power not granted by the Constitution. The South imported heavily from Great Britain; therefore all tariffs must be as low as possible, and to keep them low the expenses of Government must be reduced to a minimum. Thus on the three questions of the hour—the tariff, internal improvements, and the protection of American industries—there was a great gulf fixed between the cotton-growing States on the one hand and the manufacturing and trading States on the other.

The rapid settlement of the West and South, and the purchase of large tracts of land by settlers and by speculators, brought up yet another economic question for serious discussion. Neither in the East nor in the West was the manner of selling and using the public lands satisfactory to the people. In the opening year of the century Congress, abandoning the old system especially favorable to the rich man, adopted another especially favorable to the poor man, and having fixed the minimum price at two dollars, and reduced the minimum number of acres to be sold to one hundred and sixty, gave the purchaser four years in which to make his payments.* For a while the credit system worked well. The quantity of land sold was considerable; but the times were good, and, till the prostration of business and the ruin of commerce by the Long Embargo in 1808, the forfeitures for non-payment were few in number and far between. With the enforcement of that dreadful restrictive measure, and of the equally fruitless and ruinous non-intercourse and non-importation laws, the effect of the loss of commerce, trade, and foreign markets on the ability of the settler to pay for his land was quickly manifest, and in 1809 and 1810 Congress found it expedient to extend the time of payment. In 1811 no indulgence was granted, and tens of thousands of acres reverted to the Government. With the opening of the war times grew worse instead of better, and year after year, in 1812, 1813, 1814, and 1815, Congress was forced to be lenient with a great army of debtors.

But the hard times and business distress which made it impossible for the settlers in the West to pay for their land was the cause of a movement of population from the seaboard, where trade and commerce were prostrate, where land was costly and rents were high, to the West, where farms were to be had for a few dollars an acre, were free from taxation for five years from the day of sale, and could be purchased on four years' credit. A wild speculation in Government or, as the phrase went, Congress lands followed. To speculate was easy, for in the dark days of the war, when the credit of the Government was almost gone, when loans could hardly be negotiated, and when bonds and Treasury notes were depreciated twenty-five per cent., the Treasury Department made a bargain with the State banks in the West. If they, on the one hand, would receive and reissue Treasury notes, the Treasury, on the other hand, would accept their bills in pay-

---

* History of the People of the United States, vol. iii, pp. 124, 125.

the West. Nor was it slow in doing so. Ohio, where much of the public land had been sold, was indifferent. But from Indiana, Illinois, Missouri, and Alabama came memorials praying for a graduated scale of prices. A distinction, said Illinois, ought to be made between land recently offered for sale and that long in the market. In the latter case, the best having been taken up by bidders at the public auctions, by non-residents who buy on speculation, and by the early settlers, what remains is either poor in quality or is subject to some local disadvantage, and the price ought to be reduced. The emigrant seeking a home will not pay for it the price asked for better soil in better situations. He is therefore driven to new and distant settlements, where few have preceded him. The tide of population is thus made to roll over immense regions, creating feeble and thinly scattered settlements, separated by vast tracts of wilderness. In such a state public institutions are not established, systems of education are not matured, moral restraints are tardily enforced, laws feebly executed, and revenue raised with difficulty and at great cost. Land unsold after being offered for five years should, Illinois proposed, be valued at fifty cents an acre.*

A graduation of price, said Indiana,† will stop the wild rush westward, will make settlements compact, and will bring into the market land which otherwise will remain wilderness or be made valueless by interlopers and trespassers, whose rude and temporary settlements are a nuisance to society. Finding that no attention was paid to her memorial, Indiana, in 1826, instructed her senators and requested her representatives to do their best to secure a law graduating the prices of public lands.‡ Then, for the third time, Benton introduced his bill described by his colleague as " a compound of electioneering and speculation," and defended it in a speech which the same fellow-senator called a " studied, popularity-hunting, Senate-distressing harangue." # Nevertheless, the Legislature of Alabama approved the bill, and bade her sena-

---

* American State Papers, Public Lands, vol. iv, p. 148, December 24, 1824.
† Ibid., vol. iv, pp. 429, 430, January 21, 1825.
‡ American State Papers, Public Lands, vol. iv, p. 483.
# Debates in Congress, 1825–'26, vol. ii, part i, pp. 720–753, May 16, 1826.

tors endeavor to secure its passage,* and Indiana and Illinois each again memorialized Congress to scale down the price of land. There are in Illinois, said the memorial, some forty millions of acres, of which one million and a half have been sold. At this rate, and if the present price of a dollar and a quarter is held to, " it will be several hundred years before all the soil of the State passes to other hands." †

While the Western States, or, as many in the East believed, combinations of speculators who controlled the Legislatures, were begging Congress to reduce the price of the public domain, greed for land in the South bred a serious quarrel between Georgia, the President of the United States, and the Creek and Cherokee Indians. In 1802, when Georgia ceded the territory now part of Alabama and Mississippi, it was stipulated that the United States should extinguish the Indian title to land within the State of Georgia " as early as the same can be peaceably obtained on reasonable terms." When this agreement was made the Indian possessed in Georgia not far from twenty-six million acres, a tract larger than the State of Maine, larger than South Carolina, larger, indeed, than all New England if Maine be excluded. Of this immense area, eighteen million acres belonged to the Creeks and more than seven millions to the Cherokees. True to its pledge, the Federal Government began at once to negotiate for the purchase of the Indian rights, and in the course of twenty years concluded seven treaties, by which fourteen million acres were acquired from the Creeks and one million from the Cherokees.

Yet the Georgians were far from satisfied. The deliberate course of the Government was too slow for them, and in their impatience they charged the United States with bad faith, with a violation of the agreement of 1802, and threatened to take the matter into their own hands. That they would have done so is not likely. Nevertheless, when the great rush of population into the West began after the war with Great Britain, when cotton was selling at thirty cents a pound, and

---

* American State Papers, Public Lands, vol. iv, p. 892.

† Senate Document No. 17, Nineteenth Congress, Second Session, vol. ii. The Indiana Memorial is No. 37 in the same volume.

was determined to have their land at any cost; and that if they did not yield it willingly the United States must either aid Georgia in taking it or fight her. The memorial from the Legislature, the letter from the Governor, and another from the members of Congress from Georgia * again aroused Monroe, and led him to defend the Indian policy of the Government in a special message to Congress.† The Cherokees having positively refused to cede their land, it was manifest, he said, that they could be removed only by force. But, in his opinion, there was no obligation resting on the United States to use force. The language of the compact was " peaceably " and " on reasonable terms." The Cherokee agent soon after was commanded " without delay and in the most effectual manner forthwith to expel white intruders from Cherokee lands."

By this time the Creeks, well knowing that their turn would come next, had become so uneasy that a meeting of their chiefs and head men was held at a place called Tuckebachee. After " deep and solemn reflection," it was decided " with one voice " to follow the example set by the Cherokees, and " on no account to sell one foot of our land, neither by exchange nor otherwise." Lest any chief should think lightly of this resolution, the meeting went further, and decreed that death should be the penalty for any infraction of this law.‡

Not long after this determination had been reached the same commissioners who had been treating with the Cherokees summoned the chiefs of the Creeks to meet them in December at Broken Arrow. Alarmed at the summons, the chiefs met a second time, at Polecat Springs, and, having reaffirmed the decision reached at Tuckebachee, issued an appeal for justice to " our white and Christian brothers," * and went at the appointed time to Broken Arrow. Nothing

---

* March 10, 1824.

† Senate Documents No. 63, Eighteenth Congress, First Session, vol. iii. Messages and Papers of the Presidents. Richardson. Vol. ii, pp. 234–237.

‡ "We have guns and ropes, and if any of our people should break these laws those guns and ropes are to be their end." The Tuckebachee Resolutions are printed in Niles's Register, vol. xxvii, pp. 222–223.

⁂ See Niles's Register for December 4, 1824, vol. xxvii, pp. 222–223.

was accomplished; but it was clear to the commissioners that there were a few chiefs and head men who, for a consideration, were ready and willing to sacrifice the interests of their people. With these a treaty was concluded some weeks later at Indian Springs,* was hurried to Washington, and, despite the protestations of the Indian agent, was ratified by the Senate in the last moments of Monroe's term of office.† In consideration of four hundred thousand dollars and land beyond the Mississippi, these chiefs sold to the United States almost all the territory the Creeks owned within the State of Georgia. Dishonesty, fraud, and conspiracy tainted the treaty; yet Adams, without stopping to examine into the manner in which it was obtained, signed and made it law.‡

As the news spread among the Creeks that they had been betrayed, that their land was sold, and that in a little while, abandoning all that they held most dear, they must begin a long pilgrimage to new homes in a country a thousand miles away, their grief gave place to rage and excitement. True to the law of Tuckebachee, the chiefs made haste to execute it, and early in May three of those who signed the treaty of Indian Springs—McIntosh, Tustunugge, and Hawkins by name—were put to death. Instantly the whole Georgia frontier was aflame. Hundreds of Creeks, followers of the slaughtered chiefs, deserting their homes, fled with wives and children across the border and sought protection of Governor Troup. A grand jury of the United States District Court presented the killing of the chiefs, called for the vigorous prosecution of any white men concerned, and recommended the fugitives to the protection and succor of the State.# For a time it was feared that an Indian uprising and a border war was imminent. But the fear was an idle one. The Indians had murdered no man. Exercising an unquestionable right, they had put three men to death under a law of whose existence the culprits were well aware, and, having done this, they stopped. No thought of war upon the whites had ever been entertained. Indeed, at a meeting of the chiefs of the

---

* February 12, 1825.   † March 3, 1825.   ‡ March 5, 1825.
# Niles's Register, May 28, 1825, vol. xxviii, pp. 196, 197.

said, began with the compact of 1802, when the United States agreed to extinguish the Indian title to land within the bounds of Georgia as soon as the same could be done peaceably and on reasonable terms—a compact which bound the Federal Government not merely to use every opportunity that might come in its way, but to seek earnestly for opportunities to make good the pledge. Had the United States kept the agreement? On the contrary, she had deliberately violated it; she had been so indifferent that Georgia had been forced again and again to remonstrate; she had entirely removed the Indians from Ohio, from Kentucky, from North and South Carolina, from Tennessee and Missouri; she had removed almost all from Arkansas; she had acquired great areas of land in Michigan, Illinois, Mississippi, and Florida, and had secured for herself five times as much territory in Alabama as the Indians occupied in Georgia. Nay, more; she had not merely failed to hold out inducements to the Indians to quit Georgia; not merely failed to use her opportunities, but she had so added to their comfort, so instructed them in husbandry and farming as to attach them to their homes and destroy the last hope that they would ever part with their lands on peaceable and reasonable considerations.

After thus disposing of the charge of bad faith, the committee took up the question of title. Prior to the Revolution, it was said, the sovereignty of Great Britain over Georgia was complete and perfect; the soil was hers, the Indians were under her protection, and their possession and occupation of the land was by her permission; when the war for independence ended, the sovereignty once claimed, owned and exercised by the mother country over the lands and Indians of Georgia, passed to and vested in the people of the State, who then acquired all the rights and powers over the lands and Indians that had once belonged to Great Britain; that since this acquisition Georgia had never divested herself, either under the confederation or under the Constitution, of any right or power so acquired, and therefore was at liberty and had full right and power to possess herself by any means she might choose of the lands in dispute, and to spread over them her laws and authority.

In view of these facts, the committee recommended that

one last appeal be made to the General Government to remove the Cherokees; that if no attempt so to do was made, or, if made, was not successful, then the next Legislature should be asked to consider the propriety of taking the lands by any means they thought proper.   " The lands in question," said the committee, " belong to Georgia—she must and will have them."

So clearly was this the sentiment of the people, that both House and Senate adopted a set of resolutions declaring that the United States had palpably violated the contract with Georgia; that this breach of good faith was the cause of all the troubles with the Cherokees; that all lands within the limits of Georgia belonged to her absolutely; that the Indians were mere tenants at will; that she could at any time take possession; that she had a right to spread her laws over the whole territory in dispute, and extort obedience from all who dwelt therein, were they white, red, or black.*

Nor was her assertion of right an idle threat.   Indeed, the day before the House approved the resolutions a law was enacted which extended the criminal jurisdiction of Georgia over part of the Cherokee territory by adding it to her counties of Carroll and De Kalb.†   This was too much for even an Indian to stand, and a delegation of Cherokees was sent to Washington, where, in the closing days of Adams's term,‡ a protest was entered against the encroachments and aggressions of Georgia.   It was then too late for the outgoing President to act, so the matter was referred to his successor.

But the people of Georgia had yet another quarrel with the Federal Government.   In the opinion of their Governor and Legislature, Congress and the administration had assumed a position so hostile to slavery as to justify secession.   Both North and South the negro problem was now fast becoming a serious issue.

---

* Adopted December 19 and 27, 1827.   Report of a Committee and Resolutions of the Legislature of the State of Georgia in relation to certain lands occupied by the Cherokee Indians.   Executive Documents of the Twenty-third Congress, First Session, vol. iii, No. 102.

† Laws of Georgia, December 26, 1827.   ‡ February 11, 1829.

CHAPTER XLV.

THE NEGRO PROBLEM.

THE existence of such a problem in the Northern States was due to the presence in them of large bodies of negroes, made free by the labors of the early abolition societies and by the operation of immediate or gradual abolition laws. Since Pennsylvania led the way in 1780, Rhode Island, Connecticut, New York, and New Jersey * had followed her, and had each decreed that after a certain day in a certain year slavery should be prohibited; that men and women who were slaves on that day should remain so, but that children born thereafter of slave parents should be free on attaining a certain age. Massachusetts, New Hampshire, and Vermont had abolished slavery outright, and in them all blacks and mulattoes were free. Had freedom brought with it the rights and privileges of citizenship, the presence of this class in the communities would have been of little moment. But nowhere did the black man have all the rights of the white. Here he could not vote; there he could not serve in the militia; nowhere was he summoned to be a juror. Race prejudice shut him out of a long line of trades and occupations, and condemned him to a state of gross ignorance. No carpenter, no blacksmith, wheelwright, mason, or shoemaker would take him as an apprentice; no shopkeeper would have him as a clerk. He was excluded from every hotel, inn, and tavern, and from every school save such as benevolent persons had established for the especial benefit of his race.

---

* Rhode Island in 1784, Connecticut in 1784, New York in 1799, New Jersey in 1804.

Delaware forbade free negroes or mulattoes to enter her territory for the purpose of becoming inhabitants. If any did, the nearest justice of the peace must bid him depart. Should he refuse to go, a fine of ten dollars a week must be imposed, and if not paid the offender must be seized and sold into slavery.* Any free negro living in idleness in Maryland, or going at large through the State, must give security for good behavior, or leave the State within fifteen days after he was ordered to depart. Failing to go, he might be fined thirty dollars. If he did not pay the fine, he must be sold for not more than six months.† Nobody could buy tobacco from a free negro who could not show a certificate from a justice of the peace, granted on the sworn testimony of two white persons, and stating that what he offered had been grown or honestly acquired by him.‡ When a free negro imprisoned for any offence was pardoned or served out his term, the directors of the penitentiary were required to give him thirty dollars and banish him from the State. Should he be found in Maryland after the lapse of sixty days, he must be sold into slavery for the term of his original conviction.# Virginia would not suffer a negro made free in any other State to take up residence on her soil. Such as were emancipated must be numbered and duly registered in a book kept by the county clerks or clerks of the cities, boroughs, and corporations. A copy of the registration, specifying his age, color, name, by what court emancipated, and describing any marks or scars on face and hands, must be given him annually, for without such certificate he could not go at large, nor seek employment, nor be employed by anybody under the penalty of the law. ||

Tennessee had a very similar restriction,△ but permitted free negroes to come within the State provided they registered their freedom papers. ◊ In the District of Columbia, as in the

---

* Laws of Delaware, 1811, Chapter CXLV.
† Laws of Maryland, 1825. Chapter CLXI.
‡ Ibid., 1825, Chapter CXCIX.
# Ibid., 1826, Chapter CCXXIX.
|| Laws of Virginia, Revised Code, 1819, Chapter III.
△ Laws of Tennessee, 1806, Chapter XXXII; 1807, Chapter C.
◊ Ibid., 1825, Chapter LXXIX.

slave-holding States in general, every negro or mulatto who could not prove freedom by documentary evidence might be seized and sold into slavery. To teach a free negro to read or write was an offence punishable here by a fine of thirty dollars, there of five hundred dollars, and elsewhere by lashes. Should free negroes or their children gather at a school in Virginia for the purpose of instruction, the justice of the peace must break it up and lay twenty lashes on the back of each pupil; in South Carolina the nearest magistrate must perform the same duty and inflict the same punishment. In many slave States free negroes might not assemble for any purpose to a number greater than seven; might not preach the Gospel; might not buy, sell, or trade outside of the towns or cities in which they dwelt; might not enter the State without incurring a fine and running the risk of being sold into slavery; might not remain in the State after they had gained their freedom.

Restrictions of these kinds were to be expected in States where slavery still existed; they might easily be accounted for in States where slavery was slowly disappearing under the workings of gradual abolition laws; but if there was any portion of our country where a free negro should have been accorded the common rights of man, it was on the soil dedicated to freedom by the Ordinance of 1787. Unhappily, this was far from being the case, for the constitution of Ohio deprived him of the franchise, and the first Legislature under that constitution had not ended its second session when by a law " to regulate black and mulatto persons " it laid on the negro the burden of proving his right to be free. Henceforth no such person could enter Ohio with intent to reside or settle unless provided with a " certificate of actual freedom," which must be put on record. Blacks already in the State must have their names recorded and secure a certificate, for without it nobody could hire or employ them, nor could they even leave the State.

In Indiana their condition was, if possible, worse. The constitution did not deprive them of the right to vote, but the law forbade them to be witnesses except in pleas of the State against negroes or mulattoes, or in civil cases where such persons were the only parties. Illinois began her career as a slave-holding Territory. She prohibited free negroes to come upon her soil; she decreed that all such as did must leave within fifteen days after notice or receive thirty-nine lashes; * she accepted the Indiana † " act concerning the introduction of negroes and mulattoes," and so continued the system of registered and indentured slavery begun when a part of Indiana; she permitted non-resident slave-owners to hire their slaves to citizens of Illinois for a period of twelve months, yet not give the slave his freedom; and justified her act with the excuse that laborers were wanted to erect mills and open up the country, and that salt could not be profitably manufactured by white men. ‡ Once, indeed, an effort was made to break down slavery, and in 1817 the Legislature passed a bill to repeal so much of the act concerning the introduction of negroes and mulattoes into the Territory as authorized their importation and indenture; but the Governor defeated the attempt with his veto.

That he expressed the sentiments of a very large majority of the people cannot be doubted, for when, a year later, a convention framed and adopted a State constitution, it limited the franchise to " free white men," excluded the negro from the militia, and inserted the provision that each and every person bound to service by contract or indenture in the Territory of Illinois should be held to serve out his time under the State government; but that children thereafter born of such persons should be free, the males at twenty-four and the females at eighteen. The first General Assembly under the constitution fastened slavery on Illinois more firmly than ever by re-enacting the old laws regarding free negroes, mulattoes, servants, and slaves, and by adopting what in the Southern States would have been a slave code. Thenceforth no negro, no mulatto, either by himself or with his family, was to be suffered to live in the State unless he produced a certificate of freedom bearing the seal of some court of record of the State or Territory whence he came; nor until the certificate, with a long description of himself and of each member of his

---

* December, 1813.   † Laws of Indiana, 1817, chapter iii, section 52.
‡ Preamble to the law of 1814.

her deed of cession that the settlers at Kaskaskia, Vincennes, and elsewhere " should have their possessions and titles confirmed to them," could not be disregarded and their slaves set free, and ended with a resolution that the Legislature should recommend the voters at the next election for members of the General Assembly to vote for or against a convention to amend the constitution and make Illinois a slave State. The report was adopted, but to pass the resolution required a two-third vote in both branches. The Senate was almost unanimously in favor; in the House one vote was wanted, and to get it the pro-slavery men perpetrated that foul deed of which the history of legislation in our country affords many instances. At the opening of the session a contested election case had been heard and settled in favor of a member who agreed to give his vote for the re-election of United States Senator Jesse B. Thomas, who bore so conspicuous a part in the Missouri Compromise as the originator in the Senate of the thirty-six-thirty provision.* So far the member was willing to go; but when nothing could induce him to give the one vote needed to send down to the people the question of a constitutional convention, he was unseated and his place given to his contestant, a strong pro-slavery man, by the help of whose vote the resolution passed the House of Representatives.

While the resolution to unseat was under debate the citizens of Vandalia, then the capital of Illinois, carried away by excitement, marched about the streets one night with a burning effigy of the sitting member, and demanded a " convention or death." When the resolution was carried and the old member unseated, the pro-slavery party went wild with delight, lit up the town, formed a procession, headed by the judges, candidates for the governorship, senators, and members of the Legislature, and marched to the home of Governor Coles, whom they grossly insulted. Still later their joy found vent in public dinners, where such toasts were drunk as " The enemies of the convention: may they ride a porcupine saddle on a hard trotting horse a long journey without money or friends "; " May those individuals who are opposed to our

---

* History of the People of the United States, vol. iv, pp. 589–591.

cause, before the next election abandon Illinois "; " The
State of Illinois: the ground is good, prairie in abundance;
give us plenty of negroes, a little industry, and she will distribute her treasures." *

The question whether Illinois should or should not become
a slave State having thus been referred to the people, the
most exciting canvass they had yet known commenced in
earnest. One who lived at the time and saw it declares that
men and women took part; that families and neighbor-
hoods were divided and arrayed one against another; that
personal encounters were of constant occurrence; and that
at times the whole State seemed ready to settle the question by an appeal to arms.† Every known means of electioneering was resorted to and vigorously used. Newspapers were
established, and their columns crowded with articles written
by the ablest men. Pamphlets were printed by thousands
and circulated broadcast. Men were sent over the State scattering handbills. Antislavery societies were organized with
branches everywhere. Ministers of the Gospel ranged the
counties, distributing tracts and pamphlets. The stump orators were ceaseless in their exertions. Denominational disputes
far more bitter then than now were forgotten for the moment,
and Sunday after Sunday the preachers thundered their denunciations against "spreading the great sin." After eighteen
months of such canvassing, the election day came, on August
second, 1824. When it ended, the pro-slavery men were
beaten; the people had decided against a convention by a majority of nearly seventeen hundred votes.‡ Never had such an
election been held; more than eleven thousand voters went to
the polls.# How deeply the people were moved is well shown
by the fact that seven thousand more votes were given in August, 1824, on the question of calling a convention than were
cast at the presidential election three months later.‖

* A History of Illinois. Thomas Ford. Pp. 52, 53. A Complete History of
Illinois from 1673 to 1873. Davidson and Stuvé. Pp. 323–325.
† My Own Time. John Reynolds. P. 153.
‡ For a convention, 4,972; against it, 6,640.
# On the convention question, 11,612; all presidential candidates, 4,532.
‖ For details of the vote by counties, see Illinois, Historical and Statistical.
John Moses. Vol. i, p. 324.

every State, teem with descriptions of the free blacks. They are held up to the community as " a horde of miserable people, subsisting by plunder "; * as " a greater nuisance than slaves "; as " a vile excrescence upon society "; as " a curse and contagion "; as " the most degraded, the most abandoned race on earth." Even Clay joined heartily in these denunciations, and repeatedly gave it as his belief that of all descriptions of our population they were the very worst.

In justice to the men who spoke and wrote in this wise, it must be remembered that they were animated by no spirit of hatred of the negro, free or slave. They were, in their own opinion and in the opinion of a large part of the community, a band of philanthropic gentlemen earnestly laboring for the welfare of a down-trodden race. But this welfare could not be secured in America. Our habits, our feelings, our prejudices, they would argue—prejudices which neither refinement, nor education, nor reason, nor religion can overcome—doom the negro to a degradation inevitable and incurable. The blackness of their skins, a constant reminder of their origin and former condition of servitude, sets up a barrier which is to stand forever between them and the white. They belong by birth to the very lowest rank in society, and from that rank, be their industry, their enterprise, their wealth ever so great, they cannot rise. They form a class out of which no individual can be elevated, and below which none can be sunk. There is not a State in the Union in which a negro or a mulatto can be elected to Congress, or sent to the

---

* From the African Repository a few extracts may be taken as specimens :

" There is a class among us, introduced by violence, notoriously ignorant, degraded, and miserable, mentally diseased, broken spirited, acted upon by no motives to honorable exertions, scarcely reached in their debasement by the heavenly light—the class is the free blacks."—African Repository, vol. i, p. 68.

" Free blacks are a greater nuisance than even slaves themselves."—Ibid., vol. ii, p. 189.

" This class of persons a curse and contagion wherever they reside."—Ibid., vol. iii, p. 203.

" Averse to labor, with no incentives to industry, or motives to respect, they maintain a precarious existence by petty thefts and plunder."—Ibid., vol. vi, p. 135.

" An anomalous race of beings the most depraved upon earth."—Ibid., vol. vii, p. 230.

Legislature, or seated on the bench, or made a justice of the peace, or put in command of a company of militia. Where can they ride in the same coach, or sit at the same table, or mingle in society with the white? Where will the white working-man labor at the same bench, or plough in the same field, or toil on the same building with a black man? Every incentive to industry and good conduct which arises from the hope of advancement in this world is taken from him. What can it profit him to be educated, or refined, or rich? Looking forward to no honorable distinction, aiming at no excellence, the negro makes no efforts beyond such as are necessary to supply his daily wants. With loss of hope comes loss of desire, and the debasement which as a slave was compulsory becomes habitual and voluntary with the free negro and his children after him. No wonder, then, that the statistics of crime present him in a horrible light. A million three hundred and forty thousand whites in New York furnish four hundred and eighty convicts, while thirty-nine thousand negroes contribute one hundred and fifty. In Pennsylvania it is worse. Her million whites send three hundred and ten convicts to the penitentiaries, and her thirty thousand free blacks one hundred and sixty.

In the main, this description of the status of the free black man was true. But, however praiseworthy in the eyes of the friends of colonization may have been the purpose for which the picture was drawn, the effect of it on the community was bad. The degradation, the misery, the viciousness of the free negro was held up before the people not for the purpose of exciting sympathy, not for the purpose of impressing the fact that this degradation was the result of unjust prejudices and cruel laws which it was the duty of Christians and civilized men to overcome and repeal, but in order to persuade them to contribute money to get rid of the despised class by sending it to Africa. The feeling aroused was not such as prompted States to establish penitentiaries for the reform of criminals; to give the prisoners in the jails good food, clothes, and warm cells, and not such as force the creditor to be merciful to the debtor; led men to found Bible societies, tract societies, and temperance societies; send missionaries to the ends of the earth, and educate children of evil-disposed parents that they might become honest men and women, but one of hostility. The negro was past all reformation. He must be encouraged to go to Africa, and no easier way of inducing him to go could be devised than to keep him in a debased condition in the United States. All attempts for his betterment, therefore, were frowned down or openly resisted by the Colonization Society. Slavery must not be abolished, either immediately or gradually, because that would increase the evil by making the free negroes ten times more numerous. The slave must not be manumitted save on condition that he would go to Africa.

Had this view been confined to a few men, it would have been serious enough in its consequences. But, unhappily, it was vigorously indorsed by legislatures, by religious bodies, by churches, by statesmen, and by Congress, till the people were quite convinced that the African race was past all redemption, and that the deportation to Africa was all the consideration to which a free negro was entitled.

It was natural that results of this state of feeling toward the black man should be quick to show themselves, and that a willingness to strip him of the few privileges he possessed should be widely manifest. Statistics had often been cited to prove that free blacks furnished more criminals in proportion to their numbers than whites. But when the census of 1820 revealed the fact that in Massachusetts, where the negroes made one seventy-fifth of the total population, they contributed one sixth of the criminals,* the House of Representatives took the alarm at what it considered " the increase of a species of population which threatened to become both injurious and burdensome," † and determined to take the necessary steps to check it by legislation. A committee was therefore appointed and bidden to consider the expediency of making alterations in the laws concerning the admission into residence in Massachusetts of free negroes and mulattoes.

---

* The population was 523,000, of which 7,000 were negroes. The convicts in 1820 were 314, of whom 50 were blacks.

† Notes on the History of Slavery in Massachusetts. G. H. Moore, pp. 237–239.

The duty thus assigned was far from a pleasant one, and the report when made was a curious mixture of apologies for the appointment of the committee, and excuses for doing nothing. On the first of January, 1821, the black convicts in the State prison, the committee said, formed the one hundred and forty-sixth part of the black population of the State, while the white convicts were but the twenty-one hundred and fortieth part of the white population. This was reason enough for considering the expediency of suffering such a disorderly set of persons to remain in Massachusetts. But just what kind of legislation was needed the committee " found it impossible " to decide.

No decision was needed, for there was then on the statute-books of Massachusetts a law enacted in 1788,* and entitled " an act for suppressing and punishing of rogues, vagabonds, common beggars, and other idle, disorderly, and lewd persons." It provided that no person " being an African or negro " should tarry within the Commonwealth for more than two months, unless he were a subject of the Emperor of Morocco or a citizen of one of the United States. It decreed that if he did, any justice of the peace on complaint must order him to depart within ten days, and, failing to go, must commit him to await the action of a Court of Sessions of the Peace, and it gave that Court power, should he be found guilty, to sentence him to be whipped ten stripes, to be again ordered to depart out of the Commonwealth, and to repeat the punishment as often as the offender failed to obey.

The committee having unearthed this old law, and supposing that it had never been enforced, cited it as an illustration of the folly of such legislation, condemned it as arbitrary in its principles, and in its operations repugnant to the institutions, feelings, and practices of the people of Massachusetts, and asked to be discharged from further consideration of the matter. In two respects the committee erred. In the first place, the law was not repugnant to the feelings of the people of Massachusetts, and remained on the statute-books till 1834.

---

* March 26, 1788. An account of the law is given in G. H. Moore's History of Slavery in Massachusetts, pp. 228–229.

to the facilities for confederating afforded by the extreme indulgence with which masters in Charleston treated their slaves, and to the course which certain discussions had lately taken in Congress.* For each of these a remedy was found immediately. The African Church, described as "a hotbed in which the germ [of insurrection] might well be expected to spring into life and vigor" was dissolved. Masters put a more careful watch on their slaves. The Corporation rigorously enforced the negro ordinance, and when the Legislature met a law was enacted especially directed against negroes from foreign parts. The testimony at the trials brought out the fact that efforts had again and again been made to secure aid from San Domingo, and that letters on the subject had been carried back and forth by negroes on the ships visiting Charleston. The new law, therefore, provided that the moment a vessel entered a port of South Carolina with a free negro or a person of color on board he should be seized. He might be serving as cook, steward, mariner, or in some other capacity, and have no intention of remaining in the State; he might be a subject of a foreign power; he might be a citizen of a free State; but it mattered not. The sheriff must board the vessel, drag the negro to the jail, and keep him there till the ship had cleared out and was ready to sail. Then the master must pay all costs of detention and carry the man away, or he would become liable to a fine of one thousand dollars or imprisonment for two months, and the negro would be sold as a slave.

Scarcely had the law been placed on the statute-books when a general seizure of negro cooks and sailors began, and in a little while forty-one ships in the harbor of Charleston alone were deprived of one or more hands. Indeed, from a British trader almost the entire crew was taken. The captains of the vessels at once applied for relief to the judge of the United States District Court, who urged them to seek redress in the courts of the State, and requested the district attorney to lend his aid. A test case was accordingly made up, a writ of *habeas corpus*, to inquire into the cause of the arrest of the men, was sued out, and, the sheriff having re-

* An Account of the Late Intended Insurrection, etc., pp. 29, 30.

turned that they were arrested under the law of 1822, a motion was made for a discharge on the ground that the law was unconstitutional. But the lower Court decided that it was constitutional; the upper Court, on appeal, was divided, and the prisoners remained in custody of the sheriff.* Ultimately they were released; but meantime the American captains addressed Congress, while such as were British subjects complained to Canning. He remonstrated vigorously,† and was assured by Adams that the practice should be put a stop to; yet it went on, and very soon another British subject— a negro seaman born in Jamaica—was in the clutches of the law.

This time suit was brought in the United States District Court for a writ of *habeas corpus ad subjiciendum,* discharging the man from confinement absolutely; or, failing this, for a writ *de homine replegiando,* for his release on bail. The purpose was to try the validity of the law under which he was held. Council for the plaintiff argued that the act of 1822 was unconstitutional for two reasons: In the first place, it violated the sole power of Congress to regulate trade, because it interfered with the freedom of navigation and the employment of seamen, and drove from the ports of South Carolina all ships, foreign or domestic, with free negroes on board. In the second place, it violated the treaty with Great Britain, by which the right to engage in commerce with the United States was guaranteed to every British subject.

To this the defence made answer that a sovereign State has the right to interdict the entry of foreigners into her dominion; that South Carolina was a sovereign State prior to and at the time of her entrance into the Federal compact; that her sovereign right to exclude free negroes from other States was one she had not, and from the peculiar circumstances of her slave population could not, surrender to the Federal Gov-

---

* The Memorial of Sundry Masters of Vessels lying in the Port of Charleston, South Carolina, to the House of Representatives is in the American Daily Advertiser, March 26, 1823 ; in Niles's Register, March 15, 1823, pp. 31, 32 ; Executive Papers, No. 76, Seventeenth Congress, Second Session, vol. v.

† For Canning's note and Adams's reply, see Niles's Register, November 25 1824.

ernment; that from the very foundation of the Government
each State made such laws regarding the entry and stay of foreigners as its local policy required; that New York and Pennsylvania had established health laws to prevent the importation of diseased men; that Massachusetts had forbidden the
entry of felons and paupers of Europe; and that by exactly the
same right South Carolina had stopped the importation of free
negroes. When New York quarantined ships from South
Carolina, and made it felony for a citizen of Charleston to leave
the quarantine ground, nobody protested. But when South
Carolina confined a negro cook from New York to a particular
spot in Charleston, the cry of unconstitutionality was heard.
New York thought men from disease-infected regions dangerous to her safety; South Carolina thought free negroes fresh
from the lectures of an abolition society equally menacing to
her safety and welfare, and required them to live on a particular enclosure. Each was exercising the right which Nature
and necessity sanctioned, and which South Carolina had no
intention of relinquishing.* That the law could not be enforced without clashing with the Federal right to regulate
commerce was admitted.

The defence were careful not to point out the fact that New
York did not charge quarantined negro sailors with board,
lodging, and fees, and sell them into slavery if they could
not pay. Nevertheless, it was absolutely necessary for the
State to enact the law in question; *ex necessitate*, it was a
power South Carolina must and would use, and, " if a dissolution of the Union must be the alternative, they were ready to
abide by the result." †

The Court decided that the act was unconstitutional, and
went so far as to say that it was equivalent to a declaration
of war on Great Britain. No little excitement followed the
decision; but the seizure of negroes went on just the same,
and before the close of the year another British ship was

---

* These views are elaborately stated in The Argument of Benjamin Faneuil
Hunt, in the case of the arrest of the Person claiming to be a British seaman,
under the third section of the State Act of December, 1822, in relation to Negroes,
etc., before the Hon. Judge Johnson, etc., Charleston, 1823.

† See Judge Johnson's decision in Niles's Register, September 6, 1823.

boarded and four free blacks, subjects of Great Britain, were dragged by the sheriff from the deck. The master was put to heavy expense in securing the release of his men, and, on reaching Liverpool, complained to the president of His Majesty's Board of Trade.* Another protest, more vigorous than the first, now came from the British Minister, and Adams referred the law to Attorney-General Wirt for an opinion. Wirt pronounced it a violation of the treaty, a regulation of trade by a State, and therefore unconstitutional and void; and this opinion, together with the protest of the British Minister, was sent by Adams to the Governor of South Carolina, who transmitted them to the Legislature when it met.†

Each branch passed resolutions which the other would not accept. Those from the Senate declared that it was the duty of the State to guard against insurrections among its colored population, and to regulate any cause which might produce it; that " this duty is paramount to all laws, all treaties, all constitutions "; that it arose from the law of self-preservation, and would " never by this State be renounced, compromised, controlled, or participated with any power whatever "; that the Legislature " was aware of the dangerous and insidious conduct of a party in Great Britain and the United States, who were ever ready to indulge their benevolent propensities at the expense of their neighbors "; that South Carolina protested against the United States meddling with her slaves, which property she would " not permit to be meddled with or tampered with, or in any way ordered, regulated, or controlled by any other power, foreign or domestic, than this Legislature."

The House, having rejected these resolutions as too bitter,‡ passed a milder set of its own, asserting that the law was not a commercial regulation, but part of a system of domestic policy, that it was absolutely necessary, and ought not to be repealed. These the Senate rejected, and, both branches

---

* His letter dated January, 1824, is in Niles's Register, December 25, 1824.

† The documents and the message are in Niles's Register, December 25, 1824.

‡ The resolutions passed the Senate 36 to 6, and were rejected by the House 97 to 17.—Niles's Register, December 25, 1824; January 8, 1825.

having refused to repeal the act of 1822, it remained on the statute-book at the opening of the civil war.

The South Carolina act and the unseemly dispute that arose from its enforcement deeply impressed the people everywhere, and went far to strengthen the belief that the solution of the negro problem lay in the removal of the free blacks to Africa. Indeed, the matter was serious enough to call out expressions of opinion from States both slave and free. Georgia proposed an amendment to the Federal Constitution, declaring that no part of it should be construed to authorize the importation or ingress of persons of color into any one of the United States contrary to the laws of such State.* The General Assembly of Ohio declared that a system of colonization might be adopted which would, in due time, effect the emancipation of all slaves without violating the rights of individuals, and recommended the passage of an act by Congress providing that the children of persons then held as slaves born after the passage of the law should be free when twenty-one years old, provided they would consent to be transported to some place of colonization.† Delaware declared that it was requisite for the prosperity of the country, and, what was of far more importance, essential to its safety, that measures should be taken for the removal of all free negroes and mulattoes from the United States. New Jersey pronounced the existence of slavery in the United States a great national evil, declared that the people of New Jersey and of her sister States ought to share in the burden of removing it, and advocated the colonization of free negroes as a reasonable way of securing emancipation. New Jersey believed that colonization would be conducive of emancipation, and would furnish an asylum for free blacks without any violation of the " national compact " or infringement of the rights of individuals. South Carolina, Mississippi, and Missouri approved the amendment proposed by Georgia. Illinois indorsed the suggestion of Ohio. The lower branch of the

---

* Passed by Georgia, December 22, 1823. Presented to the House of Representatives of Congress, February 6, 1824.

† Passed January 17, 1824.

Legislature of Georgia, led on by the excitable Governor Troup, seemed for a time quite ready for civil war.

The Governor had been aroused by the action of Senator King, of New York, who, inspired by the sentiment of the hour, moved that when the national debt had been paid to the last cent the public lands with the net proceeds of their sales should constitute a fund to be used in aiding the emancipation of slaves and the removal of free negroes to Africa. A motion of like import had been laid before the House of Representatives by a member from Virginia, who proposed that a part of the United States west of the Rocky Mountains should be reserved for the colonization of free people of color. But, passing this by, Troup selected the motion of Mr. King and a supposed argument of Mr. Wirt, and made them the subject of special complaint to the Legislature. Since your meeting last year, said he, our feelings have again been outraged by officious and impertinent intermeddling with our domestic concerns. Besides the motion of Mr. King, it is understood that the Attorney-General, who may be supposed to speak the sentiments of the administration, has maintained doctrines before the Supreme Court which, if sanctioned by that tribunal, will make it easy for Congress by a short decree to abolish slavery without the cost of one dollar or the loss of one acre of public land. " Temporize," therefore, " no longer. Make known your resolution that this subject shall not be touched by them but at their peril," and while " it is not too late, stand forth and, having exhausted the argument, stand by your arms."

The committee to whom his remarks were referred reported that in their opinion " the hour is come, or is rapidly approaching, when the States from Virginia to Georgia, from Missouri to Louisiana, must confederate, and as one man say to the Union: We will no longer submit our retained rights to the snivelling insinuations of bad men on the floor of Congress, our constitutional rights to the dark and strained constructions of designing men upon judicial benches; that we protest the doctrine and disclaim the principle of unlimited submission to the General Government; that we concur with the Governor in the sentiment that, having exhausted the argument, we stand by our arms; and that, in support of this declaration, we pledge to each other our lives, our fortunes, and our sacred honor." * Happily, the House took no action for the accomplishment of such a purpose.

The fears of Troup were wholly groundless. The district attorney had made no such argument as was attributed to him. The Supreme Court was not at all likely to be called on to attack slavery; Congress had not the most remote intention of exchanging public lands for slaves in order to set them free; nor did the motion of Mr. King call for such action till the national debt, then more than eighty-three million dollars, had been paid in full. Yet Troup's fears were very real, and were intensified a few months later by the action of the American Society for the Colonization of Free People of Color.

Encouraged by the rising popularity of its antislavery scheme and the hearty indorsement of its purpose by the Legislatures of six States, the society, early in 1827, applied to Congress for aid, and succeeded so well that a select committee reported that were it not that the session had almost ended and that the matter could not then be considered, it would have recommended a grant of money.† This again excited the Georgia Legislature, and drew from it a strong remonstrance and a flat denial of the right of Congress to use the public funds for any such purpose. No one, the Legislature contended, can have the hardiness to assert that there is a word in the Constitution which expressly gives to Congress the power to make the appropriation in question; or that the exercise of it is necessary to give full effect to any power which is expressly granted; or that it comes under the flimsy covering of the words " provide for the common defence and general welfare." The establishment of an African colony on a barbarous and pestilential coast three thousand miles away, and the liberation of the slave population of the South are not essential to the common defence nor conducive of the

* The message of the Governor is printed in Niles's Register, June 11, 1825. The report of the committee is in the Register for June 25, 1825.

† Executive Documents, Nineteenth Congress, Second Session, vol. iv, No. 64, January 25, 1827.

general welfare. When the Colonization Society was established the people of the South were led to believe that its purpose was the removal from the United States of the free people of color and none others. But this impression, it now appears, was erroneous. The society boldly avows that its object is, and ever has been, to remove the whole colored population of the Union from our own to another land, and to accomplish the purpose so wild, so fanatical, so destructive to Southern interests, they ask that the general fund of the United States be used—a fund to which the slave-holding States have contributed so largely. The cold-blooded selfishness, the unthinking zeal which prompts so many of our fellow-citizens in other States to meddle with our internal concerns and domestic relations—an interference totally unwarranted either by humanity or constitutional right—cannot be too severely reprobated. The result of such meddling if continued is awful and inevitable. The people of Georgia know and feel the advantages of the Union; but they cannot and will not, even for the preservation of that Union, permit their rights to be assailed. But how is this evil to be met? Nothing can be hoped from remonstrance. Our own Legislature cannot check it by laws. It can be met and stopped only " by a union of the people and the States of the South, declaring through their legislative bodies, in a voice that must be heard, that they are ready and willing to make any sacrifice rather than submit longer to such ruinous interference, and warning their enemies that they are unwittingly preparing a mine which, once exploded, will lay our much loved country in one common ruin.*

In these remonstrances and threatenings Georgia was soon joined by South Carolina. A committee of her Senate, to which the question was referred, reported that it had no hesitation in saying that on such a subject there could be no reasoning between South Carolina and any other government. In the whole catalogue of human evils the worst was that state of affairs in which the slaves should be encouraged to look for emancipation to any other body than the Legislature.† On

* Executive Documents, Twentieth Congress, First Session, vol. iii, No. 126.

† Executive Documents, Twentieth Congress, First Session, vol. iii, No. 65. The Legislature resolved " that the American Colonization Society is not an ob-

the other hand, the border slave States approved of the purpose
of the society.   Maryland voted it one thousand dollars annually for ten years.'*   Kentucky expressed her deepest interest in the colonization movement, and requested her senators
and representatives in Congress to use their best efforts to secure the protection and patronage of the General Government
for the society.†   Ohio ‡ and Vermont # did the same; Virginia on two occasions gave the society money.

Yet, despite this widespread interest, the work of emancipation was not to be done by the Colonization Society.   Already
a little band of men, whose names were quite unknown to the
mass of their fellow-citizens, had set in motion agents which
in the course of time proved far more effective.

Foremost among these antislavery leaders was Benjamin
Lundy, a native of Handwich, Sussex County, New Jersey,
where he was born in 1789.   Like so many of those who had
labored in the cause of abolition since the day when the first
public protest against slave-holding was made at Germantown, Lundy came of Quaker stock.   His hatred of slavery
seems to have begun when, as a lad of nineteen, he went to
learn the saddler's trade at Wheeling, Virginia, then a rival
of Pittsburg as a place where emigrants obtained their outfits
for the West, and a thoroughfare on the route of the interstate slave-trade.   Hardly a week passed but coffles of negroes,
gathered from the plantations of Virginia or bought from the
dealers in the slave marts of Baltimore and Washington, were
driven through its streets.   The misery and suffering of these
unhappy people deeply affected Lundy.   From a sympathizer
he became an earnest worker in their behalf, and, on removing
to St. Clairsville, in eastern Ohio, he founded an antislavery
association, which he called the Union Humane Society, wrote
an appeal to antislavery people in the United States urging
them to form like associations, and began to contribute antislavery articles to the Philanthropist, a weekly journal pub-

ject of national interest, and that Congress has no power in any way to patronize
or direct appropriations for the benefit of this or any other society."
* Laws of Maryland, Act 172, Session of 1826–'27.
† Niles's Weekly Register, March 24, 1827.
‡ January 24–26, 1828.   # November 12, 1827.

lished at Mount Pleasant, and devoted to the interests of peace, temperance, and antislavery.* The editor was a Quaker preacher named Charles Osborn, who, after visiting most of the meetings in the South, urging immediate emancipation and encouraging the establishment of manumission societies, had settled at Mount Pleasant and begun the publication of the first newspaper that ever advocated immediate and uncompensated emancipation in the United States.

To the Philanthropist Lundy became a steady contributor, and when, in 1818, a partnership was offered him by Osborn, willingly accepted it, and set off for St. Louis, there to dispose of his stock in trade. On a second trip, made in the autumn of 1819, he reached the city just at the time when excitement over the admission of Missouri as a slave State was at its height, and, entering the contest, wrote vigorously against slavery and the compromise. Meantime Osborn, despairing of Lundy's return, sold his paper, and another Friend, Elihu Embree, of Jonesborough, in East Tennessee, established The Emancipator, the first newspaper in our country founded for the sole purpose of attacking slavery. When Lundy heard of these things, he seems to have abandoned all thought of becoming an editor. Nevertheless, he determined to return to Ohio, and, having no money, he made the journey of more than seven hundred miles on foot in the dead of winter. But, as he trudged along, news of Embree's death reached him, and he thereupon decided to found an antislavery periodical at Mount Pleasant. He had no press and no money, yet when six subscribers were secured Lundy walked with his manuscript to Steubenville, ten miles away, and carried home on his back the little edition of the first number of the Genius of Universal Emancipation. This resounding name, borrowed from a phrase that dropped from the lips of Curran in the course of one of his great speeches, was bestowed on a small sixteen-page monthly of most humble appearance. The paper was poor, the printing was bad, but the vigor and earnestness of the matter brought a hearty support and a long subscription list before the fourth number was published. Such was his

* Life of Benjamin Lundy.—Earle.

success that within a year the friends of Embree persuaded Lundy to remove his paper to Jonesborough, where he stayed till 1824, when he carried out a long-meditated plan and started East to establish the Genius at Baltimore.

In Maryland at that time the antislavery sentiment was strong. A public meeting at Baltimore had protested against the Missouri Compromise; nearly one thousand abolition votes were cast at the polls, and the day seemed near when the State would accept gradual emancipation and take her place with the free States of the North and West. From the start, therefore, the Genius was well received, well supported, and widely circulated. But the day of prosperity was short. The events of the next three years wrought a change in public opinion in the slave-holding States. Subscriptions to the Genius fell off, and in the spring of 1828 the list was so short that Lundy made a tour of the free States in search of new subscribers. He went as far north as Albany and as far east as Boston, where, at a boarding house, he met William Lloyd Garrison, then a young man of twenty-three.

Garrison was a native of Newburyport, Massachusetts, where he was born in 1805. After a boyhood passed in great poverty, he was apprenticed at thirteen to a printer of his native town, and began to set type in the office of the Newburyport Herald, but rose quickly to the position of foreman, and before he was seventeen was contributing anonymous articles of no mean kind on current topics of importance. His apprenticeship over, Garrison, at twenty, became editor and publisher of the Newburyport Free Press, and when, a few months later, that journal closed its career, went to Boston, and at twenty-three was editor of the National Philanthropist, the first temperance newspaper in the United States.* It was at this time that Garrison met Lundy, heard him explain his views to a little meeting of Boston clergymen, and, when they failed to respond, indorsed the Genius in the columns of the Philanthropist.

With a few new subscribers as the fruit of this visit to

---

* The National Philanthropist was founded in 1826 by Rev. William Collier, and was "devoted to the suppression of intemperance and its kindred vices, and to the promotion of industry, education, and morality."

the North, Lundy went back to Baltimore, but almost immediately returned to Boston, where, one midsummer evening, he spoke to a public meeting in the vestry of the Baptist Church. He dwelt on the folly of seeking to abolish slavery by the method used by the Colonization Society, told his hearers that the increase in slave population for one year was greater than the diminution the society could effect in fifty years, and urged them to found an antislavery society and petition Congress to abolish slavery in the District of Columbia.

Scarcely had Lundy finished speaking when the pastor of the church denounced the agitation of the slavery question in New England, declared that the people of the North had no business to meddle with the institution, and dismissed the meeting. Garrison was present, and it was largely by his influence that another meeting was held, that an antislavery committee was formed, and a petition written, circulated, signed, and sent to Congress. Again Lundy obtained new subscribers; but the support was of no avail, and in January, 1829, the Genius of Universal Emancipation ceased to appear. It was suspended. "It shall never be abandoned," said Lundy, "while the labor of my own hands will support life and produce revenue sufficient to print and publish one sheet per annum." *

True to his pledge, Lundy began at once to canvass for new subscribers, to collect unpaid subscriptions, and, what was far more important, he now persuaded Garrison to come to Baltimore and join him in the effort to revive the Genius. Garrison had retired from the National Philanthropist, had gone to Bennington, and was there editing The Journal of the Times, a newspaper whose mission it was to advocate the cause of antislavery, temperance, peace, and moral reform.† To quit the Journal at once was not possible; but as soon as he could, Garrison left Bennington, and in the autumn of 1829 joined Lundy at Baltimore, where, in September, the publication of the Genius was again resumed.‡

---

* Genius of Universal Emancipation, January 3, 1829.   James G. Birney and his Times.   William Birney, p. 396.

† The first number appeared October 3, 1828.   ‡ September 5, 1829.

The list of antislavery journals was then a long one. Since the day when Osborn issued the first number of the Philanthropist at Mount Pleasant, no period of three years had gone by without a new journal appearing somewhere. The Philanthropist began in 1817; the Emancipator, in Tennessee, in 1819; the Genius of Universal Emancipation in 1821; and the Abolition Intelligencer, in Kentucky, in 1822. The great struggle over slavery in Illinois called into existence the Edwardsville Spectator and the Illinois Intelligencer in 1822 and 1823; the African Observer, in Philadelphia, dates from 1826, and Freedom's Journal, in New York city, from 1827. The editor was a negro. Collier founded the National Philanthropist in Boston in 1826, and William Goodell the Investigator at Providence in 1827. One year later, the Free Press was started at Bennington, and the Liberalist at New Orleans. These were distinctively antislavery journals; but the daily and weekly newspapers whose columns were not closed to antislavery literature numbered upward of fifty.*

Besides this antislavery journalism, there was also a great body of antislavery literature. Of books of this sort, there had never been a dearth for a hundred years past; but now not a twelvemonth elapsed but appeals, orations, thoughts, letters, pictures, brief views, treatises, remarks, sketches, reports, tracts, and pamphlets, all bearing on some phase of the question, came teeming from the press. The works of Clarkson, Wilberforce, Cooper, Stephen, and Elizabeth Heyrick, and a host of other British agitators, were not merely republished in our country, they were widely read. It was at this time that Rankin wrote his " Letters on Slavery in America " ; Duncan his " Treatise on Slavery " ; Lundy his " Life of Elisha Tyson " ; Stroud his " Sketch of the Laws relating to Slavery in the Several States." But the list need not be called. Hostility to slavery as a moral and political wrong was spreading and growing in intensity. The issue between slavery and freedom had now been raised never to be abandoned till settled forever, and on this issue the great geographical sections of our country were taking sides.

---

* The list of such newspapers is given in James G. Birney and his Times, by William Birney, p. 405.

The people of the cotton belt, holding that slavery was a domestic State institution, denied the right of Congress to touch it in any way, and denounced the work of antislavery men and colonizationists as fanaticism. New England, bound to the cotton States by ties of business interest, was indifferent. In the middle belt of States, from Pennsylvania to North Carolina and from the Atlantic to the Mississippi, the friends of the negro were all activity. Of one hundred and one antislavery societies in existence in 1826, ninety-five were in this region, and seventy-seven of the ninety-five were in the slaveholding States of Delaware, Maryland, Virginia, North Carolina, Kentucky, and Tennessee. Of fifty-seven societies auxiliary to the American Colonization Society in 1826, forty-four were in the slave-holding States of Delaware, Maryland, Virginia, and North Carolina.* Two years later,

* STATE.	ANTISLAVERY SOCIETIES.	AMERICAN COLONIAL SOCIETIES.	
	1826.	1826.	1828.
Maine	0	1	1
New Hampshire	0	1	1
Vermont	0	1	1
Massachusetts	0	0	1
Rhode Island	1	0	0
Connecticut	0	0	1
New York	1	8	9
New Jersey	0	1	1
Pennsylvania	4	1	10
Delaware	1	2	2
Maryland	4	8	11
District of Columbia	0	0	2
Virginia	2	23	28
North Carolina	41	7	8
South Carolina	0	0	0
Georgia	0	3	2
Kentucky	6	1	3
Tennessee	23	0	0
Ohio	6	0	16
Indiana	0	0	0
Illinois	12	0	0
Missouri	0	0	1
	101 †	57	98 ‡

† Address of the Maryland Antislavery Society, American Daily Advertiser, November 22, 1825.

‡ Memorial of the Colonization Society to Congress, 1828. Executive Documents, Twentieth Congress, First Session, vol. iii, No. 99.

when the number had risen to ninety-eight, more than half were still to be found in the border slave States, although during the interval twenty-five societies devoted to the cause of colonization sprang up in Pennsylvania and Ohio. Some of the people were in favor of immediate abolition; some demanded gradual emancipation without compensation; some insisted on immediate emancipation with compensation; others threw all their influence in support of emigration and colonization.*

The existence of a society or of a host of societies is, indeed, no indication of vigorous activity, but the work done by these antislavery organizations before 1829 is manifest in many ways. In North Carolina the Friends, who composed the great body of the antislavery party, procured the freedom of two thousand slaves between 1824 and 1826, and, as the law required, removed them from the State. In Maryland, in 1825 and 1826, the State Antislavery Society nominated a candidate for the House of Delegates on an abolition platform, and polled almost a thousand votes.† In Delaware the Friend Wilmington Monthly Meeting sent a long memorial to the Legislature praying for the abolition of slavery within that State. It appealed to reason, to justice, to humanity; to the self-evident truths and requisitions of the Christian religion; to reasons of state, motives of expediency, the common interest and general welfare; pointed out how much more profitable voluntary rewarded labor was than the compulsory, unrequited

---

* In 1825 the managers of the Manumission Society of North Carolina sent out a series of questions to be answered by its branches. One of the questions was, "Is a majority of the citizens of North Carolina opposed to slavery?" The answer as based on the census of opinions gathered in forty-five different localities in the State was: "One thirtieth of the people are crying out for immediate emancipation among us; one twentieth are for gradual emancipation; one fifteenth are supporting schemes of emigration and colonization; three fifths are ready to support emancipation by paying their money and otherwise; one twentieth have never thought on the subject and neither know nor care anything about it; three twentieths are moderately opposed to emancipation, merely because they think it impracticable; and one twentieth are bitterly opposed to it in almost every shape." Queries proposed by the Board of Managers of the Manumission Society of North Carolina. Genius of Universal Emancipation, September, 1825. James G. Birney and his Times, by William Birney, pp. 78, 79.

† James G. Birney and his Times. William Birney, pp. 83, 84. Genius of Universal Emancipation, September 2, 1825. Ibid., October 7, 1826.

drudgery of slaves; how since Independence the States that had abolished slavery had outstripped those retaining it; how the first glance of the eye over the regions burdened with it betrayed its presence; how the fields, fences, roads, buildings, the price of property all declared it; how where it no longer existed property had risen, internal improvements had advanced with astonishing rapidity, and the happiness of all classes had been increased.*

The Legislature made no response. Indeed, it had just placed on the statute-book a law whose enactment aroused no little popular indignation, for of all the incidents to slavery there were none more irritating in the border States—both slave and free—than the rendition of fugitive slaves and the kidnapping of free negroes. The constitutional obligation to deliver up fugitives from labor or service on demand of those to whom such labor or service was due, had been embodied in an act of Congress which depended for its execution on the judiciary of the States. Under the provisions of this law the owner of a runaway slave, or a duly appointed agent of the owner, might seize and arrest the fugitive, take him before a judge of a circuit or district court of the United States, or before a magistrate of a county, city, or corporate town, claim the negro as a slave, and, having proved the claim to the satisfaction of the magistrate, become entitled to a certificate empowering him to convey the wretched creature out of the State and back to the plantation.

No warrant was required for the seizure and arrest; no opportunity was given the negro to be heard in his own defence, or to summon witnesses, or be represented by council, for the testimony of the claimant was all-sufficient. The fugitive in the eye of the law was a chattel, a piece of property, a human being destitute of the rights of man, and, having no legal standing in the State whence he fled, he was entitled to none in the State where he sought a refuge. The purpose of the law was to make easy the return of fugitive slaves, but at the same time it made easy the kidnapping and condemnation to slavery of free negroes living in the border States.

---

* Gazette of the United States, April 16, 1826.

Evilly disposed men had but to visit some little town in a free State, or, indeed, in any State where free negroes were allowed to dwell, select their intended victim, lure him from home on some pretext, seize and hurry him off by night to another town, and there claim him as a slave. If the lie they told imposed on the magistrate, a certificate was granted which enabled them openly and in the light of day to take their prisoner out of the State and sell him for transportation to that place of terrors—the far South.

Again and again the attention of Congress had been called to the crimes thus perpetrated with impunity under the law, and a remedy had as often been sought in vain. Respectful petitions of free negroes were treated with every mark of indignity.* From time to time committees were appointed to inquire into the expediency of amending the fugitive slave law, and either did nothing † or reported bills which failed to pass. One of these went so far as to require that every free negro in the United States should provide himself with a certificate of freedom bearing the seal of the county in which he resided, and made it a misdemeanor for a white man to employ a negro not so certificated.‡ Infamous as the bill was, it came within three votes of passing the House of Representatives.# Another, which did pass the House, was amended in the Senate, and then tabled in the House. A third never came to a final vote.

Meantime kidnapping grew more and more frequent. The high price of cotton expanded the cotton-raising area and increased the demand for slaves. With the demand for slaves went a rise in their market value, which made the kidnappers and negro-stealers bolder than ever. Pennsylvania, as a free State and the home of thousands of free negroes, was so infested that a stringent law against the crime of negro-stealing was enacted. No warrant for the arrest of the fugitive was required. But justices of the peace and aldermen were forbidden to take cognizance of such cases or grant certificates of

---

* History of the People of the United States, vol. ii, pp. 454–456.
† Annals of Congress, 1799–1801.
‡ Annals of Congress, 1801–'03, p. 317.
# December 18, 1802. Ibid., p. 423.

removal; the claimant was required to bring his prisoner before a judge or recorder of a court of record, and heavy fines and long terms of imprisonment were provided for kidnappers.*

The effect of the law was to insure a more careful examination of claimants, and to that extent guard the liberty of free negroes. But no warrant was required for the seizure and arrest, the sympathy of the people was almost always sure to be with the negro seized, and not infrequently that sympathy led to vigorous measures in his behalf and to a rescue. Such instances were constantly occurring. Thus, in 1821, a citizen of Maryland with his overseer, traced a runaway to Kennett Square, a little town in Pennsylvania not far from the Delaware border, where the negro was found. But in the attempt to seize him the people interfered, a struggle followed, and both owner and overseer lost their lives. A year later another Maryland planter in search of a slave went to Darby; but there also the people rose, threatened him with imprisonment as a kidnapper, and compelled him to allow the negro to escape.

These two incidents aroused such excitement in Maryland that the Legislature was forced to interfere, and address Pennsylvania on the subject. The existence of slavery, the letter set forth, was an evil as deeply regretted by Maryland as it could be by Pennsylvania. Friends of freedom everywhere would rejoice to see it exterminated. But the end of slavery could not be expected for many years to come, and until that time did come such citizens of Maryland as saw fit to own slaves were as much entitled to this as to any other kind of property, and it was the duty of the sister State to protect owners in its enjoyment. But Pennsylvania did not do so, for of all the slaves that each year sought a refuge on her soil very few were brought back to Maryland. Aside from the constitutional obligation to return fugitives from service and labor, it was bad policy for Pennsylvania not to stop the settlement of negroes on her soil. They could never assimilate with the whites, and must always be a burden and a menace.†

---

* Act of March 27, 1820. The fine might range from $500 to $2,000; with the fine went a term of imprisonment of from seven to twenty-one years.

† Journal of the Senate of Pennsylvania, 1822–'23, pp. 232–235. The letter was laid on the table.

No action followed the appeal, and, after enduring what she considered a great injustice for three more years, Maryland renewed her efforts, and sent a commission to visit the Legislatures of Delaware, New Jersey, and Pennsylvania, remonstrate in her name, and ask for a better enforcement of the fugitive slave law of 1793. The Legislature of New Jersey was not in session; but those of Delaware and Pennsylvania promptly complied with the request and, despite the loud and indignant protests of the antislavery people, enacted laws more in accordance with the wishes of Maryland.* Delaware made it a crime for a runaway slave to come within her bounds; forbade negroes free or slave to leave her soil unless provided with a legal pass, and punished kidnapping with a fine of at least a thousand dollars, with one hour on the pillory, with sixty lashes on the bare back, with imprisonment for not less than three years, and at the end of the term of imprisonment with the sale of the offender as a servant for seven years to the highest bidder. †

Pennsylvania‡ now required that the claimant should obtain a warrant # for the arrest of the negro, and that the prisoner should be examined before a judge.

All this was in the interest of the free negro. But concessions were also made to the owner seeking his slave. He might obtain his warrant from a justice of the peace or an alderman; he might, when the examination took place before the judge, have the trial postponed and the negro sent to jail until he gathered more evidence, and if any judge, magistrate, or sheriff did not aid him to secure the full benefit of the law a heavy penalty awaited the delinquent official.

In the District of Columbia it might be, indeed it was carried on with impunity. At that time the District consisted of two distinct and separate parts. The one, called the County of

---

* Journal of the Senate of Pennsylvania, 1825–'26. For the opposition in Delaware, see American Daily Advertiser, February 11, 1826. For the debate in the Pennsylvania Legislature and the opposition of the people, see American Daily Advertiser, February 10, 11, 14, 15, 18, 20, 1826.

† Laws of Delaware, Chapter CCCLXII, 1826. See also act of January 19, 1826, Chapter CCCXVI.

‡ Laws of Pennsylvania, March 25, 1826.

The warrant might be issued by a judge, justice of the peace, or alderman.

Alexandria, lay in Virginia, and was subject to such laws as were on the statute-books of Virginia at the time of the cession to the United States. The other, known as the County of Washington, is the present District, is entirely in Maryland, and was subject to such laws as were in force in Maryland in 1790. On the Virginia side of the Potomac no negro could be arrested as a fugitive slave who could produce evidence of freedom. But if such evidence could not be produced within three months after being demanded, he might be arrested and hired out till it was procured, when he must be discharged without costs, and must be given a certificate of freedom to be annually renewed. Should he be unable to secure satisfactory evidence within a year after his arrest, he must be sold as a slave.

On the Maryland side the law was very different. There all free persons of color, whether natives or emigrants, were required to register with the clerk of the County Court and procure a certificate. Negroes found at large without it must be examined before a magistrate. If adjudged runaways they must be sold as slaves. If declared freemen they must be discharged, subject, however, to all the fees, costs, and rewards usual in the case of runaways, and on failure to pay them must be sold into slavery.

Favored by situation and by the laws on the Maryland side, Washington had become a veritable slave mart. To it every week numbers of negroes bought in Maryland and Virginia were carried by the slave-dealers, there to be kept till the coffles were ready to be sent to the plantations of the South. It was the custom to deliver the blacks, immediately after arrival, to the sheriff, who confined them for safe keeping in the public jails; or take them to one of the private prisons, of which there were several in the city. In the public jails they were treated as common malefactors, though guilty of absolutely no offence whatever. In the private prisons, duly provided with cells, fetters, and chains, they were treated with a cruelty that often drove the victims to attempt suicide. When by one means and another a dealer had gathered twenty or more likely young negro men and girls, he would bring them forth from their cells; would

an unclaimed slave for jail fees and other charges.* Such a thing, the committee reported,† was just possible in Alexandria County, was possible in Washington County, but quite unlikely to occur. No change was therefore recommended for the Virginia side of the District, but a bill was reported providing that when free persons of color were arrested on the Maryland side on suspicion and discharged, the jail fees and charges should be paid by the county. Against this the corporations of Georgetown and Washington city protested, and the bill was never considered.

But the manumission, abolition, and antislavery societies had been aroused. That slavery in the States was subject to State control and no other was generally admitted. In the District of Columbia, however, where no State had jurisdiction, where, in the language of the Constitution, Congress had "exclusive legislation in all cases whatsoever," Congress, it was claimed, was fully empowered to abolish it, and was in duty bound to do so. The Twentieth Congress had not been long in session, therefore, when petitions praying for the passage of a gradual abolition law for the District were presented by dozens.‡ It was the earnest wish of the petitioners that the domestic slave-trade should cease; that the importation of negroes from the nearby States for sale in the District should cease; that the private slave pens should be suppressed, the public prisons no longer used for the safe-keeping of slaves the property of dealers; and that a day should be named after which all children born of slave parents should be free on attaining a certain age. One of the petitions bore the signatures of one thousand inhabitants of the District. #

But neither the number of signatures, nor the number of the petitions, nor the sources whence they came availed

---

* December 26 and 27, 1826. Journal of the House of Representatives, Nineteenth Congress, Second Session, pp. 146, 406.

† Reports of Committee, No. 43, Nineteenth Congress, Second Session.

‡ House Executive Documents, No. 215, Twentieth Congress, First Session, vol. v. Presented March 24, 1828.

Journal of the House of Representatives, Twentieth Congress, First Session, pp. 224, 280, 309, 341, 367, 438, 457, 727.

anything. The House went through the decent form of referring them to the committee for the District. The committee reported a bill that was not considered, and the petitioners, nothing discouraged, besieged the Twentieth Congress during its second session with the same energy with which they beset it during the first. The cause, moreover, again found a champion in Mr. Miner, who forced the House to action by offering a set of resolutions of his own.

Mr. Miner prefaced his resolutions with a long preamble setting forth that slave-dealers made the seat of Federal Government their headquarters for carrying on the domestic slave-trade; that the public prisons were extensively used for the same purpose; that it afforded occupation and profit to officers of the Federal Government; that private and secret prisons existed in the District for furthering this traffic in human beings; that persons having but a limited time to serve were bought by slave-dealers and sent where redress was impossible; that freemen were kidnapped and hurried away before they could be rescued; that free people of color coming into the District were liable to arrest, imprisonment, and sale into slavery for life for jail fees; that advertisements beginning " We will give cash for one hundred likely young negroes, of both sexes, from eight to twenty-five years old," which appeared in the District newspapers showed the openness and extent of the traffic; that scenes of human beings exposed for sale were of constant occurrence; that a grand jury had presented the slave-trade as a grievance; that a writer in a public print had declared that those who had never seen the spectacles presented by the slave-trade could form no conception of its horrors; that petitions from various parts of the Union had been presented praying for gradual abolition in the District, and that Congress ought to exact such a law. Mr. Miner moved, therefore, that the committee for the District be instructed to take their allegations into consideration, inquire into the truth of them, examine into the slave code and the slave-trade, report any needed legislation, and state whether it was or was not expedient to provide for the gradual abolition of slavery in the District.*

* Register of Debates in Congress, vol. v, 1828–'29, p. 167.

hibited the introduction of slaves into the Commonwealth; therefore they could not come into that part of the District which lay in Virginia. Maryland having no such law in force, slaves were brought in and sold in the city of Washington. Such trading as went on was chiefly for the purpose of sending the slaves South, which was one way not only of getting rid of them, but of ameliorating their condition by removing them to a genial and beautiful climate.

To the complaint that the public jails were used for confining slaves bought for the purpose of being sold elsewhere, the committee declared that the custom was good. In the jails the negroes were protected from the weather, were open to public inspection, and so afforded an opportunity to detect such as were kidnapped or improperly held to servitude; for if a negro claimed to be free, the marshal always refused to release him till ordered to do so by one of the judges of the Circuit Court,

Situated as the District was, with a slave population on all sides of it, abolition of the slave-trade was most impolitic. It was best, the committee therefore reported, to let the matter rest.* A few evils resulting from the quartering of large numbers of slaves in the city for a long time did need correction, and this was provided for in a bill which died in Committee of the Whole.

---

* Reports of Committees, No. 60, Twentieth Congress, Second Session.

CHAPTER XLVI.

THE INDUSTRIAL REVOLUTION.

To the many causes of misunderstanding which were thus springing up between the North and West, on the one hand, and the South on the other, and were fast making them two separate nations, must be added yet another directly due to the industrial revolution through which the country was passing. Never before in our history had the contrast been so marked. The invention of the Whitney gin had made cotton-growing wonderfully profitable. The inventions of Hargreaves and Crompton and Arkwright had stimulated the demand for cotton, and these two conditions combined—the existence of a market and the possibility of supplying it with ease and profit —had already made cotton-planting the one absorbing industry of the South. From a petty yield of two million pounds in 1791, the crop increased with astonishing rapidity year by year till it reached thirty-five million pounds in 1800, eighty millions in 1811, and two hundred and eighty millions in 1821, a product worth thirty-five million dollars. Under the influence of this ruling industry the enterprise, the capital, the development of the South became confined to a few restricted lines. Arts and sciences were little cultivated. Mechanical inventions were disregarded. Great natural resources were left untouched. Her deposits of iron ore were enormous. Her coal fields exceeded thirty-nine thousand square miles in area. She had boundless tracts of lumber land and farm land, and factory and mill sites the equal of any in New England. Yet her people neglected the opportunities afforded by the bounteous gifts of Nature, and concentrated all their energies on the cultivation of one plant. Every year at the same time they

sowed cotton seed. Every year at the same time they gathered
the wool, and ginned, pressed, and sent it to market at New
Orleans or Charleston or Savannah. One third was sold for
home consumption, two thirds were shipped to Great Britain
or Europe, and with the money so obtained goods, wares, and
merchandise were purchased for use on the plantations.
Every ship that came from Liverpool to Charleston or Savannah for cotton was laden with china, glass, crockery,
hardware and cutlery, grindstones and brooms, edged tools,
pipes, cotton cloth, shoes, and a hundred other articles the
planters consumed. In the course of time, therefore, an
immense trade had grown up between Great Britain and
the South to the ruin of a like trade which might have
existed between the North and the South. It is indeed true
that when this trade began very many of the articles thus imported could not possibly have been furnished by the North;
but it is also true that it continued long after every want of
the planter could have been as fully and as cheaply supplied
by the American as by the British manufacturer.

These industrial conditions deeply affected the South politically, socially, and economically. The existence of seven
States whose population was engaged in growing and market-
ing one staple gave them an identity of interest and a common
point of view. The firm belief that cotton could not be successfully cultivated save by the black man, and that the negro
would not work unless compelled to, fastened slavery on the
South, shut out the free laborer, and deprived that section of
all the blessings that flow from a state of society where every
man, from the richest to the poorest, has the right and is
earnestly seeking to better his condition. No thrifty, industrious middle class existed.

The belief that slave labor could not be utilized in mills
and factories prevented the introduction of manufactures.
Therefore machine shops, workshops, cotton mills, rolling
mills, foundries, mines, and all the many benefits that spring
from diversified industry were unknown in the South. To
the great forces which in the course of the nineteenth century
were to radically change the condition of civilized man she
was indifferent.

Not so the North. There every art and science which could add to the wealth, increase the prosperity and comfort of the people, and develop the material resources of the country was already assiduously cultivated. Of seventy-five million dollars invested in manufactures in 1825, less than fifteen were in the States south of Pennsylvania and the Ohio, and twelve of the fifteen millions were in Maryland, Virginia, and Kentucky. The change which five years had wrought in the industrial development of the North was astonishing.

The failure of the tariff of 1816 to accomplish all the good expected, the evils of a disordered currency, the hard times of 1819, the enormous importation of British goods to be sold at auction well-nigh destroyed manufactures before 1820. But with the return of better times and the general revival of business which speedily followed the dark days of 1819, manufactures once more began to thrive and multiply all over the Eastern and Middle States. When the first quarter of the century ended, Saco, in Maine, was soon to boast of the largest cotton mill in our country. Sixty others could be counted in New Hampshire, where such towns as Salmon Falls, Newmarket, and Somersworth were growing rapidly on spots which five years before were in the wilderness. In the same State were more than three hundred tanneries, more than two hundred bark mills, and half a score of paper mills. The men of northern Vermont, stirred to activity by the opportunity opened to them by the Hudson and Champlain Canal, had turned Middlebury into a factory town, had covered their hills with sheep, and were sending to New York iron, copperas, and wool. Within an area seventeen miles square in Massachusetts were five towns making fifty thousand pieces of flannel yearly, and giving employment to twenty-one hundred people. The mills and factories in the State numbered one hundred and sixty-one, with a capital of thirty million dollars. But Rhode Island surpassed this, for in Providence and its neighborhood, including a small district of Massachusetts, were one hundred and fifty manufacturing establishments, employing thirty thousand men and women. Providence now claimed to be the richest city of its size and population in the world. From the cotton and woollen mills of New York came each year cloth valued at eighteen million dollars. But her people also raised wool, and made salt, paper, glass, iron, and leather in immense quantities. The Hudson from Albany to New York city is described as " teeming with manufacturing establishments," and the counties of Dutchess and Oneida as " filled with factories." At Jersey City were carpet, glass, and porcelain works owned by New Yorkers. At Paterson five thousand dollars a week were paid out to the hands in the cotton, flax, and iron factories.

In Philadelphia were four thousand weavers. About its suburbs were growing up towns such as Manayunk, whose population was supported entirely by manufactures. Reading was a great hat town. The little county of Delaware contained one hundred and fifty-seven mills and factories. The coal and iron industries were developing with wonderful rapidity, while in Pittsburg was the great manufacturing centre of the Mississippi Valley. Steubenville and Cincinnati were her only rivals.

But it is useless to attempt a summary. It is sufficient to know that from Maine to Maryland and from Maryland to Missouri new industries of a hundred sorts were now pursued with untiring energy. In 1820 it was estimated that two hundred thousand persons and a capital of seventy-five million dollars were employed in manufacturing. In 1825 the capital used had been expanded to one hundred and sixty millions and the number of workers to two millions.

That the development of innumerable manufactures in the North should give rise to new interests, and that the rise of new interests should be accompanied by a steadily increasing demand for their protection by Government was inevitable. Just as the ship-builder, the ship-owner, the importer, and the merchant had long insisted that Government should make such treaties, pass such laws, impose such duties as were most conducive to the welfare of his business; just as the planter and the farmer had steadily resisted every attempt to do anything which in their opinion would tend to shut their produce from foreign markets, lead other nations to retaliate, or in any way lessen the number of customers at home or abroad, so the manufacturers, the holders of stock in manufacturing companies, those who derived a livelihood from labor in mills and factories, machine shops, and foundries, or furnished raw material for consumption, now united in a persistent effort to secure a really protective tariff.

The bill introduced in 1820, mild as it was, had suffered defeat in the Senate * by the union of commercial and agricultural interests. The bill of 1821 had never been put upon its passage in either house.† When the Seventeenth Congress met the great champion of protection was not a member, the speakership was given to a Virginian ‡ opposed to protection, and the Committee on Manufactures was so arranged that it would not report a bill, nor would the House consider that presented by its Ways and Means Committee. Much the same fate befell the fourth attempt in 1823. Monroe in his annual message had asked for further protection; his remarks had been referred to the Committee on Manufactures, and a bill so increasing the existing duties on iron, coarse woollen cloths, and dyed cottons as to prohibit their importation was quickly reported; but no vote was ever reached, and it perished in Committee of the Whole.

That the Eighteenth Congress would be more friendly to the protection of domestic industries was fully expected, for Clay was again a congressman, and in his old seat in the Speaker's chair presided over a House to which the States strongly in favor of a new tariff sent more members than ever before. It was therefore with a fine prospect of success that Monroe for the second time appealed to Congress to protect " those articles which we are prepared to manufacture or which are more immediately connected with the defence and independence of the country."

His words were referred to the Committee on Manufactures, which soon presented a bill arranging all imported goods, wares, and merchandise in two classes.* In the first were silks, linens, spices from the Indies, cutlery from Great Britain, and a long list of articles which were not made in our country, and whose importation would not interfere with home manufac-

---

* History of the People of the United States, vol. iv, pp. 510–515.
† Ibid., pp. 518–521.   ‡ P. P. Barbour.
* January 9, 1824.

tures in the least. On these a tariff for revenue was to be imposed. In the second class were iron, glass, lead, hemp, cotton-bagging, cotton cloth, wool, and woollen goods, and on these were laid highly protective duties.

While the committee was at work on its bill, petitions and memorials both for and against a revision of the tariff came pouring in from the East, the Middle States, and the South. Those who favored such a tariff as would encourage manufactures and build up domestic industries were the growers of wool, the manufacturers of woollen and cotton cloth, the farmers eager for a home market for their produce, the mechanics of the great cities, the people of New Bedford and Nantucket—then the centres of the whale fishing and the whale-oil industry—and all whose business was languishing because of the importation of British goods to be sold at auction.*

The opposers of a revision were the tallow-chandlers of New York and Boston, the cordage manufacturers, the Chambers of Commerce at New York, New Haven, and Philadelphia, the merchants of Portland, Portsmouth, and Boston, the hardware dealers, and the citizens of Baltimore, Richmond, Petersburg, Norfolk, Beaufort, Charleston, and of sundry towns in North Carolina, South Carolina, and Georgia.†

---

* Citizens of New Bedford, Executive Papers, No. 107, Eighteenth Congress, First Session, vol. vi. Citizens of Nantucket, ibid., No. 108. Samuel Slater and others, Senate Documents, No. 18, Eighteenth Congress, First Session, vol. i. Connecticut Manufacturers, Executive Papers, No. 36, vol. ii. Farmers and Mechanics of New York, Executive Papers, No. 48, vol. ii. Albany Merchants, Executive Papers, No. 66, vol. iv. Citizens of South Carolina, Executive Papers, No. 10, vol. v. Pennsylvania Farmers, ibid., No. 117, vol. vi. Citizens of Philadelphia, ibid., 123, vol. vi. Pennsylvania Manufacturers, ibid., No. 116, vol. vi.

† New York Tallow-chandlers, Executive Papers, No. 106, Eighteenth Congress, First Session, vol. vi. Boston Tallow-chandlers, Executive Papers, No. 105, ibid. Cordage Makers, Executive Papers, No. 9, vol. i. New York Chamber of Commerce, Senate Documents, No. 31, vol. ii. George Jones and others, Senate Documents, No. 48, vol. iii. Citizens of Charleston, S. C., Executive Papers, No. 64, vol. iv. New York Hardware Dealers, Executive Papers, No. 65, vol. iv. Boston Merchants, ibid., No. 67. Portland Merchants, No. 71, ibid., vol. iv. Citizens of Richmond, ibid., No. 74. Citizens of Petersburg, Executive Papers, No. 88, vol. v. Citizens of Beaufort, Executive Papers, No. 81, vol. v. Portsmouth Merchants, No. 87, ibid., vol. v. Philadelphia Chamber of Com-

The reasons and arguments of the antiprotectionists as set forth in their memorials were, that Congress had no power to tax imports for the purpose of building up manufactures; that the rapid and unprecedented decline in the price of agricultural products in the South, causing a like decline in the value of property, had produced an amount of distress that was simply appalling; that many of the articles to be taxed could not be dispensed with by the South, and would have to be purchased from the North at a greatly advanced price; that this increase was in effect a tribute taken by law from the agriculturalists and given to the manufacturers; and that the European market for cotton would be ruined. The commercial section declared that it saw with alarm a bill which, under the pretence of regulating commerce, really sought to destroy it, and compel thousands of ship-builders, caulkers, riggers, and rope-makers to seek employment in arts whose rudiments they had yet to master.

In the House much the same argument was used. Pass this bill, it was said, and foreign nations will shut our products out of their markets; pass this bill and our mercantile interests will be ruined; the noble art of ship-building will decline till it becomes a lost art; our navigation will be ruined, our sailors will be driven from the sea; a great arm of national defence—the navy—will be annihilated, and a shaft, " a fatal shaft," will be aimed at agriculture. With a decrease of imports will come a diminution of revenue, which means increase of debt and increase of taxation. The policy of protection is of British origin, and if adopted will entail on us what it has brought to Great Britain—pauperism, taxes, and a debt of countless millions. We shall see our artisans toiling seventeen hours out of twenty-four, never tasting meat, and living on a vegetable diet that they may eke out a livelihood on their wretched wages. Viewed from any standpoint, the policy is

merce, Executive Papers, No. 94, vol. v.   New Haven Chamber of Commerce, ibid., No. 96.   Citizens of Baltimore, ibid., No. 99.   Citizens of Georgia, ibid., No. 98.   Pennsylvania Farmers, ibid., No. 100.   Citizens of Morgan County, Ga., ibid., No. 110, vol. vi.   Citizens of Norfolk, ibid., No. 112, vol. vi.   Citizens of Georgia, ibid., No. 114, vol. vi.   Citizens of North Carolina, ibid., No. 109, vol. vi.   Citizens of South Carolina, ibid., No. 124, vol. vi.

ruinous in its tendency.   Protection of manufacture is unequal, burdensome, unjust.   The West and the South cannot
manufacture; the East and the North can manufacture.   The
North has capital, dense population, free labor.   The West
has no capital.   The South has little capital, sparse population, and slave labor.   If persisted in, this policy " will drive
the South to ruin or resistance."   Our burdens are already
greater than we can bear; endurance can go no further.   Pass
this bill and you will cut off our supply of specie.   We have no
gold, no silver mines.   Our specie comes from abroad as the
fruit of commerce.   Cut off this commerce—and that a protective tariff will surely do—and our supply of specie stops,
and paper money will become exclusively our circulating
medium.

The Constitution, said a member from South Carolina,*
contains no specific grant of power to encourage manufactures.
It has been found under the clause giving the power to levy
duties on imports for the exclusive purpose of revenue.   But
every revenue law must be uniform throughout the United
States, and this proposed measure is destructive to that uniformity of taxation which the Constitution enjoins.   Pass it
and the people of South Carolina will pay five hundred and
sixty-three thousand dollars on the cotton bagging, the Osna-
burgs, plains, and woollens they consume each year—a sum
raised by taxation for the avowed purpose of being given to
the cotton-bagging makers of Kentucky and the woollen manufacturers of the North.   This is an oppressive, an unjustifiable
wrong.   We are not a consolidated empire.   We are independent States.   Our league merely looks to a common defence,
external and internal commerce, an army, navy, judiciary,
and the powers necessary to carry these into effect.   No member of the confederation could have contemplated joining a
Union in which the common defence and general welfare
meant a sacrifice of any part of it to the good of the whole.

The sentiments of the friends of protection were best expressed by Clay, who, when the discussion had shifted from
details to the great principle which underlay the bill, took the

---

* James Hamilton, Annals of Congress, 1823–'24, pp. 2207, 2208.

floor and delivered what may justly be considered one of the epoch-making speeches of his life. He began by drawing for his hearers a picture of the distressed state of the country, which was true to some extent of the West, but was chiefly the product of his own imagination.

"In casting our eyes around us the most prominent circumstance which fixes our attention and challenges our deepest regret," said he, "is the general distress which pervades the whole country. It is forced upon us by numerous facts of the most incontestable character. It is indicated by the diminished exports of native produce; by the depressed and reduced state of our foreign navigation; by our diminished commerce; by successive unthreshed crops of grain, perishing in our barns and barnyards for want of a market; by the alarming diminution of the circulating medium; by the numerous bankruptcies; by a universal complaint of the want of employment, and a consequent reduction of the wages of labor; by the ravenous pursuit after public situations, not for the sake of their honors, but as a means of private subsistence; by the reluctant resort to the perilous use of paper money; by the intervention of legislation in the delicate relation between debtor and creditor; and, above all, by the low and depressed state of the value of almost every description of the whole mass of property of the nation, which has, on the average, sunk not less than fifty per cent.

"What is the cause of this widespreading distress, of this deep depression which we behold stamped on the public countenance? It is to be found in the fact that during almost the whole existence of the Government we have shaped our industry, our navigation, and our commerce in reference to an extraordinary war in Europe and to foreign markets which no longer exist; in the fact that we have depended too much upon foreign sources of supply and excited too little the native; in the fact that while we have cultivated with assiduous care our foreign resources, we have suffered those at home to wither in a state of neglect and abandonment.

"The greatest want of civilized society is a market for the sale and exchange of the surplus of the produce of the labor of its members. This market may exist at home, or

tation of foreign states an ' American policy,' and a preference for our own established system as it now exists and always has existed 'a foreign policy.' This favorite American policy is what America has never tried, and this odious foreign policy is what, as we are told, foreign states have never pursued."

With this sarcasm Webster passed to Clay's picture of the distressed state of the country, and declared he did not know where the reality existed. Exports had not fallen below the average; the foreign market was not lost; the means of subsistence and enjoyment had not been limited. The progress of internal improvements, the investment of capital in roads, bridges, canals; the amount paid by parents for the education of their children; the endowment of public charities; the contributions to objects of general benevolence; the munificence of individuals toward whatever promised to benefit the community, were all so many proofs of national prosperity, were all evidence that there was a surplus of profits which the generation then living was wisely vesting for the good of the generation yet to come.

The real condition was a considerable depression of prices and curtailment of profit, and in some parts of the country an inability to pay debts contracted when prices were high. This fall in the prices of commodities, this stagnation of business, this diminution of exports on which Mr. Speaker had laid so much stress was, in truth, the necessary result of circumstances. No government could prevent them, and no government could altogether relieve the people from their effects. We had enjoyed a day of extraordinary prosperity, we had been neutral while all the world was at war, and had found an extraordinary demand for our products, our navigation, and our labor. We had no right to expect that such a state of things would continue always. With the return of peace foreign nations began to supply themselves and to compete with us, and, connected as we are with all the commercial nations of the world, we must of necessity feel the serious effects of such a change. What, then, was the remedy? What the course of policy suited to our actual condition?

Webster now passed in review the arguments of the

Speaker.   Clay had cited the prosperity of Great Britain as
an example of the benefit of the protective system.   Webster
asserted and labored to prove that Great Britain was every day
growing more and more in favor of free trade, and that if we
adopted protection we should " show our affection for what
others had discarded, and be attempting to ornament ourselves
with cast-off apparel."   Clay had cited the rate of exchange
to prove that we were on the downward road to ruin.   Webster
claimed that a rise in price of London exchange meant nothing more than that money was wanted in England for commercial purposes to be carried on there or elsewhere.   Clay
" argued the question as if all domestic industry were confined
to the production of manufactured industry."   Webster held
that catching fish and whales, building ships and sailing them
were as emphatically domestic industry as any other occupation, and just as deserving of protection.   Clay had argued as
if his " American system " was something new, as if manufactures had never been protected.   Webster reminded the
House that they were already protected by the tariff of 1816,
and that the purpose of the bill under debate was to greatly
increase that protection.   Clay held up the policy of protection
as the only policy that could make American industries prosperous.   Webster described the doctrine of prohibition as preposterous.

   Turning to the details of the bill, Webster took them up
one by one and argued that it would afford no relief to the
varied interests Clay had described as languishing; that it
would lay new and crushing burdens on the shipping interests; that heavy duties were laid on certain articles absolutely
necessary to certain classes of the people, as raw wool, iron,
hemp, which could not then be produced at home in sufficient
quantity to supply the demand; and that this duty was an
oppressive tax imposed on those who used the articles for the
benefit of the few who manufactured them.   Webster closed
his speech with the words: " There are some parts of this bill
which I highly approve, there are others in which I should
acquiesce; but those to which I have now stated my objections
appear to me so destitute of all justice, so burdensome, and so
dangerous to that interest which has steadily enriched, gal-

tection to woollen manufactures.* The wool-growers of Berkshire joined in the cry for higher duties, and from them came another memorial; the manufacturers despatched a committee to Washington, and in January, 1827, a bill granting all they asked was reported in the House of Representatives,† which in time passed it by eleven majority. In the Senate, though both senators from Massachusetts gave the measure a hearty support, the vote was a tie, and the bill was laid on the table by the casting vote of Calhoun.

As the news of the defeat of the bill spread over the South, the people hailed it with delight. To them the measure was offensive and oppressive for many reasons. Were this proposed tariff, they would say, intended and needed to fill a depleted treasury, we would willingly accept it and cheerfully pay the duties imposed, heavy though the tax would be. But there is no such need, no such intention. Our Treasury is full, our debt is steadily diminishing year by year, and the real purpose of the measure is to produce a new distribution of capital, to force it into channels into which it would not naturally flow, and to produce a ruinous change in the pursuits of the people of the Southern States. The South is wholly agricultural. Of the six hundred or seven hundred thousand bales of cotton grown on her soil, but one third finds a market in the United States. Two thirds are sent to foreign countries, from whose ports come back to the South almost every article consumed in her cities, towns, villages, or on her plantations. This prosperity the tariff will surely destroy. By forcing us to buy at home it will lessen our purchases abroad, and to that extent will diminish the purchases which foreigners make of

---

* House Executive Documents, No. 70, Nineteenth Congress, Second Session, vol. iv.

† The nominal duty on woollen goods was still to remain at thirty-three and a third per cent. But it was ordered that cloth, the value of which at the place of importation was forty cents or less a square yard, should be considered to have cost forty cents; that all costing more than forty and less than two dollars and a half should be valued at two dollars and a half; and that all costing between two dollars and a half and four dollars a square yard should be valued at four dollars, and pay duty accordingly. Raw wool was to pay thirty-five per cent. duty after June 1, 1828, and forty-five per cent. after June 1, 1829. Wool costing from ten to forty cents a pound was to be rated as having cost forty cents.

us; for if we do not buy of them they will not buy of us; if we shut out their goods, they will in return exclude our products. But the loss of our foreign cotton market means the destruction of the industry of cotton-growing, for the manufacturers of the North cannot consume all the cotton we even now produce.

Again, many of the duties contemplated in the bill will fall with especial severity on the people of the South. Not the least important of our imports is a coarse grade of woollen cloth used for the sole purpose of clothing slaves. The duty on such cloth is therefore a tax on capital under the guise of a tax on consumption. Slaves must be clad according to the standard of comfort which both interest and humanity prescribe, and this too, under all conditions and at all times, whether the markets are rising or falling, in periods of adversity, as well as in seasons of prosperity. All duties which enhance the cost of clothing slaves fall, therefore, with peculiar severity on the owners. They cannot be lessened, as many other taxes on consumption, by a reduction of expenditure, for the outlay for clothing a slave is always brought within the narrowest limit consistent with humanity. The proposed duty is therefore in the nature of a direct tax on the capital invested in slaves, and under the tariff of 1824 amounts to an annual assessment of three sixteenths per cent.

Over and above this oppressive character of the proposed duty, a tariff for any other purpose than revenue is unconstitutional. There is, indeed, no limitation on the right to raise revenue by imposts, but it would have been restricted to the sole purpose of collecting money with which to pay the debts of the United States if the framers of the Constitution could have foreseen the present course of national policy.

As the summer wore away these sentiments found expression, and often an angry one, in many parts of South Carolina. At Charleston the Chamber of Commerce thanked Robert Y. Hayne, a senator, and William Drayton, a representative from South Carolina, for their faithful exertions against the passage of the bill, and listened to a speech from Hayne in reply. In his opinion, the measure, both in principle and in detail, was one of the most odious that could possibly be presented to Congress. Rich men, the owners of millions of property transferred from commerce and agriculture to manufactures, originated it that they might secure a monopoly of the home market and enhance their profits, already greater than those of other pursuits. He warned his hearers that the Woollens Bill would be revived at the next session, and urged with all the zeal, activity, and perseverance which private interests, whetted by bounties and privileges could excite. He predicted that the bill was but the first of a series of measures, all having for their object the extension of bounties on manufactures at the expense of the consumer. He declared that the foreign commerce and cotton trade of the South were in jeopardy, and assured the Chamber that nothing but the firm and unanimous remonstrance of the Southern States could avert a calamity compared with which war itself would almost lose its terrors.[*]

The St. Paul's Agricultural Society of Charleston resolved that Congress has no power to encourage domestic manufactures at the expense of every other industry; that the exercise of such a power is ruinous and oppressive to the agricultural interests, and uncalled for by any public exigency; and that the Woollens Bill was an insult to the American people.[†] James Hamilton, a member of the House of Representatives, was the guest on that occasion, and in his speech observed that it would be a curious fact, and one eminently illustrative of the instability of human schemes of happiness, if, after all the blood and treasure expended to escape the taxation of Great Britain, the Union should be dissolved by imposts devised to glut the avarice of New England, which but ten years before was in hot array against the greed of other sections.[‡]

Acting on the advice of Hayne, the Charleston Chamber of Commerce framed a remonstrance to Congress and submitted it to the people for adoption. In it the ground was taken that the proposed tariff would increase an already unequal and burdensome tax on the consumption of the Southern States; that foreign nations would retaliate; that a tariff for protection was

* Niles's Weekly Register, June 16, 1827, pp. 265, 266.
† Ibid., June 30, 1827, p. 294.
‡ Ibid., June 16, 1827, p. 266.

unconstitutional, and that Congress would do well to give heed
to the rising spirit of opposition. History was replete with
illustrations of the consequences of such neglect, and, admonished by such teaching, the petitioners could not but see with
alarm the growth of a spirit of disaffection toward the Constitution as the source of unequal burdens. They felt in duty
bound to warn Congress not to depend on devotion to the
federal compact while it went on forcing on the South a prohibitory and exclusive policy.*

The people of the Colleton District were more outspoken.
" Have you," said they in a memorial addressed to Congress,
" ascertained beyond the possibility of deception how far the
patience of the people of the South exceeds their indignation,
and at what precise point resistance may begin and submission
end? If you have not, permit us, with all due deference to
your superior wisdom, most earnestly to recommend these
subjects to your most solemn consideration." †

While the excitement was rising to fever heat in South
Carolina, the farmers and wool-growers of Pennsylvania were
uniting for action. One of them in a public appeal reminded
his fellows that while all friends of the American system were
agreed that the grower of wool needed further protection, they
were far from agreeing on the amount. This was largely due
to a want of statistical information, and to a lack of concert
on the part of those directly interested. He proposed, therefore, that a meeting of farmers and friends of the American
System should be held at the town of Washington; that a
number of committees should be appointed to ascertain how
many merino sheep there were in each township, how many
common sheep, how much wool was used in the family of each
farmer, how much remained for sale to the manufacturer, and
what was the number and capacity of the woollen mills in the
county.‡

Information so gathered was to be reported to a county
committee, which was to endeavor to have like committees for

---

* Niles's Weekly Register, June 30, 1827, pp. 297, 298.

† Ibid., July 21, 1827, pp. 348, 349.

‡ A Farmer, in Washington Reporter, April 30, 1827; also Niles's Weekly
Register, June 16, 1827.

a like purpose chosen in each county of the State, and the statistics they gathered sent to a central committee at Harrisburg to be by it forwarded to Congress. The plan was well received, was acted on, and at a public meeting * at the Court-House in the borough of Washington a formal call was issued for a meeting at Pittsburg, in June, of delegates from all the counties of Pennsylvania and any other State whose people were interested in growing or manufacturing wool. No response was made, for a call for a national convention of farmers and manufacturers had already gone forth from a much more important body—the Pennsylvania Society for the Promotion of Manufactures and the Mechanic Arts. The invitation which was extended to the friends of the American System in all parts of the Union, urging them to hold State conventions and there select five delegates to a national convention at Harrisburg in July, was accompanied by an address to the citizens of the United States.

They were reminded that about eighty per cent. of the people were engaged in agricultural pursuits; that this important industry was undeniably in a depressed state, and that the depression was due to the loss of markets abroad and to the failure to build up others at home. While a state of war in Europe forced her to take the grain and flour of the Western and Middle States, the farming interests of those States flourished exceedingly. But when these conditions passed away, when the necessity no longer existed, she closed her ports to American products, and for nine years past our breadstuffs had been excluded. In 1817 one million and a half barrels of flour, valued at eighteen million dollars, went from the United States to Europe. In that year Great Britain shut her ports, and in 1826 but eight hundred and thirteen thousand barrels went abroad, which was ten thousand less than left the country in 1792. What was true of flour was equally true of wheat and of Indian corn, yet the States which produce these commodities which would not sell abroad import each year ten million dollars' worth of foreign goods.

---

* Held May 21, 1827. For a report of the proceedings, see Niles's Weekly Register, June 16, 1827, p. 265.

How is this debt paid? We answer, by remittance to Europe of a great part of our public and private securities; by the mortgaging of the country, as it were, for the discharge of an unnecessary debt, and by the taxing of our laborers two million dollars annually to meet the interest on that debt.

The tariff of 1824 it was expected would remedy much of this, would build up manufactures and establish a home market. But in the case of the wool and woollens industry it had signally failed, and unless the original intent of the tariff was carried out by a new duty sufficient to shut British woollen cloths from the market, both the farmer and the manufacturer would be driven into other occupations. The seven millions of people engaged in sheep-farming would go to swell the number of cultivators of the soil, and the fifty millions of capital invested in manufacturing woollen goods would be directed to cotton spinning, to the serious injury of that industry. When these things were considered, the society felt impelled to make a solemn appeal to the Middle, Western, and Eastern States, not from sectional motives, but because they were most deeply interested in the policy of protection.*

A hearty response met this appeal, and before the end of June State conventions and county conventions were held all over the Middle and Eastern States, and delegates appointed to attend the Harrisburg meeting. In South Carolina this action of farmers and manufacturers was a new cause of offence. The merchants of Charleston in their address had asked for the co-operation of towns in the interior of the State, and, moved by the call, the people of Columbia and the planters around about it met and listened to a speech, famous in its day, by Dr. Thomas Cooper. "It is high time," said he, "that we should ' up and be doing..' We thought it hard enough to have to combat the tariff in favor of the cotton manufacture, the woollen manufacture, the iron manufacture; but now there is not a petty manufacturer in the Union, from the owner of a spinning factory to the maker of a hobnail, who is not pressing forward to the plunder; who may not be expected

---

* The address is given in full in Niles's Weekly Register, June 9, 1827, pp. 238–240.

to worry Congress for permission to put his hand into the planter's pocket." At this stage in his speech the doctor read from the newspapers accounts of the election of delegates to the Harrisburg Convention, and, having done so, said: "You see, then, that this is a combined attack of the whole manufacturing interest. The avowed object is to tax us for their own emolument; to force us to cease to buy of our most valuable customers; to force on us a system which will sacrifice the South to the North, which will convert us into colonies and tributaries.

" We had fully hoped that by yielding continually during ten years' discussion of the tariff principle, the pretensions of the manufacturer would erelong come to a close. But our hopes were in vain. We found, as we still find, that the voracious appetite of monopoly is insatiable; that the more we give up, the more are we required to abandon. The motto of a manufacturer, now and always, here and everywhere, is monopoly; his purpose is to put down all competition, to command exclusively every market, to compel every one to buy at his prices and sell at his prices. This is far from a republican system, least of all is it an American system. I had always supposed that equality of rights, equality of duties, equality of burdens, equality of protection, equality of laws, constituted the prevailing features of our happy institutions. But I am now to learn for the first time that in the canting, cheating, cajoling slang of these monopolists, the American system is one by which the earnings of the South are to be transferred to the North; by which the many are to be sacrificed to the few; by which unequal rights, unequal burdens, unequal protection, unequal laws, and unequal taxes are to be enacted and made permanent; that the farmer and the planter are to be considered inferior beings to the spinner, the bleacher, and the dyer; that we of the South are to hold our plantations as the serfs of the North, subject to the orders of the master minds of Massachusetts, the lords of the spinning jenny, the peers of the loom, who have a right to tax our earnings in order to swell their riches! We shall erelong be forced to calculate the value of our union; to ask of what use is this unequal alliance by which the South has always been the

loser and the North always the gainer? Is it worth our while
to continue this union of States where the North demands to
be our master? The question is fast approaching the alternative of submission or separation. Most anxiously do we wish
to avoid it, but if the monopolists are bent on forcing the decision on us, with them be the consequences." *

When Dr. Cooper finished his speech he moved the adoption of a set of resolutions which had been previously prepared and published. These declared that equality of rights
was the pervading principle of the American Union; that any
law which infringed this principle was not constitutional; that
fostering or protecting one class of citizens at the expense of
the rest was such an infringement; that all investments of
capital that do not yield a reasonable profit are unworthy of
protection; that if they do yield such a fair return they
need no protection; that the only American system Americans ought to support was that of equal liberty, equal rights,
and equal laws—a system prostrated by that of taxing the productive industry of one man to support the unproductive industry of another. The resolutions closed with a flat denial
of the right of Congress to levy taxes for the purpose of protection, and with the assertion of the principle " millions for
defence, but not a cent for tribute."

A set of resolutions adopted at Georgetown, South Carolina, set forth that whenever Government by a course of partial legislation makes one branch of industry subsidiary to
another, whenever it causes taxation direct or indirect to fall
unequally on the people, there is in such action not only a
departure from, but a deliberate violation of the social compact; that the late attempt of the National Legislature to
pass a tariff bill was an attack on the rights of agriculturists,
was an effort to impose unequal burdens on the people, and a
deliberate violation of the Constitution.

While the people of South Carolina were thus denouncing
the North and uttering threats of disunion, a hundred delegates from thirteen of the Eastern, Middle, and Western States

---

* Niles's Weekly Register, September 8, 1827. The Columbia meeting took
place July 2d.

assembled at Harrisburg.* As originally planned, the convention was to be a meeting of wool-growers and wool manufacturers for the purpose of considering how best to promote their own particular interests. But when the people chose delegates to the State conventions, which were in turn to appoint representatives to the Harrisburg meeting, demands were made for protection for many industries which it was supposed had been amply provided for by the tariff of 1824. A presidential election was near at hand, the candidates were already in the field, voters and politicians were rallying about Adams or Jackson, and when the State conventions met they fell more or less under the control of the friends of the one or the other candidate. To Harrisburg, as a consequence, came men of all sorts, representing many interests and bent on many aims. In the chair, as presiding officer, sat Joseph Ritner, Governor of Pennsylvania. Before him, in the crowd of delegates, were members of the United States Senate, such as Samuel Bell, of New Hampshire, and Ashur Robbins, of Rhode Island; members of the House of Representatives, such as John C. Wright, of Ohio, Walter Forward, of Pennsylvania, and Rollin C. Mallory, of Vermont, soon to be made chairman of the Committee on Manufactures; party leaders, such as Gideon Wells and Thomas Ewing, Secretary of the Treasury under Harrison, Charles J. Ingersoll, a candidate for the Vice-Presidency in 1812; Judge Enos T. Throop, soon to be Governor of New York; Peter Sharpe, who led the People's Party against Tammany in New York city; and Francis Granger, an anti-Mason and leader of the Adams men; political economists, such as Matthew Carey and Hezekiah Niles; and great manufacturers, such as Abbot Lawrence, of Massachusetts.

After a session of five days the convention ended its labors by appointing a committee to write an address to the people of the United States, and by adopting a memorial to Congress to which ninety-seven members affixed their names. It called on Congress " to save, to protect, and promote what has uniformly been treated by Government as one of the principal

---

* July 30, 1827.

elements of independence, prosperity, and greatness of the Republic," named the duties on wool and woollens necessary to afford such protection, and recommended a further advance on hammered bar iron and steel, on flax, hemp and their products, and on plain and printed cotton goods.

The House of Representatives to which this memorial was to be presented had been elected in 1826, when the old party divisions of 1824 were breaking down, when the new lines were yet to be drawn, and contained many members whose position was so ill-defined that to the day of organization it was a matter of some doubt which party would be in control.

On that day, however, a Jackson Democrat from Virginia was elected Speaker, and by him the Committee on Manufacturers was so constituted that a majority of its eight members were friends of Jackson, while the minority, including the chairman, Rollin C. Mallory, were supporters of Adams and protection. To this committee were now referred the tariff and anti-tariff memorials as they came pouring in from all parts of the country; but no action was taken till after the Speaker sent it the memorial from the Harrisburg Convention.* Led on by Silas Wright, of New York, the majority of the committee refused to accept this as the basis of a bill, and forced their chairman to move in the House for power to send for persons and papers, a request which the House promptly granted.

While the committee was summoning manufacturers and conducting an investigation of its own as to the condition of the woollen industry, memorials of a very serious kind began to come in from the Legislatures of the States. Those from Rhode Island,† New York,‡ and Pennsylvania # approved of a revision of the tariff, and instructed their senators and requested their representatives to endeavor to secure adequate protection for cotton, wool, hemp, flax, and iron.

In North Carolina so much of the Governor's message as related to the Woollens Bill was sent to a joint select commit-

---

* December 24, 1827. Journal of the House of Representatives, Twentieth Congress, First Session.

† Executive Documents, Twentieth Congress, First Session, vol. iii, No. 98.

‡ Ibid., vol. iii, No. 123.   # Ibid., vol. iii, No. 97.

not interpose the most unyielding and determined resistance. Let it be distinctly understood that Alabama, in common with the Southern and Southwestern States, regarded the power assumed by the General Government to lay a tariff for protection as a palpable usurpation of a power not given by the Constitution; that she saw in the proposed Woollens Bill a species of little less than legalized pillage of the property of her citizens, to which she could never submit until every constitutional means of resistance had been exhausted.*

Ohio expressed the belief that the rights of the original States to promote domestic industries by tonnage and import duties had been given to Congress, which by the Constitution had full power to protect manufactures.† New Jersey took the same view, and made a long answer to the remonstrances of South Carolina and Georgia.‡

To the protests and memorials of the State Legislatures were added upward of threescore petitions from societies, farmers, wool-growers, manufacturers, chambers of commerce, and citizens.# Twenty-five asked for an increase of duties. Thirty-two opposed an increase. Thirty-eight came from States north of Maryland, nineteen came from States south of Pennsylvania, and of these thirteen were sent up by the citizens of South Carolina, where feeling against the tariff, the North, and the Union ran high. They were convinced, and justly, that duties laid for protection bore with especial weight on the slave-holding States, and they believed most firmly that imposing duties for such a purpose was a deliberate and palpable violation of what they called the compact.

Toward the close of January, 1828, the Committee on Manufactures having finished its examination and matured its plan, reported a bill ‖ which it fully expected would never

---

* Executive Documents, Twentieth Congress, First Session, vol. iii, No. 113.
† Ibid., vol. iv, No. 156.   ‡ Ibid., vol. v, No. 198.
# These petitions may be found in Executive Documents, First Session, Twentieth Congress, vol. ii, Nos. 13, 14, 15, 16, 20, 21, 23, 24, 27, 28, 29, 30, 31, 33, 36, 42; vol. iii, Nos. 62, 63, 64, 65, 80–82, 84, 85, 91, 93–98, 111, 112, 114, 118, 123; vol. iv, Nos. 124, 132, 133, 142, 147, 155–157, 160; vol. v, Nos. 174–178, 181, 188, 191, 198, 202, 209, 213; vol. vi, Nos. 227–229, 239.
‖ The bill is printed in Congressional Debates, vol. iv, p. 1727.

pass. Indeed, it had been most carefully prepared to invite defeat. In the first place, all duties were high in order to satisfy the demands of the protectionists of the Middle and Western States, and so keep as many as possible in the Jackson party. In the second place, the duties were excessively high on such raw material as New England manufacturers wished them to be low. Thus Smyrna wool was highly taxed in order to stop its importation and put an end to the manufacture of negro cloth; the tariff rates on iron, hemp, and cordage were advanced in order to check the business of ship-building, and a heavy duty was placed on molasses, which was nowhere consumed in such quantity as in New England. In the third place, it was agreed that the friends of Jackson, whether Southern men or Northern men, free-traders or protectionists, were to unite, put down every attempt at amendment, and force a vote on this bill and on no other. When the yeas and nays were taken, the Jackson men from Southern States were to turn about and vote nay, and, as it was supposed, the New England men would be forced to do likewise and the bill would be lost. The Jackson men of the North were to vote yea, which would cast the odium of defeat on the Adams men and leave the Northern supporters of the hero of New Orleans to pose as the friends of the American system. But the plan, shrewd as it was, failed. The Senate made some amendments, the House concurred, the New England men did not vote nay, and the bill, with all its odious provisions, passed House, Senate, and President, and became " the tariff of abominations." *

As the news of the passage of this hated bill spread slowly over the country, the mutterings of discontent gave place to angry threats and open resistance. At Charleston the shipping in the harbor displayed their flags at half mast and the people of the North heard with indignation that many a British flag was seen in that position. At a great anti-tariff meeting at Walterborough, in the Colleton District of South

---

* The details of the plan for the defeat of the tariff are given by Calhoun in a speech in the Senate in 1837. See Calhoun's Works, vol. iii, pp. 46–51. See also the account given by Hammond in Political History of New York, vol. iii, p. 159.

or, if thou depart to the right hand, then will I go to the left." The same newspaper urged an anti-tariff congress to recommend to the Legislatures and the people the best measures for preventing the introduction and use of the " tariffied articles." When the twenty-eighth of June came, the day being the anniversary of the battle of Monmouth, the secessionists seized the occasion and celebrated the event with toasts and speeches of a seditious sort.*

Much the same sentiments were expressed by Mr. McDuffie at a dinner given in his honor by the people of Charleston. He hoped that the citizens of South Carolina would appear on the fourth of July clothed in homespun, the manufacture of the South, and thereby express in a public manner their determination not to submit to the unjust exactions imposed by the tariff. He, too, advocated a prohibitory tax on Northern goods. To do so was perfectly constitutional. The moment the original packages were broken and the goods mixed up and made a component part of the stock and capital of the country, they ceased to be imports and became subject to taxation, as property, by the State. To single them out for taxation was then just as legal as to single out horses or slaves. The expediency was manifest. The commerce of

---

* At Charleston, C. C. Pinckney offered the toast, " The battle of the 28th of June and the tariff of June 28th.   Let *New* England beware how she imitates the *Old*."

By Henry Rutledge : " The rattlesnake of the South !   Caveant Moniti.   Warned by its rattle, let the foe beware."

Among the fourth of July toasts are these :

" The river Potomac : notable as a barrier between Southern independence and Northern despotism.   May its current be the protector of the former to the destruction of the latter."

" The union and independence of the States.   Let us never forget that we united to secure our independence.   If the choice must be made, we must not prefer the *means* to the *end*."

" The union of the States ; but, if separation must come, let us separate in peace."

" Internal improvements and the tariff—the firebrands of discord.   Let the South look to State rights and State sovereignty."

" The crisis to which we have come.   To hesitate now is to submit, and to submit is ruin."

" Down with the tariff, the accursed upas beneath whose poisonous shade the prosperity, the life, perhaps, of this great confederacy is destined to expire."

Kentucky was trifling except in hogs, horses, mules, and cattle bought by the Southern States. Yet the Kentucky delegation was unanimously in favor of the tariff. She had done all she could to injure South Carolina; let her feel the effects. Nothing on earth should induce a Carolinian to buy a hog, a horse, a mule from Kentucky. The students of Franklin College followed the example set by those of South Carolina College, and refused to use for apparel goods made in the North. At a public meeting at Milledgeville, it was resolved to abstain, as far as possible, from the use of everything made in the tariff States; to request the Legislature to lay prohibitory taxes on the hogs, mules, horses, cattle, bagging, whiskey, pork, beef, bacon, flax, and hemp of the Western States, and on all the productions and manufactures of the Northern and Eastern.

The Charleston Mercury published a letter from a correspondent at Columbia declaring that on the subject of the tariff the people of the interior were exasperated beyond measure. Not the stump orators, not the court-yard politicians, but the substantial citizens. Such was the state of feeling toward the General Government arising from the repeated and insulting injuries received from it, that, if the delegations from the Southern States to Congress were to secede and recommend the States to call a convention and organize a government for themselves, the recommendation would be received with bonfires and rejoicings all over the State.*

By July fourth sentiments of a different kind began to find expression. The Governor of South Carolina, in response to the address of the people of the Colleton District, positively refused to assemble the Legislature, and at a public dinner spoke strongly against disunion. " This severing of a member from an established confederation," said he, " is by no means so easy as some seem to think. The plan I see discussed in the newspapers of calling conventions and withdrawing our senators and representatives will repeal no law now binding on the whole. Those who act under the authority of the Gen-

---

* Niles's Weekly Register, July 26, 1828, p. 356.

eral Government, if they do their duty, must bring the two authorities into collision, and then—but I will not go on. I rely on the ballot box. I have not despaired. I see nothing yet to make me willing to give up the ship. If I have any firmness it will be exerted to preserve the Union—to preserve, protect, and defend the Constitution of this State and of the United States."

A member of Congress from Alabama told his constituents that while he was the last man in the world to submit to oppression, he would be among the first to resist disunion. He for one would not ask, "Of what value is this union to Alabama?" If the Union was ever dissolved, it would be the result of the most awful revolution that ever stained the pages of history. Newspaper after newspaper now made haste to protest. Said one, We are in favor of a temperate and independent opposition. We are by no means willing that the emissaries of Great Britain shall creep in among us, laugh at our simplicity and glory in the idea of a dissolution of the Union. Another urged the people to rely on themselves, to manufacture for themselves, and pay no heed to the protestations of mouthing patriots. A third remarked that in the mercantile centres of Georgia—in Savannah and Augusta, places where the burdens imposed by the tariff, if any, would surely be felt—there were no complaints, no meetings, no resolutions, no threats of disunion. Yet in the back country, among the middling farmers, where nine people out of ten had always worn homespun, and never bought a yard of broadcloth in the whole course of their lives, the belief was prevalent that the tariff would be their ruin. Those who knew nothing about commerce, who could not tell a wheelbarrow from a ship, were crying out that their shipping interests would suffer. Did not this prove that ignorance had much to do with the excitement? *

Ignorance, in truth, had very little to do with the excitement. No man was more eager for disunion, more active in preparing the way, than Doctor Thomas Cooper, President of South Carolina College. McDuffie, in toasts and speeches,

---

* Niles's Weekly Register, September 20, 1828, p. 59.

never lost an opportunity to recommend even an appeal to arms.* A writer under the name of Sidney openly urged nullification, and called on the people to uphold the sovereignty of South Carolina and, "if necessary, die in the ditch." † When, said he, our sovereignty, using its delegated powers, declares a certain law to be constitutional, and another sovereignty, using its reserved powers, declares the same law to be no law, who is to decide between them? Not the Supreme Court surely, for it is the creature of one of the sovereignties. Plainly the right of judgment rests with the power that made the Constitution. The Legislature of South Carolina, therefore, should meet, cite the tariff acts of 1824 and 1828, declare them null and void, open the ports, and force the General Government to act. An amendment to the Constitution or attempted coercion would follow. With one fourth of the States on her side an amendment would be impossible. If coercion were attempted, the course of the minority would be glorious.‡ No man in all South Carolina was more respected than Charles Cotesworth Pinckney. Yet he, too, repeatedly gave public expression to sentiments that were seditious. At one dinner his toast was: "The battle of the 28th of June, and the tariff June 28th—Let *New* England beware how she imitates the Old." At another he proposed, and those present drank to, "Southern rights and Northern avarice—When the Constitution is degraded to destroy one and support the other, resistance is a virtue."

Led on by such men, the people spoke more plainly than ever. From grand juries, from the muster ground, from meetings called for the especial purpose of protesting, came demands for resistance and appeals to the Legislature to defend the insulted rights of the State. #

---

* "The Stamp Act of 1765 and the tariff of 1828—kindred acts of despotism. When our oppressors trace this parallel, let them remember that we are the descendants of a noble ancestry, and profit by the admonitions of history."

† Charleston Mercury, July 3, 1828.

‡ Charleston Mercury, July 3, 4, 8, 1828.

See the resolutions adopted at Coosawhatchie, at Edgefield, Beaufort, Abbeville, St. Helena's Parish, All Saints' Parish, Barnwell, and others, as given in Niles's Weekly Register, September 20, 1828, pp. 60–63.

In Georgia the people were less violent, and confined their indignation to solemn resolutions not to use anything made in the North; not to buy the horses, mules, pigs, cotton-bagging, whiskey, pork, bacon, beef, or hemp of the West, and to ask the Legislature at the next session to impose heavy taxes on the manufactures and produce of States favorable to the tariff.*

The meetings of the Legislatures of Georgia and South Carolina were looked forward to, it may well be believed, with interest of no common kind. That something must be done, that something would be done, no one doubted. But for the action of South Carolina very few were prepared. The Governor in his annual message urged a firm stand, but prudent action. Congress, in his opinion, had indeed been guilty of " a deliberate, palpable, and dangerous exercise of powers not granted by the compact." But the object of South Carolina was reform, not revolution. Let her, therefore, once again declare the tariff act unconstitutional, void, and not binding on her people. Let her send forth this declaration as her solemn and deliberate opinion. Let her bring this momentous question for trial before every tribunal known to the Constitution and the laws, and let her invite the other States to do likewise. But let her not separate her interests from those of the other suffering States, nor adopt a course that would excite the hostile feelings of the North and West.†

In the expression of such sentiments the Governor was almost alone. Both House and Senate, by large majorities, were eager not merely to denounce the tariff, but to defy the Government, and if needs be to secede. Indeed, hardly a member of note in either body failed to submit resolutions calling for such action. One proposed that if the tariff law was not repealed at the next session of Congress the people should be called on to send delegates to a convention, to meet at Columbia, " and devise such means of redress as the crisis

---

* See the resolutions passed at the meetings in Baldwin, Montgomery, Wilkes, Glynn, Twiggs, Harris, Putnam, and Oglethorpe counties.—Niles's Weekly Register, September 20, 1828, pp. 63, 64.

† For the message see Niles's Weekly Register, December 20, 1828, pp. 274, 275.

demands." *   Another asked that South Carolina apply to
Congress to summon a convention to propose such amendments
to the Federal Constitution as should define the powers of
Congress, and limit them to the purpose plainly expressed on
the face of the instrument.†   One set announced that the
General Government was a confederacy of sovereign and independent States; that it was made by the States, and not by
the people; that it was subordinate to and dependent on and
responsible to the States for the exercise of its delegated
powers; that the States and no one else had the right to decide
on the constitutionality of its laws, and, in cases of dangerous
and palpable usurpations of power, to pronounce them void;
that the charter of the Bank of the United States, all acts for
surveys in States or Territories, all appropriations to aid in
the construction of roads or canals, and the tariff laws, were
dangerous usurpations of power, and if not repealed by Congress ought to be declared null and void by the State.

The sentiments common to all were that duties imposed
for purposes other than revenue were unconstitutional; that
the tariff acts of 1824 and 1828 were for other purposes than
revenue; that they were therefore deliberate, palpable, and
dangerous infractions of the Constitution, and that the duty of
South Carolina was to interpose to stop the progress of the
evil.   Some were in favor of referring the time and manner
of interposition to a State Convention.   Others of deferring
action for at least one more session of Congress.   In the
end this plan prevailed, and the House, about the middle of
December, ordered a committee of seven to prepare a solemn
protest again the constitutionality and oppression of the system of protective duties for entry on the journal of the Senate
of the United States; to make a public exposition of the
wrongs done South Carolina, and of the remedy within her
power; and to prepare an appeal to her sister States to join
with her—if the tariff laws were not repealed—in such measures as might be necessary for arresting the evil.

Three days later the committee of seven presented a paper
of great length, written months before by John C. Calhoun,

---

* Mr. Nixon.   † Mr. N. A. DeSaussure.

and now known as the South Carolina Exposition of 1828.*
During the summer, when the excitement over the tariff was
running high in the State, the Vice-President had been visited
by many of the political leaders eager for his advice and support.   By one of them, William C. Preston, he was asked to
prepare such a paper as could be used by the Legislature when
it met in the autumn, and did so.   Having the report in hand,
it was necessary to fit the action of the Legislature to its contents, which was done by the passage of the resolution.

The Exposition begins with the deliberate assertion that
the tariff act of 1828 is unconstitutional, unequal, oppressive,
and calculated to corrupt the public virtue and destroy the
liberty of the country, goes on to prove each one of these assertions, and ends with a statement of the remedy.

The tariff was unconstitutional because the General Government is one of specific powers, expressly granted; because
these only, and such others as may be necessary to carry them
into effect, can rightfully be used by Congress; and because the
power to protect manufactures is neither one of those granted,
nor necessary to such as are specifically given.   It was true
that the advocates of the tariff found the right in that article
of the Constitution which authorized Congress to levy and
collect impost duty.   But the purpose, the sole purpose, of such
duties is the raising of revenue, and the conversion of them
into an instrument for the rearing of the industry of one section of the country on the ruins of that of another is a deliberate violation of the meaning of the Constitution, which does
not at all differ from a violation of its letter.

The tariff, in the second place, was unequal and oppressive
because its burden fell on the South and not on the North.
That it did not oppress the North was manifest from the fact
that the people of that section had urgently and repeatedly
demanded an increase, had welcomed every addition as a blessing, and had looked on each failure to secure high rates with
keen regret.   That it oppressed the South was manifest from
the character of the Southern trade.   The South exported in

---

* The Exposition, as originally drawn, is printed in the Works of Calhoun,
vol. vi, pp. 1–57.   As adopted by the Legislature, it is printed in Dr. Thomas
Cooper's edition of Statutes at Large of South Carolina, 1836, vol. i, pp. 247–273.

order to import. Soil and climate enabled her to raise great staples—cotton, rice, and tobacco—which the Old World needed. Dense population and accumulated capital enabled older countries to manufacture articles well suited to her use, and thus the foundation was laid for an exchange of commodities advantageous to both parties. Of the $53,000,000 worth of domestic produce sent out of the country each year, the cotton, rice, and tobacco-growing States contributed a part valued at $37,500,000, or more than two thirds. But it was by a tax on the goods brought back as the fruit of this exchange that the Government was chiefly supported. At that time the duty was forty-five per cent., which on the $37,500,-000 exported by the South gave $16,650,000 as the share which she contributed of the $23,000,000 the tariff yielded the Government annually.

The system again tended to corrupt the Government and destroy the liberty of the country because on all industrial interests it divided the country into two great parties, because this division was sectional, and because, unless arrested, it must be followed by all the evils which spring from the exercise of irresponsible power. We want free-trade. The tariff men want restrictions. We want low taxes, frugality in the Government, economy, accountability, and a rigid application of the public money to the payment of the debt and to the objects authorized by the Constitution. They want precisely the opposite of these things. They feel and act on all questions connected with the American system as sovereigns, as men who impose burdens on others for their own benefit; and we as men on whom such burdens are imposed. Differences of interest must exist, but the rights of the majority must not be unchecked. No government based on the naked principle that the majority ought to govern can preserve its liberty for a single generation. Governments which provide checks, which limit and restrain the power of the majority, are the only ones that live long and give happiness to the people.

It would therefore be extraordinary if our system, resting as it does on its recognized diversity of geographical interests, provided no check against the dangers which diversity of interests must produce. What means, then, are provided by

CHAPTER XLVII.

EARLY LITERATURE.

IT has often been remarked—and the remark is true—that literature pure and simple never existed in America till Washington Irving began to write. There is, indeed, no portion of our history which presents a spectacle of so much dreariness as our literary annals during the two hundred years which followed the landing at Jamestown. In all that time no one great work of the imagination was produced. It could not have been otherwise. Men were too busy clearing farms, cutting roads, building towns, acquiring wealth, to have any time for literature. During the stormy years which immediately preceded the rebellion of the colonies, when events turned the thoughts of men into new channels, and forced them to take up the pen before they ventured to take up the sword, our countrymen, it is true, began to make lasting contributions to the world's stock of literature. Great questions were then to be settled; great principles of government explained and expounded. The people were to be educated as to the rights of man and the duties of kings and parliaments, and to this end a mass of political literature of the very highest order was produced. Nothing superior to the declarations, the remonstrances, the petitions, the State papers, the State constitutions, the treatises on government, and the pamphlets on the public questions of the day, which teemed from the press in the ten years before and in the fifteen years which immediately followed the Declaration of Independence, has ever been produced by any people at any time. That quarter of a century was pre-eminently the age of political writing. The authors appealed to a living audience, and, treating of questions which were then present and which soon passed away, their writings have come to be much praised and little read.

But the men whose writings will not soon pass away; the men who founded our national literature; the men whose works and names we have come to regard as classic, belong to a later generation. With scarce an exception all were born after the Revolution had ended. Between these two periods—the period when our ancestors were reading and writing political tracts and fast-day sermons, and the period when they read "Salmagundi," "Knickerbocker's History," "Thanatopsis," and "The Spy"—is an interval of some thirty years. Yet that interval, so destitute of native authors, is precisely the one during which the most serious efforts were made to establish that sort of literature which depends for success on nothing so much as on the number and variety of well-trained writers. That was the age of magazines, asylums, museums, censors, repositories, repertories, registers, and impartial reviews, very few of which ever lived through a presidential term. On a list by no means complete of magazines which saw the light during the administrations of Washington and Adams, there are forty-one titles. Eleven of these were published at New York, five at Boston, and sixteen at Philadelphia, which was then and long remained the literary centre of the country. Two were issued in Vermont, three in Connecticut, and one at Charleston. Two mark an early effort to establish medical journals. Five were devoted to matters of religion.

If the statements of the projectors of our early periodicals may be trusted, they were moved by a spirit very different from that which animates their successors. It was with no idea of filling a long-felt want, or their own pockets, or the coffers of a corporation, that they began to till this field of letters. They were moralists, philanthropists, censors whose high duty it was to lead, not to follow. They were purveyors of that sort of mental food which the people ought to have; not caterers to every passing fad, or commentators on the topic or sensation of the hour. One of them in his prospectus is at great pains to assure the public that guardians and tutors will find his Miscellany worthy of recommendation to the

children and youth committed to their care, for it is his purpose to awaken attention, cultivate benevolence, improve the
understanding, and amend the heart. Another is content
with the assurance that his Monthly Mirror " shall contain
a variety of matter calculated to improve and amend the
mind." A third, waiving such assurances as unnecessary, appeals to State pride on behalf of his Monthly Repository of
Knowledge and Rational Entertainment. Every State, he
informs the people of Connecticut, has such a Repository.
Even New Hampshire supports one. Surely, therefore, the
enlightened people of Connecticut will not be behind in a
magazine of their own.

Not infrequently the prospectus would fill a column of
some local newspaper, and would set forth with the utmost
detail the character and object of the projected Museum. In
it the editor would promise there should be found miscellaneous essays—some original, some selected—on philosophy,
natural history, the useful and ornamental arts, on politics,
travel, and on subjects " calculated to amuse the mind and
advance the best interests of society." From time to time
there should also be " agreeable and entertaining moral tales,"
short novels, anecdotes, and what were called " elegant dis-
sertations and lively sallies of wit and humor." A promise
was always made that nothing should be admitted that could
" call a blush to the cheek of innocence," and was strictly
kept.

When at last, after two or three months of advertising,
two or three hundred subscribers were secured, the first number would appear, and would contain a jumble of articles
such as cannot now be found in any magazine or journal.
Everybody was to be instructed. There were, therefore, articles to instruct everybody—" medical facts and observations "
for the doctors; notes on law cases and comments on decisions
for the lawyer; State papers for the politician; " intelligence " respecting the arts, the sciences, agriculture, and
manufactures for the general reader; and poetry and book
reviews for such as affected literature. A monthly chronicle
of events, compiled from the newspapers, a list of marriages
and deaths, a catalogue of the names of persons appointed to

office, and the rates of exchange, completed the usual table of contents.

Such a publication existed in every city of importance in the country, and was sure to have some high-sounding and pretentious name. Thus in Boston there was the Columbian Phœnix and Boston Review. The Polyanthus, a magazine whose editor aimed " to please the learned and enlighten the ignorant, to allure the idle from folly and confirm the timid in virtue." " Is there," said he, " a gem that sparkles yet unknown? Ours be the task to place it where its radiance may illuminate society. We will transplant the rose that has hitherto blushed unseen on the field of science, and select flowers of the noblest kind from the variegated carpet of Nature." This was fine writing in 1805, and was closely imitated, in 1806, by the editor of the Boston Magazine when he announced that its successor, The Emerald, would " be polished by the labors of the learned and occasionally glitter with the gayety of wit, and would be found worthy to shine among the gems which sparkle on the regalia of literature."

In New York there was the Monthly Magazine and American Review. Philadelphia had the Philadelphia Monthly Magazine, or Universal Repository of Knowledge and Entertainment; The Repository of Knowledge, Historical, Literary, Miscellaneous, and Theological; the Philadelphisches Magazin oder unterpollender Gesellschafter für die Deutschen in Amerika; and The American Review and Literary Journal.

Baltimore, as early as 1804, could boast of The Orphan's Friend, a monthly magazine whose mission it was to amuse the mind, strengthen the judgment, affect the heart, and awaken the fancy; and The Companion, a weekly periodical, whose editor frankly and wisely declared that he wanted no profits. In Virginia there was then The Virginia Religious Magazine. At Charleston, in South Carolina, the first number of the Monthly Register and Review of the United States was announced to appear in January, 1805; but as " no good paper could be had out of Philadelphia," and as the vessel carrying the paper purchased in that city was " ice-bound in the Delaware," the publication of number one of volume one was postponed till June.

The year 1804 may be taken arbitrarily as the beginning of a new epoch in the history of magazine enterprise. The spread of education, the great increase of population, the prosperity of the people, the improved means of communication, and, above all, the opening of the mails to books and packages, enabled the magazine publisher not merely to find a larger class of general readers, but a large class whose interests were centred on a common object or profession. Then for the first time magazines devoted not to general literature but to particular interests began to appear in quick succession. There had, indeed, been a Medical Examiner in Philadelphia as early as 1788, and an Arminian Magazine, a Theological Magazine, an Experienced Christian Magazine, a Monthly Military Repository, a Methodist Magazine, and a Medical Repository before 1800. But each had been feebly conducted and poorly supported, and, after dragging along for a few numbers or a few volumes, had died and been forgotten. They were the pioneers in a great movement, which, after 1804, went steadily on, growing stronger and stronger year by year, till now there is not a trade, not a profession, not an industry, calling, business, sect, or creed but has at least one magazine or journal devoted to its interests, and to its interests alone.

Specialization began with what were then the three professions—medicine, theology, and law—and, as the home of medicine was Philadelphia, it was there that the Philadelphia Medical and Physical Journal and the Medical Museum were founded, and became the first of a long and unbroken series of periodicals devoted to medicine.* The way once opened, others followed, and there was soon a Medical and Physical Recorder at Baltimore, a New England Journal of Medicine

---

* The Museum ran on to 1810, and was followed in 1812 by The Emporium of all the Arts and Sciences. In 1811 came forth the first number of The Eclectic Repository and Analytic Review, Medical and Philosophical, which continued till 1820, when it took the name of The Journal of Foreign Medical Science and Literature, and continued as such till 1824. In 1818 the American Medical Recorder was begun as a quarterly. This in 1824 became the Medical Recorder of Original Papers and Intelligence in Medicine and Surgery. In 1829 it was merged in the American Journal of the Arts and Sciences, which Silliman had established at New York in 1818.

and Surgery at Boston, and a Medical Repertory at Philadelphia. From medicine to science was but a step, which was quickly taken; and before 1820 Silliman's Journal of the Arts and Sciences, and the American Mineralogical Journal, the first purely scientific magazine supported by original American contributions, were founded at New York.

The first legal magazine in our country, and the second in the English language, was the American Law Journal, established at Baltimore in 1809. Of the magazines and repositories given up to theology, some were in the interests of a particular sect and some in the interests of Christianity. For the Presbyterians there was the Assembly's Missionary Magazine at New Haven, and the Virginia Religious Magazine, edited by a committee of the Virginia Synod, and devoted to " religious intelligence," biographical essays, and the solution of difficult texts of Scripture. The profits were pledged to the support of missionaries; but it is not likely that many were maintained by the profits of a magazine each of whose five hundred subscribers paid a dollar and a half a year. For the New Jerusalem Church there was for a few months the Halcyon Luminary and Theological Repository at New York. For the Episcopalians there was the Churchman's Magazine, published at New Haven, and its rival, the Magazine of Ecclesiastical History, Religion, and Morality. A certain printer of New Haven had been chosen to publish the Churchman's Magazine, and had been sent to the southward to canvass for subscribers. While so engaged the printing was taken from him, and in revenge he started the Magazine of Ecclesiastical History. Later a quarterly Theological Magazine and Religious Repository was published in the interests of the Episcopal Church in Vermont. This, the editor declared, he was led to do because most of the monthly magazines " calculated to convey religious instruction were dropped," and because he believed that if the church would not support monthlies it might a quarterly.*

---

* Other religious magazines were: The Religious Instructor, Carlisle, 1810; The Christian Register and Moral and Theological Review (semi-annual), New York city, 1816; The Evangelical Guardian and Review, New York city, 1817; The Quarterly Theological Review, Philadelphia, 1818; The Latter-Day Luminary

In supposing that the church magazines languished because they came out but once a month he was much mistaken. If the date of issue affected them at all, they suffered from infrequency; for in the very year in which he announced his quarterly a weekly newspaper, the Religious Remembrancer began its career at Philadelphia. It was followed in rapid succession by ten others,* and from its appearance, in 1813, may be dated the beginning of religious newspapers in our country. Once started, the new journalism grew with astonishing rapidity—both in number of journals and in circulation. Before 1826 the Boston Recorder and Telegraph, and Zion's Herald, the great Methodist weekly, had each a circulation of five thousand copies, while the Watchman, the Christian Register, and the Universalist Magazine each printed a thousand copies a week. In 1828 there were in the United States thirty-seven religious newspapers, one of which, the Christian Advocate, had a weekly circulation of fifteen thousand copies, the largest, it was

---

(Baptist quarterly), Philadelphia, 1818; The Methodist Magazine, New York city, 1818; The American Baptist Magazine and Missionary Intelligencer (bi-monthly), Boston, 1817; The Christian Herald, Portsmouth, N. H. (monthly), 1818; The Virginia Evangelical and Literary Magazine (monthly), Richmond, 1818; The Christian Monthly Spectator, New Haven, 1819; The Episcopal Magazine, Philadelphia, 1820; The Presbyterian Magazine (later, The Christian Advocate) (monthly), Philadelphia, 1821; The Religious Inquirer (Universalist, fortnightly), Hartford, 1821; Unitarian Miscellany, 1821; The Theological Review and General Repository of Religious and Moral Information (quarterly), Baltimore, 1822; The Utica Christian Repository (monthly), Utica, 1822; The American Sunday-School Magazine (monthly), Philadelphia, 1823; The Christian Advocate, Philadelphia, 1823; The Evangelist (monthly), Hartford, 1824; The Christian Telescope (quarterly), Providence, 1824; The Church Register (weekly), Philadelphia, 1826; The Christian Examiner, Boston, 1824.

* The Religious Remembrancer, September 4, 1813, was the first of its kind in America, and the founder of religious weekly journalism. The second was The Recorder, at Chillicothe, Ohio, 1814. The third, the Recorder, at Boston, 1816. The fourth, The Christian Herald, New York, 1816. The fifth, The Christian Journal and Literary Register (fortnightly), New York, 1817. The sixth, The Sunday Visitant or Weekly Repository of Christian Knowledge. The seventh, The Watchman and Reflector (Baptist), 1819. The eighth, The Christian Disciple, a Methodist weekly at Boston, 1819. The New York Observer was started at New York city in 1820, and The Christian Register, a Unitarian weekly, at Boston in 1821.

claimed, then reached by any newspaper in the world, the London Times not excepted.

Around these imposing scientific and religious magazines and weeklies a host of minor secular periodicals sprung up, flourished for a day, and perished. There were The Thespian Mirror * and Theatrical Censor,† published weekly during the theatrical season, and devoted to criticism on current plays and living actors. There were juvenile magazines;‡ an attempt at a comic newspaper,# and a journal devoted solely to the interests of agriculture—the first of its kind in America.‖ There were musical journals, designed chiefly for the publication of good music for the piano, flute, and violin; ladies' journals; ᴬ a repository intended to "rescue from oblivion historical facts connected with Western history; ◊ and a review of reviews, which owed its existence to a desire to provide American readers with "the spirit of foreign magazines." It was better, the prospectus set forth, that Americans should have the spirit than the magazines, for in them were often to be found views corrupting to the morals of

---

* The Thespian Mirror, published at New York, 1806, and edited by John Howard Payne, then a lad of fourteen years.

† The Theatrical Censor, Philadelphia, 1805–'06. Theatrical Censor and Critical Miscellany, Philadelphia, 1806. Thespian Monitor and Dramatic Miscellany, Philadelphia, 1809. Mirror of Taste and Dramatic Censor, Philadelphia, 1810.

‡ The first of these was the Juvenile Magazine or Miscellaneous Repository of Useful Information, Philadelphia, 1802. The second was the Juvenile Olio, Philadelphia, 1802. These died young, and were followed in 1811 by a periodical with the child-repelling title of The Juvenile Magazine, Religious, Moral, and Entertaining Pieces in Prose and Verse. In 1813 there appeared a weekly called the Juvenile Port Folio.

The Fool, edited by Tom Brainless, at Salem.

‖ The American Farmer, Baltimore, 1819.

ᴬ The Weekly Visitor and Ladies' Museum, New York city, 1817. The Ladies' Literary Cabinet (weekly), New York city, 1819. The Ladies' Magazine (weekly), Savannah, 1819. The New York Mirror and Ladies' Literary Gazette (weekly), New York city, 1823. One of the most curious was The Intellectual Regale or Ladies' Tea Tray, by Mrs. Carr, of Baltimore. The prospectus states that Mrs. Carr knew that the malignant part of mankind would scoff at a woman editor, but a mother would brave death for the support of her offspring, and "she had five."

◊ Tennessee Repository, 1810.

republican youth, and criticisms which perverted public taste.*
In short, there were ventures in every kind of journalism;
even to the publication of weeklies whose purpose was to " castigate the age," supply the town with social gossip, and satirize
the fashionable follies of the hour. In every city of importance there was now sure to be a band of young lawyers without cases, or young beaux with a taste for letters and some
claims to wit, who found a congenial occupation in furnishing
essays, criticisms, and satirical effusions to weeklies of the
lighter vein † long since forgotten.

It must not be supposed, however, that what the fine
writers of the day called the destroying hand of time was laid
on every periodical that arose during the first quarter of our
century. The Port Folio, founded in 1801 by Joseph
Dennie, was still published in Philadelphia. The North
American Review of the present day was then ten years old,
and represented the intellectual activity of Boston.

The contrast between these two periodicals in character
and purpose, contributors and success, marks an epoch in our
literary annals. The Port Folio, just about to perish after
a long career of usefulness and prosperity, represented the literary tastes and aims of the past. The North American Review represented the literary aims and aspirations that were
to rule in the future. The Port Folio was essentially and intentionally English. The North American, as its name was
intended to imply, was essentially American. On the long
list of men who in their youthful days contributed to the Port
Folio were many who in later life became famous as politicians, political economists, lawyers, bankers, men of affairs,
but few who have any claim to distinction in the world of
letters. Literature with them was a pastime. The men who

---

* Select Reviews and Spirit of the Foreign Magazines, Philadelphia, 1809,
vol. i. In 1812 the name was changed to The Analectic. Washington Irving was
the editor, 1813–'14.

† The list is too long to cite. The Trangram or Fashionable Trifler, by Chris-
topher Crog, Esq., his Grandmother, and Uncle; The Beacon, erected and supported by Lucidantus and his Thirteen Friends; The Luncheon, boiled for People
about Six Feet High, by Simon Pure; The Tickler, by Toby Scratch 'Em; The
Rainbow, edited by the Richmond Literary Club; The Observer, by Beatrice Iron-
sides, Baltimore; The Critic, by Geoffry Juvenile, Esq., are but specimens.

from the very start contributed to the North American made writing a serious occupation, laid the foundation of a distinctly national literature, and left behind them works that are classics.

The magazine of early times was not intended to be read by the masses. It was for the professional class, for men and women of means and leisure, for people of education, and rarely contained what could be called light literature. The people when they read anything read newpapers, political pamphlets, novels of English origin, poetry sometimes the product of native authors, fast-day sermons, fourth-of-July orations, treatises on manners and morals, and such literature as was especially prepared for them.

For young women there was a class of books designed to inculcate a morality of the most unhealthy sort. That any woman was ever the better for their perusal seems scarcely possible. Yet they were popular, and the list is long. On it may be placed the Young Ladies' Mentor; Mrs. Pilkington's Mentorial Tales for young ladies just leaving school and entering on the theatre of life; the Young Ladies' Parental Mentor; the Ladies' Literary Companion, "a collection of essays adapted for the instruction and amusement of the fair sex"; and the Young Gentlemen and Ladies' Monitor, made up of collections of what were called select pieces from the best modern writers, and intended "to eradicate vulgar prejudice and rusticity of manners, improve the understanding, rectify the will, purify the passions, and direct the mind of youth to the pursuit of proper objects." There was a collection of dramatic pieces designed "to exemplify the mode of conduct which will render young ladies both amiable and happy when their school education is completed," and containing such delightful reading as "The Good Mother-in-law," "The Good Daughter-in-law," "The Maternal Sister-in-law." In another book, which seems to have been quite popular, called the "Ladies' Library," were gathered Miss Moore's "Essays," Dr. Gregory's "Legacy to his Daughter," Lady Pennington's "Unfortunate Mother's Advice to her Daughter," Marchioness de Lambert's "Advice of a Mother to her Daughter," Swift's "Letter to a Young Lady newly

Married," and Mrs. Chapone "On the Government of Temper," very few of which have ever been heard of by the young women of our day.

The Misses' Magazine, which appeared in 1795, was not a periodical, as the name might seem to imply, but a single volume, a storehouse of moral lectures in the form of a series of dialogues "between a governess and several young ladies of quality—her scholars—in which each is made to speak according to her peculiar genius." The several faults of each were pointed out, an easy way of mending them was shown, and an effort made, the author declared, "no less to form the young readers' hearts to goodness than to enlighten their understandings with useful knowledge."

The aim of the Literary Miscellany, which for a time was issued fortnightly, was "to excite humane and sympathetic affections" in children and "to cultivate the benevolent and virtuous dispositions, improve the understanding, and amend the heart." The literature selected as likely to accomplish this purpose was Sterne's "Dead Ass," Collins's "Ode to the Passions," Wharton's "Dying Indian," Gray's "Elegy," and Goldsmith's "Edwin and Angelina." That splendid and wholesome literature, now the delight of every intelligent boy and girl, had no existence, and its place was supplied by such books as "The Father's Gift," "The Mother's Gift," "The Present for a Little Boy," "The Prize for Youthful Obedience," with its four-and-thirty "handsome cuts," and "The Hieroglyphic Bible," a collection of five hundred cuts and curious passages, "represented with emblematic figures for the amusement of youth, designed chiefly to familiarize tender age in a pleasing manner with early ideas of the Bible."

For children of a larger growth there was a political literature, now forgotten, but well written and widely read in its day. Scarcely a public man of note but made at least one contribution. The times were stirring. The question of ratification of the Constitution, the interpretation of the document after it became the supreme law of the land, the first proclamation of neutrality, the first treaty of amity and commerce with Great Britain, the struggle for neutrality, the insolence of the French Directory, the quarrel with Great

Britain, the embargo, the orders in council, the Berlin and
Milan decrees, and the great questions of international law,
brought to the discussion of public matters the ablest men
of the day. The pamphlets of Hamilton, Madison, Jay,
Elbridge Gerry, Oliver Ellsworth, Roger Sherman, George
Clinton, Samuel Chase, James Sullivan, John Dickinson,
James Iredell, Charles Pinckney, Luther Martin, Daniel Car-
roll, Noah Webster, Pelatiah Webster, Randolph, Mason,
Richard Henry Lee, defending or attacking the Constitution;
the letters of Helvidius and Pacificus, in which Madison and
Hamilton discussed the proclamation of neutrality; the let-
ters of Marcellus, Columbus, and Barneveldt, in which John
Quincy Adams held up the conduct of Genet, and explained
our neutral rights and duties; the letters of Camillus, in which
Hamilton defended Jay's treaty; Monroe's " Review of the
Conduct of the Executive "; Fauchet's " Sketch of the Relations of France and the United States "; Charles Pinckney's
three letters on impressment, expatriation, and neutral
rights; Gallatin's " Sketch of the Finances of the United
States "; Madison's " Examination of the British Doctrine ";
and a hundred others that might well be named form a library
of political history of the highest order. Around these books
and pamphlets might be grouped others of no mean order by
men of lesser note in our time, but well known in their own.
The political writings of Joseph Priestley, of Thomas Cooper,
of Goodloe Harper, William Cobbett, James Thomson Cal-
lender, Matthew Carey, were once eagerly read, and powerful
for good and evil. Bitterly partisan, slanderous, malignant
as some of these men were, their writings must not be ignored
in a review of the popular reading of the last year of the century.

The deep interest taken in the French revolution, and the
presence in our seaboard cities of thousands of refugees from
San Domingo and *émigré* from France, made everything
French, or, as the phrase went, everything Gallic, *à la mode.*
The wild craze of 1793, with its liberty poles and red caps,
civic feasts, Citizen This and Citizen That, the intense outburst
of democracy which made it impossible for a true republican
to walk on Prince Street, or Queen Street, or King Street,

or worship God in a church on whose wall was a rude imitation of the royal arms—all this passed rapidly away.   But
French influence continued to be felt in the cities and by
those who affected fashion.   Dancing schools, fencing schools,
language schools conducted by Frenchmen, French dishes,
names, expressions, customs, dress, music, books, were the rage.
Inns and taverns became hotels, bakers and pastry cooks became *restaurateurs*, French advertisements appeared in the
newspapers.   Indeed, the important cities had their French
newspapers.   That at New York was the Gazette Française;
Philadelphia had Le Courrier Politique de l'Univers, Le Courrier de l'Amérique, and La Chronique des Mois ou les Cahiers
Patriotique; Charleston had Le Moniteur Français, and
later L'Oracle.   In Philadelphia was a French circulating
library claiming to possess twelve hundred and fifty volumes.

But the great mass of popular literature was of English
origin, and composed of books of all sorts brought from across
the sea.   Booksellers and printers in each city and important
town regularly imported and sometimes reprinted the great
English classics, and such literature of the day as could not fail
to find readers.   The novels of Miss Burney and Mrs. Rad-
cliffe, of Madame de Genlis and Mrs. Rawson, the writings of
Dryden and Pope, Shenstone and Akenside, Burke, Johnson,
and Chesterfield were sure of a reasonable sale, and seem,
from the advertisements in the newspapers, to have been regularly imported.   But standard works that cost more than five
dollars, works in two, three, or four volumes, or such as were
likely to have a large sale, were generally reprinted, because
they could be profitably sold much below the price of the
English copies.   A proposal for reprinting Robertson's "History of America" stated the situation precisely.   Without
many native writers of our own, said the publisher, we naturally turn to the country whence we derive our origin and
our language.   But the moderate fortunes possessed by most
men and the expensive form in which English books come to
us forbid free indulgence.   Hence the utility of reprinting
the best of them in order that by the lessening of their cost
they may be put within the reach of many.

Books of this sort generally went to press when three or four hundred subscribers had been secured, and it is no uncommon thing to find the names of the subscribers printed at the back of the last volume. Thus Goldsmith's " Earth and Animated Nature " was reprinted and sold by subscription in twenty-four weekly parts at a quarter of a dollar each, and Maynard's translation of " Flavius Josephus " in sixty numbers at one shilling fourpence ha'penny each.

So far as our country could be said to have a literary centre at that time, it was Philadelphia. The enterprise of her publishers and the long period over which their enterprise extended, the character of the books they printed and her citizens read, justly entitle her to that distinction. It was at Philadelphia that the first newspaper in the middle colonies,* the first secular magazine in North America,† the first religious magazine,‡ the first religious weekly,# and the first daily newspapers in the United States || were established. The first American edition of the Bible in any European language,▲ and the first American edition of the Bible and New Testament in English,◊ and the first American editions of a long list of standard works by British writers, came from Phila-

---

* American Weekly Mercury, 1719.

† The American Monthly Magazine, 1741.

‡ Ein Geistliches Magazin, 1764.

The Religious Remembrancer, 1813.

|| Pennsylvania Packet, begun in 1771, became the first daily newspaper in the United States on September 21, 1784.

▲ Biblia, Das ist: Die Heilige Schrift Altes und Neues Testaments, noch der deutschen Uebersetzung D. Martin Luthers, etc., Germantown, Gedruckt by Christoph Saur, 1743.

◊ The war for Independence cut off the supply of Bibles from England, and produced such a scarcity that Dr. Allison, of the First Presbyterian Church, Philadelphia, with many other citizens, petitioned Congress for aid. On September 11, 1777, that body appointed a committee of three to consult the printers in the city, and if possible arrange for the publication of 30,000 copies at the expense of Congress. But the scarcity of paper and the impossibility of procuring proper type led the committee to advise Congress to order the Committee on Commerce to import 20,000 English Bibles from Holland, Scotland, or anywhere. The importation, though ordered, was never made, and the expediency of printing the Bible in the United States was again referred to a committee, under whose encouragement Mr. Robert Aitken, a Philadelphia printer, went on with the work of printing. The task was a hard one for those days, but after four years of labor

delphia presses. On that list, before 1790, are "Epictetus, his Morals," "Pamela," "Rasselas," "Robinson Crusoe," "The Sentimental Journey," "The Deserted Village," "The Vicar of Wakefield," "Paradise Lost," Blackstone's "Commentaries," Robertson's "Scotland," Leland's "Ireland," Chesterfield's "Letters," Lady Mary Wortley Montagu's "Letters and Pastimes," Adam Smith's "Wealth of Nations," and an abridgment of "The Lives of the British Poets."

Between 1790 and 1800 Adam Smith's "Wealth of Na-

---

was completed, and early in 1781 Congress was asked to "approve the pious and laudable undertaking," which it did in the manner following:

The Committee, consisting of Mr. Duane, Mr. McKean, and Mr. Witherspoon, to whom was referred a Memorial of Robert Aitken, Printer, dated 21st January, 1781, respecting an edition of the Holy Scriptures, report: That Mr. Aitken has, at a great expense, now finished an American edition of the Holy Scriptures in English; that the Committee have from time to time attended to his progress in the work; that they also recommended it to the two chaplains of Congress to examine and give their opinion of the execution, who have accordingly reported thereon; the recommendation and report being as follows:

PHILADELPHIA, 1st September, 1782.

REVEREND GENTLEMEN.—Our knowledge of your piety and public spirit leads us without apology to recommend to your particular attention the edition of the Holy Scriptures publishing by Mr. Aitken. He undertook this expensive work at a time when from the circumstances of the war, an English edition of the Bible could not be imported, nor any opinion formed how long the obstruction might continue. On this account particularly he deserves applause and encouragement. We therefore wish you, Reverend Gentlemen, to examine the execution of the work, and if approved, to give it the sanction of your judgment, and the weight of your recommendation. We are, with very great respect,

Your most obedient, humble servants,

(Signed)   JAMES DUANE,
Chairman in behalf of a Committee of Congress on Mr. Aitken's Memorial.
Reverend Doctor WHITE and Rev. Mr. DUFFIELD,
Chaplains of the United States in Congress assembled.

GENTLEMEN.—Agreeably to your desire we have paid attention to Mr. Aitken's impression of the Holy Scriptures of the Old and New Testaments. Having selected and examined a variety of passages throughout the work, we are of opinion that it is executed with great accuracy as to the sense, and with as few grammatical and typographical errors as could have been expected in an undertaking of such magnitude. Being ourselves witnesses of the demand for this invaluable work, we rejoice in the present prospect of a supply; hoping that it will prove as advantageous as it is honorable to the gentleman who has exerted himself to fur-

tions," Paley's " Moral Philosophy," " The Letters of Junius,"
Robertson's " Histories," Russell's " Modern Europe," Aristo-
tle's " Ethics and Politics," Johnson's " Dictionary," the plays
of Shakespeare, the " British Classics," in thirty-eight volumes, and a shelf full of other works quite as solid reading
were reprinted by Philadelphia publishers.

Reading of a lighter sort was confined to a class of novels
which was fast driving the old favorites to the wall.   " Tom
Jones " and " Tristram Shandy," " Sir Charles Grandison "
and " Camilla " were, indeed, widely read, but a new school of
fiction of a distinctly different type was already in high favor.
The very names of these novels is indicative of the change.
" The Mysteries of Udolpho," " Trials of the Human Heart,"
" Solitary Castle," " Castle of Inchvalley," " Mysteries of
the Castle," " Spirit of the Castle," " Castle Zitwar," " Bel-
grave Castle, or the Horrid Spectre," " Aurora, or the Mysterious Beauty "—these and a score of others, in two, three,
and even four volumes, made the popular prose fiction of the
day.   Castles, dungeons, mystery, ghosts, women led astray,
seducers, uncanny incidents, were the essential ingredients of
them all.

To this school our country contributed one writer of note
—Charles Brockden Brown, who has a double claim to re-

---

nish it, at the evident risque of private fortune. We are, gentlemen, your very
respectful and humble servants,
            (Signed)   WILLIAM WHITE,
                                                  GEORGE DUFFIELD.
    PHILADELPHIA, *September 10th*, 1782.
Honorable JAMES DUANE, Esq., Chairman, and the other Honorable Gentlemen of
    the Committee of Congress on Mr. Aitken's Memorial.

    Whereupon, RESOLVED,
    That the United States in Congress assembled, highly approve the pious and
laudable undertaking of Mr. Aitken, as subservient to the interest of religion, as
well as an instance of the progress of arts in this country; and being satisfied
from the above report, of his care and accuracy in the execution of the work,
they recommend this edition of the Bible, to the inhabitants of the United States,
and hereby authorize him to publish this recommendation in the manner he shall
think proper.   CHA. THOMSON, *Secretary.*

    Scarcely had Mr. Aitken issued his Bible when peace was declared, when the
ports were opened, when commerce was resumed, and Bibles were imported from
Great Britain so cheaply that the American copy was driven from the market, and
a loss " of more than three thousand pounds in specie " entailed on the printer.

membrance, for he was the first man in the New World who made letters a profession, as he was the first whose writings entitle him to be called a novelist. Brown was born at Philadelphia in 1771, and while still a very young man began the study of law. But the natural bent of his mind was toward literature, and, after encountering the usual vicissitudes of youthful authors, he began, when twenty-six years of age, to write romances which were hailed as works of genius by his countrymen and won him fame abroad.* That they should have been so regarded is but another sign of the unwholesome literary taste of the time, for no such men and women, no such scenery, no such supernatural machinery, no such horrible adventures, are permissible even in romantic fiction. Yet the story is always well told, and many of the scenes, as those in Philadelphia during the plague of 1793, are described with great skill. But the truly American novel of that day was " Modern Chivalry," a prose satire on democracy, by a man who was himself an extreme democrat.

Humble as the efforts of our countrymen may seem, there was scarcely a branch of literature in which some of them, judged by the standards of the time, had not risen to note. The poetry of Philip Freneau, the " McFingal " of John Trumbull, the epics and pastorals of Timothy Dwight, and " The Vision of Columbus," by Joel Barlow, were hailed as indisputable evidence that the spirit of democracy was not hostile to the Muses. Ramsey's " History of the Revolution in South Carolina," Gordon's " Rise, Progress, and Establishment of the Independence of the United States," Thomas's " History of Printing," Brackenridge's " Incidents of the Western Insurrection," have lived down to our day, and are still authorities; while Murray's " English Grammar " and Noah Webster's " Speller," both published before 1800, have had a national reputation for three generations.

All this was encouraging. There were those, indeed, who utterly despaired of the existence of literature in a democracy, and missed no chance to abuse their countrymen for a neglect

---

* The writings on which rests the fame of Brown are Alcuin: A Dialogue on the Rights of Women; Wieland; Ormond; Arthur Mervyn; Edgar Huntly; Clara Howard, and Jane Talbot.

too well deserved. " To study with a view to becoming an author by profession in America," exclaimed one, " is a prospect of no less flattering promise than to publish among the Eskimos an essay on delicacy of taste, or to found an academy of sciences in Lapland." " We know," said another, " that in this land, where the spirit of democracy is everywhere diffused, we are exposed, as it were, to a poisonous atmosphere which blasts everything beautiful in Nature and corrodes everything elegant in art; we know that ' the rose leaves fall ungathered.' " A third describes his country as " these cold shades," " these shifting skies—

> Where Fancy sickens and where Genius dies,
> Where few and feeble are the Muses' strains,
> And no fine frenzy riots in the veins."

But there were others with more hopeful views. The prospect before us, said one of this class, is brightening. America, despite the aspersions of English reviewers, has reached an eminence in literature which, to say the least, is respectable. Like Hercules in his cradle, she has manifested a gigantic grasp, and discovered that she will be great. The wisdom, penetration, and eloquence of her statesmen are undoubted. Her judges and lawyers are distinguished for powers of reason and plausibility of address. Her writers of history are not many, yet they raise our expectations and claim our praise. Her poetry, it is to be hoped, has not yet assumed its most elevated form. Yet it is not true that beneath her skies " Fancy sickens and Genius dies." The exhibitions of American talent already made justify the warmest expectation. Miltons, Newtons, and Robertsons will surely arise in the New World, and in time to come " the sun of genius " will pour " his meridian beams " on our land. The editor of a projected magazine, in commenting on the state of literature, declared that it soothed the observant mind to contemplate the gradual and general cultivation of letters which had marked the progress of the United States since the adoption of the Constitution. Our men of learning, said he, were then rare; our booksellers were few and poor; our students were content with the scanty sale of literature which chance and charity threw in their way. Books imported from Europe were found only in the houses of the rich, and but one or two native periodicals spread the gleams of literature among the middle classes. Now it is rare to find a village without a circulating library.

The charge, said another, of neglect of native genius is not well founded. He who knows the wide circulation of the Port Folio and of the Analectic Magazine of Philadelphia, and of the Polyanthus of Boston, cannot maintain such a proposition for a moment. On the contrary, there is not on earth a people more indulgent to their home productions or more prompt to foster the offsprings of native genius than the people of the United States. The ready sale of certain works of merit—such works, for example, as "Salmagundi," "John Bull and Brother Jonathan," and "Knickerbocker's History of New York"—is proof positive that an English origin is not necessary to the success in this country of works of sterling merit. If it be a good book, no American will think the worse of it for being American. If bad, none will like it the better for being English. But so long as Great Britain is richer than the United States, so long will London be the mart of literature. So long as her population shall afford a greater number of persons who can live by their pens, so long will her men of letters outrank our own.*

Now and then some writer, encouraged by what had been done, would protest against the subserviency of the literary class in America to that in England; would "resent the British scoff that when separated from England the colonies would become mere illiterate orang-outangs"; would denounce "the unjust manner" in which our native authors were "treated by reviewers of England"; and would lament that in the eyes even of American critics "if an individual has the temerity to jingle a couplet and to avow himself descended from America, the offence is absolutely unpardonable." No one not familiar with the periodical literature of the first fifty years of our political independence can form any conception of the universality and persistence of the charge

---

* The Port Folio, 1815, p. 193.

that our forefathers were intellectually the slaves of Britain. The longing for English praise, the submission to English literary judgment, the fear of English censure, and the base humility with which it was received, was dwelt on incessantly in magazines, in newspapers, in addresses, in recollections of distinguished men, and in the prefaces to books.

When we examine an American literary production, said the reviewer of a wretched book written in imitation of English models, the first thing we do is to determine whether the author has or has not adopted an English fashionable model. If he has, we then hasten to find out if he derived his characters, views, and opinions from the same source, and we confess that if we find he has, our estimate of him is lowered. We consider it a breach of duty to the republic of letters in America to assist, by servile conformity, the fashion now prevalent for everything foreign in literature. The inevitable consequence of such a taste is a state of colonization of intellect, of subserviency to the critical opinion of the once mother country.

Another, reviewing Paulding's "Backwoodsman," had much to say in praise of a man hardy enough to select for his poem an American character with American life and scenery. We have, said the reviewer, no ferocious giants, no frowning battlements, no lordly knights, no damsels in distress. With us all is plain, simple, unsophisticated Nature. The most terrible necromancer among us is the sheriff; but even his gates readily open on the exhibition of a bit of paper. In such utter absence of anything like a hero, or even a suitable scene for a poetic eye in a fine frenzy to roll upon, it requires uncommon nerves and powerful motives to publish an epic lay which deals with American scenery and life on the frontier.

Much the same condition prevailed, another critic remarked, in the literary as in the industrial world. In the manufacture of coarse fabrics we distanced Great Britain. In the manufacture of fine goods we could not approach her. So in literature. The great literary staple of our country was the newspaper, on which the very best talent was spent and wasted. Next must be placed pamphlets, magazines, and periodicals, which, with a few books of travel and some popular histories, generally succeeded and were widely read. But in

men in 1825 should prefer " Marmion," " The Lay of the Last Minstrel," " The Lady of the Lake," " Lalla Rookh," " The Corsair," " Marino Faliero," " The Lyrical Ballads," " The Excursion," " Waverley," and " Guy Mannering," to the novels of Brown, the poetry of Trumbull and Dwight, and the odes and laments that abound in the reviews, museums, and repositories of the time, was right. We do so to-day. Their preference was not subserviency, but sound literary judgment. Never in the course of two centuries had Great Britain produced at one time such a goodly company of men of letters. Jane Austen and Maria Edgeworth, Mrs. Hemans, Burns, Byron, Hallam, Coleridge, Keats, Moore, Wordsworth, Scott, were authors with whom our countrymen could not compete. Their novels and poems went everywhere, sold everywhere, were read everywhere, not because the Americans were without literary judgment, but because they possessed it in the highest degree. That a nation which produced such writers should be deferred to in literary matters was to be expected. This gathering of men and women was phenomenal, and the influence of English literary opinion was phenomenal. Our countrymen deferred to it just as we defer to the advice of the ablest physicians, the skill of the greatest surgeons, the leadership of the most successful commanders.

On the other hand, it was no more than human that our own writers should feel this influence keenly, and that American literary journals should resent it bitterly. They correctly stated a condition, but attributed it to a wrong cause. Yet it would be a great mistake to suppose that we were without American men of letters. Indeed, it was during the first quarter of the nineteenth century that some of the most typical of American books were produced by some of the most original American writers.

First in point of time was Irving. He was born in New York city, April third, 1783, just a few days before peace with Great Britain was proclaimed throughout the land, and in token of gratitude to the great man who led our armies through the struggle so happily ended received the name of Washington. The youngest of a family of eleven children, he inherited from his mother the traits both of mind and character that so distinguished him in after life, and grew up a vivacious, mischief-loving lad, delighting in books, music, and the theatre, fond of companionship, and averse to methodical study and protracted mental work. At sixteen he became a student in a law office; but the literary spirit was strong within him, and in 1802 Irving began to write for the Morning Chronicle over the name of Jonathan Oldstyle. The letters are of no value save as an additional illustration of the enormous influence of Addison and Steele on the young writers of the day, for the letters were closely modelled on the Spectator and the Tatler.

In 1804 Irving was sent abroad to improve his health, but returned to New York in 1806, where his literary tastes and good fellowship made him one of a band of lively young men who as " The Nine Worthies " or " The Lads of Kilkenny " frequented the city taverns, and held what they considered wild revelries on the banks of the Passaic in an old house they called Cockloft Hall. In company with two of these companions, Irving, in 1806, began the publication of Salmagundi, a semi-monthly periodical in the manner of the Spectator, and especially designed to " instruct the young, reform the old, correct the town, and castigate the age." But the partners soon wearied of supplying the town with a fortnightly allowance of wit and humor, and after twenty numbers the publication ceased, though the success had been surprising.

This venture determined Irving's career. He now practically abandoned law, devoted himself more and more to literature, and was soon at work on " The History of New York." Dr. Samuel L. Mitchell had published what he called a " Picture of New York," which seemed so fair a mark for ridicule that Irving and his brother Peter determined to satirize it, and had their book well under way when Peter Irving was called by business to Europe, and the completion of the task fell on Washington. As Philadelphia was then the centre of the book trade and of letters, the manuscript was sent to a Philadelphia publisher, and when all was ready announcements of a novel sort appeared in the newspapers. First came the statement that a " small, elderly gentleman, dressed in

an old black coat and cocked hat, by the name of Knickerbocker," had disappeared from his lodgings in New York city.
Next from week to week came other notices, setting forth
that an elderly gentleman answering the description had been
seen in a north-bound Albany stage; that he owed his landlord for room rent and board; that he had left behind a curious sort of written book, and that unless he returned and paid
his score the manuscript would be sold to satisfy the debt.
The identity of the fictitious author having thus been established, " A History of New York, by Diedrich Knickerbocker," was given to the world in 1809. Of all the books
up to that time written by Americans, this was the most original. The reality which Franklin gave to the " clean old man,"
Poor Richard, was surpassed by the semblance of actual existence with which Irving invested the little old gentleman
in black coat and knee breeches. He became the type of a
great class. What the Puritan is to New England, what the
Cavalier is to Virginia, and the Quaker to Pennsylvania,
Father Knickerbocker has ever since been to New York.
Many a reader with Dutch blood in his veins failed to see
the humor of the book. One, indeed, a scholar of no mean
repute, described it as a " coarse caricature." But the verdict
of our countrymen has pronounced it a masterpiece of humor.

That literature, not law, was Irving's calling was now
more apparent than ever. But a strange mental laziness overcame him, and during ten years he did nothing worthy of his
powers. For a short time he edited the Analectic Magazine,*
and contributed to its pages two essays,† which now appear in
" The Sketch Book," some reviews of popular writers,‡ and
short biographies of naval heroes.# But it was not till stern
necessity drove him to it that he went seriously to work, and
put forth book after book with what for him was great rapid-

---

* This magazine was published in Philadelphia, and from 1809–'12 was known
as Select Reviews and Spirit of the Foreign Magazines. In January, 1813, the
name was changed to the Analectic Magazine. From 1813–'14 Irving was the
editor.

† Traits of Indian Character, and Philip of Pokanoket.

‡ R. T. Paine, Paulding, Lord Byron, E. C. Holland.

Perry, Lawrence, Burrows, Porter.

ity. He published " The Sketch Book " in 1819, " Brace-bridge Hall " in 1821, " The Tales of a Traveller " in 1824, and began seriously to contemplate a life of Washington. From this for the time being he was diverted by a visit to Spain. Irving's purpose was merely to translate a mass of historical documents extracted from the papers of Las Casas and the journals of Columbus, edited by M. Navarrete, and in course of publication at Madrid.* But, while he pored over this mass of history in the rough, his lively imagination reproduced the age of discovery and exploration with all its characters in their habit, as they lived, made him almost the contemporary of Ferdinand and Isabella, and enabled him to write the best " Life of Columbus " now extant in any tongue.

" The Life of Columbus " appeared in 1828, by which time our literature had been enriched by many noble contri-butions. Marshall had written his " Life of Washington," Temple Franklin had published the writings of his illustri-ous grandfather, Sparks was doing pioneer work in the do-main of history, while the people of Great Britain and the United States were eagerly reading " The Spy," " The Pilot," " The Last of the Mohicans," and " The Pioneers." Mar-shall's " Life of Washington " does little credit to the great chief justice. He began it against his will, completed it with unseemly haste, and produced a biography which is one long eulogy of a man who needed none, and is too Federalistic in tone to be fair. The period covered by the last fifty years of Washington's life is full of events of the deepest historical interest. It was during these years that the English settlers, long moving steadily westward up the Atlantic slope, crossed the mountains, entered the valley of of the Mississippi, came face to face with the French at the sources of the Ohio, and brought on that final struggle for possession which ended in the triumph of Great Britain, in the expulsion of France from the continent of North America, and in the enormous expansion of the dominion of the British Crown. These new

---

* Coleccion de los viages y descubrimientos que hicieron por mar los Españoles desde fines del siglo XV, Madrid, 1824–'37, 5 vols.

acquisitions made necessary a new colonial policy, which provoked the rebellion of thirteen colonies, which had long ceased to be English and had long since become American, and led step by step to the establishment of the United States. At every part of this procession of events Washington was always a conspicuous, and often the most conspicuous, figure. Rarely does the world's history present so striking a character, dealing with such dramatic incident, surrounded by such a varied company, tried by so many vicissitudes, and dying at last with every undertaking accomplished, and leaving behind no act of which posterity need be ashamed. The opportunity was a great one; but Marshall threw it away, and, unprepared, unfitted for the task, rushed through a pile of dreary papers and wrote with such rapidity that in two years' time four octavo volumes were ready for the press. The subject, the writer, the popular interest in them, all gave expectations of a great success. Thirty thousand volumes, it was thought, would be subscribed for. But the high price, and the report spread abroad by the Republicans that the work was a Federalist history of the United States, and intended chiefly to affect the presidential election * of 1804, kept down the subscriptions to eight thousand.

While Jefferson and the Republicans were accusing the biographer of Washington of being a tool of the Federalists, the newspapers were asserting that the editor of Franklin's writings was a tool of Great Britain. After the death of the doctor in 1790, his papers and manuscripts passed by will to his grandson, William Temple Franklin, who promptly announced that they should be published, and issued a call for

---

* No one held this view more fully than Jefferson. In a letter to Joel Barlow begging him to write a history of the United States, the President said: "John Marshall is writing a life of General Washington from his papers. It is intended to come out just in time to influence the next presidential election. It is written, therefore, principally with a view to electioneering purposes. It will consequently be out in time to aid you with information, as well as to point out the perversions of truth necessary to be rectified."—Jefferson to Barlow. Works, vol. iv, p. 437.

In a letter to his publisher Marshall wrote: "The Democrats may say what they please, and I have expected they would say a great deal, but this is at least not intended to be a party work, nor will any candid man have cause to make this charge."

the return of such as had been scattered by the vicissitudes of war. But Temple Franklin went abroad a few months later, and for seven-and-twenty years the promise was unfulfilled.

Meanwhile book-makers, reviewers, and newspaper critics, weary at the delay, abused him roundly. In those days if anything went wrong in our country and the reason was not easy to find, it was customary to ascribe the evil to the action of Great Britain. Why the promised edition of Franklin's writings was not forthcoming, though a decade and more had passed since his death, was unaccountable. It must, therefore, be due to the malignity of Great Britain, to whom Temple Franklin was now openly accused of having sold himself. The charge was first made by the National Intelligencer, a Jeffersonian newspaper published in Washington. The public, said the editor, is tired with waiting for the appearance of Dr. Franklin's works. Something is wrong. An ugly rumor is afloat that the papers of the great man never will be published. It's time for his descendants to explain. No explanation was made; whereupon the National Intelligencer returned to the charge in 1804. Silence, said the editor, had given the subject increased weight. More than eight years ago assurances were given repeatedly that an edition was to appear at the same time in Europe and America. Why has it not appeared? Some say because Mr. Temple Franklin sold his copyright to a London bookseller, who in turn sold it for a much greater sum to the British Government, in order that the papers might be suppressed.*

This plain statement seems to have had some effect at home, for the next year William Duane, editor of the Aurora, and husband of the widow of Benjamin Franklin Bache, advertised for subscriptions to a three-volume edition of Franklin's works. But even this dragged on for thirteen years, when, instead of three, six volumes had been issued.†

The charge of suppressing once started in this country, crossed the Atlantic, and in 1806 appeared in the preface to

---

* The same charge appears in The (Boston) Democrat, August 22, 1804.
† The first volume appeared in 1808; the last in 1818.

a three-volume edition of Franklin's writings, edited by his old friend, Benjamin Vaughan, at London.* When, says Vaughan, Temple Franklin thought his manuscript ready for the press, he offered it to the London printers; but his terms were too high, the printers demurred, and nothing more has been heard of the offer. " The reason is plain. The proprietor, it seems, has found a bidder of a different description in some emissary of government, whose object is to withhold the manuscripts from the world, not to benefit it by their publication, and they either passed into other hands, or the person to whom they were bequeathed received a remuneration for suppressing them."

The Edinburgh Review sifted, denied, and pronounced the accusation foolish.† But it again crossed the Atlantic, and was once more set afloat by the American Citizen, a newspaper published in New York. " William Temple Franklin," said the writer, " without shame, without remorse, mean and mercenary, has sold the sacred deposit committed to his care by Dr. Franklin to the British Government. Franklin's works are lost to the world forever." ‡ Idle as the story was, it would not down, but was next taken up by a Paris journal, called the Argus, or London Review,# in which it is quite likely the slander for the first time reached the eyes of Temple Franklin. He promptly branded the charge as false; the editor accepted his statement as final, the London Chronicle republished it, and through this channel the denial made its way back to the United States, where respectable journals reprinted it and respectable men went on disbelieving it till Franklin began to issue his volumes in 1817. Even then there were some who remained unconvinced, and as late as 1829 it was reiterated by the publication of Jefferson's Anas.

Such delay in the case of most men would have been fatal to the success of the book. But nothing could dim the popular interest in Franklin the world over. Since his death in 1790 there had been published twenty-eight editions of such of his

---

* The preface is dated April 7, 1806.
† Edinburgh Review, July, 1806.
‡ American Citizen, September, 1806.
# March 28, 1807.

writings as could be collected, thirty-three editions of his life in English, and thirteen in French, some twenty editions of " Father Abraham's Speech " and " The Way to Wealth," besides innumerable reprints of his famous tracts and pamphlets. The writings of no other American were so scattered over Europe. Save Irving and Cooper, no other American writer had yet approached him in fame even in England.

James Fenimore Cooper, the son of William and Elizabeth Fenimore Cooper, was born at Burlington, New Jersey, September fifteenth, 1789. He was the eleventh child of a family of twelve, and when little more than a year old was taken by his parents to the shore of Otsego Lake, New York, where four years before his father had laid out the village of Cooperstown. In this frontier settlement, in the heart of the wilderness, the boy grew up, surrounded by the most majestic scenery and in contact with all the incidents and characters of pioneer life. When the rudiments of education had been mastered in the village school-house, Cooper was sent to reside in the family of an Albany minister, and at thirteen entered the class of 1806 at Yale. There a boyish escapade brought his course to a sudden ending, after which his father decided to fit him for the navy.

In those early days, when the academy at Annapolis had no existence, the lad who aspired to rank in the navy began his nautical experience on the deck of a merchant trader, and on such a vessel Cooper as a common seaman sailed from New York, in the autumn of 1806, for " Cowes and a market." A year of experience before the mast furnished him with many an incident for his sea novels, and gained for him a commission as midshipman in the United States navy, in which he served for three years.*

Cooper when he resigned in 1811 was twenty-one, and had as yet shown neither literary tastes nor the smallest disposition to become an author. Indeed, he was thirty before a casual remark of his wife turned him from an idler into one

---

* The facts regarding Cooper's early life are taken from the Life of Cooper, by Thomas R. Lounsbury, in American Men of Letters. The book is a model biography.

of the most prolific of American writers. The story is told that as he sat one day reading to his wife from an English society novel he laid down the book with the remark, " I believe I could write a better novel myself." " Do so," was the calm reply; and, thus challenged, he went to work, and in November, 1820, " Precaution: a Novel, by an Englishman," appeared in New York. The work as a piece of printing, as a piece of fiction, as a story was bad. It was below the average of the wretched school to which it belonged. Yet, poor as it was, his friends considered it good enough to urge him to go on, and in 1821 he brought out the first truly American novel. In " Precaution " Cooper had gone to England for his incidents and characters, and had attempted to draw a picture of a life of which he knew nothing whatever. We are informed that he was now advised to stay on this side of the Atlantic, and to deal with men and manners well known to him, that he had the good sense to take the advice, and that he chose as the foundation of " The Spy " the adventures of a real spy employed by John Jay during the Revolution.*

As Cooper may be said to have stumbled on the profession of author, so he may be said to have stumbled into fame. Neither he nor the publisher had the smallest conception of the merits of " The Spy," nor of the reception to be given it by the public. The writing of the book was half perfunctory. The manuscript as finished passed to the type-setter unrevised and uncorrected, and the first volume was printed and bound some months before Cooper had the heart to begin on the second. When at last the task was resumed the end seemed so far away that the publisher protested lest the work should exceed all reasonable limits; whereupon Cooper, to satisfy him, actually wrote the last chapter and had it set up, paged, and printed before a word of the intervening chapters were written or the incidents so much as imagined. Nothing short of merit of a high order could save such a piece of composition from contempt. But that merit " The Spy " contained, for it is a story of adventure remarkably well told,

---

* Lounsbury's Cooper, pp. 28, 29.

and as such won a speedy recognition.   Within six months of the day of issue the book passed through three editions in America, was dramatized and acted with success, was published in England, was translated into French, and gained for the unknown * writer the title of " a distinguished American novelist."

The success of " The Spy " at home was a signal refutation of the charge so long and vigorously made that no American would read a book by one of his countrymen.   It was read everywhere, and secured for Cooper a popularity which aroused the greatest expectation when the announcement was made that " The Spy " would soon be followed by " The Pioneers."   Such was the eagerness to read the promised book that thirty-five hundred copies were sold during the forenoon of the day of publication.   Nor was expectation disappointed. Though by no means the best of the five fine stories known to us as "The Leatherstocking Tales," " The Pioneers " is indeed a vivid picture of frontier life and frontier character drawn by one who knew both well.   It was the first truly American book by an intensely American author, and in Leatherstocking the readers of Cooper's day were introduced to the first and only original character our countrymen have ever yet given to literature.†

This of itself would have entitled him to lasting distinction.   But while " The Pioneers " was still on the press Cooper began another novel destined to increase his fame yet more, and to make him the founder of a new school of fiction.   His biographer assures us that while at a dinner party in New York in 1822 the puzzle of the literary world, Who is the author of the Waverley Novels? came up for solution, and that Cooper attributed them to Scott.   Those who denied his authorship cited " The Pirate," pointed to the incidents of the story as proof positive that none but a seafaring man could have written it, and maintained that, as Scott knew nothing of life aboard ship, " The Pirate " could not be his work.   Cooper contended that the novel showed no evidence

* The novel was published as The Spy : A Tale of the Neutral Ground, by the author of Precaution.   2 vols.   New York : Wiley & Halsted, 1821.

† Lounsbury's Cooper, p. 283.

in the North American Review, a periodical to which Bryant now became a contributor of prose and verse. One of these prose articles is of more than passing interest, for it was a review by him, then a young poet of four-and-twenty, of the state of poetry in America. In 1817 Mr. Solyman Brown published an " Essay on American Poetry," with specimens of his own handiwork. Neither the essay nor the verse was very good, but it afforded Bryant an excuse for some remarks on the condition of his art in the United States. It was his belief that our national poetry began with independence. Before that time we could hardly be said to have such a thing. The few quaint and unskilful specimens of rhyme that had come down from colonial times were objects of curiosity rather than value. Some men of taste and learning had amused their leisure with these trifles, but a people struggling with the difficulties of colonization and possessing no superfluous wealth had small use for writers. Not till the contest for independence awakened an ambition to be distinguished in all that makes a nation did native literature, and poetry in particular, begin to thrive in America. Then for the first time could we be said to have poets. Yet the effusions of most of the men he hailed as such—Francis Hopkinson, Church, Freneau, Trumbull, Dwight, Barlow, Humphreys, Honeywood, and Clifton—long ago came to be considered objects of curiosity. Their themes were " The Progress of Dulness," " The Conquest of Canaan," " The Triumph of Infidelity," " The Vision of Columbus," and were treated with a sameness of imagery, a coldness of manner, a monotony of versification, tiresome in the extreme. They were feeble imitators of English bards who flourished when they began to write.

This custom of imitating the peculiar manner of the last popular English author was still prevalent, and went far to account for the neglect of native writers. There was more good taste among those who read than among those who wrote poetry, and in the long run the judgment of the people was sound. Mr. Bryant could recall no instance when great poetical merit had come forward, and, finding its claim disallowed, had been forced to retire to the shade whence it emerged. The fondness for literature was growing. The popular English books of the day were reprinted in America, were scattered everywhere, were in everybody's hands, and were the subject of everybody's conversation. What, then, should hinder native works of equal merit from meeting with an equally favorable reception? *

There might indeed be no good reason why meritorious works by American authors should find small favor with the reading public, yet the fact remained that they certainly did not, as Bryant discovered to his cost, when, in 1821, he published a small volume of forty-four pages containing some of his best efforts.† Seven hundred and fifty copies were issued, but so little were book buyers interested in good poetry that at the end of five years but two hundred and seventy copies had been sold, yielding Bryant a profit of not quite fifteen dollars,‡ or less than two dollars each for such poems as " Thanatopsis," " The Yellow Violet," and " The Water-Fowl." Still, the return, small as it was, seemed ample, and when, in 1825, after contributing some thirty poems to the United States Literary Gazette, Bryant was invited to name his compensation, he thought two dollars apiece sufficient.

Compared with the compensation made by the Gazette to another poet, the sum paid Bryant was large. The United States Literary Gazette, was edited by Theophilus Parsons, now remembered as one of Massachusetts' great judges, was issued simultaneously at Boston and New York, and had among its contributors most of the rising young writers of the day. One of these was Henry Wadsworth Longfellow, a native of Portland, Maine, where he was born in 1807. While a student at Bowdoin, Longfellow made contributions to the Gazette, and when a dozen or more had been printed, received, by way of reward, a copy of Coleridge's poems. In those days the returns of authorship were small. Cooper, whose novels sold by the thousands on the day of issue, Irving, and Payne, whose plays commanded a high price and ready sale, were among the few who found literary labor profitable. Ten

---

* Essay on American Poetry. North American Review, July, 1818.

† Among them were Thanatopsis, The Ages, To a Water-Fowl, The Yellow Violet, Green River, and The Inscription for the Entrance to a Wood.

‡ $14.92.

This new venture settled, Sparks went seriously to work on the Washington papers, spent nearly a year at Mount Vernon, visited Europe, searched the archives of England and France, and came home in 1829. But five years slipped by before the Writings of Washington began to be published, and during these years Sparks prepared the Life and Writings of Gouverneur Morris.

The field of history and biography was now being well tilled. Trumbull's Connecticut, Burk's Virginia, Ramsay's South Carolina, Williamson's North Carolina, Stoddard's Louisiana, Bradford's Massachusetts, Winthrop's New England, Gordon's Pennsylvania, Gibbs's Administration of Washington and Adams, and the lives of Patrick Henry, James Otis, General Greene, and Richard Henry Lee, were all published before 1830. Before that date, too, Coxe and Seybert and Pitkin had published their works on statistics, and Waite his collection of State Papers, while Congress had made public the Journal of the Convention that framed the Constitution.

Mingled with writers of this sort were a host of others, whose names are now almost forgotten, and whose novels, plays, and poems are rarely read. They supplied the magazines and newspapers with wit and poetry; they kept the printing presses busy, contributed largely to the prosperity of the booksellers, and occasionally some one among them would strike the popular fancy with verses so good that half a century has not lessened their popularity. Woodworth's " Old Oaken Bucket," Payne's " Home, Sweet Home," Clement C. Moore's " Visit from St. Nicholas," and Mrs. Hale's " Mary's Lamb " have suffered no decline in popular favor.

CHAPTER XLVIII.

BRITISH CRITICISM OF THE UNITED STATES.

WHILE one part of our countrymen was lamenting the neglect of letters and complaining bitterly of the blind subserviency with which authors and writers in America followed English models, another part repelled with vehemcnce the slanders heaped on the people of the United States by the magazines, reviews, and journals of Great Britain. For a generation past it had been the fashion for English travellers in America on their return home to write books narrating their adventures in the New World and describing the manners, customs, usages, languages, peculiarities, and forms of government of the people of the great republic. Whoever has travelled in foreign parts is well aware that such descriptions are of little value; that generalizations made from data picked up during a hasty trip are of necessity crude, if, indeed, they are not wholly false, and that of all sources of information books of travel are the least reliable. For a time our countrymen seem to have remembered this, and to have treated such travellers' tales as found their way to the United States with indifference or good-natured criticism. The amusing blunders, the patriotic conceit, the confident predictions that the republic would not hold together for fifty years, the assurances that democracy had but to be seen in all its hideousness to be despised, with which such books abounded were often held up to laughter, but rarely were honored with a reply. But, as the commercial quarrel between America and Great Britain grew fiercer and fiercer, and the second war approached, the belief gained ground that behind these attacks of travellers lay a deeply premeditated policy of the British ministry; that it was their deliberate purpose to belittle and abuse the United States; and that the men who seemed to be travellers were hired lampooners in disguise. It is contrary, it was said,* to every principle of human nature to suppose that men not influenced by the all-powerful motive of self-interest can be so degraded as to prefer downright and palpable falsehood when truth is within their reach. It cannot for a moment be doubted that such men as Smyth and Moore, Ashe and Parkinson, have been well paid by the ministry for their tours and travels through the United States. A government under whose benign influence all are happy, all are equal, must be an eternal reproach to the tyrants of Europe. It is their hellish policy to exclude from their deluded subjects everything which might tend in any way to awaken inquiry into natural right. They are therefore taught to believe that in the only free country under heaven the people are savage, poor, illiterate, uncivilized, and un-social. Nay, they have been told that in this unbounded continent Nature herself droops and languishes; that the very animals, trees, and plants want the vigor which a royal clime imparts to the productions of the earth. Were it not that the falsehoods of these sordid adventurers are designed to hold us up to the contempt and derision of other countries, to contradict them would be a waste of time. Mother-country is a favorite term with these sons of St. George. But with what consistency is it applied to a country discovered by an Italian and settled by English, Spanish, Irish, Scotch, Dutch, French, and Germans? It would, indeed, be hard, as Mr. Ashe observes, to conjecture " what kind of character is hereafter to arise from an amalgamation of such discordant materials." But is it not strange that England should avow herself the mother of such a race? of a country " where bigotry, pride, and malignant hatred of her characterizes the inhabitants "? of a country " where sordid speculators alone succeed, where classic fame is held in derision, where grace and taste are unknown, and the ornaments of style are condemned or forgotten?" of a

---

* Travellers in America. Niles's Weekly Register, April 11, 1812, pp. 94–96 April 18, 114–118; May 2, 141–143; May 9, 162, 163.

country where the men are "turbulent citizens, abandoned Christians, inconstant husbands, unnatural fathers, and treacherous friends"? That our countrymen may know how deeply indebted they are for this condescension, it is but necessary to point out the many proofs of their unworthiness as detailed by the "legitimate" sons of the mother-country who have lived and travelled among them, who have seen them in all their nakedness, and who must, therefore, be competent to form a correct judgment. Then followed a scathing review of the book of each "hired traveller."

After the second war with Great Britain, however, this criticism of America took on a more serious form. Critics of reputation, men of influence, periodicals of standing, began to join in the hue and cry, till readers on this side of the water were convinced that a deliberate and well-laid scheme to decry the United States was on foot in Great Britain. Some thought the purpose was to stop immigration; others attributed it to a desire for revenge aroused by the events of the war; still others declared that the calumniators were bent on disgracing us in the eyes of Europe. But whatever the aim, all agreed that the time for silence was gone; that the false statements must be refuted and the slanders once for all put at rest. As might have been expected, the sharp retorts from this side of the water drew forth yet more bitter rejoinders from Great Britain, which were answered in turn, only to be replied to in course till an international controversy sprang up, and for ten years was waged in a manner far from creditable to either side. Reviews and magazines whose pages might well have been put to a better use, men of parts and learning whose ability might well have been expended in a better cause were not ashamed to engage in the fruitless and unseemly wrangle. And when at last the dispute ended where it began there had been engendered in this country a hearty detestation of Great Britain which strongly affected international relations for many years to come.

This phase of the dispute may be said to have become serious in January, 1814, when the Quarterly Review published an article entitled "Inchiquin's Favorable View of the United

States." * The author of the review was declared to be the poet laureate Southey. The event which called it forth was the publication of Macon's report on the conduct of the British † in the war then waging. Mr. Macon was chairman of a committee of the House of Representatives appointed to report on the spirit and manner in which the war had been conducted by the British. The report was made late in 1813, and consisted of a mass of documents setting forth that American prisoners had been cruelly treated in British prisons; that naturalized citizens had been held as British subjects; that American sailors who happened to be in British ports when war was declared had been held as prisoners, though other citizens were allowed to depart; that American sailors had been pressed and forced to fight their fellow-countrymen; that flags of truce had not been respected; that private property had been pillaged and destroyed along the shores of Chesapeake Bay; that outrages of the foulest sort had been perpetrated on women at Hampton; and the cruelty and barbarity practised on American prisoners after the battle of the Raisin River far exceeded what was currently believed. To have replied to these serious charges, supported as they were by an array of documents and sworn testimony of eye-witnesses, would have been a difficult task. The writer, therefore, resorted to another method, and in the form of what pretended to be a review of Charles J. Ingersoll's Inchiquin's " Jesuit's Letters " ‡ made what was in reality a savage attack on the people of the United States based on half a dozen books of travel written by French and English visitors.

With Mr. Macon, the reviewer assured his readers, he would deal later, unless, indeed, the sober and more enlightened part of Congress, finding Macon's facts to be forgeries, forced him

---

* The Quarterly Review, No. 20, January, 1814.

† Report of the committee to whom was referred that part of the President's message which relates to the spirit and manner in which the war has been waged by the enemy. House Documents, Thirteenth Congress.

‡ Inchiquin, The Jesuit's Letters during a Late Residence in the United States of America. Being a fragment of a private correspondence accidentally discovered in Europe, etc., by some unknown foreigner. New York, 1810.

1814. THE LONDON QUARTERLY REVIEW. **311**

to put his report in the fire. Meanwhile it might be interesting and amusing to inquire into the character of the people who were being thus excited against Great Britain by their Government. Such an inquiry, said he, will enable us to appreciate the probable chances of forming cordial and sincere relations with our kindred on the other side of the Atlantic, and will tend to console us for the failure of our many attempts to effect such relations. Then followed a long account of our public men, of our Government, and of Congress; of our system of representation, our judiciary, suffrage, religious toleration, manners, morals, literature, and general depravity, based on the stories of French and English travellers. A public man in America was a man of the people, and a man of the people was one who frequented grog-shops, smoked cigars, and harangued the people with violent abuse of the opposing faction. Every free man, nay, every free woman,* in the United States was a voter, and every one was free who declared himself worth fifty pounds. Such extension of the suffrage produced a debased and ignorant body of representatives, and in proof of this the story of the Lyon-Griswold fracas was retold in full. As our national judges were elected by the President and the Senate and received but an uncertain compensation at stated periods, they were the creatures of the President and the Senate. As they held office during good behavior they were careful to act in all matters as the Government wished. The divorce of Church and state had been productive of a host of illegitimate sects—Presbyterians, Baptists, Methodists, Universalists, Moravians, Quakers, Dunkers, Shakers—all equally thriving under the neglect of the parent state, and finely illustrating the fanatical extravagance to which men are driven in the absence of a national church and established form of worship. An irreligious people must of necessity be an immoral people, and in evidence of this our magistrates, merchants, farmers, planters, tavern-keepers, were described and vilified in turn. Finally, the citizens of the United States were declared to be a people with little taste, not much manners, still less literature, and no genius at all, given up to dram-

---

* History of the People of the United States, vol. iii, p. 147.

drinking, gouging, fighting, duelling, boasting, and the sordid pursuit of gain.

The picture was too absurd to be a good caricature. The statements refuted themselves. No such people as the reviewer described ever existed in any civilized land. Yet the bitterness of the attack went home, and called forth two serious replies, the one * by James Kirke Paulding and the other † by Timothy Dwight. Paulding complained that, not content with the swaggering abuse of the people of the United States constantly appearing in such journals as the London Times and the London Sun, the British Government had of late sent paid agents to this country for the sole purpose of gathering material wherewith to misrepresent our national character and manners. Hired travellers, like Parkinson, poor and contemptible Grub Street hacks dressed out as gentlemen, had been employed to wander about from one American city to another, search out solitary instances of ignorance, brutality, and corruption, and from these draw general conclusions of national vulgarity and widespread depravity. This had been done on the one hand to stop the emigration of the working classes of England, and on the other to keep alive the stupid and bitter prejudice existing among the educated classes, which think themselves the most liberal and enlightened people of Great Britain. For years the British Government has glutted the markets of Europe with gross calumnies intended to harm us and our cause in the eyes of Europe. She has employed a standing army of hired critics to invent libels, and has even caused them to be published in the newspapers of Paris and Vienna. The governments of Europe have been made to believe that we are a people little better than barbarous, that we are without education and the habits and customs of civilized men, and that in America society is a bear garden in which men and women mix and riot without distinction as to character or rank.

---

* The United States and England. Being a reply to the criticisms on Inchiquin's Letters contained in the Quarterly Review for January, 1814. New York, 1815.

† Remarks on the Review of Inchiquin's Letters published in the Quarterly Review, addressed to the Right Honorable George Canning, Esq. By an Inhabitant of New England. Boston, 1815.

Dwight opened his reply with a strong expression of regret that two peoples which ought to be firm friends were rapidly becoming implacable enemies. Great Britain and the United States were bound together by the strongest of natural ties—by a common origin, by a common language, by similar laws, customs, manners, institutions, and by a scarcely less strong tie of common interests. The fruit of such a union carefully cultivated could not fail to be beneficial to both nations, but a severance of the ties must inevitably be prolific of untold evils. It was no slight matter, therefore, to see the journals of both countries bent on destroying every vestige of good feeling, and those of Great Britain most active in the work. Both her travellers and her journals, for reasons idle to seek, had long thought it proper to caricature America. Their pens were dipped in gall; their descriptions of our country were mixtures of maliciousness and falsehood, while their persistence showed a settled hostility toward the United States.

With these statements of the reasons which led them to reply, Paulding and Dwight took up, one by one, the many charges brought against our countrymen by the Quarterly Review, paralleled each instance of brutality, each case of vulgarity, of bad manners, of dishonesty, immorality, legislative or judicial indecorum, by another taken from English history, and showed that just such a caricature might be drawn of Great Britain as the Review had presented of the United States. At home the replies were thought to be final, but abroad they were not thought of at all, and year after year travellers from the British Isles continued to put forth books which cannot be described as other than lampoons on our country. The petty annoyances, the little inconveniences and unpleasant incidents met with in all journeys, were grossly exaggerated and cited as characteristic of daily life in the States. Men and women met with at the inns and taverns, in the stage-coaches and far-away country towns, were described not as so many types, but as the typical Americans. The abuse heaped on public men by partisan newspapers, the charges of corruption made by one faction against the other, the scandals of the day, were all cited as solemn truth. We were a whittling, spitting, guessing, reckoning, gambling, slave-beating, dram-drinking people, and a parody on the race whose language we spoke. To the amazing things going on about them these travellers were intentionally oblivious. A nation was in the making. Great principles of government of infinite importance to the human race were being applied and tested. A vast population was pushing its way westward, cutting down the forests, opening the prairie, founding towns and commonwealths, building roads, clearing rivers, joining great lakes and water-ways by canals, creating manufactures, and dealing with the gravest economic and financial problems on a gigantic scale and in a manner hitherto untried. Never within historic times had any other people presented so interesting a spectacle to observers. Yet all these phases of life were passed over in silence, or if mentioned were mentioned as fit subjects for ridicule and contempt.

Left to themselves, these books would have done little harm. Irritation produced by them would soon have been allayed, or, at most, would have called forth a few counterblasts in return. But they were not left to themselves. They were taken up by the great periodicals, by the Edinburgh Review, by Blackwood's, by the British Review, and by the Quarterly were reviewed at length, were cited as authorities, and were made the subjects of long and savage articles on life in the United States, abounding in false statements, ignorant assertions, and malicious perversions of the truth. Readers were gravely told that " in the United States a debt contracted in one State cannot be sued for in the next, and a man who has committed murder in Virginia cannot be apprehended if he makes his way into the neighboring lands of Kentucky."

That " the States of America can never have a native literature any more than they can have a native character. Even their wildernesses and deserts, their mountains, lakes, and forests, will produce nothing romantic or pastoral, for these remote regions are only relinquished by pagan savages to receive into their deep recesses hordes of discontented Democrats, mad, unnatural enthusiasts, and needy or desperate adventurers."

That " when the American captains could not fight to advantage during the last war they ran away, and in some instances most shamefully. Their Frolic, for instance, after vainly endeavoring to escape by flight, surrendered to the Orpheus and Shelburne without firing a single shot."

That " in the southern parts of the Union the rites of our holy faith are almost never practised."

" The North American Republicans are the most vain, egotistical, insolent, rodomontade sort of people that are any-where to be found.   They give themselves airs."

" The Americans have no history—nothing on which to exercise genius and kindle imagination."

" One third of the people have no church at all.   Three and a half millions enjoy no means of religious instruction. The religious principle is gaining ground in the northern parts of the Union; it is becoming fashionable among the better orders of society to go to church."

" The greater number of States declare it to be unconsti-tutional to refer to the providence of God in any of their public acts."

" Every freeman in America—ay, and free woman, too— is a voter, and every one is free who declares himself worth fifty pounds; none think of boggling if required to answer to this qualification; none more expert at an evasion or equivoca-tion than a citizen of the United States.   Besides, a man must be of little value if he is not worth fifty pounds; he would fetch that sum as a redemptioner.*   The supreme felicity of a true-born American is inaction of body and inanity of mind.†   No such character as a respectable country gen-tleman is known in America.   For the practitioners of law, physic, and surgery no preparatory course of study, no testi-monial of competency, no board of examination, no particular qualification, no diploma, no license, are required.‡   America is all a parody—a mimicry of her parent.   It is, however, the mimicry of a child, tetchy and wayward in its infancy, abandoned to bad nurses, and educated in low habits."

" We do not mean to deny the charges against the litera-ture and learning of the Americans.   Literature is one of those finer manufactures which a new country will always find it easier to import than to raise.   There must be a great accu-

---

* Quarterly Review, No. 20.   † Ibid., No. 38.   ‡ Ibid., No. 20.

officials, the success of universal suffrage, the cheapness and speediness of justice, administered by a judge "without a calorific wig and particolored gown, in coat and pantaloons." He had much to say that was complimentary, but he had something to say concerning our bad manners, our lack of a literature, our slave-holding, and closed with a statement that, after all, England was a far happier land. "Native literature," said he, "the Americans have none. It is all imported. They had indeed a Franklin, and he may live for half a century more on his fame. There is, or was, a Mr. Dwight who wrote some poems, and his baptismal name was Timothy. There is also a small account of Virginia by Jefferson, and one epic by Joel Barlow, and some pieces of pleasantry by Mr. Irving. But why should the Americans write books when a six weeks' passage brings them in their own tongue our sense, science, and genius in bales and hogsheads? Prairies, steamboats, grist-mills, are their natural objects for centuries to come. By and by, when they have got to the Pacific Ocean, they may have epic poems, plays, pleasures of memory, and all the elegant gratifications proper to an ancient people who have tamed the wild earth and sat down to amuse themselves."

This was galling enough, but his remarks on slavery were exasperating. "If nations," said he, "rank according to their wisdom and their virtue, what right has the American, a scourger and murderer of slaves, to compare himself with the least and lowest of European nations? much more with this great and humane country, where the greatest lord dare not lay a finger upon the meanest peasant? What is freedom where all are not free? And these are the men who taunt the English with their corrupt Parliament, with their buying and selling votes. Let the world judge which is the more liable to censure, we who, in the midst of our rottenness, have torn off the manacles of slaves all over the world, or they who, with their idle purity and useless perfection, have remained mute and careless while groans echoed and whips cracked round the very walls of their spotless Congress."

"As for emigration, every man must of course determine for himself. A carpenter under thirty years of age who finds himself at Cincinnati with an axe over his shoulder and ten pounds in his pocket will get rich in America. But any man with tolerable prosperity here had better remain where he is." *

In the same vessels that brought copies of the Edinburgh Review to Boston, New York, Philadelphia, and Charleston went bundles of another British periodical—the Quarterly Review, January–March, 1819—with two articles on America more savage still. The books selected for review were Fearon's " Narrative of a Journey through the Eastern and Western States " and Bristed's " Resources of the United States." † Of all the descriptions of our country yet published, Fearon's was the favorite with the reviewers. He had been sent over by a colony of weavers to see if the stories of the prosperity and happiness of the people of the United States were true, and if there was in our land a spot where they could settle and be less burdened with taxes and blessed with more wages than they were in Great Britain. He went, it was said, as a serious investigator with a definite purpose. He represented men eager to seek homes in the New World. Yet he returns with an account which must be most discouraging.

At New York the streets were narrow, dirty, and infested with pigs; the laboring classes no better clothed than in Europe, but less careworn; the mercantile population were in appearance loose, slovenly, careless, and not remarkable for cleanliness. The whole white population—men, women, and children alike —was sallow. To have a tinge of color in the cheeks was a sure indication of English birth. The shopkeepers were a cold, indifferent set, who stood with their hats on or sat or lay along their counters smoking cigars and spitting in every direction. The existence of slavery, the advertisements of negroes and wenches for sale, the ostracism of free blacks, and the stories which he hears of slave-beatings and maltreatings, shock his ideas of liberty and give occasion for his reviewer to exclaim: " No man valuing genuine freedom or possessing real sentiments of humanity could for a moment tolerate the idea of

---

* Travellers in America. The Edinburgh Review, or Critical Journal, for December, 1818, to March, 1819.

† Resources of the United States, or a View of the Agricultural, Commercial, Financial, Political, Literary, Moral, and Religious Character of the American People. By John Bristed, Counsellor-at-Law, New York, 1818.

passing his days in a country where such brutalizing scenes are perpetually before his eyes."

Unlimited liberty of conscience charmed Mr. Fearon, but he was horrified to notice a total absence of devotion and the gross bigotry of sects. Religious duties seemed to be performed without one spark of true devotion. Men and women went to particular churches because they knew the preachers, or because their great-grandmothers went there before the Revolution, or because their interest would be best served by so doing, or because the churches were frequented by the fashionable set. As for the countless sects, they differed from the English sectaries in being more bigoted, more intolerant, more ignorant of the Scriptures. He stumbles into the bar-room of a roadside tavern and notes the absence of tables and chairs; he enters a grog-shop and is surprised that he can get nothing to eat.

Boston strikes him as offensively religious and strongly tinged with aristocracy, and affords him some fine specimens of Yankee inquisitiveness. Philadelphia has less business, less gayety, less life than New York. The men are given to the excessive use of liquor and tobacco, the women to rouging and reading the novels of Lady Morgan. There he witnesses a foul and corrupting spectacle known as an election of a governor, there he examines a cargo of newly arrived redemptioners, and attends a revival in a negro church, and is shocked at the brutality of the one and the blasphemy of the other.

From Philadelphia he travels westward to Pittsburg, which he finds full of English goods that command a ready sale, and English artisans longing to be home, and then goes on across the prairie of Ohio. " It is not to him," says the reviewer, " that we are indebted for the information that it is not all the French word signifies, ' green grass bespangled with daisies and cowslips '; *he* does not tell us that it is a wide expanse covered with rank, coarse, rushlike grass sometimes flooded middle-deep and wearing the appearance of an inland sea; but such is the fact. In Ohio, too, he sees negro slavery on the indenture system, and finds himself in a land where Spanish dollars cut into halves, quarters, and eighths, and paper bills torn into halves and quarters, constitute the circulating medium."

Kentucky affords him a sight of a hideous negro flogging, and brings him in contact with a population given over to drinking, swearing, gambling, gouging, and gander-pulling. To this the reviewer adds Indian scalping, and, supposing the River Raisin to be in Kentucky, turns that famous massacre into an American victory and describes the Kentuckians as cutting razor-strops from the backs of dead savages! Illinois is described as one unbounded flat of swamps and forests tenanted by a motley group of Indian hunters, squatters, land jobbers, lawyers, doctors, and farmers occupying land on speculation. At Washington the people seemed a century behind those of Boston, and half a century behind those of New York. They spent their time in place-hunting all day, and talking, chewing tobacco, and spitting all the evening. At the taverns the door-knobs were broken, the floors of the coffee-room strewn with bricks that had fallen from the walls and with plaster that had dropped from the ceiling.

Such pictures were well suited to the purpose of the reviewer, which was to discourage emigration. " There are in England," said he, " a numerous class of people who, having grown inordinately rich under its protecting shield, while the rest of the civilized world lay exposed to the ravages of war, have become feverish and discontented because the return of peace has not instantaneously shaken from their shoulders the burdens created by a protracted war. Too selfish to endure any reduction of their extravagant profits, they leave their country to bear its burdens as best it can and take wing for a foreign shore. The love of country, once the peculiar boast of Englishmen, the ties of blood, of society, of early friendships, of kindred habits, are all sacrificed by them to the one sordid passion, while they rush in crowds to deposit their wealth where it will be safe from the claim of their native land."

That such ungrateful and short-sighted persons might be deterred from wasting their lives and substances in our inhospitable land the reviewer then proceeds, with the aid of Fearon and Bristed, to construct a most dismal account of life in

America. The United States, in his opinion, was doomed to destruction. It was in a revolutionary condition and contained within it " the seeds of those sudden changes which scatter upon the wings of ruin all the labors and products of past experience." We had no established church, therefore we were an immoral and irreligious people. A church establishment, founded on liberal principles, was one of those blessings to which Englishmen were indebted for innumerable benefits. An order of men selected from all descriptions and classes, from the sons of the peer to those of the farmer and the trader, and set apart to cultivate knowledge, diffuse religion, and preserve virtue, must produce a more beneficial and abundant influence than can be dispensed by any other means. This blessing we could not enjoy. Upward of three million souls in the United States were destitute of all religious ordinances and worship. In the Southern and Western States societies existed for the sole purpose of rooting out every vestige of Christianity. Many serious people doubted the permanence of the Federal Constitution because it made no reference to the providence of God. " We, the People," was the constitutional substitute for Jehovah. A few State governments, as in New England and New York, did acknowledge God as the governor among nations, and occasionally recommended a day of general fasting, thanksgiving, and prayer. But the greater number declared it unconstitutional to refer to the providence of God. Virginia would not allow a chaplain to officiate in her State Legislature. Louisiana had rejected by an immense majority a bill for the better observance of the Sabbath.

The consequences of this were visible and awful. Among the many institutions to which England stood indebted for her comfort, her security, her prosperity, the courts of law were first in importance. " A peculiar character of dignity attaches to our judges, which gives them respectability allied almost to religious veneration. The nature of their education and their station, which forbids them from being foremost in the circles of even innocent levity, have a tendency to raise their characters and inspire a confidence in their decisions which must be unknown to the people of America. We hear of one of their judges appearing on the bench with a countenance battered in a boxing match; of another shot because he had approached to attack his neighbor with pistols and a dagger hidden in his bosom; of some engaged in duels as principals and seconds; of others posted as cowards for declining such contests."

As was the bench, so was the bar. The practitioners were advocates, solicitors, attorneys, proctors, conveyancers, and special pleaders all in one. The law was the repository of American talent—a talent which did not find its way to the bench, but was spent in intrigue for offices of state. Hence the bar was the school in which American statesmen learned the vulgar chicanery, so easily imbibed in a profession that teaches acuteness but does not inspire integrity. " All the Presidents since Washington and Adams have been lawyers, and so have almost all the secretaries of State, war, treasury, and navy. America, if not priest-ridden like Spain, is in a worse state— she is lawyer-ridden."

Besides being an irreligious, immoral, and lawyer-ridden people, we were ignorant. The number of books published in America which had any tendency to improve the mind or enlighten the understanding were few indeed. It was true that many of the most popular English writings were reprinted in America. But they seemed to be little read. Ages must pass away before America could find either leisure or inclination for the study of Bacon, Locke, and Newton. In every part of our vast country education was on too low a scale. The schools could do no more than create mediocrity in learning. " Meantime she may derive what consolation she can from the reflection that this low state of learning is the natural consequence of that spirit of republicanism on which she prides herself." We had a post-office; but such was the state of ignorance that little correspondence took place, and the post-office could not defray the cost of operating.*

" In America the emigrant must expect to find not an economical or cleanly people, not a social or generous people, not a people of enlarged ideas, not a people of liberal opinions or to whom one could express his thoughts free as air, not a

* The Quarterly Review, January, 1819, Statistical View of America.

people friendly to the advocate of liberty in Europe, not a people who understand liberty from investigation or from principle, not a people who comprehend the meaning of the words honor and generosity. On the other hand, he would find a country possessing the most enlightened civil and political advantages, a people reaping the full reward of their own labors, a people not paying tithes and not subject to heavy taxation without representation, a people with a small national debt and no standing army, and he would find little else." *

The attack of the Edinburgh in January was followed in February and March by Blackwood's Magazine with two articles on " The Means of Education " and on " The State of Learning in the United States." " Learning, in the true sense of the word," says the writer, " is not to be found in America, for the business of a scholar is not one of the occupations öf life. There every man of liberal education must have an occupation, and as there are no fellowships or scholarships in the colleges there can be no classes of society with sufficient leisure for the cultivation of science and general literature. The low standing of America in the world of letters and the poor showing she makes in our libraries is due to bad education, to want of learning, and the peculiar uses to which talent is applied. Franklin is their only philosopher whose discoveries have been of use to mankind, and if all the books ever written in the United States were set on fire to-morrow no scholar would miss them. We do not mean to say they have produced nothing worth preserving, but we do assert that they have not one master production of the mind in whose safe keeping all the world is interested. Mr. Irving has much talent and great humor, and ' Knickerbocker ' and ' Salmagundi ' are exceedingly pleasant reading; Belknap, Minot, Ramsay, Jefferson, and Marshall have written valuable histories; the sermons of Freeman, Buckminster, and Channing are fine specimens of eloquence and taste; in essays of the lighter kind Wirt and Dennie excel; but of works of the imagination very little has been produced. There is nothing to awaken fancy in that

---

* Fearon's Sketches of America. The Quarterly Review, January, 1819, pp. 124–167.

land of dull realities. No objects carry the mind back to contemplation of a remote antiquity. No mouldering ruins excite interest in the history of the past. No memorials commemorative of noble deeds arouse enthusiasm and reverence. No traditions, legends, fables, afford material for poetry and romance. America has gone through no period of infancy, no pastoral state. The whole course of life is there a round of dull practical duties. There is a task for each person each day. No man stops to admire the heavens over his head or to scan the charms of the earth under his feet. No one has time to study Nature or acquire a love for the beauties she spreads around." *

By this time it had become the fashion to assail the United States, and the fashion having been set, the British Review, or London Critical Journal, followed, and in May, 1819, regaled its readers with an account of the actual condition of the United States. At the head of the article stood a list of seventeen titles of books printed in or relating to America, but it was from two of them—Bristed's "Resources of the United States" and Fearon's "Narrative"—that the reviewer drew his stock of information. He began with the usual remarks on the infancy of our literature, and assigned the reasons. The thinness of our population, spread over an immense area of country, the lack of wealthy families to create a demand for original works, the want of competition and of rewards and honors capable of exciting emulation, were all so many obstacles to the production and circulation of literature. The man who compiled a heavy, dull, and tasteless political journal was sure to be richly repaid for his pains. But a literary work in which genius, wit, and learning combined to amuse and instruct was just as sure to be neglected. There were, as a consequence, few authors by profession in America. If here and there one existed he drudged along in his gainless calling, solitary and alone. He did not repose in the bowers of academic learning, surrounded and encouraged by the wise of other nations. Among his contemporaries there were no

* On the State of Learning in the United States of America. Blackwood's Edinburgh Magazine, March, 1819.

congenial minds with which to hold communion. And when his work was done there were no institutions, no publishers, ready to print his books on terms honorable and profitable to himself. " His labors do not end when the manuscript is delivered. A distant day is assigned for the payment of what he has earned, a day which too often never comes, and he is forced to be content with the assurances of his printer that delinquent subscribers, dull sales, and bankrupt agents have reduced his profits to nothing.

" It is quite possible that the Americans may become a powerful people, but they lack the elements of greatness. They may overcome a portion of the world, but they will never civilize those whom they conquer. The mass of the North Americans are too proud to learn and too ignorant to teach, and having established by act of Congress that they are already the most enlightened people of the world, they bid fair to retain their barbarism from mere regard to consistency." *

Continued criticism of this sort having become unbearable, the North American Review felt called on to reply to so much of it as related to the low state of letters. It was pointed out that, with a few exceptions, the age was one of critics and compilers rather than of men of genius; that while we could not claim for our poets a place with Scott and Byron, Campbell and Wordsworth, we could at least see indications of poetic genius which gave promise of great things in the near future; and that it was unwise to make an elaborate and voluminous defence of America in answer to the faultfindings of certain British critics and travellers. They could not much longer impose on the intelligent and impartial classes of foreigners. It was better to wait for our vindication as the result of our becoming better known and more justly estimated.†

But the vindication of our country was not to be the work of time. The task had already been attempted, and a few days after the North American Review appeared at Boston a portly volume, by Robert Walsh, Jr., issued from the press at Philadelphia. Mr. Walsh called his book " An Appeal

---

* The British Review, or London Critical Journal. Actual Condition of the United States, May, 1819.

† North American Review, September, 1819.

from the Judgments of Great Britain respecting the United
States of America." He began by stating in the preface that
he had been driven to write the book in the hope that it might
serve to refute the slanders incessantly heaped on his country
by British writers. In common with such Americans as were
well affected toward Great Britain he had hoped that the
false and contumelious language of the better class of British
critics would cease as time brought our true condition and
character into strong relief. But his disappointment was complete, for no one who paid attention to the tenor of speeches and
writings of late in Great Britain wherein reference was made
to the United States, no one familiar with the Edinburgh
and Quarterly Reviews of the past year, could fail to see that
no amount of evidence could silence the defamers. The desire to emigrate to America had spread among the rural population of England to an extent deemed hurtful, and the British
politicians, thrown into paroxysms of jealousy, had enlisted the
great reviews and journals in a common scheme of misrepresentation, to the end that the British farmer and artisan might
be filled with horror of republican America, and the nations
of the world with a distrust of the spirit of her Government.
The Edinburgh and Quarterly had assailed us with a fierce-
ness and rancor no provocation could excuse. The Whig journals had begun to rail in the same strain. The Opposition
had joined with the ministerial party in a hue and cry against
American ambition and cruelty, and credit had been given
to the coarse inventions of English travellers who visited us
for the express purpose of manufacturing libels, or had be-
taken themselves to this form of abuse after their return home
as a profitable speculation.

Thus beset by a band of implacable and indefatigable foes
who moved the public mind and directed the public affairs
of Great Britain, we were in duty bound to combat them by
every means in our power. A true showing of our character
and principles having failed, nothing was left but retort in
kind, for the British orators and writers never reproached
America without putting England in glorious contrast. It
was the excellent government, the liberty, the purity, and the
comfort they had at home which, they would have us believe,

quickened their sensibility of the evils and abuses existing on our side of the water and embittered the expressions of their hate.

True to this purpose, Mr. Walsh undertook to show, by the use of British authorities of the highest order, historians, and legislators, records of Parliament, nay, by the very journals employed to pour British venom on the American people, that Great Britain was as miserable and wicked as any nation on earth. He reviewed the political mercantile jealousy of Great Britain from early colonial times, and quoted in evidence Evelyn, Hume, Postlethwayt, Sir Josiah Child, and Adam Smith. He reviewed the general character of the early colonists, and cited Burke, Chalmers, and the Quarterly Review in their defence. He set forth the difficulties that beset the colonists, the conquest of the wilderness, the struggles with the French and Indians, the sacrifices made for the good of the mother country, and her ungrateful return. He summed up the many titles of the United States to British respect; reminded his readers that slavery had been planted, fostered, and maintained in the colonies by Great Britain despite every effort to get rid of it; and showed from British sources that the treatment of the Catholics and the state of her prisons, jails, and paupers surpassed anything ever known in America; that the condition of her law courts, her chancery courts, her Parliament, was as bad as ours, while the fondness of the British people for prize-fights and cock-mains exhibited a degree of brutality wanting in the American character.

To this defence the Edinburgh Review in time replied vigorously. Meanwhile, in the number of that periodical for the first quarter of 1820 was published the only one of the long series of attacks that has lived down to our day—the famous article by the Reverend Sydney Smith. The book he selected for review was Adam Seybert's " Statistical Annals of the United States," and the first part of the article was given up to a short epitome of its contents. He passed in review the statistics of population, trade and commerce, imports, tonnage and navigation, lands, the post-office, the revenue, the army, the navy, the national debt, and the cost of carrying on the Government; and having done this he exclaimed: " Such is the land of Jonathan, and thus has it been governed. In his honest endeavors to better his condition and in his manly purpose of resisting injury and insult we most cordially sympathize. Thus far we are friends and admirers of Jonathan. But he must not grow vain and ambitious, or allow himself to be dazzled by that galaxy of epithets by which his orators and newspaper scribblers endeavor to persuade their supporters that they are the greatest, the most refined, the most enlightened, and the most moral people upon earth. The effect of this is unspeakably ludicrous on this side of the Atlantic. The Americans are a brave, industrious, and acute people, but they have hitherto given no indications of genius and have made no approaches to the heroic either in their morality or character. They are but a recent offset, indeed, from England, and should make it their chief boast for many generations to come that they are sprung from the same race with Bacon and Shakespeare and Newton. Considering their numbers, indeed, and the favorable circumstances in which they have been placed, they have done marvellously little to assert the boast of such a descent, or to show that their English blood has been exalted or refined by their republican training and institutions. Their Franklins and Washingtons, and all the other sages and heroes of the Revolution, were born and bred subjects of the King of England— and not among the freest or most valued of his subjects. And since the period of their separation a far greater proportion of their statesmen and artists and political writers have been foreigners than ever occurred before in the history of any civilized and educated people. During the thirty or forty years of their independence they have done absolutely nothing for the sciences, for the arts, for literature, or even for the statesmen-like studies of politics or political economy. Confining ourselves to our own country and to the period that has elapsed since they had an independent existence, we would ask: Where are their Foxes, their Burkes, their Sheridans, their Windhams, their Horners, their Wilberforces? where their Arkwrights, their Watts, their Davys? their Robertsons, Blairs, Smiths, Stewarts, Paleys, and Malthuses? their Porsons, Parrs, Burneys, or Blomfields? their Scotts, Campbells, Byrons, Moores, or Crabbes? Their Siddonses, Kembles, Keans, or O'Neils?

their Wilkies, Lawrences, Chantreys? or their parallels to the hundred other names that have spread themselves over the world from our little island in the course of the last thirty years, and blessed or delighted mankind by their works, inventions, or examples? In so far as we know, there is no such parallel to be produced from the whole annals of this self-adulating race. In the four quarters of the globe, who reads an American book? or goes to an American play? or looks at an American picture or statue? What does the world yet owe to American physicians or surgeons? What new substances have their chemists discovered, or what old ones have they analyzed? What new constellations have been discovered by the telescopes of Americans? What have they done in the mathematics? Who drinks out of American glasses? or eats from American plates? or wears American coats or gowns? or sleeps in American blankets? Finally, under which of the old tyrannical governments of Europe is every sixth man a slave, whom his fellow-creatures may buy and sell and torture? When these questions are fairly and favorably answered their laudatory epithets may be allowed." *

In the following number of the Review was an article on Mr. Walsh's Appeal, and in this some attempt was made to atone for the bitterness of the previous attack and to soothe the animosity now assuming serious proportions.

It was, the reviewer admitted, a fact which required no proof even in America that there existed a party in England unfriendly to political liberty and decidedly hostile to all extension of popular rights. It was quite true that the party disliked America, and was apt enough to insult and decry her. Its adherents had never forgiven the success of her war for independence, her supposed rivalry in trade, and, above all, the tranquillity and happiness she enjoyed under a republican form of government. Such a spectacle of democratic prosperity was unspeakably mortifying to their high monarchical principles and easily imagined to be dangerous to their safety. Their first wish was that the States would quarrel among them-

---

* The Edinburgh Review, or Critical Journal, for January, 1820, to May, 1820, pp. 69-80.

selves and be thankful to be again received under British protection. That hope lost, they longed to find that republican institutions had made the Americans poor, turbulent, and depraved—incapable of civil wisdom, regardless of national honor, and as intractable to their own chosen rulers as they had been to their hereditary sovereign. " To those who are capable of such wishes and such expectations the happiness and good order of the United States, the wisdom and authority of its Government, and the unparalleled rapidity of their progress in wealth, population, and refinement, has been an ungrateful spectacle, and a subject of scurrility by the journals of this party at once disgusting and despicable. But need we tell the well-informed American that neither this party nor its journals can be allowed to stand for the people of England? that there is among that people another and a far more numerous party whose sentiments are opposed to the former, who are friends to America and to all that Americans most value in their character and institutions? who as Englishmen are proud to have great and glorious nations descend from them? who as freemen rejoice to see freedom spreading itself with giant steps over the fairest regions of the earth? and who know that when the drivelling advocates of hierarchy and legitimacy vent their sophistries with some shadow of plausibility on the Old World they can turn with decisive triumph to the unequivocal example of the New, and demonstrate the unspeakable advantages of free government by the unprecedented prosperity of America? Where then, we ask, is the justice or the policy of seeking to render a quarrel national when the cause of quarrel is only with an inconsiderable and declining party of its members ; why labor to excite animosity against a whole people, the majority of whom must be your sincere friends, merely because some prejudiced or interested persons among them have disgusted the great body of their own countrymen by the senselessness and scurrility of their attacks on yours? " *

---

* Dispositions of England and America. The Edinburgh Review, May, 1820, pp. 395–431. A Review of Walsh's Appeal from the Judgments of Great Britain.

The North American Review* now hastened to defend Mr. Walsh, only to draw out a yet more patronizing criticism from another English periodical, which up to this time had held aloof from the dispute.

"Several citizens of the United States," said the writer, " addicted to writing books or, like ourselves, given to the less ambitious composition of periodical reviews, consider themselves in a state of declared and justifiable hostility against the British press for what they are pleased to call the ' indiscriminate and virulent abuse ' heaped on their country. If the questions at issue were confined to the respective merits of Mr. Walsh, the American appellant against the calumnies of English writers and our periodical reviews he so bitterly assails, we should be content to let the belligerents fight out their differences in a course of harmless missile warfare across the Atlantic. But it is quite plain, from the tone of Mr. Walsh's Appeal and of his Boston reviewer, that they have taken up the affair in a spirit far exceeding that of a common literary quarrel. They have labored hard to impress on America that she is an object of systematic hatred and contumely in Great Britain, have revived obsolete questions for the mere purpose of exasperation, and have discussed them in a tone of the fiercest recrimination. Now, the generality of Englishmen know of their own knowledge that in this country America is not the object of hatred and contempt. On the contrary, we take a very anxious interest in all that relates to her. We feel the endearing influence of consanguinity in all its force. We cannot forget that the men he is seeking to inflame against us are chiefly the children of British subjects; we cannot forget that our fathers were the countrymen of Washington and Franklin; we cannot bring ourselves to look on their land as absolutely foreign ground. Many generations must pass away and great changes in our common sentiments and relations mark the close of each before a contest between America and Great Britain can be anything else than what the late one was—an unnatural civil war. We cannot but feel that the character of the principles and institutions that most attach us to our own country is vitally connected with the moral and political destiny of

---

* North American Review, 1820.

the United States; that, in spite of the violent separations and of many changes of forms and titles that have since taken place, the Americans of future times will be regarded by the world as a race either of improved or degenerate Englishmen."

Entertaining such sentiments, the writer went on to defend the British press from the sweeping charges made against it by Mr. Walsh and Mr. Everett; pointed out the many complimentary things said by Mr. Smith in the review which had excited so much wrath; declared that nothing worse had been said of America than was said every day about kings and queens, ministers and judges, the Bourbons, the Holy Allies, and even of that august representative of what was most monarchical in the eyes of men, the Emperor of all the Russias; reminded our countrymen that no wise or sober American need feel alarm for the character and dignity of his nation, even though a Scotch critic did make light of Mr. Joel Barlow's inspiration, or Mr. Sydney Smith's pen in an hour of thoughtless gayety did address some friendly admonition to the United States under the homely appellation of Jonathan, and then proceeded to find the cause of this American sensitiveness.

The critic found it in a peculiarity of our national vanity. "Other nations," said he, "boast of what they are or have been, but the true citizen of the United States exalts his head to the skies in the contemplation of what the grandeur of his country is going to be. Others claim respect and honor because of the things done by a long line of ancestors; an American glories in the achievements of a distant posterity. Others appeal to history; an American appeals to prophecy, and with Malthus in one hand and a map of the back country in the other he boldly defies us to a comparison with America as she is to be, and chuckles in delight over the splendors the geometrical ratio is to shed over her story. This appeal to the future is his never-failing resource. If an English traveller complains of their inns and hints his dislike to sleeping four in a bed he is first denounced as a calumniator and then told to wait a hundred years and see the superiority of American inns to British. If Shakespeare, Milton, Newton, are named, he is again told to 'wait till we have cleared our land, till we have idle time to attend to other things; wait till 1900, and then see how much nobler our poets and profounder our astronomers and longer our telescopes than any that decrepit old hemisphere of yours will produce.'

" The American propensity to look forward with confidence to the future greatness of their country may be natural and laudable. But when they go further and refer to the wished-for period as one in which the glory of England shall be extinguished forever, their hopes become absurdities. Let us suppose the day is come when their proudest predictions are accomplished, when the continent shall be theirs from sea to sea; when it shall be covered by contiguous circles of independent states, each a kingdom in itself, with the great Federal Constitution like a vast circumference binding them together in strength and union, and when it shall be the home of countless millions of free and enlightened Americans. Let us suppose the time arrived when American fleets shall cover every sea and ride in every harbor for purposes of commerce, of chastisement, or protection; when the land shall be the seat of freedom, learning, taste, morals, all that is most admirable in the eyes of man, and when England, sinking under the weight of years and the manifold casualties by which the pride of empires is levelled in the dust, shall have fallen from her high estate. In that day of her extremity, what language might an Englishman hold to an American boasting of the superior grandeurs of his country? Might he not truly say: America has reason to be proud; but let her not forget whence came the original stock of glory she has laid out to such good account. Might we not say: Who were the men who first cleared the barren tracts that have since become a garden? Englishmen. Who taught you the art of navigation? Englishmen. From what code did you catch the first spirit of freedom which won and has so happily maintained your independence? From the laws and institutions of England. Where did your infant science and literature find their models of deep thought, of exquisite composition, of sublime conception? In the writings of immortal Englishmen, your ancestors and instructors. No, America can achieve no glory in which England has not a share. Let the name of England fade from the list of nations, let her long line of statesmen, heroes, scholars, be buried in oblivion; yet so long as an empire of Americans survives, speaking her language, cherishing her institutions, and imitating her example, her name shall be pronounced with veneration throughout the world, and her memory be celebrated by a glorious monument.

" We think America is doing wonders. We heartily congratulate her. But she is yet in her infancy, and must not, like a forward child born to a great estate and the dupe of domestic adulators, assume the tone of riper years. She must be docile, industrious, patient of rebuke that conveys instruction. She must not talk much of glory till it comes." *

The review was clearly intended to be friendly. But it was not so received in America. The very moderation of its language, the very seriousness of its effort to be just, made its patronizing air and unasked advice most offensive, and led the North American to review the reviewer.

" American writers," said Mr. Everett, " who defend the United States against injuries done her by the English press are accused of ambition to create a bustle about themselves or of being troubled with fretfulness in behalf of their country. But when one looks at the present case and considers how much has been said in abuse of this country in England; when we recall the number of low-bred persons who have fled from justice in their native land and crossed the Atlantic to traverse and vilify ours; when we see their slanders incorporated into respectable literary journals and given an importance they would not otherwise attain; when we consider that from the correspondence of a minister of state down to the school-boy's declamation the English public has shown itself a too willing patron of abuse of America, we fail to understand how any reply on our part can be called fretful and irritable. Our press was long, very long, silent. It did little else than meekly reprint the calumnies sent over to us, as our brethren at Edinburgh justly state, ' by the bale and the ship-load.' And now that Mr. Walsh has most amply refuted their base charges,

---

* Complaints in America against the British Press. The New Monthly Magazine and Literary Journal. London, February, 1821.

and we have reviewed the book, we are accused of bad motives and a bad spirit.

" The reviewer has accused us of smarting under a Scotch critic's treatment of Joel Barlow's inspiration. Now, nothing is more notorious than that the ' Columbiad ' has ever been regarded by the judicious public in our country as a total failure, that it has been read little and liked less, and that on its appearance the critical journals of America handled it as severely as those on the banks of the Forth and the Thames. The multitude of new and worthless words the poet coined were the cause of far more unsparing criticism here than in England. Nor is this all. The persecution of Americanisms at large has nowhere in Great Britain been pursued with such keenness as in America. We stated in our review of Mr. Walsh's book, and we repeat it now, that, on the whole, the English language is better spoken here than in England. We do not say that it is better spoken by well-educated people in America than by well-educated persons in Great Britain, but we do say that there is no part of America in which the corruption of the language has gone so far as in the heart of the English counties. As for the specimens of pretended American dialect found in the books of travellers, we pity the Englishman who cannot see that they are fabrications compiled from local observations made in the porter-houses and oyster-cellars of Boston, New York, and Philadelphia. Whence should we learn bad English? We are derided and taunted with our dependence on the English press. We are scorned for the poverty of our literature. It is well known that our children's books are English; that many of our text-books used in the colleges are English; that our standard professional works are English; that our stage is supplied from England; that Byron, Campbell, Southey, Scott, are as familiar to us as to their own countrymen; that we receive the first sheets of the new novel before the last one is thrown off at Edinburgh; that we reprint every English work of merit before it is dry from the English press; and that the English version of the Scriptures is the great source whence the majority of Americans imbibe their English language. How, then, is it possible that we should not speak good English?

" Had the English critics who have exercised themselves on Americanisms remembered that language is a fluctuating thing, never stable, constantly improving or declining, always changing, they would have saved themselves trouble and us abuse. They would have remembered that many a good and useful word brought to America by the first settlers and of approved use in its day has survived here while lost in Great Britain, and recollecting, they would have asked whether we or they have done the language most harm. They would have remembered that such words as presidential, of, or belonging to a chief magistrate ruling by the consent of the people, and congressional, of, or belonging to a body of representatives equally chosen by the people, represent political ideas utterly unknown in Great Britain, are terms forced on us by our institutions and are not corruptions of the language. To charge us with affecting a new language is a calumny; to charge us with actually writing or speaking a corrupt dialect is equally so." *

Arguments of this sort availed nothing, and in a few months the Quarterly was attacking America as violently as ever in a review of four of the many recent books of travel.† The writers of each were abused for reporting what little good they saw in the United States, extracts were taken from their books to show the bad manners and vulgarity of the Americans, their shiftless ways, their want of refinement and general intelligence, and the conclusion reached that the praise so grudgingly given by travellers was not supported by the facts they recited, and that the republic was on the high road to ruin. " None," the reviewer said, " but the servile flatterer or the sour and discontented sectary in whose bosom no spark of patriotism now glows could think of placing the people of the United States in comparison with those of England."

---

* England and America. North American Review, July, 1821, No. xxxii; new series, vii.

† Views, Visits, and Tours in North America. Quarterly Review, April, 1822. The books were: Remarks made During a Tour through the United States, etc., William Tell Harris. A Visit to North America, etc., Adlard Welby. Letters from the Illinois, etc., Richard Flower. Views of Society and Manners in America, by an Englishwoman (Frances Wright).

Every fact stated by such persons belies their panegyrics and proves how vain it is to look for the arts and elegances of life, for refinement and general intelligence in so heterogeneous a population as that of the United States. Among a people so circumstanced the refinement of intellectual and polished society is not to be found or expected, and whether it ever can exist under a republican form of government may well be doubted. There is good reason to believe that as population grows more dense in the Western States the existing form of government will be found inadequate, and that the United States will, of necessity, become two, if not more, rival nations."

The horrors of democracy as displayed in America was a theme of which the editor of the Quarterly never wearied. He was at all times loath to lay it down. Each book of travels in our country was a new incentive to attack us. When, therefore, in an evil hour Faux published his " Memorable Days in America," * Gifford once again took up his favorite task and outdid all former efforts.† So intemperate was the article that the Boston publisher of the Quarterly refused it a place in the American edition,‡ and the editor of the North American Review prepared an elaborate answer.

The charges brought against us by Gifford, and supported

---

* Memorable Days in America. Being a Journal of a Tour in the United States, principally undertaken to ascertain by Positive Evidence the Condition and Probable Prospects of British Emigrants, etc. By W. Faux, an English farmer.

† Memorable Days in America. The Quarterly Review, July, 1823.

‡ The publishers of the American edition of the Quarterly Review have hitherto reprinted the whole in exact conformity with the original. Some articles they would gladly have omitted or curtailed as disgracing the high literary character of the journal by abuse and misrepresentation of the manners and character of the United States. These articles have generally been written in a style of great vulgarity, and by persons who are either entirely ignorant of the country, or who studiously misrepresent or falsify. With regard to this article the case is different. It brings forward wantonly and unnecessarily the names of private individuals whose feelings must be outraged by being thus dragged before the public. It goes further. The publishers have received a communication stating that this article contains a libel upon the character of a distinguished individual at Washington, which must be canvassed in a court of justice in his native country, and cautioning the American publisher against being accessory to this offence. The article, therefore, has been wholly omitted.

by citations from the pages of Faux, were the old ones of
ten years' standing. We were a dishonest, cunning, cruel,
lawless, godless nation. We held slaves, tolerated rowdy
juries, met civil officers with violent resistance, kept such
peace as we had by regulators and lynch law, could not speak
the English language correctly, and in our Constitution did
not acknowledge the existence of a God. " We are very much
inclined," said Mr. Gifford, " to ascribe the vicious and heartless conduct of the Americans, with which every page of Mr.
Faux's book teems, to the total disregard of religion on the
part of the Government. This fatal mistake in framing their
Constitution has been productive of the most injurious consequences to the morals of the people; for to expect men will
cultivate virtue and morality and neglect religion is to know
little of human nature. The want of an established national
religion has made the bulk of the people either infidels or
fanatics. In the back settlements here and there a fanatic
sectarian holds forth in a hovel or under a tree, and in the
old States no kindly associations are connected with the
gloomy and heartless performance of religious worship. The
village church, with its spiry steeple, its bells, its clock, and
well-fenced churchyard, with its ancient yew tree and its
numerous monumental records of the dead, are here utterly
unknown."

To this and to much more in the same strain the North
American replied in spirit and in kind. Gifford and Faux
were reminded that so long as slavery existed in the British
West Indies it was not for an Englishman to be horrified at
the sight of slavery in the United States; the instances of
American brutality they cited were matched by precisely
like instances drawn from the pages of British reviews; and
Gifford was warned that if he continued his abuse the North
American would read him such a lesson from English works
of standard authority as should force him to be silent or change
his tone. He was assured that what the political feuds of the
past had failed to do was rapidly being done by such publications as the Quarterly Review; that it was a matter of notoriety that the feeling entertained in this country toward Great
Britain was less friendly in 1824 than it had been ten years

before at the height of the war; that he and his review were
largely responsible for alienating two nations that ought to
be friends; and that it merited consideration whether or not
it was wise to do all that could be done by a literary journal
of commanding influence " to turn into bitterness the last drop
of good-will toward England that exists in this country." *

And now Blackwood's assumed the task of peacemaker.
" Let us calmly consider," the editor said, " whether such a
cause ought to have produced such an effect. Let us dispas-
sionately examine whether any article, in the Quarterly or
elsewhere, of the kind complained of should bring forth such
threats of retaliation, such hints that a repetition of Quarterly
reviewings of American manners will ' turn into bitterness
the last drop of good-will toward England that exists in the
United States.'

" The Americans complain that our travellers misrepresent
them by describing and exaggerating scenes of low life; that
our journals make ridiculous or angry comments on these and
similar details; that we deride their literature; and that several among us do not show for their government, their legislators, and their administration of justice the veneration with
which such things are regarded across the Atlantic. It is
made a matter of mortal offence that tourists who visit America
complain of bad roads, promiscuous inns, intruding companions,
bundling three in a bed, mosquitoes, smoky log huts, swamps,
rude servants, and vaporing associates. Why should Americans wonder at these complaints? In thinly settled countries
such as theirs, roads will occasionally be bad and inns indifferent. In States governed as theirs, men will be found who think
impertinence is freedom and reviling other countries doing
their own honor. But is the mouth of the traveller going among
them to be gagged? Must he see everything white or golden,
without a tint or dark shadow? Nobody but an habitual in-
mate of grog-shops supposes that the descriptions of coarse
habits and vulgar conversations, whether caricatures or real pictures of the inn, steamboat, and mail-coach manners, are intended to represent the manners of American ladies and gen-

---

* North American Review, July, 1824.

tlemen.   But if a traveller must of necessity mix with such society, must he hold his tongue?   Is not this sort of life worth description?   Let the American who feels sore read our travellers' stories of foreign countries.   Is there any conceal-ment of the sorry fare, garlicked dishes, filthy rooms, swarming vermin, and haughty landlords of Spain?   Do we fail to notice the awkward lumbering diligence of the French? the obstinate postmaster of the Germans?   Are our travellers more compli-mentary of the domain of the autocrat Alexander than of that of the democrat Jonathan?

" If we turn from travellers to critics on American litera-ture we find that America has no cause to complain of us as a nation.   We say the United States has produced no great writer.   Is it not so?   Classical learning is there underrated and neglected.   Knowledge of any kind is valued as a prepa-ration for some intended vocation, and not as a source of en-joyment.   The demand for business talent is so great and the rewards so tempting that men are drawn away from study. It is not to be expected that America will produce scholars, poets, dramatists, novelists, for many a year to come." *

A few months later the editor returned to the subject, and in the course of a review of another book of travels † in our country adopted a manner yet more conciliatory.   " Why is it," said he, " that up to this hour we have no such trav-ellers in America as we have in other countries—scholars, gentlemen, philosophers, profound and liberal thinkers, lovers of plain dealing?   Why is it that up to 1824 the statesman, the man of science, the yeoman of Great Britain, are ac-quainted with America only through the representations of such persons as Hewlett, Weld, Ashe, Parkinson, Welby, Fearon, Faux, Hall, and Miss Wright—persons who would not have been permitted to write essays on anything in a pro-vincial newspaper or poetry magazine? " ‡

---

* Blackwood's Edinburgh Magazine, October, 1824.

† A Summary View of America, comprising a Description of the Face of the Country and of Several of the Principal Cities, and Remarks on the Social, Moral, and Political Character of the People.   Being the Result of Observation and In-quiries during a Journey in the United States.   By an Englishman.   1824.

‡ Blackwood's Edinburgh Magazine, December, 1824.

But the editor of the Quarterly was not convinced. He did, indeed, for the time cease to abuse our institutions and our people; but he was soon denouncing our foreign policy, our diplomacy, our persistence in the matters of the Maine boundary, the right to navigate the St. Lawrence, and the ownership of the Oregon country.*

---

* London Quarterly Review, January, 1828. Answered in North American Review, October, 1828.

CHAPTER XLIX.

THE COMMON SCHOOL IN THE FIRST HALF CENTURY.

In the long list of institutions of which our countrymen have just cause to be proud, few hold so high a place in the estimation of the people, or show so marvellous a progress, as the American common school. To-day, in the five-and-forty States comprising the Union, more than fourteen millions of children are being educated at public expense by an army of four hundred thousand teachers, and at an annual cost of one hundred and seventy millions of dollars. When John Quincy Adams took the oath of office as President of the United States there were not fourteen million inhabitants in our entire country, nor did the common school exist as an American institution. In some States it was slowly struggling into existence; in others it was quite unknown. Here the maintenance was voluntary. There free education was limited to children of paupers or of parents too poor to educate their sons and daughters at their own expense. Elsewhere State aid was coupled with local taxation. Scarcely anywhere did the common-school system really flourish. Parents were indifferent. Teachers as a class were ill-fitted for the work before them, and many a plan which seemed most promising as displayed in the laws accomplished little for the children of the State.

The story of the rise and development of the common school in the United States may well begin with the passage of an act by the General Court of Massachusetts as far back as 1647. Each township of fifty householders was then required to employ some one to teach reading and writing to such children as might come to him, and each township of one hundred householders to set up a grammar-school and hire such masters as could fit youth for the university. A previous law, enacted in 1742, made it the duty of parents and masters to teach their children and apprentices to read the English tongue, to know the capital laws, and to be able to repeat by rote some orthodox catechism. These two acts—the one requiring parents to see to it that their children had the rudiments of education, and the other requiring towns to provide schools— form together the foundation of the earliest common-school system in our country.

As time passed and population increased and towns grew in size, the provisions of 1647 seemed to be too meagre, whereupon it was ordered, in 1683, that in every town of more than five hundred families two grammar and two writing-schools (primary they would now be called) should be maintained. But this was a step too far in advance. The number of parents who wished to give their children more than the plainest sort of an education did not increase rapidly with the growth of population, the grammar-schools became a burden on the people and after the union of the Plymouth Colony and Eastern Maine with Massachusetts a step backward was taken and their maintenance was no longer required.

Each town of fifty householders must, however, have one reading-and-writing school. This gave the people all they desired, and when the Revolution opened there was not a school of any importance in Massachusetts save one, which was not founded and supported by the people.

With the Revolution came the transition from colony to Commonwealth, the adoption in 1780 of a written Constitution which made it the duty of the General Court to cherish public and grammar-schools, and nine years later the enactment of a law which arranged the towns in four great classes,*

---

* In the first class were those of less than fifty families, where no schools were required to be kept. In the second were those of from fifty to one hundred householders, where a school or schools to teach children reading, writing, arithmetic, orthography, the English language, and " decent behavior " must be kept for such time as should be equivalent to six months each year. Towns of from one hundred to one hundred and fifty householders made the third class, and were required not only to maintain the schools of the second class, but in addition to provide masters to give instruction in the English language for such time as should be equivalent to twelve months. Towns and districts of two hundred and more families

specified the kind and number of schools that each must support, and planted the district system in New England. In many parts of Massachusetts the people were scattered far and wide. To force the children to come long distances over bad roads and in foul weather to attend one school would be such a hardship that the framers of the law most wisely provided that the inhabitants of each town should mark out as many districts as they saw fit, establish one school in each, and pay the salary of the master by a tax on polls and ratable estates. Not till 1800 were the towns authorized to raise money to build and furnish school-houses. Prior to that year, and indeed long after, district schools were kept in the basements of churches or in rude cabins erected by the voluntary labor of the people.

Funds for school uses were raised by a tax laid by the legal voters in town meeting assembled. At these gatherings each freeman might propose such a sum as he thought sufficient, and on the amounts so named the mind of the town was taken, beginning with the highest and going down in order till one received the approval of the majority. The tax so voted was then assessed on property within the town, was collected in the usual way, and the money divided among the districts in proportion to the number of children of school age, and paid to the trustees. These officials, one for each district, were elected by the people in public meeting at the school-house, and charged with the duty of hiring the teachers, caring for the school property, and receiving and expending the school money. Two school sessions were held each year. That in summer was for young children and girls, was conducted by a young woman, and extended over a term of from five to thirteen weeks, during which the subjects taught were reading, writing, and spelling. That in the winter was kept by a young man, and was attended by both girls and boys, who received instruction in reading, writing, arithmetic, English grammar, geography, the Constitution of the United States, the Constitution of Massachusetts, and the dictionary. From time to time poems, fragments of orations, and extracts from plays were committed

---

were further required to support a grammar-school to afford instruction in Latin, Greek, and English.

to memory and delivered by some scholar in the upper class as an exercise in public speaking.

Prior to 1800 there were few text-books deserving of the name. Indeed, at that date, in some subjects there were no text-books used. But a quarter of a century witnessed great changes, and the task of the master was now made easier by the readers and spellers of Noah Webster; the geographies of Woodbridge, Willard, and Morse; the grammars of Murray and Greenleaf; the arithmetics of Adams and Smith; and the fine series of readers prepared by John Pierpont.

Improvement in the appliances for teaching was not accompanied by a like improvement in the art of teaching. As a rule district teachers were not persons trained for their work, nor were they zealous in the cause of education. Some were young men studying at Harvard, or preparing for a profession, or casting about for something to do. These seem to have given satisfaction. But with the work done by another class, those who taught because it was easier to teach than to plough, who became pedagogues because, after many trials in many fields of labor, they despaired of eking out a livelihood in any other, very serious fault was found. The law of 1789 ordered that no one should be a school-master who could not produce evidence of good moral character, who had not been educated at a university or college, or who could not procure a certificate of fitness from a minister settled in the town where the school was to be kept or from two others in the vicinity. But the law was not carefully enforced; men and women utterly unfit for the task were constantly appointed, sometimes because the district could not afford to hire better, sometimes because the trustee was careless, sometimes because he did not know the good from the bad. Governor Levi Lincoln stated no more than the truth when, in 1827, he assured the General Court that the cause of learning languished both from the indifference of parents and the incompetence of instructors.

Worse than all was the condition of the grammar-schools. They had never been popular, but had always been looked on by the people as costly, unnecessary, and undemocratic. Only a small number could afford to give their boys and girls any higher education than was provided for in the common schools. That such as could not should be taxed for the benefit of such as could was taxing the many for the benefit of the few, which, was unfair, unjust, and contrary to democratic principles. When the educational system was revised in 1789 this feeling was so strong that the provision of the old law was swept away, and no town of less than two hundred families was required to support a grammar-school, and even with this not every such town complied.

The grammar-school, however, was little missed, for its place had already been taken and its work better done by academies founded by towns, individuals, or denominations. Some were merely chartered by the Commonwealth and empowered to hold property and educational funds. Of these, fourteen were flourishing in Massachusetts before 1800. Others were directly aided with gifts of land or money.*

None of them were free, but the cost of tuition was not beyond the reach of such as chose to strive for it; they were open to girls and boys alike on equal terms, and fully met the needs of the few who were not content to end their education with reading, writing, and arithmetic.

Excellent as was the educational system of Massachusetts in theory, time had shown it faulty in practice. Lack of proper and constant supervision of the districts led to the employment of unfit teachers. There was too wide an interval between the common school and the college, and these two defects the Commonwealth sought to remedy by the law of 1826. Thenceforth every town of five hundred families was required to maintain a free English high-school; every town of four thousand inhabitants a high-school of such grade as to fit students for college; and all towns to elect a school committee of three, or some multiple of three, to which was expressly assigned the duty of examining teachers and supervising the schools in their district. But this law in turn was

---

* Before 1797 four such institutions in Maine and three in Massachusetts had received each a township of land. With the immense tracts of forest in Maine to draw on, it was easy to be generous, and in 1797 several other academies were given half a township of wild land in Maine in order that there might be one academy for every twenty-five thousand people.

undid the work of 1793, ordered that the money to be derived from the sale of lands in the Western Reserve should be a permanent and irreducible fund; stripped the church societies or parishes of all " power to act on the subject of schooling "; authorized " all the inhabitants living within the limits of the located societies who by law have or may have the right to vote in town meeting " to assemble annually in October, bade them organize for the transaction of all business concerning education, and left to these societies the free use of their shares of the interest yielded annually.

A few months after the enactment of the law the committee in whose hands its execution was left sold the land for $1,200,000, payable in five years, and the first State school fund in our history was created. Interest was allowed to accumulate till 1799, when $60,000 was distributed on the basis of polls and ratable estates.

From 1795 to 1800 the trust was managed by the men who sold the land; but in 1800 the care of it was assigned to a commission of four, who seem to have been both unfit and negligent. The investments were bad, the interest was not collected, and the whole fund threatened with extinction, when the commission was abolished, and James Hillhouse called from the United States Senate to assume the duty of " commissioner of the school fund." By him it was finely administered. Old debts due from the original purchasers of the land were recovered, overdue interest collected, good securities substituted for bad, the principal raised in fifteen years to $1,719,000, and more than three quarters of a million dollars divided among the societies. Education, however, steadily declined. Now that the maintenance of high-schools was not obligatory, they were no longer founded. The steady increase of the principal and the large dividends, averaging fifty thousand dollars a year, made the people less and less inclined to tax themselves, and more and more disposed to depend on the annual distribution and the State allowance of two dollars on every one thousand raised by taxation. But in 1820, when the income of the school fund reached sixty-two thousand dollars, the State abolished the annual allowance from its treasury, and the dividend became practically the sole means of support. Then the school system went down rapidly, till it became little more than a number of commonplace district schools held for a few weeks in summer and a few in winter in wretched school-houses, taught by teachers of little ability and destitute of aids, and closed when the money obtained from the State was expended.*

Between Massachusetts and Connecticut, the earliest Commonwealths to attempt the free education of the people, lay the little State of Rhode Island, where as yet, save in Providence, no free-school system existed. Town records do indeed show that efforts were early made to help the poor to educate their children. Newport, in 1640, set apart a hundred acres and appropriated the income " for a school for encouragement of the poorer sort to train up their youth in learning." Providence, in 1663, ordered that one hundred acres of upland and six acres of meadow, or, in lieu of it, eight acres of lowland, should be laid out, reserved for the maintenance of a school, and the tract called " the school lands of Providence." Bristol, in 1682, voted that parents having children of school age should pay threepence a week to a school-master, and that the town should raise enough more by taxes to make his salary twenty-four pounds a year. Later the license fees paid by keepers of inns and taverns were used for support of the town school. Kingston, in 1696, gave land to Harvard for the education of youths whose parents could not afford to support them. Excellent as all this was, the aid afforded was small, and down almost to the Revolution the private school seems to have been the seat of education. After the close of the French and Indian War, however, the people of Providence thought seriously of founding a free-school system, and went so far as to listen to reports on buildings and on a scheme of management for four schools. But the voters were in nowise

---

* The history of education in Connecticut is fully covered by History of Education in Connecticut, by Bernard C. Steiner, Bureau of Education Circular of Information, No. 2, 1893. Barnard's History of Common Schools in Connecticut. The American Journal of Education, vol. iv. The American Common School in New England. Rev. A. D. Mayo. Educational Report, 1894–'95, chap. xxxix. Report of the Connecticut Board of Education for 1876.

before 1799. As the five-year limit was then fast expiring, with no prospect of renewal, a lottery was chartered to raise one hundred thousand dollars in four drawings.

By this time the school system had utterly collapsed, and Clinton, the steady friend and unflinching advocate of free education for the people, once more appealed to the Legislature. "The system of common schools," said he, "having been discontinued and the advantage to morals, religion, liberty, and good government arising from the general diffusion of knowledge being universally admitted, permit me to recommend this subject to your deliberate attention. The failure of one experiment for the attainment of an important object ought not to discourage other attempts." But failure did discourage other attempts, and though Clinton returned to the subject year after year till he ceased to be Governor, and though his successor took up the good work where he laid it down, every appeal went unheeded till 1805. In that year Governor Morgan Lewis urged the Legislature to set apart the State lands as a school fund, give the management of the fund to the Regents of the University, authorize them to mark out school-districts, appoint trustees, and levy taxes when needed to supplement the fund. The plan was far too radical for the ideas of the time. Nevertheless the Legislature made bold to take one step, and ordered five hundred thousand acres of vacant land to be sold and the proceeds invested till the annual interest should amount to fifty thousand dollars, when it should be used for the support of free schools.

Meanwhile a band of public-spirited men in New York city, deeply sensible of the importance of educating the horde of children growing up as outcasts in the slums, and weary of waiting for the State to act, formed a society and applied for a charter. "Your memorialists," they assured the Legislature, "have seen with painful anxiety the many evils which have arisen from the neglected education of the children of the poor." Especially deplorable was the condition of such as did not belong to any church and were not provided for by any religious organization. Cared for by no one, neglected by parents who were too indifferent, too intemperate, or too poor to even seek to give them an education, they were growing up in the densest ignorance, a prey to every vice. That something might be done to save these unfortunate little ones it seemed expedient to establish free schools in the city for their education, and for this laudable purpose the petitioners asked to be incorporated. The prayer was willingly granted, and in 1805 " The Society for Establishing a Free School in the City of New York for the Education of such Poor Children as do not belong to or are not provided for by any Religious Society " was created.

An appeal was next made to the public, with such success that it soon became necessary to decide on some scheme of education, and, after due consideration, what was then known as the Lancastrian method was adopted and put in operation for the first time in this country. Joseph Lancaster was born in London in 1778 of well-to-do parents. By nature he belonged to that class of men whose mission it is to labor unrequited for the welfare of their fellows. For one so constituted no better field existed than that afforded by the great city of London. The misery, vice, and crime fostered by ignorance that was itself the product of abject poverty deeply affected him, and, prompted by a strong love of children, he opened a free school in his father's house for the instruction of those whose parents could not pay the cost of education. Success with a few attracted others and still others, till the little room became too small and a school-house was built, in which, it is said, as many as a thousand boys and girls were often gathered.

Increase in numbers of scholars made necessary an increase in the teaching force; but to employ many teachers was beyond the limited means of Lancaster, who therefore met the need by an expedient which at once became the peculiarity of his system. Selecting the brightest of the advanced pupils, he made them monitors and sent them to teach little classes of younger children the rudiments of such knowledge as they had acquired.

In later years, when Lancastrian schools were high in public favor a hot dispute was waged over the merits and defects of the " monitorial or pupil-teacher system." The faults were many; but it should never be forgotten that Lancaster succeeded in deeply interesting in the cause of popular education large numbers of men to whom no other system appealed; that he provided a way of doing the greatest amount of good at the least expense, and that he gave an impetus to the movement in behalf of the public schools at the very moment an impetus was most needed.

Such was the experience of the society at New York. The work done was manifestly good; the Legislature, the city, and the people helped it on, and in 1808 the name was changed to the Free-School Society of New York, and its doors opened to all children who were proper objects of free education.

While the State fund was slowly growing the Legislature bade the Governor appoint five commissioners to plan a general system of State schools, and from them came a report which led to the law of 1812. Electors in each town were authorized to choose three commissioners to mark out as many school-districts as seemed proper. The voters of each district were then to elect three trustees to manage the local school, which was to be supported by the State and the people, for each town was required to raise as much money by taxation as it received from the literary fund. At the head of the system was placed a Superintendent of Education. To the office thus created Gideon Hawley was appointed, and on him, in 1813, fell the duty of putting the system in operation. The task was a hard one, for town after town refused to tax itself, lost its share of the State fund by so doing, and failed to establish a free school. At the urgent request of the Superintendent the tax was therefore made compulsory. Then success attended his efforts, and when, in 1821, the office of State Superintendent was abolished and the free schools placed under the charge of the Secretary of State, three hundred thousand children were receiving instruction in six thousand three hundred school-districts, at an annual cost of two hundred thousand dollars.*

In New Jersey there were no common schools. There

---

* The American Common School in New York, New Jersey, and Pennsylvania during the First Half Century of the Republic. Rev. A. D. Mayo. Report, Commissioner of Education, 1895–'96, chap. vi. University of the State of New York. Sidney Sherwood.

were private schools of various grades and parochial schools maintained by the several religious bodies.   There was a school fund created in 1816 and enlarged in 1817; there was on the statute-book a law authorizing the towns to tax themselves for the tuition of children of paupers and poor parents, but no system of schools open alike to the children of rich and poor without charge and supported by the public treasury.

Delaware was equally backward.   There, too, were private and denominational schools, and there, as elsewhere, in colonial times laws were occasionally enacted which may be construed into State aid to education.   Nevertheless the first legislation in behalf of popular instruction was a law charging the State Treasurer to set apart all moneys accruing from marriage and tavern licenses for twenty years to come, and such donations, gifts, and bequests as might be received from individuals, as a fund for the establishment of public schools. A little later the law was continued till 1820; but twenty-one years passed away before the first draft was made on the fund and a thousand dollars given each of the three counties to be used for the instruction of children of poor parents in reading, writing, and arithmetic.   The limitation to one class in the community defeated the purpose sought.   In the eyes of the people the money was no better than an appropriation for the relief of paupers, and neither the law of 1817 nor a modification of it in 1821 ever met with popular favor.   Not till 1829 was the common school really established in Delaware.

Pennsylvania, too, was very slow beginning her system. Her Constitution of 1776 did indeed enjoin it on the Legislature to establish in every county a school for what it termed the correct education of youth and provide for the masters such pay as might enable them to "instruct youth at low prices."   But in the stormy days of the Revolution and during the years of distress that immediately followed, the injunction went unheeded.   So, too, the Constitution of 1790, which replaced that of 1776, bade the Legislature establish schools throughout the State "in such manner that the poor shall be taught gratis."   But this also was disregarded for twelve years, and not till 1802 was the first step taken toward its execution.   Then the overseers of the poor in every county were commanded to find out the names of all persons unable to educate their offspring, notify them that their boys and girls might be sent to school at the expense of the State, and to pay the cost with money collected as the poor rates.

The law was regarded as a bold and hazardous experiment, and was to expire in a little more than three years; but ere that day came an amendment was necessary. Teachers, it seems, were not always willing to admit into their schools children they regarded as paupers. Another law, therefore, made it obligatory on all school-masters and school-mistresses who taught reading and writing in the English or German language and arithmetic to receive any child sent by the overseers of the poor or recommended by a justice of the peace and two freeholders.

The purpose of these laws was most praiseworthy. They fell, indeed, far short of establishing a free-school system, yet they were steps in the right direction, and, had the people been so disposed, might have been productive of some good. Most happily they were not so disposed. The law of 1802 was undemocratic; it set off the children of the rich from those children of the poor, invited the parents of the latter to come forward, make a public confession of pauperism, and ask that their boys and girls be sent at State expense to some school to become the object of contempt by both teacher and scholars. In 1804 the people of Northampton County therefore petitioned the Legislature to establish separate schools for the poor, to which their children could go without question. The committee having the petition in charge reported that in their opinion the children of all citizens ought to be taught at public expense, that there ought to be no invidious distinction of rich and poor, that the pay schools were wretchedly conducted, that the larger part of the teachers were utterly ignorant of the language in which they taught, that to acquire any degree of useful knowledge in such institutions required an immense waste of time, and that, considering these facts, it was no wonder so few of the poor had made use of the opportunity to educate their children without cost.

The committee went so far as to outline a plan for a system of free district-schools maintained by the State and open to all children under fourteen.   But the report was promptly laid on the table, and, in spite of appeals from the governors and the efforts of the reformers, the old method was contin-ued for twenty years.

Meantime the people took the matter into their own hands, opened Sunday-schools, established the Society for the Free Instruction of Female Children, the Aimwell School Association, the Philadelphia Society for the Establishment and Support of Charity Schools, the Philadelphia Union, the Philadelphia Friends' Association for the Instruction of Poor Children, and put in operation numbers of schools for white children and black.   The object lesson thus given was not wasted, and in 1812 the Legislature was persuaded to authorize the county commissioners to establish public schools in such manner as the city council should approve.   This too failed, and in 1818 the city and county of Philadelphia was made the first school-district of Pennsylvania and empowered to found free schools on the Lancastrian system for the education of children of indigent parents.   Joseph Lancaster was at once sent for, and within a year thirteen schools, with three thou-sand pupils, were in full operation.   Later other school-dis-tricts on the same plan were established at Pittsburg and Lancaster.

The history of the Lancastrian schools in Philadelphia, as set forth in the yearly reports of the commissioners, is full of interest.   The time of their establishment was one of great commercial and industrial depression, of hard times all over the Union.   Years afterward those who passed the dismal period 1816–1820 used to speak of it as " eighteen hundred and starve to death."   As no one would take an apprentice, no manufacturing establishment employ a young boy or girl, parents of the better class of working people gladly seized the chance to give their children an education, and by 1820 more than five thousand pupils were on the rolls of the pub-lic schools of Philadelphia.*   But with 1820 came better times.   Business was resumed, manufactures were springing

* Third Annual Report of the Controllers of the Public Schools of the First School District of the State of Pennsylvania, 1821, p. 4.

up, a demand for child laborers increased, attendance fell off rapidly, and in 1821 less than three thousand boys and girls were in the schools, and the controllers called loudly for legislative action. " If," said they, " the employment of youth in the manufacturing establishments be not accompanied with due attention to their mental and physical health and improvement, they will grow up unfit to discharge the duties of social life, and from bodily infirmities and vicious habits become burdens on the community. Employment of children in factories should be stopped until they have had an opportunity to obtain the rudiments of an education in the public schools." In 1822 the attendance was four hundred and fifty less than in 1821, and in 1823 was less than half what it had been in 1820.

" Of the children who have entered the schools, many," said the controllers, "have been taken away because of the high wages, which vary from fifty cents to a dollar and a quarter a week, according to the demand for labor by the manufacturers. The rising generation may thus sustain irretrievable loss in the abandonment of means for acquiring useful learning. Employers of large numbers of young persons in manufactories should be made to give them a useful education, and care for their health and morals. Something should also be done to rid the streets and wharves of the little children, who as beggars and petty depredators wander about in search of a pittance for the support of idle and worthless parents." An attempt to reach these children was made by associations of charitable persons, and infant schools were opened. But five years passed before the controllers were authorized to establish like institutions as part of the public-school system.

In the Lancastrian schools children were taught the alphabet, spelling, reading, arithmetic, and, when advanced enough, writing on slates and, finally, on paper. To this rudimentary education in the case of the girls was added knitting, useful needlework, plaiting of straw, and sewing on canvas. Down to 1822 none but white children were received; but in that year the controllers grew bold and opened a negro school, and were astonished at the large attendance and capacity of the scholars. Their apology for this daring act throws not a little light on the status of the free negro. " One of the most important acts of the controllers," they say, " since the last annual report, is the opening of a school for colored children." As this was to be the first instance within the district of the extension of the law to " this friendless and degraded portion of society, it became the controllers to examine the ground which they were about to occupy." Legal advice was therefore sought, and under the assurance that the practice was sanctioned in other parts of the State, was not forbidden by the Constitution, and was quite within the limits of the school law, the controllers ventured to make the experiment, trusting that the expediency of the act would not be questioned by the public.

Outside of Philadelphia, Lancaster, and Pittsburg the old system was in use, growing worse and worse each year. A committee appointed by one branch of the Legislature in 1822 to report on the state of education declared that the law of 1809 was not enforced in some counties and was much abused in others; that here the people were paying for the schooling of children whose names were on the registers but whose faces had never been seen in any school-house; that there the gross neglect and incompetency of the teacher defeated the purpose of the law; that elsewhere children were being sent to schools they were not fitted to attend; that it was nobody's business to correct these evils, and that nobody could tell positively whether pupils anywhere were so much as taught their letters. In 1824 reform was once more attempted, the law of 1809 was repealed, and all communities were authorized, if they wished, to establish free schools open to all children and supported by taxation. But before the law could go into effect such a storm of opposition was aroused that in 1826 it was repealed, the old one of 1809 was re-enacted, and the old order of things continued for eight years longer. Once, in 1829, the workingmen in Philadelphia endeavored to break it down, held a mass meeting, and chose a committee to report on the educational methods in Pennsylvania and suggest a remedy. With the exception of the cities of Pittsburg and Lancaster and the city and county of Philadelphia they found the educational system in shocking condition. The elementary schools were irresponsible institutions, owned by individuals, sometimes destitute of all moral character, often grossly ignorant, and always carried on solely with a view to private gain. In some parts of the State there were none even of this sort, and there ignorance and its attendants vice and crime held full sway. The defects of the law of 1809 were thus made worse by local conditions. Sometimes the provisions could not be enforced, for there were no schools. Sometimes to enforce them was but to put children under the influence of an ignorant, brutal, and immoral teacher. Instances were not wanting where the funds appropriated were embezzled or ignorantly misapplied or culpably neglected. Time and again, in order to save a few dollars, county commissioners had deliberately selected the most worthless schools, because they were the cheapest, and made them the only ones open to the poor.

Back of the whole system lay one radical defect. The ruling idea was pauperism. State aid was confined exclusively to the children of the poor. Many a one in consequence went without an education because the parents were too self-respecting to make their offspring an object of public charity, or of such standing in the community that they would not take the benefit of a poor law. The remedy suggested by the workingmen was " a system of universal free and equal public education " *—in a word, the common school of to-day.

What was true of Pennsylvania and Delaware was equally true of Maryland. There in every county was at least one academy aided by the State, and in return giving free instruction to a certain number of pupils. There, too, were innumerable pay schools, taught sometimes by men of character, but more generally by vagrant school-masters, redemptioners, or indentured servants. There, too, in Baltimore were all sorts of religious and benevolent associations for the education of boys and girls. There were the Female Humane Association Charity School; the Male Free School, maintained by the Methodists; the Roman Catholic Free School; the school

---

* A Report on the State of Education in Pennsylvania, accompanied with two bills, for the establishment of a general system of public instruction, etc., adopted by a town meeting of workingmen, July 11, 1830.

founded by the Carpenters' Humane Society; St. Peter's School; and another for poor girls conducted by the Benevolent Society of the City and County of Baltimore. But not till 1812 did the State begin the foundation of a system of county primary schools for the education of poor children by taxing the capital stock of each State bank, and setting apart the proceeds as a literary fund. In 1816 fifty thousand dollars a year for five years was ordered to be raised by lotteries, and the money added to the fund, and the levy courts of five counties bidden to appoint seven trustees, charge them with the education of poor children in each election district, and assess a property tax of twelve dollars for each child they might assign to any school. In 1819 the Governor laid before the Legislature a plan for raising money without taxation, and urged that an application should be made at once to Congress for a share of the public lands.

Federal aid to education began with the passage of the great land ordinance of 1785, which reserved every sixteenth section for the maintenance of public schools within the township. Not a word was said as to who should establish them, or of what kind or grade they should be. The land was set apart and reserved and nothing more. So, again, in the ordinance of 1787—the famous ordinance for the establishment of government in the territory of the United States northwest of the river Ohio—one article declared that religion, morality, and knowledge being necessary to good government and the happiness of mankind, schools and the means of education should forever be encouraged, and, obedient to this injunction, the Continental Congress ten days later ordained that the sixteenth section should be given perpetually for the purpose of maintaining public schools. But not an acre was actually given till the organization of the State of Ohio in 1802. Then, as one of three considerations offered by Congress in return for the exemption from State taxation, for five years from the date of sale, of land sold by the United States within Ohio, it was promised that the sixteenth section should be granted to the inhabitants of each township for the use of schools. Ohio accepted the conditions, and the next year Congress vested the title to all such sections in the Legislature of Ohio in trust for the use of schools, and for no other use, intent, or purpose whatever. But Congress, not content with this, gave two entire townships to be used by the Legislature for the purposes of a university.

What was done for Ohio was done for Indiana, Illinois, Alabama, and Mississippi. Louisiana over and above her grant had received an additional township of 23,040 acres; Connecticut another for the benefit of her Asylum for Deaf and Dumb; and Tennessee one hundred thousand acres for two colleges, and a like quantity for the founding of one academy in each county. As a result of this wise and liberal policy, great tracts had been ceded to the Western States before 1820, and it was these cessions which suggested to the Governor of Maryland the idea of demanding from the Governments similar grants to the old States.

The committee to which his remarks were sent reported favorably in 1821. The public lands of the United States, the report said, whether acquired by conquest or by cession, by treaty or by purchase, had been secured by the common effort or paid for by the common treasure of all the States, were therefore the common property of all, and ought not to be used for the benefits of any particular set of States to the exclusion of the others. Yet the domain was constantly so used, for never had a State (save Tennessee) or a Territory been carved out of it, but one thirty-sixth part was reserved for the use of schools. Grants, moreover, had been made to Western States for universities, colleges, and academies, till in the course of a generation the Government had parted, or was pledged by precedent to part, with fifteen million acres. Not a foot of this magnificent tract, larger than the State of Ohio, belonged or ever would belong to any State east of the Alleghany Mountains, though some of them gave much of the land in question and all contributed to the fund for the purchase of Louisiana. This, in the opinion of the committee, was unfair and unjust. It was using lands for State, not national purposes. It was converting the common property of the Union to the exclusive benefit of a small section.

Maryland proposed, therefore, to Congress and to her sisters that the Atlantic States, which had never received land to be used for the purposes of education, should be given tracts corresponding to those already granted or pledged to the States beyond the mountains.

In Congress the proposition met with small favor. Ohio, Indiana, and Illinois, Alabama, Mississippi, and Louisiana (Missouri was not yet admitted) said a committee to whom the matter was referred have received the sixteenth section of each surveyed township for schools, and two townships in addition for colleges and academies; Tennessee has been allotted two hundred thousand acres for universities and academies; and Connecticut one whole township in aid of her Asylum for the Deaf and Dumb. Land so disposed of is not subject to taxation by the State in which it lies. If, therefore, this policy be extended to the old States a large part of the soil of the new will be taken up with donation tracts, which cannot be taxed or settled without the consent of the sovereignties that own them. A far wiser course would be to set apart a certain percentage of the money derived from land sales, distribute it among the old States according to population, and subject the land when sold to taxation by the States or Territories in which it happened to be.

The States, on the other hand, were divided in opinion. All in New England save Massachusetts, and all in the middle section save New York, together with Virginia, North Carolina, and Kentucky, heartily approved. Massachusetts dissented because, in her opinion, the public lands are the property of the United States, and no State may claim a share of them, and because the reservation of townships and sections for the support of schools are not donations to the State within whose limits they happened to be, and no other, therefore, is entitled to demand an equivalent.

Failing to secure congressional aid, Maryland fell back on her own resources, and in 1825 adopted a system of district schools which each county was at liberty to adopt or reject. The people at their own cost were to buy the sites, put up the school-buildings, and supply fuel, books, and stationery. The State was to pay the salaries of the teachers. But so strong was the prejudice against taxation for school purposes that six counties rejected the system. Thirteen, indeed, adopted it, but not one ever put it fully into operation, and when, in 1828, the Governor declared the plan a failure, the office of State Superintendent was abolished.

In Virginia the history of popular education, with that of many another movement in behalf of the rights of man, goes back to Thomas Jefferson. To his labors Virginia owes the abolition of primogeniture, the abolition of entail of property, the divorce of Church and state, and the establishment of religious liberty, and had his efforts been attended with a like success she would have owed to him the abolition of slavery and the establishment of the common school. As early as 1779, while the country was still distracted by the Revolution, Jefferson had laid before the House of Burgesses a complete and characteristic plan of universal education. The counties, he urged, should be cut into sections five or six miles square, called hundreds, in each of which there should be a free school for teaching reading, writing, and arithmetic, supported by the people and open to all children. Once a year a " visitor " should pick from each school the brightest boy whose parents were too poor to continue his education, and send him to one of twenty grammar-schools to be founded and scattered over the State. From the batch thus sent annually to each grammar-school one scholar was to be chosen at the end of a year to go on with his studies and the rest dismissed. Six years later the lads thus selected were to be again sifted, one half dropped and one half sent for three years to William and Mary College.

Unhappily, the ruling class in Virginia was not at all disposed to be taxed for the education of the children of poor whites, and the plan was accorded no serious consideration for seventeen years. By that time the rising tide of democracy had reached even Virginia, and in 1796 it was ordained that a majority of the justices of any county, if they saw fit, might establish schools to be maintained by taxation. But they did not see fit so to do, and when the half century of independence closed Virginia was still educating her children in the old way—in " field schools," by the clergy, in academies, and in such colleges as then existed at home or in her sister States.

So was it in North Carolina. She too, like Virginia, had her State university, graduating four or five students each

year, and, scattered over the counties, male academies and
charity schools, and female academies supported by female
benevolent societies, female charitable societies, female orphan societies, aided to a small degree by the State.   Towns
in which the schools were might grant the use of the common
as a building site; money might be raised by lotteries; teachers and scholars were often exempt from military duty; but
as yet no common free school existed.

To the great educational movement which spread over our
country after 1800 North Carolina was indeed responsive.
Governor after governor appealed to the Legislature to spread
education into every corner of the State; * to put a certain
amount of education within the reach of every child in the
State; † to remember that if the wealthy alone be admitted
to the temple of science the most dangerous species of aristocracy may be apprehended.‡   But not till 1816 did the Committee on Education respond with two reports.#   One came
from a member; the other was presented in the name of
the committee by Archibald D. Murphy, whose splendid work
at a later day earned for him the enviable title of " father
of the common schools."   After listening to this report,
the General Assembly ordered a committee of three to be
appointed to digest a system of public instruction, and submit
it to the Legislature in 1817.   The plan then presented began
with the district school and ended with the college.   The
counties were to be cut into townships, these again, when containing more than one hundred families, were to be parted
into wards, in each of which one primary school was to be
established.   This was a feature plainly borrowed from New
England.   The next was as plainly taken from the Middle
States, for it required those who could to pay, and made the
schools free to such and such alone as could not afford to educate their sons and daughters.   Even these children were not

---

* Governor James Turner.   November 21, 1804.

† Governor William Hawkins.   November 20, 1811.

‡ These reports will be found in The Common Schools of South Carolina,
Stephen B. Weeks.   Report of the Commissioner of Education, 1896–'97, chap.
xxix.   Mr. Weeks's monograph is a model of its kind.

Governor William Miller, November 20, 1816.

to receive free instruction for more than three years. Above the primary schools were to be academies, one in each of ten academical districts, and above them the university, then twenty years old. Like many another fine scheme for the public good, the plan of the committee was too far in advance of the means of the State and the ideas of the people, and never took the form of law.

South Carolina, on the other hand, had established what might have been, but was not, a system of free common schools. Her law, enacted in 1811, required the people in each election district to provide as many school-houses as they had representatives in the lower branch of the Legislature, pledged the Legislature to appropriate annually three hundred dollars for the support of each school to be open to all white children, rich and poor alike, but provided that when the sum of money appropriated was too little to pay for the instruction of all who applied, preference should be given to destitute orphans and children of the poor. By this provision the intent of the law is made manifest. Schools were to be founded at public expense for the sole purpose of educating poor children. Only when the funds were sufficient could children of well-to-do parents be admitted. With this excellent intent the State went on year after year appropriating money till, in the course of ten years, three hundred thousand dollars had been drawn from the treasury, without producing any such result as the State desired. The districts took the money given them, rarely made any report on its use, and spent it as they saw fit. Generally they saw fit to expend it on some private or sectarian school, which in return gave free instruction to such poor children as the commissioners were pleased to send, and institutions of this class fed by the State came rapidly into existence. In 1812 there were one hundred and thirty-three, and in 1828 eight hundred and forty. But they were a very different sort from that contemplated by the framers of the law. Instead of free schools for the poor to which children of the rich might be admitted if the funds held out, they were generally private or denominational pay schools, which received the State's money and admitted in return a certain number of poor children sent by the commissioners.

To the educational system thus prevalent in all the States southward of New England, a system which aided with land and money academies and colleges of use to none save the prosperous, and ignored the poor or educated their children as paupers, Georgia affords no exception. The war for independence was scarcely over, indeed the British army was still at New York, when the State entered with zeal on a scheme of public instruction highly creditable to its framers. Land was set apart in Augusta for a university, a thousand acres were granted in each county for the benefit of a free school, and provision made for one academy in each of three counties. The year following the university was founded, endowed with forty thousand acres of wild land, and made the head of an educational body of which all public schools " supported by funds or public money " were parts.

To provide on paper for the creation of schools and colleges was an easy matter. But to actually bring them into existence, to put up the buildings, secure the teachers, and assemble the pupils required money. The money was not to be had, and 1801 came before the university began its career in a one-room building in a city of two houses. A half dozen schools had been started meantime, and a number of county academies, which the State aided as much as it could. But they were all pay schools, were far beyond the reach of the great body of the plain people, who received small consideration before 1817. Then two hundred and fifty thousand dollars, and in 1821 a like sum, was set apart and the interest appropriated " for the support and encouragement of free schools." It was a poor fund for the free schooling of indigent children, was scorned by the people, and, as committees assured the Legislature after ten years of trial, was " wasted," " misapplied," " dissipated with comparatively little benefit."

In the far Northwest, in the region once under the ordinance of 1787, but now parted into the States of Ohio, Indiana, Illinois, and the Territory of Michigan, the sixteenth section of each township had been set aside by the great land ordinance of 1785 for the support of public schools within the township. With so liberal a provision as this it should seem at first sight that from the very start the settled regions of the

Northwest Territory ought to have been dotted over with public schools. But this was far from the case, for many causes that could not be foreseen combined to hinder and delay the rise of the common-school system. Great tracts had been reserved by Connecticut and Virginia, and in these the Government did not own one section of land to dedicate to school purposes. Again and again it happened that, for geographical reasons, a township would be but a fraction and would not contain the sixteenth section. Sometimes the section would be swamp land or wholly or in part under water. For many years it was not settled whether the schools endowed with public lands should be controlled and managed by the local or the Federal Government. These obstacles in turn were removed, but others meantime had arisen. Save the emigrants who came from New England in the early days, the mass of the pioneers was composed of people from Pennsylvania and Virginia, who knew nothing of the common school, cared nothing for it, and went on educating their children in the way they themselves had been. The dire poverty of the settlers, the hardships of frontier life, the long Indian wars, the pittance which the lands yielded even when used for school purposes, were all so many hindrances. There were plenty of universities and colleges of the frontier type—a dozen students, a teacher, and a cabin. There were academies quite as good as the needs of the people required; but no common-school system, though the importance of such an institution was again and again urged on the authorities. As early as 1800 the Territorial Legislature, then assembled for the first time, bade the delegate to Congress do his best " to secure equal rights to school lands for all children," poor as well as rich. So strongly did this neglect of the poor appeal to the leaders of the movement for statehood that when Ohio made her first Constitution, in 1802, one section forbade the enactment of any law to deprive the poor of equal rights in the schools, academies, colleges, and universities endowed in whole or in part from the revenue arising from the Government land grants, and required their doors to be open to all scholars, students, and teachers, without any distinction or preference whatsoever.

Unhappily, the provision could not enforce itself, there was nobody to enforce it, and no change for the better is apparent. Here and there was what may be called a district school, but the custom of using the money obtained by selling or leasing the lands to pay for the instruction of poor children at a private school was almost universal. At last, in 1806, part of the State was laid out into districts and the revenue yielded by each sixteenth section was set apart for the support of free schools. But not till 1824 was a law forced through a reluctant Legislature to provide for the establishment of a common-school system supported by taxation.

The story of education in Indiana is but a repetition of that of Ohio. There, too, from the beginning of its separate Territorial existence, what passed for higher education was encouraged, while primary education for the people was neglected. There, too, was a struggling university and a host of academies, but no common schools. The first State constitution, however, required the Legislature to provide by law " for a general system of education, ascending in a regular gradation from township schools to a State university, wherein tuition shall be gratis, and equally open to all "; and under this, in 1816, was made the first attempt at a common-school system. Electors in each township might, if they saw fit, establish schools; but no money was provided, and few came into existence.

In Illinois the struggle was short and decisive. By an act of 1825, voters in any county might create districts, establish schools for white children between the ages of five and twenty, and maintain them by a tax of one-half mill on each dollar of taxable property. The law was not compulsory. Unless a majority of the voters favored a school, none would exist. Yet the idea of a free people being taxed for the support of schools was vigorously resisted, and in 1829 the Legislature repealed so much of the law as provided State aid, and declared that no man should be taxed for the maintenance of schools unless he first gave his consent in writing.

South of the Ohio lay the growing State of Kentucky. There, too, education had never been wholly neglected. From her earliest days schools of the frontier type, academies, and universities were endowed with land grants by Virginia and by her own Legislature. But the first serious effort at the education of the people by the establishment of elementary common schools was the creation of a literary fund in 1821. Into this fund was to go one half the net profits of the Bank of the Commonwealth. But in less than five years the Legislature diverted the money to other purposes, and no good came of the attempt.

Of Tennessee her historian says, with absolute truth, " The history of the common school is the history of her public lands, and the history of her public lands is the history of confusion." * Until 1829 no attempt was made to establish them, and that attempt was for many years a failure. Of colleges and universities there was no lack throughout the Union. Sixty-two were in full operation. But the common school, the school for the children of the people, was still to become a great American institution.

---

* History of Tennessee, James Phelan, p. 233.

CHAPTER L.

POLITICAL IDEAS IN THE FIRST HALF CENTURY.

WHEN our forefathers threw off their allegiance to Great Britain, and founded the republic of the United States, they announced to the world certain political ideas, all of which they firmly believed, but very few of which they ventured to put in practice. They declared that all men are created equal, and endowed by their Creator with the inalienable rights of life, liberty, and the pursuit of happiness; that government is constituted among men for the sole purpose of securing these rights; that it derives its just powers from the consent of the governed; and that, failing to accomplish the high purpose for which it is established, it becomes the duty of the people to alter or destroy it. Had they attempted to apply these new truths generally, the whole social fabric would have gone to pieces. Happily, they were not so applied. They were ideals to be held up and attained to gradually, and the very men whose lips were constantly heard demanding the rights of man, the inalienable rights of man, went on and set up State governments in which these rights were very little regarded.

Nor could it have been otherwise. In the confusion which followed the outbreak of the war for independence the colonial governments were swept away, and the people, taking authority into their own hands, established others of their own making. As the dispute was not supposed to be of long duration, the new governments were regarded as makeshifts, to serve till the question with the mother-country was settled. They were, therefore, of the simplest kind, and consisted of Provincial Congresses, Provincial Conventions, and Committees of Safety or Committees of Correspondence. In every case the Provincial Congress exercised all legislative authority, and consisted of one house, to which came delegates elected by the people, or chosen at a mass meeting of citizens, or appointed by the municipal authorities of cities or towns. The Committees of Safety were composed of men elected by the Provincial Congresses, and were intrusted with the duties of governors.

These bodies, however, had scarcely been set up when colony after colony was forced to consider the expediency of adopting a more regular and permanent form. Naturally enough, the first to feel this need was Massachusetts, and from her came a letter to the second Continental Congress, which met at Philadelphia on the tenth of May, 1775, describing the trouble the people labored under for want of " a regular form of government," and asking for " explicit advice respecting the taking up and exercising the powers of civil government." To this appeal answer was made that no obedience was due to the act of Parliament changing the charter of Massachusetts, nor to the Governor and Lieutenant-Governor who endeavored to subvert the charter; that these men should be considered as absent and their offices vacant; that the Provincial Convention should call on the people to elect assemblymen; that the assembly so chosen should elect a council; and that the assembly and council should rule till it pleased his Majesty to appoint a governor who would govern in accordance with the charter.

New Hampshire was next to apply " for the advice and direction of Congress with respect to a method of administering justice and regulating our civil police." She was told to set up such a form of government as " will best produce the happiness of the people "; and before 1775 ended, the very same advice in the very same words was given to South Carolina and Virginia. By May of 1776 all idea of submission had disappeared, and Congress, declaring it necessary " to suppress every kind of authority under the Crown," urged the colonies to take up civil government.*

Acting accordingly, all save two made constitutions of

---

* May 15, 1776.

government.* Connecticut and Rhode Island went on under their old charters, the one till 1818, and the other till 1842.

The instruments thus framed in the course of the war consisted in general of a preamble, a bill or declaration of rights, and the Constitution proper. In the preambles were set forth the principles of popular government, the purposes for which each particular government was constituted, and the reasons which induced the people to establish it at the time they did. The bills or declarations of rights consisted in every case of a summary of what were understood to be the inalienable rights of man. They declared that all men are born free and equal; that they have certain natural, inherent, and inalienable rights, among which are to be reckoned life, liberty, and the pursuit of happiness; that for the protection of these it is necessary that there should be freedom of conscience, liberty of speech and of the press, trial by jury, *habeas corpus*, no cruel punishments, no excessive fines, no *ex-post facto* legislation; that the military should be subordinate to the civil power; that no soldiers should be quartered on the people in time of peace; that the right to bear arms, the right to petition for the redress of grievances, the right to be secure from unreasonable search or seizure of papers or person should not be abridged, nor property taken without due compensation.

The Constitution proper provided in each State a government composed of three branches—the executive, the legislative, and judicial. The legislative branch passed by different names in different States: in some it was the General Court; in others, the Legislature; in yet others, the Assembly or the General Assembly; but in all save Pennsylvania, Georgia, and Vermont, there were two houses. No principle of popular government was more frequently and positively asserted than that taxation and representation go hand in hand. It is not surprising, therefore, that an examination

---

* 1776, July 2d, New Jersey; July 5th, Virginia; July 15th, Pennsylvania; August 14th, Maryland; September 10th, Delaware; December 18th, North Carolina. 1777, February 5th, Georgia; April 20th, New York. 1778, March 19th, South Carolina. 1780, March 2d, Massachusetts. 1783, October 31st, New Hampshire.

of these early constitutions reveals the fact that proportional representation in the Legislature based on population did not exist; that the number of men who sat in any House or Senate depended not on how many human beings resided in the State, but on how many taxpayers, or how many freeholders, or how many electors lived in the counties, or the cities, or the towns from which the delegates came. The Massachusetts Senate consisted of forty men apportioned among the counties according to the amount of taxes each paid. The more taxes the more senators. The same rule applied in New Hampshire, where the Senate numbered twelve. In New York representation was according to electors.* In Pennsylvania there was no Senate. In New Jersey, in Delaware, in North Carolina, population was utterly ignored, and each county, no matter what the number of its inhabitants, had an equal representation in the State Senate.

Nor did the people receive any more consideration in the lower branches of the Legislatures. In Connecticut each town, and in six other States each county, whether large or small, populous or thinly settled, sent exactly the same number of representatives.† Four others ‡ restricted representation to property owners, and apportioned the delegates among the towns or counties according to taxable polls.

No principle, again, of popular government had been more loudly proclaimed than the great truth that all governments derive their just powers from the consent of the

---

* The counties were arranged in four great senatorial districts, to one of which nine, to another three, and to each of two others six senators were apportioned. But it was also ordered that seven years after the close of the war for independence a census should be taken; that if it should then appear that the number was not justly apportioned, the Legislature should "adjust the proportion as near as may be to the number of qualified" *voters* in each district; and that when the number of voters in any district had increased by one twenty-fourth of that returned by the census, one more senator should be given to the district.

† Connecticut, two from each town; New Jersey, three from each county; Delaware, seven from each county; Maryland, four from each county and two from Baltimore and two from Annapolis; Virginia, two from each county; North Carolina, two from each county; Georgia, ten from each county, save Liberty, which had fourteen, the port and town of Savannah had four, and that of Sunbury, two.

‡ New Hampshire, Massachusetts, New York, Pennsylvania.

governed. Yet under most of these early constitutions none but property-owning, tax-paying men could give that consent from which government derives its just powers. The government set up by many a constitution, despite the principle announced in its preamble, was that of a class. Nowhere, save in Vermont, did manhood suffrage exist. Elsewhere no man voted who did not pay a property tax, or rent a house, or own a specified number of acres of land, or have a specified yearly income.* Each one of the State constitutions guaranteed liberty of conscience; but the man who did not exercise that liberty of conscience in such wise as to become a Protestant or a Catholic, a trinitarian or a believer in the divine inspiration of the Old and New Testament, must give up all hope of political preferment.† Even to such as could subscribe to creeds and doctrines the way to public office was barred by property qualifications, which increased with the dignity of the office till it became absolutely impossible for a poor man to become a candidate for the State Senate or the governorship.‡

When election day had passed, when the taxable poll, the house-renter, the man with fifty pounds' worth of real estate, the owner of fifty acres freehold had cast his ballot or given his *viva-voce* vote, his part in the government of his State was played. The Legislature, the General Court, did the rest, elected the Governor in most cases, chose his council, appointed and removed the judges of the courts, the justices of the peace, the sheriffs of the counties, the civil officers, and all militia officers down to the grade of captain. Nor was the Governor when elected invested with a tithe of the power now exercised by his successor. The early State constitutions were made at a time when the people were still smarting under the effect of the vetoes, the prorogations, the tyranny of the royal governors, and were still under the influence of the principles and teachings set forth by the revolutionary leaders. They were of no mind to repeat a bitter experience, and from preamble to schedule their constitutions are marked all through

---

* History of the People of the United States, vol. iii, pp. 146, 147.
† Ibid., p. 148.   ‡ Ibid., p. 148.

with unmistakable signs of distrust of the one-man power and a perfect trust of the popular Legislature. The executive of revolutionary days had no extensive patronage, no well-paid offices at his disposal. In eleven States he had no veto; in one he was given a qualified veto, and in another this power was vested in a Council of Revision, of which he was a member. Everywhere he was checked by an executive council. Everywhere, save in New Jersey and Maryland, he could be impeached, tried, and, if found guilty, removed from office, and nowhere did he exercise an unrestricted power to pardon. So great was the power of the Legislatures that the constitutions of nine States could be amended without in any way consulting the people.

Yet our forefathers must not be accused of inconsistency, however much their practice departed from their theory. Their faces were set in the right direction. They were determining on just what principles governments should be founded, and, having announced and defined these principles, they went on to put them in practice as quickly as they could. But they had not gone very far when it became evident that by a timid adherence to custom and to precedent many things had found a place in the constitutions which had no place there, and these, the moment an opportunity offered, were removed. How greatly the experience of a few years of self-government affected the political ideas of the time was shown when New York abolished the entailment of estates, when Virginia provided for religious liberty, and in 1787, when two instruments of vast importance—the Ordinance of Government for the Territory northwest of the river Ohio, and the Constitution of the United States—were framed at New York and Philadelphia. By the first three great principles were firmly established in the new West, and by each one of them the rights of man were much extended. Estates both of resident and non-resident proprietors dying intestate were to be divided equally among the heirs; the navigable waters leading into the Mississippi and the St. Lawrence, and the carrying places between them, were to be common highways, and forever free not only to the inhabitants of the territory and of the States then existing, but to those of States yet to be admitted into the Union; and, finally, slavery and involuntary servitude, save as a punishment for crime, was forbidden. By the Federal Constitution representation in the House is apportioned according to population.

Reform was the order of the day, and in the general revision of the old State constitutions, between 1790 and 1800, and in the eight newly made or amended the rights of man were greatly extended. Pennsylvania cast away her religious test, and put the ballot in the hands of every tax-paying male. In Kentucky and Vermont manhood suffrage for the first time was made a part of the political system of the United States. New Hampshire followed and abolished the religious qualification once exacted of her Governor and her Legislature, took off poll taxes, and gave the suffrage to every male inhabitant twenty-one years old. Delaware enfranchised every free white male of age who had lived two years on her soil, and ceased to ask if he believed in the Trinity and the divine inspiration of the Testaments. South Carolina opened the polls to Catholics. Georgia did away with her religious test for civil office and the property qualification once required of all voters.

During the last decade of the eighteenth century, therefore, a great stride forward was made. Church and state began to be separated. Religious qualifications almost ceased to be a condition for the exercise of civil rights. Property qualifications were much reduced, and the democratic doctrine of universal suffrage was spreading fast. Everywhere the plain people were calling for a larger share in the management of political affairs, for speedier justice, for more elective offices, for the abolition of life-tenure, for manhood suffrage, and before 1810 serious attempts were made in Connecticut, Pennsylvania, and Virginia to secure new constitutions or amend the old in such wise as to obtain these things. They failed; the men who agitated for reform and the rights of man were denounced as disorganizers, levellers, Jacobins, malcontents of the worst sort, and in all that decade but one new constitution—that of Ohio—was produced; and but one old constitution—that of Maryland—was amended. There, in 1810, the property qualification for voters was abolished,

dicial. Without their leave no law can pass, no law can be
repealed. On them more than half the House of Assembly
is dependent for reappointment as justices, as judges, or for
promotion in the militia. By their will each year there are
brought into official life six judges of the Superior Court,
twenty-eight judges of probate courts, forty of county courts,
and five hundred and ten justices of the peace, and all the
sheriffs. Not only do the seven make laws and appoint
judges to administer the laws, but as lawyers they plead before the judges they annually appoint, and as a Court of
Errors interpret the laws of their own making. Is this, it
was asked, a constitution? Is this an instrument of government for free men? And who may be a free man in Connecticut? No one who does not have a freehold estate worth
seven dollars, or a personal estate on the tax list of one hundred and thirty-four dollars. We demand a constitution
which shall separate the legislative, executive, and judicial
powers; which shall extend the free man's oath to men who
labor on the highways, who serve in the militia, who pay
small taxes, but possess no estates. We demand the free
exercise of all religions, independent judges, and the district system of choosing assistants and representatives in Congress.

By the constitution adopted in 1818 many of these demands were secured. The three departments of government
were distinctly separated. The council was replaced by a
Senate, whose members did not sit as a Court of Errors; the
franchise was extended to men who served in the militia, or
paid a State tax, or had a freehold estate of the value of seven
dollars. Judges of the Supreme Court of Errors and the Superior Court were made independent of the Legislature, and an
injunction was inserted that no person should be required by
law to join or support or be classed with any congregation,
church, or religious association.

That all men should vote and all judges be independent;
that people should be represented, and not mere political areas
as towns and counties; that there should be fewer appointed
and more elected officials, were now self-evident truths. They
were to be applied, not justified, and in the course of the next

decade serious efforts to apply them were made in four old States.

The struggle in New York was most interesting, for it was a struggle between the rights of property and the rights of man. As the constitution then stood, any male of full age who had resided six months in any county, and was possessed of a freehold of the value of twenty pounds within the county, or had rented a tenement therein of the value of forty shillings, and had been rated and paid taxes to the State, might vote for member of assembly. But to vote for senator or governor he must be possessed of a freehold of the value of one hundred pounds over and above all debts charged thereon. The constitution apparently arranged the males in the State in three great classes: those who could not vote for any State official; the twenty-pound freeholders and forty-shilling renters, who could vote for members of the assembly; and the one-hundred-pound freeholders, who were electors of assemblymen, senators, lieutenant-governor, and governor. But the narrow interpretation which the law placed on the word freehold deprived of a vote many a man who, from the language of the constitution, would seem to be entitled to it. In the eye of the law, a man who possessed a piece of land for his own life or the life of another was a freeholder, and if the land was worth twenty or one hundred pounds—that is, fifty or two hundred and fifty dollars— he might vote. But a man who held an estate in a farm, or city lot, or tract of land for nine hundred and ninety-nine years, was a leaseholder, and could not vote, though the land was worth one hundred thousand dollars. In this class were the many lessees of Trinity Church in New York city, and the thousands of farmers who, as lessees of the great Dutch manors, held their land for nine hundred and ninety-nine years. A second class of disfranchised landholders were the equitable freeholders, as they were called—the men who, in northern and western New York, had purchased farms on the instalment plan from the Holland Land Company or the Pulteney, the Hornby, or other estates. In place of selling in fee simple, and taking back a mortgage, these great land-owners would sell on long credit, with payments at certain intervals, and execute a contract to convey by deed when the

journeymen, manufacturers, and those undefinable classes of inhabitants which a State and city like ours is calculated to invite. This is not a fancied alarm. Universal suffrage jeopardizes property, and puts it in the power of the poor and the profligate to control the affluent. This democratic principle cannot be contemplated without terror. We have seen its career in Europe, and the things done there should be a warning to us here. It is madness to expect an exemption from those passions by which other nations have been first inflamed and then destroyed, and if we borrow no wisdom from their misfortunes our posterity will deplore in sackcloth and ashes the delusions of this day.

In the ranks of those who stood up for the rights of man was Martin Van Buren, then one of the ablest lawyers and political leaders in the State. Van Buren was born on the fifth of December, 1782, in a log building at Kinderhook, an old Dutch village on the east bank of the Hudson river, where his father, Abraham Van Buren, was a thrifty farmer and tavern-keeper, if the campaign stories of the Whigs may be believed. The boy Martin obtained what education he could in such schools as the village afforded, attended the Kinderhook Academy, and at fourteen began to read law in the office of a local attorney. After the custom of the day, he was janitor, errand-boy, and student all at the same time. He swept the office, lighted the fires, carried messages, copied and served papers, and read the shelf of books members of the bar were expected to peruse. After six years spent in this wise at Kinderhook, and one at New York city—for no man could then be admitted to the bar who had not passed seven years in preparation—Van Buren returned to his native village in 1803 and plunged at once into politics. The State was torn by the struggles of the Federalists and Republicans for power, intensified by the bitter faction quarrels of the followers of the great families, the Clintonians, the Livingstonians, and the Burrites. Van Buren, who had been a Republican from boyhood, and who, before he was eighteen, had been a delegate to a Republican convention for Columbia and Rensselaer Counties, espoused the cause of the Clintonians, became a strong partisan and active worker, and soon received his reward. In 1808 he was appointed surrogate of Columbia County; was elected to the State Senate in 1812; was appointed attorney-general in 1815; was chosen United States senator in 1821, and made a member of the convention to revise the constitution of the State.

To the dismal forebodings of the chancellor, and the predictions of those who "would not bow before the idol of universal suffrage," Van Buren replied that experience was the test of government, and did not justify the dread of universal suffrage so many entertained. He pointed out that property had been just as safe in States where every man voted as in those where the franchise was restricted to the owners of lands and houses. He pointed out the injustice of giving the ballot to the holders of the two hundred and fifty-six millions of real estate, and refusing it to men who paid taxes on one hundred and fifty millions of personal property. He met the arguments of those who predicted that the fruits of universal suffrage would be agrarian laws, and the taxation of real estate exclusively, with the remark that when that time came it made little difference what was in the constitution. "When the people of this State shall have so far degenerated, when the principles of good order and good government which now happily characterize our people and afford security to our institutions, shall have so far given way to anarchy and violence as to lead to an attack on private property, either by an agrarian law or by an attempt to throw all public burdens on any particular class of men, then all constitutional provisions will be idle and unavailing, because they will have lost all their force and influence."

Yet Van Buren, Democrat though he was, would not go beyond "the verge of universal suffrage." He would not "cheapen the invaluable right." He was "disposed to go as far as any man in the extension of rational liberty, but he could not consent to undervalue the precious privilege so far as to confer it with undiscriminating hand upon every one, black or white, who would be kind enough to condescend to accept it." In the end the property qualification for white electors was abolished, and every male citizen of full age and a resident of the State who could fulfil either of three conditions * was given the right to vote " for all officers that are now or may hereafter be elective by the people."

But reform did not stop here. The free negro was recognized to be a man, and was given the ballot when he possessed a freehold worth two hundred and fifty dollars. Under the old constitution representation in the Assembly was apportioned among the counties according to the number of electors in each. Under the new, representation was according to the number of inhabitants, excluding aliens, paupers, and negroes not taxed. Under the old, the Council of Revision had the veto; under the new, it was given to the Governor. The chartering of lotteries and the sale of lottery tickets was forbidden, and thousands of officers once selected by the Council of Appointment were brought one step nearer a choice by the people.

In 1820 the people of Massachusetts amended their constitution,† and there, too, in her convention was the same hostility to universal suffrage, the same distrust of the plain people, and the old struggle between the rights of property and the rights of man. The champion of those who stood up for a property qualification was Daniel Webster. " In my opinion," said he, " there are two questions before the committee: the first is, Shall the legislative department be constructed without any other check than such as arises simply from dividing the members of this department into two houses? The second is, If such other and further check ought to exist, in what manner shall it be created?

" If the two Houses are to be chosen in the manner proposed (dividing the State into districts, and choosing a given number of senators and a given number of representatives

---

* These conditions were—the payment, if not exempt, of a State or county tax on real or personal property ; or service, if not exempt, in the militia ; or three years' residence in the State, one year in the county, and actual labor on the highways or payment of a tax equivalent.

† The convention called to amend the constitution of 1780 met in November, 1820, and submitted fourteen amendments to the people. At an election, held in April, 1821, five were rejected.

in each in proportion to population), there is obviously no other check or control than a division into separate chambers. The members of both Houses are to be chosen at the same time, by the same electors, in the same district, and for the same term of office. They will, of course, be actuated by the same feelings and interests. Whatever motives may at the moment exist to elect particular members of one House will operate equally on the choice of members of the other. There is so little real utility in this mode that, if nothing more be done, it would be more expedient to choose all the members of the Legislature, without distinction, simply as members of the Legislature, and make the division into two Houses either by lot or otherwise after these members thus chosen shall have come up to the Capitol.

"It has been said that we propose to give to property, merely as such, a control over the people, numerically considered. But this I take not to be at all the nature of the proposition. The Senate is not to be a check on the *people*, but on the House of Representatives. It is the case of an authority given to one agent to check or control the acts of another. There can be no effectual control without some difference of origin, or character, or interest, or feeling, or sentiment. And the great question in this country has been where to find or how to create this difference in a government entirely elective and popular. Various modes have been attempted in various States. In some a difference of qualification has been required in the persons to be elected. This obviously produces little or no effect. All property qualification, even the highest, is so low as to produce no exclusion to any extent in any of the States. A difference of age in the persons elected is sometimes required, but this is found to be equally unimportant. In some States a different sort of qualification in the electors is required for the two Houses, and this is probably the most proper and efficient check."

Webster's view prevailed, and the old qualification for senators remained unchanged. But the property qualification for voters was cast aside, and the ballot given to every male citizen of full age (save paupers and persons under guardianship) who has resided within the Commonwealth one year and had paid any State or county tax assessed within two years. But a proposition to change the system of representation in the House and Senate was rejected.

Next to feel the spirit of the age was Rhode Island, where, in 1824, the first constitution in her history was framed by a convention, but, unhappily, rejected by the voters. Maryland followed, and in 1826, after a struggle of more than twenty years, opened her public offices to the Jews. From the day when her constitution went into effect in 1776 every man appointed to any office of profit or trust must, before he entered on his duties, " subscribe a declaration of his belief in the Christian religion." Because of this restriction no Hebrew, no infidel, no free-thinker, no one who did not believe in the divine paternity of Jesus Christ, could hold any political office, or be an officer in the militia, or sit as a juror, or even practice law in the courts of Maryland. Over and over again the attempt was made to blot this remnant of the middle ages from the constitution of the State. But to amend it was no easy matter. A bill to alter it must pass the General Assembly, must be published at least three months before the next election, and " be confirmed by the General Assembly after a new election of delegates in the first session after such new election." Hard as was the task, there was one man in the State who thought it worth undertaking. He brought in a bill to alter the constitution and make his Hebrew fellow-men eligible to office; it failed. He tried again, a second, a third, and a fourth time. Then even his constituents turned from him and elected another representative in his place. Still he persevered in the cause of the rights of man till he again became a member of the Assembly, when his first act was to once more introduce " the Jew Bill."

Those who opposed it argued that the restriction was no hardship, because a test existed in Massachusetts,* in New

---

* " Any person chosen Governor or Lieutenant-Governor, Counsellor, Senator, Representative, accepting the trust, shall, before 'entering on his duties,' make and subscribe the following declaration, viz.—I, A. B., do declare that I believe in the Christian religion. . . ."

Jersey,* in Delaware,† in North Carolina; ‡ that if the bill passed, not only Jews, but Turks and Chinamen would be eligible to office; that the Jews were unworthy of relief; that their religion, while harmless in private life, was dangerous in the administration of government; that it was the Jew who crucified the Saviour of the world.

They were answered that the test in Massachusetts applied to none but the highest offices in the Commonwealth; that Delaware had long ago abolished hers; and that in North Carolina a few years before, when an attempt was made in the Legislature to unseat a Jew, it was decided that the test was repugnant to the Constitution of the United States, and he remained a member.   The disqualification was denounced as against the policy of our country, the spirit of the age, the principles of our governments, the Maryland declaration of rights, and against the letter of the Constitution of the United States.   "Could this question," said one friend of the bill, " be brought before some tribunal competent to decide, I would undertake to maintain that the privilege this bill professes to give is already secured by our national compact. I would boldly contend that the State of Maryland has deprived, and still continues to deprive, American citizens of their just political rights.   The man who cannot hold the most trivial office in the State of Maryland may be chosen to preside over its destinies as President of the United States. He may be commander-in-chief of the army and navy of the United States, yet he cannot be an ensign or a lieutenant in

* "All persons professing a belief in the faith of any Protestant sect . . . shall be capable of being elected into any office of profit or trust on being a member of either branch of the Legislature."

† "Every person who shall be chosen a member of either house, or appointed to any office or place of trust," before entering on his duties, " shall make and subscribe the following declaration, to wit: I, A. B., do profess faith in God the Father, and in Jesus Christ, his only Son, and the Holy Ghost, one God blessed for evermore; and I do acknowledge the Scriptures of the Old and New Testaments to be given by divine inspiration."   Constitution of 1776.   Not in that of 1792.

‡ "That no person who shall deny the being of a God, or the truth of the Protestant religion, or the divine authority either of the Old or New Testaments . . . shall be capable of holding any office, or place of trust, or profit in the civil department within this State."

the militia of Maryland. He may sit on the bench, and in the Federal courts pass judgment on the people of Maryland, but under your constitution he cannot be a justice of the peace to decide the most trifling dispute. He may be a juror in the Circuit Courts of the United States, and as such be an arbiter of the life, liberty, reputation of the first among you, yet he cannot under the laws of Maryland sit in the same box to mete out justice to a pilfering slave. He may be a United States marshal of the district, but he cannot be a constable. The Federal Constitution has guaranteed to every American citizen the right of worshipping God in such manner as he pleases, and this right is violated whenever he is made to feel the consequences of his opinions either by direct bodily inflictions or by disqualification." At last prejudice was overcome by reason. The bill passed the Legislature in 1825; the Confirmatory Act in 1826, and another of the rights of man was extended to Hebrews.

The gain in New York and in Maryland was great indeed. Yet in neither State were the people satisfied. The old agitation for manhood suffrage went on as vigorously as ever, till in 1826 the New York constitution was again amended, the tax qualification for white voters abolished, and the franchise extended to every male citizen of full age who had resided one year in the State and six months in the county in which his vote was offered.

Virginia was next to yield, and, after a contest of nearly twenty years, called a convention to revise and amend her constitution adopted in 1776. Not a word was said in it concerning the franchise, save that "the right of suffrage in the election of members of both houses shall remain as exercised at present." This left it as then defined by law, and the law gave it to a small landed aristocracy. No free negro, no mulatto, no man who refused to give assurance of fidelity to the constitution, could vote under any circumstances. Every other male citizen of the Commonwealth aged twenty-one years could vote on either of three conditions—he must be possessed, or his tenant for years, at will or at sufferance, must be possessed, of twenty-five acres of land, properly planted, on which was a house with a foundation at

least twelve feet square; or own in freehold fifty acres of un-
improved land; or have a freehold or estate interest in a lot
or part of a lot in some city or town established by law.   As
Williamsburg and the borough of Norfolk then had the right
to send one delegate each to the Assembly, a freeman in either
might vote if a housekeeper and possessed of a visible estate
of $166.66; or, having served an apprenticeship of five years
in the borough, could show a certificate of the fact from a
Court of Hustings.

The effect of this limited franchise, it was believed, had
been hurtful to Virginia in many ways.   Legislation and appointment to office had been confined to freeholders.   Migra-
tion from the State of small land-owners and of landless men
had been greatly encouraged.   Immigration of the same class
to the State had been absolutely prevented; while within the
Commonwealth had grown up a steadily increasing class of
men, numbering eighty-nine thousand, who paid taxes, yet
gave no vote for a member of the Assembly, and were therefore governed without their consent.   Again and again attempts were made to secure a convention, extend the suffrage, and give representation to men, and not merely to counties and incorporated towns and cities.   At last, in 1829, a
convention met, revised the constitution, and extended the
franchise somewhat, but still restricted it by property qualifications as curious as they were elaborate.   Representatives in
Congress were now apportioned among the counties, cities,
boroughs, and towns on the basis of population, which was
defined to be all free persons, including those bound to service,
and three fifths of the slaves.   Untaxed Indians were not to
be counted.   At all elections to office the votes must be given
viva voce, and not by ballot.   No man who fought a duel,
sent a challenge, or in any way aided or assisted in a duel,
could hold any office elective or appointive in the Commonwealth.   No law of any sort could originate in the Senate, nor
even be amended by it, without consent of the House of Delegates; nor could the abolition of any court deprive the judge
thereof of his office unless two thirds of the members of each
House consented.

Thus was it that in the course of the first fifty years of our

national existence the political ideas of the people changed
greatly, and changed for the better.   Test oaths and religious
qualifications for office-holding and voting were no longer
in use; property qualifications were fast disappearing; representation was apportioned on population rather than on electors
or tax-payers; offices elective by the people were increasing in
number; and more restraint was placed on the Legislatures and
less on the governors.

But there had developed in the course of the half century
another restraint on the legislative branch of government
which was not imposed by any constitution.   Judges had
assumed the right to set aside acts of legislation which in
their opinion were unconstitutional.   When and where this
right of the judiciary originated, what were the conditions
under which it developed, who was the first man to boldly announce it from the bench, are questions which cannot be answered.   But it is safe to assert that, like every other judicial
idea that ever existed, it is the slow outcome of circumstances.
The majority of the colonies for years before their quarrel with
the mother-country had seen their laws disallowed at pleasure
by the King or Queen in council.   They had, therefore, become used to the idea of the existence of a body that could
set aside a law enacted by a Legislature and approved by a
governor.   They were used to written charters and frames of
government, and were accustomed to appeal to them as the
source of all authority under the King.   When, therefore, in
their quarrel with the mother-country it became necessary to
find some reason for resisting the stamp tax, the colonists appealed to a written document, and declared the tax law invalid,
because it violated the provisions of Magna Charta.

Indeed, it is in this connection that one of the early nulli-
fying decisions was made by a court.   One day in February,
1766, the clerk and other officers of the Court of Hustings for
Northampton County, Virginia, appeared before the bench
and moved for an opinion on two questions: Was the law of
Parliament imposing stamp duties in America binding on Virginia?   Would they, as officers of the law, incur any penalty
by not using stamped paper?   The judges were unanimously
of the opinion that the law did not bind, affect, or concern the

inhabitants of Virginia, " inasmuch as they conceived the said act to be unconstitutional."

When the struggle for the rights of Englishmen took on the form of a struggle for independence, the same idea of judicial control of the legislative power was taken up by the leaders and asserted more broadly still.   James Otis declaring, in his great argument against the writs of assistance, that an act of Parliament " against the constitution is void," that " an act against natural equity is void," and that " if an act of Parliament should be made in the very language of this peti- tion it would be void "; Mr. Justice William Cushing charg- ing a Massachusetts jury that certain acts of Parliament are null; John Adams congratulating Cushing, and assuring him he was right; George Mason arguing against the validity of a Virginia law providing for the sale of the descendants of Indian women as slaves, because it was contrary to natural right and justice, were but so many men announcing another self-evident truth of which in time the people grasped the meaning.   But it was not till the colonies had become States, with written constitutions of government, that the courts began the continuous practice of controlling legislation by deciding laws unconstitutional.   Even then they did so with great re- luctance.   One of the earliest, if not the first, of this long line of decisions was made by the Supreme Court of New Jersey in a case argued in November, 1779.

The proximity of New Jersey to the British army on Staten Island and in New York afforded an opportunity for trade with the enemy, which many of the inhabitants gladly seized.   That a stop might be put to this shameful inter- course, the Legislature in 1778 made it lawful for any person to seize provisions, goods, wares, and merchandise coming from any place in possession of the subjects of troops of King George, and take the articles and the individual in whose hands they were before a justice of the peace of the county. Should either party demand it, the justice must grant a jury according to an act of 1775, which limited the number of jurors to six and made their decision final.   In the course of a few months a militia major named Elisha Walton seized a quantity of goods of very considerable value in the posses-

The General Assembly of that State, having emitted a certain sum of paper money, passed a tender act declaring that all citizens must take the paper at par with gold and silver, and by another law provided for the punishment of such as refused to obey, and ordered that cases arising under the law should be tried before judges without a jury. The case of Trevett *vs.* Weeden arose under these acts, and when it came on for trial Weeden answered that the act of the General Assembly on which the information was founded had expired, and that, as the court was not empowered to empanel a jury, the act was " unconstitutional and void." * The argument by Weeden's counsel was long, and was summed up by him in these words: † " We have attempted to show that the act upon which the information is founded hath expired; that by the act special jurisdictions are erected, uncontrollable by the Supreme Judiciary Court of the State; and that by the act this court is not authorized or empowered to empanel a jury to try the facts contained in the information. That the trial by jury is a fundamental, a constitutional right, ever claimed as such, ever ratified as such, ever held most dear and sacred. That the Legislature derives all its authority from the constitution; hath no power of making laws, but in subordination to it; cannot infringe or violate it. That, therefore, the act is unconstitutional and void."

The five judges gave it as their unanimous opinion that the information was not cognizable before them. They did not, indeed, declare the law unconstitutional in so many words; but, as it had made the case cognizable before them, their declaration that it was not was a denial of its validity, and was so understood.

As a consequence of this understanding, the General Assembly at its next session summoned the judges to appear and "assign the grounds and reasons for the aforesaid judgment." ‡

---

* The Case of Trevett against Weeden, etc., by James M. Varnum, pp. 2, 3.

† Ibid., p. 35.

‡ " Whereas it appears that the honorable, the justices of the Supreme Court of Judicature, at the last September term of the said court, in the county of Newport, have by the judgment of said court, adjudged an act of the supreme Legislature of this State to be unconstitutional and so absolutely void ; and whereas it

In obedience to this summons three came, and through one of their associates made answer. The order might, he said, be considered as calling on them to do either of two things— assist in matters of legislation or give the reasons for their judicial determination. As to the first, he " pointed out the objectionable parts of the act upon which the information was founded, and most clearly demonstrated, by a variety of conclusive arguments, that it was unconstitutional, had no force of a law, and could not be executed." * As to the second, he replied that " on any question judicially before them they were accountable only to God and their own consciences." † In the end the judges were discharged from further attendance on the Assembly, but when their terms expired not one of them was re-elected.

The example thus set in New York and Rhode Island was quickly followed by courts in Massachusetts and North Carolina, where laws were deliberately declared unconstitutional.

Many a year went by, however, before our countrymen quietly accepted the political idea that a court could examine the constitutionality of a law, and that a decision against it was equivalent to its repeal. So late as 1808 judges in Ohio were punished for such action; and so late as 1816 the right was denied in Georgia. The Legislature of Ohio in 1805 defined by law the duties of the justice of the peace; but the Circuit Court decided certain parts of the act to be void because they conflicted with the Constitution of the United States, and the Supreme Court of the State sustained the decision. In the opinion of the people, it was a small matter whether the justices of the peace did or did not perform the new duties assigned them. But that the courts, the creatures of the Legislature, should presume to repeal one of its acts,

---

is suggested that the aforesaid judgment is unprecedented in this State and may tend to abolish the legislative authority thereof, it is therefore voted and resolved that all of the justices of the said court be forthwith cited by the sheriffs of the respective counties in which they live or may be found, to give their immediate attendance upon this assembly, to assign the reasons and grounds for the aforesaid judgment; and that the clerk of the said court be directed to attend this assembly at the same time, with the records of the court which relate to the said judgment."

* Case of Trevett against Weeden, Varnum, p. 38.   † Ibid., p. 38.

this, too, in a State where the veto power was unknown, as a usurpation not to be endured. To appease the popular wrath, two of the judges were impeached, tried, and acquitted; but not till the House of Representatives had voted that judges were not authorized by the constitution of the State to set aside an act of the Legislature by declaring it unconstitutional, null, and void.

During the hard times that followed the war for commercial independence, Georgia had enacted a law to stay the execution of judgments for the recovery of debts. Here, too, the courts intervened and declared the law a violation of contracts and of the constitution of the State, and refused to execute it. Here, too, the Legislature indignantly resented interference, and denied the right of the judges to question the legality of its acts. In the Senate a strong majority dissented, and sought in vain to have their reasons spread on the journal. They objected, because to deny to the judicial department authority to pass on the acts of the Legislature " was to confer on the General Assembly the omnipotency of the Parliament of Great Britain; destroy the distinctive character of the two branches of government; put the Legislature above the courts; remove the last check on legislative tyranny and oppression, and leave to the people no other alternative than insurrection or servile obedience to unconstitutional edicts."

While the proceedings in Rhode Island and New York were still fresh in the memory of men, the convention that framed our Constitution assembled in Philadelphia, and in the course of its deliberations came to the questions: How shall Congress be prevented from assuming powers it does not possess? How shall the States be prevented from encroaching on the authority of the General Government? Some were in favor of a Council of Revision. Others urged that Congress should repeal State laws. Still others insisted that such matters might safely be left to the courts, and so they were. In the Virginia ratification convention, Patrick Henry declared he did not believe the Federal judges would have the fortitude to oppose any act of Congress. But time proved his fears were groundless, and before the United States courts were three years old the judges demonstrated that they had the fortitude to declare an

act of Congress unconstitutional.   A law of March, 1792, provided for the settlement of claims to invalid pensions, and of
claims of widows and orphans barred by limitation, and assigned to the Circuit Courts of the United States the duty
of passing on such claims, but gave to the Secretary of War
and to Congress power to review all decisions.

There were then three circuits—one for the Eastern, one
for the Middle, and one for the Southern States.   Yet in each
the judges were of one mind—the law could not be obeyed,
because the power conferred was not judicial within the meaning of the Constitution, and the act was therefore void.   So
bold a stand required explanation.   Jay, Cushing, and the district judge, Duane, sitting in the Eastern circuit, desiring, as
they said, to show their high respect for the National Legislature on all proper occasions and in every proper manner, were
willing to act as commissioners.   Those holding Circuit Court
for the district of Pennsylvania addressed a long letter to
Washington, explaining the distribution of the powers of government, the importance of an independent judiciary, and the
regret they felt to be forced to differ with Congress as to a
constitutional principle.   In the Southern circuit the bench
addressed the President without waiting for a case to come
before them.   Later, when a case reached the Supreme Court,[*]
the judges were so loath to come to an issue that no decision
was handed down till the law in question was amended, and
ten years passed away before the court, in plain and unmistakable language, announced its right to disregard any law
at variance with the Constitution.

Sometimes the justices on their circuits would decide now
on one side of the question and now on the other, as when
Justice Patterson declared void the Pennsylvania Quieting
and Confirming Act in 1795; as when Justice Iredell discussed
the constitutionality of the Alien and Sedition Acts at the trial
of John Fries in 1799; as when Justice Chase, in 1800, said:
" Although it is alleged that all acts of the Legislature in direct
opposition to the prohibition of the Constitution " are null,

---

* Application for a mandamus directing the district court of Pennsylvania to
hear the petition of Hayburn to be placed on the list as an invalid pensioner,
2 Dallas, United States, 409.

" it remains a question where the power resides to declare them void." * Once the Supreme Court, without filing an opinion, seemed to have decided unanimously that a certain act of Congress was not constitutional.† Once, on a like question, the court was divided. Not till John Marshall handed down the decision in the case of Marbury against Madison was the position taken that it could disregard any law, State or Federal, which in its opinion was unconstitutional. Since that day it has done so more than one hundred and ninety times.

Meantime a far more serious blow was struck at State rights in the case of Chisholm *vs.* Georgia, wherein the suability of a State was maintained. This was indeed a bold idea, and four States protested. Georgia enacted a law subjecting to death without benefit of clergy any officer who should serve a process against her. Massachusetts resolved that the power claimed by the court was " dangerous to the peace, safety, and independence of the several States, and repugnant to the first principles of a Federal government." Connecticut was of the same mind. Virginia held that a State could not be a defendant in a suit brought by any man, and that the decision was " incompatible with and dangerous to the individual State, as the same tends to a general consolidation of these confederated republics." The result was the eleventh amendment, and the establishment of another political idea more fruitful of harm than of good.

This addition to the Constitution was proclaimed in force in 1798, a year memorable for the passage of the Alien and Sedition Acts, and for a yet more vigorous denial of the authority of the Supreme Court over States. Both Virginia and Kentucky now maintained not only that a State might judge of the constitutionality of an act of Congress, but also that there was no arbiter before which a dispute between the Federal Government and a State could be tried. Seven States repudiated the doctrine, and declared, each one of them,

---

* Cooper *vs.* Telfair, 4 Dallas, 194.

† United States *vs.* Yale Todd. No opinion was filed, but the effect of the decision was to declare the act of 1792 unconstitutional. Elliott. The Legislatures and the Courts. Political Science Quarterly, vol. v, pp. 243, 244. United States *vs.* Ferreira, 13 Howard, 40, 52.

that no State Legislature ought to judge of the constitutionality of an act of Congress, and gave that power to the Supreme Court. To these answers both Virginia and Kentucky in their turn made reply, and by the latter was announced a new political idea, the right of nullification.

Shocking as this seemed to the answering States in 1800, four of them in time eagerly approved it, and down to 1833 no period of ten years elapsed but some member of the Union deliberately asserted it.

First came Pennsylvania, in armed resistance to a decision of the Supreme Court. More than thirty years before, while the war for independence was raging, Gideon Olmsted, a native of Connecticut, and three companions were captured on the sea by the British, were taken to Jamaica, and there forced on board the sloop Active, bound for New York with supplies for the British army. But Olmsted, who was no common man, aided by his companions, rose one night, shut the captain and crew below deck, and took control of the vessel. A prolonged and desperate struggle followed. The prisoners, fourteen in number, melted the pewter spoons and dishes, cast them into bullets, beat open the hatches, and swept the deck. Olmsted was wounded; but he got possession of a swivel gun, trained it on the hatchway, and brought his enemies to temporary submission. Then the captain cut a hole in the stern, wedged the rudder, and held out for two days, when hunger and thirst forced him to surrender, and the Yankee fishermen made all sail for Little Egg Harbor, on the New Jersey coast.

But land had scarcely come in sight when two armed vessels cruising in company—the Convention, owned by the State of Pennsylvania, and an American privateer, Le Gerard—hove in sight, and bore down on the Active. To the captain of the Convention the story of Olmsted was preposterous. Four men take fourteen prisoners, and that, too, on shipboard! The thing was not possible. It was a ruse of the British. So the Active was taken to Philadelphia and claimed as a prize.

The case was tried in the Admiralty Court before Judge Ross and a jury, which found that Olmsted and his men were entitled to one fourth the prize, and that the rest should be divided between the State of Pennsylvania, the owners of the privateer, and the officers of the Convention and Le Gerard. Under an act of the Assembly, which permitted an appeal on questions of law, but not of the facts, Olmsted appealed to the Continental Congress, which referred the matter to a standing committee, known as the Court of Commissioners of Appeals for the United States of America. As security was required, Olmsted, friendless and unknown, applied to another Connecticut man, Benedict Arnold, then military governor of Philadelphia. Arnold and a merchant named Stephen Collins bought a share in the claim, furnished the necessary security, and on September, 1778, the case came on for trial. When it ended the decision of Judge Ross was reversed, and the marshal ordered to sell the Active and her cargo, deduct expenses, and pay the rest of the money to Olmsted.

Deeply as Judge Ross sympathized with Olmsted, wrong as he believed the award of the jury to be, he now felt compelled to stand by his findings in defiance of the Court of Commissioners of Appeals of the United States of America. The authority of the commissioners to set aside a decision of an admiralty judge he did not pretend to deny. But the verdict of the jury was beyond their reach. It could not be reversed. The sloop and cargo must be sold and the money divided, and with this in view Judge Ross bade the marshal make the sale and pay the money into court.

News of the action of Judge Ross soon reached the ears of Arnold, who, alarmed lest he should lose his share of Olmsted's award, at once notified the commissioners, and urged them to act instantly, to act that very evening. But the commissioners took their own time, waited till the following morning, and then called before them the register of the Court of Admiralty, only to be told that one hour before the marshal had paid Judge Ross £47,981 2s. 5d. proclamation money as the proceeds of the sale of the cargo. As the Active was still unsold, the commissioners commanded the marshal at his peril to keep in his custody all the money arising from the sale of both ship and cargo. He sent them in return the receipt of Judge Ross. Both the commissioners and Olmsted now appealed to Congress, but the confederation passed away with nothing accomplished.

Meantime the Active had been sold, the money realized by the sale of sloop and cargo had been paid over to David Rittenhouse, the State treasurer, under order of the Assembly, and a bond of indemnity had been given to Judge Ross. In 1790 the judge died, whereupon his executors were sued by Olmsted, and a judgment recovered by default. The executors of Ross, in 1792, sued Rittenhouse on the bond of indemnity and won, for the Supreme Court of Pennsylvania decided that the Court of Common Pleas had no jurisdiction in admiralty matters.

All chance of success now seemed lost; but Olmsted would not give up hope, would not accept the pittance awarded by the court, and in time was rewarded for his patience. In 1795 the Supreme Court of the United States held that the district courts did have power to execute the decisions of the old Court of Appeals of the days of the Confederation.* In 1802, therefore, Olmsted sued the heirs of Rittenhouse in the District Court of Pennsylvania, and in 1803 obtained against Mrs. Sergeant and Mrs. Waters, his daughters and executrices, a decree which bade them deliver to the marshal the certificates of public debt in which years before their father had invested the money obtained by the sale of the Active and her cargo.

Once again Olmsted had triumphed, only to be again defeated. The State of Pennsylvania now interfered, a law was enacted commanding the heirs of Rittenhouse to pay the money into the State treasury, and authorizing the Governor to defend their persons and their property against any process that might issue from any United States court. During five years no process did issue, for Judge Peters, who sat on the bench of the District Court, had not the courage to defy the State of Pennsylvania with the spirit she had defied him. But at last, in 1808, Olmsted applied to the Supreme Court for a mandamus. Marshall granted it, and then Judge Peters issued the writ. The home of Mrs. Sergeant and Mrs. Waters

---

* Penhallow vs. Doane, 3 Dallas, 54.

stood on the northwest corner of Seventh and Arch Streets, Philadelphia, and about this, when the marshal went to serve the writ, he found the militia drawn up to resist him. He read his commission; he read his warrant; he made a speech; he attempted an entrance into the house; and, finding all in vain, named that day four weeks for the serving of the writ, and summoned a posse of two thousand men to assist him.

Alarmed at the serious aspect of the issue, the Legislature now yielded, and appropriated a sum of money to be used in such way as the Governor might think advisable and proper, and so opened the way to a settlement. The marshal then gained access to the house by the rear, and held the women prisoners. A writ of *habeas corpus* was sued out; but the Supreme Court dismissed it, and remanded the prisoners to the marshal; whereupon the Governor paid over the sum in dispute to save them from imprisonment.*

After a struggle of more than thirty years, Olmsted, an old man of fourscore and eight years, won, and Pennsylvania had been defeated. Her Legislature, loath to give up the contest, framed an amendment to the Federal Constitution providing for the establishment of an impartial tribunal to decide disputes in which a State was a party, and asked for an expression of opinion from the co-States. Virginia answered, and in 1810 asserted what in 1798 and 1800 she had denied—that there was a common arbiter, and that the arbiter was the Supreme Court of the United States. But Pennsylvania was not convinced, and in 1811 plainly affirmed the doctrines held by Virginia and Kentucky in 1798.

In the same year in which Pennsylvania ended her quarrel with the Federal courts, Congress enacted the Force Act of 1809, the most infamous piece of legislation which up to that time had been placed on the statute-book of the United States. What the Alien and Sedition laws were to the Republicans in 1798, that was the Force Act to the Federalists in 1809. All New England rose in open resistance. From town after town came resolutions asserting the

* The case of the sloop Active, Hampton L. Carson. The whole proceedings in the case of Olmsted *et al.*, *vs.* Rittenhouse, Richard Peters, Philadelphia, 1809.

doctrine of State interposition. Boston voted the law repugnant to the Constitution, and called on the Legislature to interfere and save the people from the ruinous consequences of its enforcement. Hallowell declared that when those delegated to make laws transcend the powers given by a fair construction of the instrument whence their powers come, such a law is null, and petitioned the General Court to interfere and stop the career of usurpation. Yielding to the wish of the people, that body enacted a law prescribing fine and imprisonment for any person who, acting under the Force Act, entered by day or by night the house of any citizen against his will, and without a warrant searched for specie, or articles of domestic growth, produce, or manufacture. This was equivalent to a nullification of the Force Act, and was vetoed by the Governor.

In Connecticut, when the Secretary of War, in obedience to an order from Jefferson, called on the Governor to name in or near each port of entry some officer of the militia having " known respect for the laws," on whom the collectors of the customs might call for help, Trumbull refused to obey. He knew, he said, of no authority for making such a request, promptly assembled the Legislature, and addressed it in the language of the Virginia resolution. When, said he, the National Legislature oversteps the bounds placed by the Constitution, it is the duty of the State to interpose and protect the people from the assumed powers of Congress. Delaware pronounced the act an invasion of the constitutional sovereignty of the States. At this crisis the Embargo and the Force Acts were repealed.

Our second war with Great Britain—the war for commercial independence—soon followed, and one week before the declaration the Secretary of War, by order of Madison, called on the States for their quotas of militia. But the governors of Massachusetts, Connecticut, and Rhode Island refused. There were, in their opinion, but three purposes for which the President could call out the State troops, and these were to repel invasion, to put down insurrection, and to execute the laws. The country was not invaded; no insurrection existed; no laws were being resisted. The call, therefore, was unconstitutional, and could not be obeyed. This interpretation was upheld in Massachusetts by the judges; in Rhode Island by the Council; in Connecticut by the Assembly, which now in turn put forth a definition of the Constitution and the rights of the States. In this declaration Connecticut is described as a sovereign, free, and independent State; the United States as a confederacy of States, and the Constitution as a compact which delegates certain powers to Congress, forbids the exercise of those not delegated, and expressly reserves them to the States respectively.

That same year (1812) the territory of Orleans, having formed a constitution, applied to Congress for admission into the Union as the State of Louisiana. The question thus raised was new and serious. For the first time in our history a State comprising territory lying wholly without the bounds of the United States at the time of the adoption of the Federal Constitution was seeking admission " into this Union." A precedent was to be established, for it was certain that if Louisiana were added to the Union other States made from the territory purchased from France would in time seek the same privilege. Is it safe to establish such a precedent? Have we power under the Constitution to admit such States? Will the commercial interests of the East be secure when there are on the floor of Congress senators and representatives from States where inhabitants own no ships, carry on no commerce—nay, have never in the whole course of their lives looked out on the wide expanse of the ocean or seen the waves of the Atlantic breaking on the sand and rocks of our seacoast? were the questions asked on every hand. The bounds of our country, it was asserted, have been set by the definitive treaty with Great Britain in 1783. They are, on the west, the Mississippi river; on the north the possessions of Great Britain; on the south the thirty-first degree from the Mississippi river to the Appalachicola; the Appalachicola to the Flint; a line from the Flint to the St. Mary's river, and by it to the sea. Such was the extent of the United States when the Constitution was framed, and such it must remain. If the framers of that instrument had intended that the area of our country should, some time in the future, be expanded, they would have said so in the Constitution. But the Constitution does not contain one word from which the right to acquire foreign soil can even be deduced. The phrase " Congress may admit new States into this Union " means this Union as it was when the Constitution was adopted, and the new States that may be admitted must be made on the soil east of the Mississippi.

These views were well stated in a speech by Josiah Quincy, a representative from Massachusetts. " This bill," said he, " which it is now proposed to pass has this assumed principle for its basis: that the three branches of this National Government, without recurrence to conventions of the people in the States, or to the Legislatures of the States, are authorized to admit new partners to a share of the political power in countries out of the original limits of the United States. Now this assumed principle I maintain to be altogether without any sanction of the Constitution. I declare it to be a manifest and atrocious usurpation of power, of a nature dissolving, according to undeniable principles of moral law, the obligations of our national compact, and leading to all the awful consequences which flow from such a state of things. Touching the general nature of the instrument called the Constitution of the United States, there is no obscurity. It has no fabled descent, like the palladiums of ancient Troy, from the heavens. Its origin is not confused by the mists of time, nor hidden by the darkness of past, unexplored ages. It is the fabric of our day. Some now living had a share in its construction. All of us stood by and saw the rising of the edifice. There can be no doubt about its nature. It is a political compact. By whom? and about what? The preamble will answer these questions. It is we the people of the United States, for ourselves and our posterity; not for the people of Louisiana, nor for the people of New Orleans, or of Canada. None of these enter into the scope of the instrument. It embraces only the United States of America.

" I know, Mr. Speaker, that the clause new States may be admitted by the Congress into this Union has been read with all the superciliousness of a grammarian's triumph, accompanied with this most consequential inquiry, Is not this a new State to be admitted? If we were now at the bar of some stall-fed justice, the inquiry would insure the victory to the maker of it. But, sir, we are now before the tribunal of the whole American people, reasoning concerning their rights, their liberties, their Constitution. The question is concerning the interests of the American people, the proprietors of the old United States when they agreed to this article. Dictionaries and spelling books are of no authority. Neither Johnson, nor Walker, nor Webster, nor Dilworth, has any voice in the matter. Sir, the question concerns the proportion of power reserved by this Constitution to every State in this Union. Have the three branches of this Government a right at will to weaken and outweigh the influence respectively secured to each State in this compact by introducing at pleasure new partners situated beyond the old limits of the United States? "

Mr. Quincy then went on to prove that not only had no power been given to Congress to admit States out of the original bounds, but that the idea of so doing had not even occurred to the framers of the Constitution. They were not madmen. They had not taken degrees at the hospital of idiocy. " I have heard," said he, " of six States, and some say more, that will surely be formed beyond the Mississippi. It has even been said that the day is coming when the mouth of the Ohio will be far to the east of the centre of empire. It is impossible such a power could be granted. It was not for these men that our fathers fought. It was not for them the Constitution was adopted." You have no right, he argued, " to throw the liberties and property of this people into hotchpotch with the wild men on the Missouri, nor with the mixed, though more respectable, race of Anglo-Hispano-Gallo-Americans who bask on the sands at the mouth of the Mississippi. Do you suppose the people of the Northern and Atlantic States will, or ought to, look with patience and see representatives and senators from the Red river and Missouri pouring themselves on this and the other floor, managing the affairs of a seaboard fifteen hundred miles at least from their residence." The bill, he asserted, if it passes, is a death-blow to the Constitution.

" It is my deliberate opinion that if this bill passes the bonds of this Union are virtually dissolved; that the States which compose it are free from their moral obligations; and that as it will be the right of all, so it will be the duty of some to prepare definitely for a separation—amicably if they can, violently if they must." Nor was Mr. Quincy alone in this opinion. When the vote was taken on the passage of the bill, twenty of the thirty-six nays were given by members from New England.

But Louisiana was admitted, and another political idea— the admission of new States lying without the original boundary of the United States—was permanently established.

As the war went on, New England found new cause for the assertion of the principle of State rights and nullification. Her coast east of Montauk Point had neither been blockaded nor molested by the British, and a brisk trade with Europe had in consequence been carried on. But Congress to stop this laid an embargo in 1813, which fell chiefly on New England (for the rest of our coast was already under British blockade), and set that region once more aflame. Thirty-two towns in Massachusetts immediately petitioned the General Court for relief. Various are the forms, said the joint committee of the House and Senate, in which the people have expressed their feelings, but the tone of and spirit in all are the same. They all discover an ardent attachment to the union of these States, and all express a reverence for the national Constitution; but they are all stamped with the melancholy conviction that the basis of that union has been destroyed by a neglect of its principles, and that the durability of the Constitution has been impaired by a perversion and abuse of its powers. After due consideration of their petitions, the committee resolved that the Embargo Act was not constitutional; that the people of Massachusetts had always enjoyed the right of sailing from port to port within the limits of the Commonwealth and of fishing along its coasts; that the power of prohibiting the exercise of their rights was never delegated to Congress; and that all laws passed by the General Government and intended to have such an effect " are therefore unconstitutional and void."

The dire need of men for the army and of men for the navy brought before Congress the conscript plan of the Secre-

party in control. Virginia, in 1810, had assured Pennsylvania that an impartial tribunal to try cases to which a State was a party was not needed, because one already existed in the Supreme Court. Now, alarmed by the action of that court in the case of McCullough *vs.* Maryland, her legislators joined in the cry for a tribunal before which might be tried all cases involving a conflict of State and Federal authority. The proposed amendment to the Federal Constitution was not offered; but the need of it became imperative when, a few months later, the famous case of Cohens *vs.* Virginia reached the supreme Court, and Marshall summoned the Commonwealth to appear on the first day of February, 1821, and ordered the papers to be served on her Governor. Then, again, Virginia went back to her position in 1793, reaffirmed the resolutions of that year, declared that the Supreme Court of the United States had no authority under the Constitution to examine and correct the judgment for which she had been cited to appear, and entered a solemn protest against the jurisdiction of that court over the matter.

Kentucky by this time found another cause for alarm in the decisions of the inferior courts in cases arising under what were known as the occupying claimant laws. In 1789, when about to sever her connection with Virginia and apply for admission into the Union as a State, Kentucky entered into articles of agreement with her parent, and promised that all private rights and interests in land within her bounds, derived from laws made by Virginia prior to the day of separation, should remain secure and be determined by those laws. But Virginia had been at once both too liberal and too careless. She had disposed of more acres than Kentucky contained, and had allowed each holder of a warrant to locate his claim wherever he pleased. It came about as a consequence that the same piece of land would be contended for by two persons, each holding warrants of equal dignity but of different date: the one an absentee, the other an actual occupant who had made a clearing, built his cabin, and cultivated the soil perhaps for a term of years. In the interest of these occupying claimants Kentucky, in 1797, placed a law on her statute-book which provided that when an occupying claimant was evicted by a better title he should be exempt from the payment of rents and profits accruing before notice of adverse title, and that the evicting claimant should be liable to a judgment against him for all valuable and lasting improvements, less the waste and deterioration of the soil by cultivation. Liberal as this was, it fell short of popular demand, and in 1812 Kentucky went further still, and decreed that the occupying claimant should be paid for all improvements made up to the day when judgment was given against him, whether the improvements were or were not valuable and lasting; and that no deduction should be made for waste and deterioration of the soil by cultivation before the day when suit was brought, but merely for the time between notice of adverse title and judgment.

In the course of a suit under these laws before the Circuit Court for the district of Kentucky the question of constitutionality was raised. The judges were unable to agree, and the question was certified to the Supreme Court, where decision was rendered that the law of 1797 had been repealed by the law of 1812, and that each was a violation of the compact of 1789, an impairment of a contract, and unconstitutional, the one until it was repealed and the other since it was enacted. By the compact of 1789, Kentucky had bound herself to decide conflicting land claims for all time to come by the laws of Virginia in force when the compact was formed.

The excitement throughout Kentucky was intense. Our occupying claimant laws, said the Governor in his message to the Legislature in 1824, measures in which the State of Kentucky and many individuals have the deepest interest, call for your attention. The decision of the Supreme Court of the United States so materially affects the sovereignty of the State, degrades us so far below the level of our sisters, and works such manifest injustice to the real occupants of our soil under titles honestly derived, that we cannot be said to be a free people. Attention was immediately given by the Legislature, a memorial of great length was drawn up and presented to Congress,* and an earnest effort was made

---

* Executive Papers, No. 69, Eighteenth Congress, first session, vol. iv. Presented February 9, 1824.

her quarrel with the President over the Indian treaties, have already been passed in review.

Thus was it that in the short space of twenty years thirteen of the four-and-twenty States then in the Union asserted the doctrine of State sovereignty in one form or another. They charged Congress with usurpation of powers; they proposed amendments to the Constitution; they defied the President; denied the jurisdiction of the Supreme Court; declared laws unconstitutional; threatened resistance if others were enacted; asserted the doctrine of nullification, and in their Legislatures talked openly of secession.

The change wrought in political ideas by a half century of independence is again manifest in the development of an Executive utterly different from that contemplated by the fathers. The men who met at Philadelphia in 1787 and framed the Constitution lived at a time when great political parties, national in extent, highly organized, ably led, and commanding a patronage of enormous value, had no existence. It was combinations of States, not of men, they feared. The evils they sought to remedy were to come from the union of large against small, free against slave, agricultural against commercial States.

They were dealing with a people few in numbers, scattered over a wide area of country, and destitute of the many mechanical appliances which in our day annihilate time and space, and reduce whole continents to the limits of a town. Small as our republic was in 1787, the lack of every sort of modern means of communication, of every device for the collection and dissemination of information—the steamboat, the railroad, the telephone, the telegraph—made it immense, and powerfully affected the Convention in its attempt to create an Executive.

The vast extent of the country; the difficulties in the way of communication; the diversity of interests in the Eastern, the Middle, and the Southern States; the ignorance of the people in each one of these sections of the wants of their fellows in the other two, led to a serious effort in the Convention to establish an Executive of three men, representing the three geographical divisions or groups of States. That a New England man, however well meaning and sincere, could understand and appreciate the needs of Southerners, or that a man born and bred in Pennsylvania could impartially administer the law to the people of Massachusetts, was declared to be impossible. When it was answered that the Executive was to be the mere instrument for carrying out the will of Congress; that the energy, despatch, and responsibility necessary for the proper carrying out of that will could not exist in an Executive of more than one; that if the administration of the laws were intrusted to three men, each would consider himself the representative of his section, responsible to his section, and would guard its special interests rather than the welfare of all, the reply was, a single Executive is " the fœtus of monarchy," and the temper of the people is opposed to even the semblance of monarchy. They will never repose confidence in an Executive consisting of one man. At last, after many postponements and many debates, the decision was made to have a President; but the difficulty was as far from a settlement as ever, for it was transferred to the next question, How shall he be chosen? Every State save one agreed that an election by the people was not to be thought of. The country was too large and the people were too little informed. It was admitted that the country was blessed with a few characters of continental reputation, but the time would come when such men would not exist, and then the people would never agree on any one man. They would vote for a citizen of their own State or their own section, and nobody would be elected. Very possibly—nay, very probably—the inhabitants of the populous States would combine and carry the elections. Did any one suppose that a native of Georgia or of South Carolina could ever, in times of peace, attain to such public importance as to be heartily supported by the voters of New England in preference to a native of Massachusetts? As one member said, " it was as unnatural to refer the choice of a proper character for Chief Magistrate to the people as it would be to refer a trial of colors to a blind man." This expressed the opinion of every State save Pennsylvania, and was the one view on which there was a general agreement.

For a while the Convention could not decide who should

elect the Executive, and plan after plan was suggested. Some were for assigning that duty to electors composed of the governors of the States; some to electors chosen by the State Legislatures, or by the people, or by the State executives, or taken by lot from the National Legislature; others were for leaving the whole matter to the Senate, or at least to the Senate and the House of Representatives. Each plan had much to recommend it, but the Convention, utterly unable to determine which was best, voted that there should be an Executive of one, that he should serve for seven years, should be elected by Congress, should not have a second term, and might be removed on impeachment and conviction of malfeasance or neglect of duty. The decision was made in sheer desperation, was not wholly acceptable to any body, and was attacked on all sides. The Executive, it was said, must be independent of the Legislature. This was admitted. But how, it was asked, can he be independent of a Legislature to which he owes his election? Is it not certain that he will be its creature, and will he not in all likelihood secure his election by chicane, by intrigue, by cabal? He ought to control the Legislature; he ought to be a check on its tendency to seize power; he ought to be the protector of the great mass of the people, and stand between them and legislative tyranny. This cannot be if the Legislature elect him or impeach him, or if his service be limited to a single term. The ideal Executive is an officer chosen directly by the people for a short term, eligible to any number of re-elections, unimpeachable by the Legislature, and endowed with power to stop legislation not in the interests of the people.

For such an Executive the Convention was not prepared; but the argument unsettled it, and led to a reversal of all that had been done. The presidential term was cut down from seven to four years; the single-term provision was stricken out; the idea of election by the National Legislature was abandoned; and in order that the President might be wholly independent of Congress, and not be subject to coercion on the one hand, and be able to protect the people against unwise laws on the other, he was given the veto. Nothing could induce the Convention to consent to an election by the people, and, as it was now fully determined that the Executive should be independent of Congress, each State was required to appoint, in such manner as its Legislature should prescribe, as many electors as it had senators and representatives in Congress; and to these electoral bodies or colleges, each meeting in its own State and acting independently of every other, was given the double task of selecting a fit character to be President of the United States, and then electing him to the office. Except for the restriction that the electors must vote by ballot for two men, one of whom must not be a resident of the same State as themselves, they were free to do as they pleased; and that their action might be as free as possible, two safeguards were provided. One forbade any senator, representative, or office-holder under the United States to act as elector. The other required the electors to meet in their own States and vote on the same day; for it was feared that, should they come from all parts of the country and gather in one grand convention, they would be subjected to that " chicane, intrigue, and cabal," the dread of which was the reason for taking the election of President away from Congress.

While the Convention was thus willing to resort to every means to secure the free election of an independent Executive, it was not unmindful of the fact that his powers must be defined and his action restrained, lest he should become too independent, and by means of the veto coerce Congress and dictate legislation. Provision was made, therefore, that his veto might be destroyed by a two-thirds vote of both Houses; and that should he become too hateful to be endured for even one term, he could be impeached, and on conviction removed from office.

As thus defined by the framers of the Constitution, the President of the United States was to be an official chosen and elected by sundry bodies of citizens having no connection with the Government, was to serve as many terms as the electors saw fit to give him, and was to be the guardian of popular rights against legislative encroachment. He was to come to his high office bound by no pledges, representing no section, advocating no policy, belonging to no party, and owing no man anything. He was to be the choice of fellow-citizens who were called for the moment to act without collusion as electors, and, this duty done, were to sink at once into private life again. But Washington had not been many months President when a change set in, and the evolution of the President as we know him began.

First came the annual speech. The Constitution requires that the President " shall from time to time give to the Congress information of the state of the Union." To a generation which had not the easy means of gathering and spreading news which we enjoy, this provision had a meaning and a use. Washington attached much importance to it, and with that love of method and system which so distinguished him, gave the information to Congress, not, as the Constitution requires, " from time to time," but regularly at the opening of each session. On such occasions, after the two Houses had organized and were ready for business, he would come, with great ceremony, in his state coach, to the room where the House sat, and, taking the Speaker's chair, would read a speech to the assembled senators and representatives. After he had finished and gone home, the two Houses would separate and appoint committees to frame answers; and when they were ready, the Senate on one day, led by the Vice-President, and the House on another day, with the Speaker at its head, would march to the President's house, and stand with solemn faces while their presiding officers read the unmeaning replies. After partaking of cakes and wine, they would return to their chambers and go on with their public duties just as if the speech had never been made.

Next came the Cabinet. No such body of advisers was thought of or intended by the men who framed the Constitution. It was, indeed, proposed to give the President a council similar to those which in many States were then associated with the governors. But this found no favor, and the Cabinet as we know it is purely the creature of Executive action. The Constitution declares that the President " may require the opinion, in writing, of the principal officer in each of the executive departments upon any subject relating to the duties of their respective offices." But that these officers should hold regular meetings, and that the Secretary of War and the Postmaster-General, the Secretary of the Interior and the Attorney-General, should advise the President, not in writing, on matters of finance or foreign policy which do not relate to the duties of their respective departments, and that these regular gatherings of the Secretaries should be looked on as one of the political institutions of our country, finds no countenance or authority in the Constitution. The first Congress, however, had no sooner established the Departments of War, State, and the Treasury—departments which had grown up under the Continental Congress—than Washington appointed the Secretaries and began to consult them. For a while the consultations were informal and their opinions were in writing, but before his first term ended the Secretaries and the Attorney-General were formally assembled at the President's house, and the Cabinet as a political institution was established.

With the refusal of Washington in 1796 to accept a third term came the first contest for the presidency, and the first real test of the system of election by electoral colleges in the States. The Federalists might easily have carried the day; but party organization was then so imperfect that, although every Federalist elector wrote the name of Adams on his ballot as first choice, there was no agreement as to who should be second choice, and Jefferson, the Republican candidate, who received three votes less than Adams, became Vice-President. The lesson taught was not lost on either party. It was clear that the wasteful scattering of votes which had enabled Jefferson to come in between Adams and Pinckney must be prevented, and that the best way to prevent it was to come to an agreement beforehand to vote for two particular men, and no others. Absolute liberty of choice was good in theory but poor in practice. Each party, therefore, made most careful preparations for 1800. The Federalists, by consultation and correspondence, decided to support Adams and Pinckney, and so perfected their organizations that all their electors wrote the name of Adams on their ballots, and all save one the name of Pinckney. Beyond this, organization could not possibly go. Nor were the Republicans much behind their opponents. They, too, organized, and at an informal caucus of Republican members of Congress selected

Jefferson and Burr as the two men to be voted for by their party electors. Unhappily, the leaders did not, as did the Federalists, select a particular electoral college and charge it to see that one of its members, and only one, failed to vote for Burr. Each elector, therefore, voted for his party candidates, and for nobody else, and the long contest in the House of Representatives followed.

Two defects in this system of presidential election were thus made manifest. The contest in 1796 proved that it was possible under certain conditions for one party to elect the President and another the Vice-President. The contest of 1800 showed that a party with a large majority of electoral votes might not always be able to elect even a President. Lest such defeats should again occur, the Republicans provided two preventives, which at the time seemed all-sufficient. They so amended the Constitution as to establish a ballot for Vice-President, and from 1804 to 1824 they did formally what in 1800 they did informally, and nominated, or, as they said, "recommended," their candidates for the presidency and the vice-presidency at caucuses of party congressmen.

The introduction of the nomination of candidates by congressional caucuses marks an epoch in our political history. The intention of the framers of the Constitution was that no elector should be pledged, that each should be free to vote for any man he liked, and that the electoral colleges as a body should be responsible for the selection of a fit man to be President and then for his election to the office. But on the day the Republican senators and representatives in Congress met in response to a written summons and named their party candidates, the presidential electors were robbed of their most important function, and degraded to the petty boards of registry they have ever since remained. The Constitution was thus, to all intents and purposes, amended.

The inauguration of Jefferson brought yet further changes in the presidential office. The ceremony attending the opening of each session of Congress, the visit of the President, the speech from the Speaker's desk, or, as the Republicans called it, the throne, the answers of the two Houses, and the parades through the streets of Philadelphia to deliver them—ceremonies borrowed from England—had always seemed to Jefferson quite out of place in a republican country, and had long been subjects of ridicule by his party. That he would have discontinued them under any circumstances is therefore quite likely. But in the summer of 1800 the seat of government was removed to Washington, and the thought of the Senate and the House marching down Pennsylvania Avenue (then a long and dusty country road) to deliver useless answers at the half-finished and not half-furnished " Palace " was too much for him, and in December, 1801, in place of appearing to deliver the annual speech, he sent a written message. The custom thus begun has never been abandoned, and since 1801 every President has communicated his " information on the state of the Union " by message.

When Jefferson retired, in 1809, the presidential office had thus in the course of twenty years been greatly modified. The heads of the executive departments had been transformed into the Cabinet, or council of advisers; the annual message had become an established institution; the electoral ballot for Vice-President had been created; the congressional caucus nomination of candidates had been introduced; the electors had practically been stripped of all power of choice; and the doctrine that two terms were enough for any President had been formally announced, had been ratified by the people, and made a part of the unwritten Constitution.

On no feature of the Executive did the framers of the Constitution bestow more patient care than on the President's term of office. Every phase of the question, from the expediency of a short term with re-election to a long term without re-election, was fully considered. At the outset the general opinion of the delegates was that Congress should elect the President, that his term should be three years, and that he should be re-eligible, lest rotation should throw out of the office men found to be well fitted to perform its duties.

Opposed to this were many members very earnest for a term of seven years and no re-election. The Executive, they said, is to be chosen by the Legislature, and will be dependent on it, and, as its creature, must do its bidding and enforce its laws. A long term with no succession will prevent a complaisance on the part of the Legislature toward an unfit man, and the temptation on the part of a bad Executive to intrigue with the Legislature for reappointment. One member begged hard for triennial election, with ineligibility after nine years; but the States by a close vote decided that the President's term should be seven years, and that no man should ever have a second. Later on in the session the members changed their minds, struck out this prohibition, and made re-election possible. But the old distrust could not be downed; even this decision was soon reconsidered, and the resolution passed that the "Executive be appointed for seven years, and be ineligible a second time."

This seemed final. But when the Committee on Detail reported, a vigorous attempt was made to take the election of the Executive from Congress. So serious was the effort that the Convention could come to no conclusion, and sent the matter to a grand committee of one from each of the eleven States represented. The report provided a plan for a choice of President by electoral colleges, or, in case this method failed, by the Senate, and reduced the term to four years. In the debate which followed, a member of the committee told the Convention that the sole purpose of the plan was to make the Executive independent of Congress and eligible to more than one term. He was told that such a scheme was wholly impracticable; that the State colleges would never elect; that the Senate would always choose the President; and that he would in consequence always be the creature of one branch of Congress. In the end the idea of re-election to many terms prevailed, and with a few slight changes the plan of the Committee of Eleven was incorporated in the Constitution.

From all this it is quite clear that the framers intended that a President might be elected over and over again as many times as the electors in the State colleges saw fit. But again their purpose was defeated and their judgment condemned by that great tribunal—the people—before which in our country all public issues sooner or later must be tried. Again the unwritten Constitution amended the written, and no President in all our history has ever been given a third term.

For much of this, precedent is alone responsible. Had our first President been willing to succeed himself many times, the people would willingly have permitted him, a precedent would have been created, and he would in all probability have been followed by others serving for twelve or even sixteen years. But Washington was weary of the presidency, and gladly laid it down at the end of eight years. "The acceptance and continuance hitherto in office," said he in the Farewell Address, "to which your suffrages have twice called me, have been a uniform sacrifice of inclination to the opinion of duty, and to a deference to what appeared to be your wishes. . . . I rejoice that the state of your concerns, external as well as internal, no longer renders the pursuit of inclination incompatible with the pursuit of duty or propriety."

No scruples about a third term troubled him in the least. He went back to private life solely because he was tired of the cares of state. No great principle underlay his act, nor did the people see anything wrong in a President holding office a third term till Jefferson pointed it out. In November, 1806, more than two years before the end of his second term, the Legislature of Vermont formally invited him to become a candidate for a third term, and the great Republican strongholds made haste to follow her. Georgia joined in the request in December, and Maryland, Rhode Island, New York, Pennsylvania, New Jersey, and North Carolina in the course of 1807. For a time Jefferson made no reply; but the day was now at hand when he must speak out, for it would soon be the duty of the congressional caucus to nominate, or, as the phrase went, recommend a candidate. In December, 1807, therefore, Jefferson broke silence, declined the invitations, and in letters to Vermont, New Jersey, and Pennsylvania set forth his reason.

"That I should lay down my charge at a proper period is as much a duty," said he, "as to have borne it faithfully. If some termination to the services of the Chief Magistrate be not fixed by the Constitution or supplied by practice, his office, nominally for years, will in fact become for life, and history shows how easily that degenerates into an inheritance.

sion to the States and the ratification by them of the eleventh amendment.

The appointment of Chief-Justice Jay to the post of Minister to Great Britain, the ratification of his treaty by the Senate, and the impossibility of Republican Legislatures recalling Federalist senators were, in the opinion of the Republicans, glaring defects in our system of government that ought to be corrected. The elevation of Jefferson to the vice-presidency in 1796, because there was not a separate ballot for the election of that official, and the presence in Congress of foreign-born citizens, seemed quite as insufferable to the Federalists. Amendments were therefore proposed, making United States judges ineligible to any other office; requiring treaties to be submitted to the House in certain cases; cutting down the term of senators to three years; authorizing electors to designate in their ballots persons voted for as President; and excluding from Congress all foreign-born citizens who were not in the country on July fourth, 1776.

The failure of the electors to choose a President in 1800, and the bitter contest in the House in 1801, were the causes of a new batch of proposed amendments touching the Executive. Fifteen times in the course of three years propositions to alter the method then in use were laid before Congress. From 1801 to 1803 the tables of the House and Senate were never free from them for a session. Then, after years of reflection, the twelfth amendment went out to the States and was adopted, and immediately the subject was up again for discussion.

The failure of the Senate to convict Judge Chase, the decision of Marshall in the case of the "midnight judges," greatly excited the Republicans, and they cried out for amendments giving States power to recall senators, and authorizing the removal of judges on the joint address of both Houses. The long embargo and its enforcement excited the Federalists, and the Legislatures of Massachusetts and Connecticut demanded that a limit should be placed on the duration of embargoes. The decision of the Supreme Court in the Olmsted case aroused Pennsylvania to call for the creation of an impartial tribunal to try cases to which a State is a party. But the strangest of all propositions were two, of which one called for the abolition of the vice-presidency and the choice of the President by lot from the retiring senators; and the other declared any citizen of the United States who accepted, received, retained, or claimed any title of nobility or of honor, or without consent of Congress accepted any present, pension, office, or emolument of any kind from any emperor, king, prince, or foreign power, should cease to be a citizen of the United States, and become incapable of holding office. Strange as it may now seem, it passed both Houses, went out to the States, was ratified by twelve, and for many years was printed in school-books and histories at the end of the Constitution as the thirteenth amendment, though it was not accepted by three fourths of the States in the Union.

The third decade of our history under the Constitution covers the years 1810 to 1820, and during this time one hundred and fifteen propositions to amend were presented in Congress. Every phase of political life and thought was expressed in them. The ruling ideas were the choice of representatives and presidential electors in districts; a shorter term for senators; the appropriation of public money for the building of roads and canals; to give Congress and the States concurrent power to train the militia; to prevent an increase in the pay of congressmen till after one election intervened; to take away the veto; to give Congress power to appoint the heads of departments, fill all vacancies in the judiciary, appoint all office-holders under the Government, and forbid it to establish banks outside the District of Columbia.

Many of these were but the passing notions of the hour, or an attempt to override the strict construction doctrines of the party in power. But with them were mingled a few which came from the Hartford Convention, and expressed the political ideas of a great section of the country. It was proposed to weaken the influence of the South by apportioning representation according to free persons; to protect the interests of New England by admitting no more new States into the Union save by a two-thirds vote of both Houses of Congress; by limiting the power of Congress to lay embargoes, impose restrictions on commerce, and declare war; to give the Execu-

and Colombia now responded, and one spring day in 1825 the Ministers from Mexico, Guatemala, and Colombia requested interviews with Clay.

Separate meetings were accorded to each, and in course of conversation each announced that his Government was most anxious that the United States should be represented at a Congress of Republics soon to be held at Panama, and that he had been empowered to extend an invitation, but had been instructed before doing so to ask if it would be agreeable to the United States to be invited.

Clay replied, after consulting Adams, that the United States could not be expected to take any part in the war with Spain, or in any council for deliberating on the means of continuing the struggle for independence, and that before expressing a willingness to receive the formal invitation it would be desirable to know what subjects would be discussed, how the Congress was to be organized and act, and what powers were to be given to the diplomatic agents composing it. The Ministers promised to report this answer to their governments, and no more was heard of the matter till November.

Clay meantime took up the task of mediation. He was deeply and sincerely concerned in the welfare of the republics; he was most anxious to see the end of the war that had so long distracted and devastated them, and he beheld with no little alarm the preparations they were making to liberate Cuba and Porto Rico.

The fate of these two Spanish islands had long been a matter of interest to the United States, and as far back as the early months of 1823 was the subject of instructions to our Minister at London. France, in obedience to the commands of the Holy Allies, had invaded Spain for the purpose of restoring the absolute rule of Ferdinand Seventh. Great Britain had disapproved the war, had avowed her intention to defend Portugal against the application of the principles under which the peninsula was attacked, and might soon, it was feared, be using her arms against the Holy Allies in defence of the Constitution and the Liberalists of Spain. That her reward for such help would be Cuba and Porto Rico seemed certain, and at the prospect of such a transfer Monroe became anxious.   The possession of the islands by a decaying power such as Spain was one thing, but their ownership by a great naval power such as Great Britain was another and a very different matter.

"These islands," said Adams in his instructions to our Minister at the Court of Madrid, "are natural appendages to the North American continent.   One of them, Cuba, lying almost within sight of our shores, is an object of transcendent importance to the commercial and political interests of our union.   It commands the entrance to the Gulf of Mexico and the West Indian seas.   The character of its population, its situation midway between our southern coast and Santo Domingo, its safe and capacious harbor of Havana fronting hundreds of miles of our coast destitute of such ports, the nature of its productions and its wants furnishing the supplies and needing the returns of a commerce immensely profitable, give to Cuba an importance in our national affairs with which no other foreign territory can be compared.   Such are the interests of that island and this country—geographical, commercial, moral, and political—that, in looking forward to the probable course of events for half a century, it is impossible to resist the conviction that the annexation of Cuba to the United States will be indispensable to the continuance of the Union itself.

"In any other state of things than that which sprang from the war between France and Spain these considerations would be premature.   But the condition of Cuba will depend on the issue of the war, and in the fate of Cuba the United States have deep and important interests peculiarly their own.   As Spanish territory, the island will be liable to invasion from France, and the only reasons for doubting that the attempt will be made are the weakness of the French navy and the probability that the effort would be resisted by Great Britain.

"Were the people of one race and one color they would without doubt make the invasion of Spain by France the occasion for a declaration of independence.   They may even do so as it is; but no reflecting man can fail to see that they cannot stand alone, that they must have foreign support, and that for such support they must look to Great Britain or the United States.

"Great Britain has indeed declared her neutrality; but the spirit of the British nation is so strongly and so unanimously against France that she may soon be engaged on the side of Spain, and that the price of such an alliance will be Cuba and Porto Rico does not admit of doubt. The transfer of Cuba to Great Britain would be an event unpropitious to the interests of the United States. The question both of our right and of our power to prevent it by force already intrudes itself on our councils, and the administration is called on to guard against and defend it. You will then," said Mr. Adams, " say that the wishes of your Government are that Cuba and Porto Rico may continue attached to Spain." *

But the war which called forth this assurance, so comforting to Spain, did not assume the magnitude expected by Adams. French troops crossed the Pyrenees early in April, occupied Madrid in May and Cadiz in August, and the purpose of the Allies, so far as old Spain was concerned, was accomplished. No declaration of independence, no servile insurrection, followed in Cuba; Great Britain gave no aid to Spain. The assertion of the Monroe Doctrine stopped the design of the Holy Allies on the New World, and when John Quincy Adams succeeded Monroe, Cuba and Porto Rico still owned the rule of Ferdinand, and what had once been his South American colonies were still independent and at war with him.

To see this struggle happily ended was the earnest desire of both Adams and Clay. The little republics, after years of heroic effort, had driven Spain from the continent, had won their independence, and had been recognized as sovereign powers by the United States and by Great Britain, and were entitled to such recognition by Spain. But there was yet another reason which weighed with the administration. Plans were on foot in Colombia for an expedition to liberate Cuba and Porto Rico. That the attempt, if undertaken, would succeed, that success would be followed by emanci-

---

* Adams to Nelson, April 28, 1823. MSS. instructions to Ministers.

pation of the slaves, and that the existence of a republic full of free negroes just off the coast of our slave States would be a source of constant danger to the South, seemed almost certain.

Such a change in the condition of these islands must therefore be prevented at all hazards, and this Clay now undertook to do. Mr. Everett, our Minister at Madrid, was instructed to bring the subject of the war to the attention of the Spanish Government.* He was to remind it that the struggle on this continent was at an end, that not one foot of land from the southern and western limits of the United States to Cape Horn owned the sway of Spain, that not one bayonet in all that vast domain remained to support her cause, nor was the peninsula able to replace the armies vanquished and annihilated by the victorious forces of the republics. The troops of these new states, flushed with victory, no longer had employment on the continent, and yet while the war continued they could not be disbanded. To what object, then, would the republics direct their conquering arms? To Cuba and Porto Rico. It was not, then, in the interest of the republics that the President wished to see the war ended. They would be the gainers by a continuance. It was for Spain herself, for humanity, for the general repose of the world, that Mr. Everett was to urge Spain to end the strife. As to the United States, he was to say that we were " satisfied with the present condition of the islands in the hands of Spain "; that we " desired no political change in that condition."

Mr. Middleton, at St. Petersburg, was next instructed to ask the Russian Government to use its best efforts to persuade Spain to end the war with her old colonies. The contest had gone on for seventeen years, had been marked in its early stages by shocking excesses on both sides, and during its continuance whole generations had passed away and others had grown to majority without knowing the blessings of peace. In this war the people of the United States had taken no part. They had been strictly neutral, but it could not be said they were indifferent spectators. Mr. Middleton

---

* Clay to Everett, April 27, 1825.

was to urge on the Russian Government the hopelessness of the attempt to conquer South America, and impress the Emperor with the fact that only by a speedy peace could Cuba and Porto Rico be saved to Spain, in whose hands the United States was quite content to have them remain.*

Russia would do nothing. Neither justice, nor the law of nations, nor the respect due to the authority of a mother country over her colonies would, the Emperor replied, permit him to offer mediation till the sentiments of Spain and of the Allies she had long been in the habit of consulting had first been ascertained.†

Stripped of its diplomatic garb, the answer was understood to mean that the Emperor would consult the Allies and act accordingly; and, with the hope of aiding the negotiations yet further, Clay turned to the Ministers from Colombia and Mexico. They were informed of the request made to the Emperor, of his reply, of the conviction that Spain would soon yield, and were asked to urge their governments, in the interests of peace, to suspend the sailing of an expedition, then fitting out at Cartagena, against Cuba and Porto Rico.‡ Such a suspension was due to the Emperor, to the United States, and would render it unnecessary for other powers to consider what they would do if the islands were invaded.

Just what this meant Clay now explained in a letter to Mr. Middleton. " On this matter," said he, " it is necessary that we should be clearly understood by Russia. For ourselves, we desire no change in the possession of Cuba. We cannot allow a transfer of the island to any European power. But if Spain should refuse to conclude a peace and obstinately go on with the war, although we do not desire to see Cuba in the possession of either Mexico or Colombia, the President cannot see any ground on which we can interfere. If the war against the island should be conducted by the republics in a desolating manner; if they should put arms into the hands of one race of the inhabitants to destroy the lives of

---

* Clay to Middleton, May 10, 1825.
† Nesselrode to Middleton, August 20, 1825.
‡ Clay to Salazar, December 20, 1825.

another; if, in fine, they should set examples which, from our neighborhood, would be dangerous to our quiet and safety, the Government of the United States might feel called on to interpose its power." *   In plain language, if the Republicans of South America invaded Cuba, stirred up a slave insurrection, and armed the negroes, the United States would interfere.   One thing was settled.   Slavery must not be abolished in Cuba and Porto Rico, and to keep the islands slave soil they must remain in the possession of Spain.

But it was not to Russia alone that this policy was announced.   Like declarations had already been made to Great Britain, France, and Mexico.   During the summer of 1825 a great French fleet suddenly appeared off the coast of Cuba, and gave color to the belief that it was the intention of France to seize the island and hold it for herself, or perhaps for Spain.   Rumor went so far as to assert that, once in the hands of France, Cuba was to be made the base of action for an attack on Mexico and subjection of her to the Crown of Spain.   Greatly alarmed at the prospect, Mexico instantly turned to the United States and asked for an application of the Monroe Doctrine in her behalf.

Clay had been but a few weeks in office when it became his duty to instruct Joel R. Poinsett, the first Minister ever sent by our country to Mexico.   The novelty of the situation appealed strongly to Clay, and in his instructions he dwelt at length on this fact, bade Poinsett remind Mexico of the warm feeling always entertained toward her by the people of the United States, of the promptness with which we recognized her independence, and of the step on our part which did so much to stop interference in her affairs by the Holy Allies.   Mr. Poinsett was especially to bring to the attention of Mexico the message of Monroe of December, 1823, in which were asserted certain important principles of "inter-continental law in the relations of Europe and America," and urge on her the utility and expediency of asserting two of them on all proper occasions.   These were that the American continents are not henceforth to be considered subject to coloni-

---

* Clay to Middleton, December 26, 1825.

zation by any European power, and that we should regard as dangerous to our peace and safety any attempt on the part of the allied powers to extend their system to any portion of this hemisphere.*

Obedient to instructions, Poinsett opened negotiations for a treaty of commerce, presented what Clay called the two principles of inter-continental law, and had scarcely done so when news reached Mexico that a French squadron was off the coast of Cuba, and her Secretary of State requested the United States to demand an explanation from the King of France.†

That Clay was influenced by Mexico's appeal may well be doubted; nevertheless, he acted and bade our Minister at Paris protest against the appearance of so large a fleet off our coast without any previous statement of its purpose, and to add to the assurances already given that we did not want Cuba and Porto Rico for ourselves, that we were satisfied with their present political condition, and could not, with indifference, see them pass from Spain to any other European power, the further avowal that we could not consent to the occupation of them by any other European power than Spain under any contingency whatever.‡

Nor was this an idle threat. A few days later, when writing to Poinsett, the Secretary returned to his statement, sent him a copy, and told him to read it to the Mexican representatives as an indication of what the United States would have done had the contingency happened.#

It was now the month of November, by which time the Ministers of Mexico, Colombia, and Guatemala, having heard from their respective governments, returned to Clay with a formal invitation to the United States to be represented at Panama, and with statements of the matters to be discussed before the Congress. Mexico suggested the kind of opposition to be made to colonization in America by European powers, and the sort of resistance to be offered to the

---

* Clay to Poinsett, March 25, 1825.
† Poinsett to Clay, August 21, 1825.
‡ Clay to Mr. Brown, October 25, 1825.
# Clay to Poinsett, November 9, 1825.

interference of any neutral in the war between the young republics and Spain. Colombia approved these and added two more—the independence of the negro republic of Hayti and a consideration of the means to be used for the abolition of the slave-trade. Guatemala urged that, as the powers of the Old World had formed a continental system and held congresses to consider their interests, the republics of the New World should meet, form an American system, and discuss American interests.

Though the answers were far from satisfactory, Adams accepted the invitation, and in his annual message aroused his enemies with the statement that " Ministers will be commissioned to attend."

The purposes for which the Congress at Panama had been called were well known to him. He had the answers of the Ministers, and he had, besides, seen, in a copy of the official Gazette of Colombia, a plain statement of what the Congress was expected to do. It was " to form a solemn compact or league by which the states whose representatives are present will be bound " to wage war against Spain or any other power that attempts to assist her; to consider the expediency of uniting to free Cuba and Porto Rico; to discuss the wisdom of joining in a war at sea and on the coast of Spain; to consider what should be done to give effect to the declaration of Monroe that the American continents are closed to European colonization; and to decide what should be done to resist foreign interference in the domestic affairs of American governments.

But Adams ignored these matters, and, in a special message to the Senate, suggested very different objects for discussion and named two envoys extraordinary and a secretary to attend the Congress.* Of his constitutional right to accept the invitation he had, he said, no doubt. Yet it seemed wise, before taking so important a step, to be sure that the Senate, by confirming his nominations, and the House, by voting an appropriation, concurred in the expediency of the measure. The United States neither intended nor were ex-

---

* Richard C. Anderson, John Sergeant, William B. Rochester, secretary.

pected to take part in deliberations of a belligerent kind, nor contract alliances, nor engage in undertakings hostile to other nations. The meeting would afford a fine chance to give our Spanish-American brethren some good advice; to secure advantageous arrangements of commercial reciprocity; to make definitions of blockade and neutral rights; to stop privateering, or rather that sort of piracy which went on under the name of privateering; to obtain united measures for the abolition of the slave-trade, and very possibly to urge " upon all the new nations of the South the just and liberal principles of religious liberty." * With these high purposes in view, he announced that " Ministers will be commissioned to attend " the Panama Congress.

The opposition began with a motion by Martin Van Buren to the effect that debate on the expediency of the mission should be conducted with open doors, unless the publication of documents necessary to be referred to in debate would be objectionable, and that the President be asked to state whether the publication of any documents would be objectionable, and if so to name them.† Adams replied that all the documents had been sent by him in confidence; that this confidential character, in his opinion and in accordance with the usages of the Senate, ought to be preserved; but that he left it with the Senate to decide whether it would or would not, for the first time in its history, depart from this usage.‡

On the receipt of the answer, the anger of the opposition flamed out, and five resolutions, amounting to a censure, were offered.

The Senate was declared to be the sole judge of what were its rules, its usages, its modes of procedure, whether at any time it was not departing from them, and whether that departure was or was not without example; that the President could not meddle in such matters without violating the constitutional rights of the Senate; that it had a right

---

* Messages and Papers of the Presidents, Richardson, vol. ii, pp. 318-320, December 26, 1825.

† Journal of the Senate, February 15, 1826.

‡ Messages and Papers of the Presidents, Richardson, vol. ii, p. 327.

to call for information, and that it was not within the power of the President to decline to give it. Each one of the five was voted down by a strict party vote of twenty-four to twenty.

A motion by one of the New England senators that the discussion of the mission should proceed with closed doors brought on another struggle, which ended with a resolution of defiance. The Senate, it was said, could not find in the answer of the President any information that the publication of the papers would or would not be prejudicial to existing negotiations. Yet it did find a strong objection on his part to such publicity, and although the Senate had the right to publish the communications and discuss the mission with open doors without the assent of the President, it would not in the present case exercise the right, so the debate was conducted in executive, or secret session.

The Senate Committee on Foreign Relations having reported that " it is not expedient at the present time for the United States to send any Ministers to the Congress of American nations assembled at Panama," the debate opened in earnest.

Those who opposed it did so on two grounds. Some declared that the purpose of the Congress was to form a league of republics and drag the United States into an entangling alliance of the most serious kind. Others announced that with their consent the day should never come when the United States should enter into any kind of a league with, or even apply the Monroe Doctrine in behalf of, republics that had abolished slavery, that wanted vigorous action taken for the suppression of the slave-trade, that were demanding recognition for the negro republic of Hayti, and sought to free Cuba and Porto Rico and emancipate the slaves. There were, according to them (and they based their belief on the statements of the official Gazette of Colombia), four topics to be discussed at the Congress.

It was asserted that the South American republics understood that the United States was pledged to resist all foreign interference in the affairs of this continent; that the pledge was contained in the famous message announcing what

a question of extreme delicacy, concerning which there is but one safe rule either for the States in which it exists or for the Union. It must ever be treated as a domestic question. To foreign governments the language of the United States must be that the question of slavery concerns the peace and safety of our political family, and that we cannot allow it to be discussed. To the free States the language of the slave States must be that they will not permit it to be brought into question either by their sister States or by the Federal Government. Let me solemnly declare, once for all, that the Southern States never will permit and never can permit any interference whatever in their domestic concerns, and that the very day on which the unhallowed attempt shall be made by the authorities of the Federal Government we will consider ourselves as driven from the Union. . . . With nothing connected with slavery can we consent to treat with other nations, and least of all ought we to touch the question of the independence of Hayti in connection with revolutionary governments. These governments have proclaimed the principles of liberty and equality. They have marched to victory under the banner of universal emancipation. You find men of color at the head of their armies, in their legislative halls, and in their executive departments. Our policy with regard to Hayti is plain. Other States will do as they please; but let us take the high ground that these questions belong to a class which the peace and safety of a large portion of our Union forbids us to discuss. Let our Government direct all our Ministers in South America and Mexico to protest against the independence of Hayti; but let us not go into council on the slave-trade and Hayti."

But there was a matter which concerned the slave-holding States and their senators far more deeply than a recognition of the independence. Should the threatened expedition for the liberation of Cuba and Porto Rico take place, should the attempt prove successful and the yoke of Spain be thrown off, it was certain that two island republics would come into existence with not a slave in one of them. But this, in the opinion of the slave-holders, would be unendurable. Never, if they could prevent it, should Cuba be without slaves; never would they willingly see a non-slave-holding republic within ninety miles of the Florida coast. Turning to Cuba, Hayne declared that the question of its liberation was one of the most important subjects to be discussed at Panama. The President, it was true, had not put one word about Cuba in his message. But he had been silent because he was powerless to act. To France and Russia Clay had said the United States " will not permit any nation except Spain to take Cuba under any circumstances whatever." To the South American states Clay had declared that " if Spain should refuse to conclude a peace, and obstinately resolve on continuing the war, although we do not desire that either Colombia or Mexico should acquire the island of Cuba, the President cannot see any justifiable grounds on which we can forcibly interfere." If this meant anything, it meant that we would not permit interference by the Old World powers, and would permit it by those of South America. " This position," said Hayne, " I would change. I would declare that the South American states shall not be permitted to take Cuba nor to revolutionize it."

" Of all the subjects that could be thought of for discussion at Panama," said White, of Tennessee, " the abolition of the slave-trade is the most unfortunate. If slavery is an infliction, all the Southern and Western States have it, and with it their peculiar modes of thinking on all subjects connected with it. Some of these new States have put it down in their constitutions that whoever owns a slave shall cease to be a citizen. Is it, then, fit that the United States should disturb the quiet of the Southern and Western States by a discussion and agreement with the new States on any subject connected with slavery? Let us then cease to talk of slavery in this House, let us cease to negotiate upon any subject connected with it."

" It is manifest from the documents before us," said Berrien, of Georgia, " that the Congress at Panama is to settle the fate of Cuba and Porto Rico. When we look at the situation of those islands we cannot be indifferent to a change of their condition. But when we reflect that they are in juxtaposition to a portion of this Union where slavery exists, that the

the people of the United States in their sovereign character; and that, in the opinion of the Senate, the appointment of deputies to the Congress at Panama would be a departure from the wise and settled policy by which the intercourse of the United States with foreign nations had hitherto been regulated. This, too, the Senate rejected.

The resolution reported by the Committee on Foreign Relations was next rejected, the committee discharged from further consideration of the matter, and the nominations of Richard C. Anderson, John Sergeant, and William B. Rochester were duly confirmed.

The Senate having consented to the appointment of commissioners, it now became the duty of the House to vote an appropriation to cover the expenses of the mission. That the call for money would be made the occasion for an attack upon the President was well known, for the matter had already been under debate in that body. Quite early in the session * a member from South Carolina offered a resolution calling on the President for copies of the papers and correspondence which had induced him to inform the House that Ministers from the United States would be sent to the Panama Congress. But the chairman of the Committee on Foreign Affairs assured him that it was the intention of the President to send the papers as soon as the Senate consented to the proposed mission, and he allowed his resolution to lie on the table. As time passed and no papers came, another member, a month later,† introduced two resolutions. One expressed the deep and anxious solicitude with which the people of the United States watched the struggle of the South American republics for independence and self-government. The other declared that the appointment of Ministers to the Congress at Panama was wise and proper, and that an appropriation to meet the cost of the mission ought to be made.

These were tabled; but when a resolution was offered ‡ calling on the President for papers and documents relative to the invitation to be represented at Panama, the House

---

* December 16, 1825.   † January 26, 1826.

‡ January 30, 1826.

could contain itself no longer, and spent two weeks in debate before the resolution passed by a vote of one hundred and twenty-five to forty.*

Adams waited ten days, and then sent the information and the papers.† At the end of another ten days the Committee on Appropriations reported a bill making provision for the mission, and the Committee on Foreign Relations a report and resolution that it was expedient to appropriate the funds necessary to enable the President to send Ministers to Panama. Both were sent to the Committee of the Whole House on the State of the Union.

First to be taken up was the resolution, to which an amendment was offered declaring that it was the settled policy of the United States, in extending commercial relations, to have as little political connection with other nations as possible, to preserve peace, commerce, and friendship with all nations, and form entangling alliances with none; that the Ministers ought to go in a diplomatic character only; that they should not be authorized to discuss, consider, or consult on any proposition of alliance between the United States and any South American government, nor make any compact or declaration binding their Government to resist interference from abroad with the domestic concerns of South American countries.

Those who opposed the amendment took two grounds: Some, led by Webster, held that to pass such a resolution was to instruct the Ministers, that the instruction of Ministers was an executive act, and that as the Constitution vested the executive power in the President the House could not use it. Others argued that, the President having recommended the mission and the Senate having approved, the plain duty of the House was to vote the appropriation, unless it believed the mission was likely to be dangerous to the peace of the country. To remove the constitutional objections of Webster and his followers, a resolution was offered by James Buchanan declaring that while the House had the warmest sympathy for the republics of South America and could not view the hostile interposition of any European power against their

---

* March 5, 1826. † March 15, 1826.

independence with indifference, yet it was not expedient, by entering into any alliance, offensive or defensive, with any nation, for the people of the United States to deprive themselves of the right to act freely in any crisis in such manner as their own honor and policy at the time might dictate.

To meet the arguments of those who held that the House was bound to act because the Senate had approved the mission and there was nothing dangerous to the peace of the country likely to result, the statement was made that the peace of the country was seriously threatened. "We will prove three things," said the supporters of the amendment. "We will show, in the first place, that two subjects of serious importance to us will be considered at Panama; in the second place, that if we send Ministers without the limitations proposed in the amendment, we stand committed to take part in the deliberations on these subjects; and, in the third place, that we shall, by so doing, endanger our peace and safety.

"What, to begin with, are these two subjects? Before the Ministers of Mexico and Colombia extended to us the invitation to be present the Secretary of State was asked if it would be agreeable to the United States to be present. The Secretary consulted the President, and then requested to be informed as to 'the subjects to which the attention of the Congress was to be directed.' The answer was full and explicit. 'Those,' said the Mexican Minister, 'which from their nature and importance the late administration characterized as of general interest to the continent,' and lest this should not be plain enough he specified two. One he described as 'resistance or opposition to the interference of any neutral nation in the question and war of independence between the new powers of America and Spain.' The other he called 'opposition to colonization in America by the powers of Europe.' These, then, are to be considered at Panama. But are we committed to consider them? What was the answer of Mr. Clay when he received this information as to 'the subjects to which the attention of the Congress was to be directed?' That the invitation was accepted, that Ministers would be sent, and that they would be fully instructed and empowered 'upon all questions likely to arise in the Congress on subjects in which the nations of America have a common interest.' The Mexican Minister, in his reply to Mr. Clay, was at great pains to mention resistance to foreign interference and colonization as 'the two principal subjects' for consultation. They will, then, beyond a doubt be discussed, and as Mr. Clay has promised that our Ministers shall be fully empowered to deliberate on all questions in which the nations of America have a common interest, we are committed to discuss them.

"It now remains for us to show that the result of our participation in the deliberation on these subjects will be the adoption of measures endangering the future peace of the country. In the first place, the principle of resistance by force is already agreed to. 'The powers of America,' said the Mexican Minister to Mr. Clay, 'are already of accord as to resistance,' and this being the case it behooves them 'to discuss the means of giving to that resistance all possible force.' But are we committed to resistance? We certainly are. In our diplomatic intercourse with the states of South America Mr. Clay has treated certain vague and oracular expressions in a message of the late President as a pledge not to permit any interference of the European powers in the war between these South American states and Spain. When, therefore, during the last summer a French fleet appeared in the West Indies with the supposed intention of occupying Cuba and Porto Rico, we were appealed to to make good this pledge. And what did Mr. Clay do? He wrote to our Minister in France and bade him say that we 'could not consent to the occupation of those islands by any European power other than Spain under any circumstances whatever.' He wrote to our Minister in Mexico and told him to read to the Mexican authorities a copy of the note to France as an interpretation of our policy toward South American powers, and in this correspondence he referred to the utterances of the late President as 'that memorable pledge.' If this does not commit us to the point of resistance on the happening of a certain event, then it is hard to see what can.

"What, in the next place, will be the probable consequences of this agreement to use force? This mission is the first step in a new scheme of foreign policy which, if taken, will lead inevitably to the adoption of the whole system. It is well known to the committee that two distinct methods of procedure toward the republics of South America are before us. The one proposes that we conduct our intercourse with them on principles of the utmost liberality and kindness, but carefully avoid embarrassing political connections. The other, under the pretext that a moral and physical necessity binds together in one common fate the destinies of North and South America, aims to unite them under one grand American confederacy in imitation of the Holy Alliance of Europe. The one is the system of Washington, of the sages and patriots of the Revolution, of the statesmen of the earlier and purer era of the republic. The other is that of a new school of politicians, is that of the present administration, is presented under the name of the American System, and is the work of the present Secretary of State.

"In a speech made by him on this floor in 1820 he drew for us the first outline of this first conception of an American policy. 'What,' said he, 'would I give could we appreciate the advantages of pursuing the course I propose. It is in our power to create a system of which we shall be the centre and in which all South America will act with us. Let us no longer watch the nod of any European politician. Let us become real and true Americans, and place ourselves at the head of the American System.'

"But this American System is not confined to the Secretary of State. The President is a proselyte. 'The fraternity of freedom,' our 'sister republics,' the 'nations of this hemisphere,' the 'powers of America,' are the phrases with which his messages abound. Nay, more! Finding the Farewell Address of George Washington an obstacle in the path of the policy he is determined to pursue, he attempts, with desperate violence, to prove that it recommends to us now a course it warned us not to take thirty years ago. 'Compare,' says the President, 'our situation and the circumstances of that time with those of the present day, and what, from the very words of Washington then, would be his counsels to his countrymen now? Europe has still her set of primary interests, with which we have little or a remote relation. Our distant and detached situation with reference to Europe remains the same. But we were then, the only independent nation on this hemisphere, and we were surrounded by European colonies, with the greater part of which we had no more intercourse than with the inhabitants of another planet. These colonies have been transformed into eight independent nations, extending to our very doors. Seven are republics like ourselves. With them we have a growing commercial, and must have, and have already, important political connections. Our situation as to them is neither distant nor detached. Their political principles and systems of government must have an action and counteraction upon us and ours, to which we cannot be indifferent. Reasoning upon this state of things from the sound and judicious principles of Washington, must we not say that the period which he predicted as then not far off has arrived? That America has a set of primary interests which have no or a remote relation to Europe? That the interference of Europe, therefore, in those concerns should be spontaneously withheld by her upon the same principles that we have never interfered with hers? That if she should interfere, as she may, we might be called on in defence of our own altars and firesides to take an attitude which would cause our neutrality to be respected, and choose peace or war, as our interests, guided by justice, should counsel?' From this American System, to which the President and his followers are pledged, nothing but evil will come."

At this stage in the discussion James K. Polk, of Tennessee, offered an amendment which was in substance that when the House was called on to appropriate money to meet the cost of foreign missions it was in duty bound to consider the expediency or inexpediency of such missions, and to act accordingly; that to send Ministers to take part in the deliberations of the Congress of South American nations at Panama would be a total departure from the uniform course of policy pursued by the United States from the adoption of the Constitution to the present time; that it might, and probably would, involve us in entangling alliances; and that it was therefore inexpedient to send Ministers to the Congress at Panama or grant an appropriation to defray their expenses.

The discussion now turned on the question whether the House was or was not bound to vote the money. James Buchanan, of Pennsylvania, was convinced that the appropriation must be made. The President had nominated the Ministers, the Senate had consented to their appointment, and they were free to start for Panama whenever they were ordered. The House could refuse to pay them, but if they went without salary their acts would be legal. He thought provision must be made, but in giving the money the House had a right to express its opinion on the necessity of the mission. The resolution before the committee, when amended and adopted, would be neither more nor less than an expression of opinion. The President, in framing the instructions of the Ministers, would give the opinion as much weight as in his judgment it deserved, and no more. He might utterly disregard it if he thought proper.

" The only question to be considered was, Did the information before the House justify an expression of opinion? It certainly did. The time was at hand to take a firm stand in defence of the old and approved policy of the country to preserve peace, commerce, and friendship with all nations, and to form entangling alliances with none.

" In the summer of 1823 the Holy Allies, at the request of Spain, were called on to assist in subjugating what she was pleased to call her revolted colonies. A serious apprehension was felt that a crusade was begun against the cause of liberty and republican government wherever it existed on the face of the earth; and, sharing this belief, Mr. Monroe, in his celebrated message, announced to the Holy Allies and to the world that we could not view with indifference the hostile interposition of any European power against the independence of the southern republics. Millions of freemen echoed the declaration. It was received with enthusiasm in every part of the Union. It answered the purpose for which it was intended, and the danger which then threatened the South American republics passed away. Did we give any pledge to foreign nations? Did we commit the faith of the nation to all or any of the southern republics? Certainly not. The declaration contained no pledge. It left us perfectly free, but it had since been converted into a pledge by the administration.

" Because of this pledge, which was a dangerous departure from the time-honored policy of Washington, a step toward the entangling alliances against which Mr. Jefferson had warned his countrymen, Buchanan was in favor of the amendments. They would enable the administration to relieve itself from a pledge it had no right to give. They would enable the President to say that, strong as was his inclination to fulfil it, the House of Representatives had declared it should never have their sanction."

Webster replied. He was convinced that the House must appropriate the money, and he was opposed to the amendments. The appointment of the ministers was a clear and unequivocal exercise of executive power. It was less connected with the duties of the House than almost any other executive act, because the office of Public Minister was not created by any statute or law of Congress. It existed under the law of nations, and was recognized as existing by the Constitution. Indeed, it was only because Ministers, like other officers, must have salaries, and because no salaries can be paid without consent of the House that the subject was referred to it at all.

Webster disapproved of the amendments because they prescribed what the Ministers should and should not discuss at Panama, because the House had no right to instruct Ministers, and because, even if it had, the instruction in question was not proper.

With this he might well, he said, be content to stop; but the discussion had extended over a broader field, and, following where others led, he would make some observations on the general topics of the debate. In the course of discussion the declaration of Mr. Monroe in 1823 had been described as loose and vague. " Not only as a member of the House, but as a citizen of the country I have an anxious desire that this part of our history should stand in its proper light. In my judgment, the country had a very high honor connected with this occurrence. I look upon it as a part of its treasures of reputation, and, for one, I intend to guard it. It was, I believe, sufficiently studied. I have understood, from good authority, that it was considered, weighed, and distinctly and decidedly approved by every one of the President's advisers at that time. Our Government could not follow precisely the course which Great Britain had taken. She threatened the immediate recognition of the provinces if the Allies should take part with Spain against them. We had already recognized them. Nothing remained but for our Government to say how we should consider a combination of the allied powers to effect objects in America which concerned ourselves, and the message was intended to say what it does say—that we should regard such combinations as dangerous to us. I agree with those who maintain the proposition, and I contend against those who deny it, that the message did mean something, that it meant much; and I maintain against both that the declaration effected much good, answered the end designed by it, did great honor to the foresight and spirit of the Government, and that it cannot now be taken back, retracted, or annulled without disgrace. I look on the message of December, 1823, as forming a bright page in our history. I will neither help to erase it nor tear it out, nor shall it be, by any act of mine, blurred or blotted. It did honor to the sagacity of the Government. It elevated the hopes and gratified the patriotism of the people. Over those hopes I will not bring a mildew, nor will I put that gratified patriotism to shame.

" But how does it happen that there is now a new-born fear on the subject of this declaration? The crisis is over. The danger is past. When made there was real ground for apprehension. Now there is none. And yet we are vehemently warned against the sentiments of the declaration. To avoid this inconsistency it is contended that new force has been given to the words of Mr. Monroe. Do gentlemen mean to say that the communication made to France was improper? Do they mean to repel and repudiate the declaration that we could not see Cuba transferred from Spain to any other

European power? If the House intends to contradict that, be it so. But I pray gentlemen to review their opinions. A member has said that if Spain chose to transfer the island to any other power she has a right to do so, and we here cannot interfere to prevent her. I must dissent from this opinion. The rights of nations in matters of this kind are much modified by circumstances. Because France or Great Britain could not rightfully complain of the transfer of Florida to us, it does not follow that we could not complain of the cession of Cuba to one of them. The transfer of Florida to us was not dangerous to the safety of either of these nations, nor fatal to any of their great and essential interests. Proximity of position, neighborhood, whatever augments the power of injuring and annoying, very properly belong to the consideration of all cases of this kind. What might otherwise never be thought of is justified for these reasons and on these grounds."

When at last the long debate ended the Committee of the Whole reported the resolution of the Committee on Foreign Relations without amendment. But the House added that of Mr. McLean, and, having done so, rejected the resolution as amended and passed the Appropriation Bill.

It was now late in April, and summer came before Anderson and Sergeant set out to attend the Congress from which Clay expected such great results. But he was doomed to disappointment. Anderson died on the way, and Sergeant reached Panama to find that the delegates had assembled and adjourned to meet again at Tacubaya, in Mexico. But when the appointed day arrived the little republics were once more the scene of domestic violence, this meeting was never held, and Sergeant came home without accomplishing anything.

Quite as futile was the attempt to move the boundary of our country farther southward into Texas. The independence of Mexico left with her the duty of executing the treaty of amity, settlement, and limits concluded with Spain in 1819. But it was in many respects so unsatisfactory that a proposal was offered to put it aside and make another. As defined, the line of demarcation between the United States and the Mexican provinces of Spain passed up the west bank

branch, thence due north to the Colorado, up that river to its source, and thence to the forty-second parallel of latitude in such wise as to head all the tributaries of the Arkansas and Red rivers Poinsett might offer a sum proportionately less.

Should Mexico refuse to sell so great a piece of Texas, he might propose as a boundary the Colorado from its mouth to its source, or the Rio Brazos from its mouth to the head of its most westerly branch, and in either case around the tributaries of the Red and the Arkansas rivers to the parallel of forty-two degrees.

The present boundary was objectionable not only because of the nearness of the Sabine to New Orleans, but because it was a shallow stream, navigable only by small craft, and never likely to become the channel of enough commerce to justify the establishment of a custom-house on its banks. For lack of such restraint, the frontier was and would remain the resort of smugglers and outlaws and the home of a most disreputable population.

The want of confidence and attachment between the Government of Mexico and the inhabitants of Texas lured there by the land-grant owners was notorious. In the short space of five years this antipathy had displayed itself in four revolts, of which one had for its avowed object the independence of the country. The United States had lost no time in assuring Mexico that the resistance to her lawful authority was without aid or countenance, direct or indirect, from us. Yet the recurrence of such scenes could not but tend to excite suspicion of our motives and produce heart-burnings ruinous to that cordiality which ought to exist between neighbors.

These and many other considerations made it most desirable that Texas, or at least a part of it, should be acquired by the United States. The small value placed on the country by Mexico, its remote and disconnected situation, the unsettled state of Mexican politics, the depressed and languishing condition of her finances, and, above all, the threatening attitude of Spain, were, in Van Buren's opinion, so many reasons why Mexico should willingly part with the province for a proper consideration.

Mexico, however, was fully determined to retain Texas,

and the line as defined in the treaty of 1819 remained unchanged for sixteen years.

Quite as unavailing were the efforts of the administrat n to bring Great Britain to an agreement on the boundai l of Oregon and Maine. Forty years and more had passed since the signing of the definitive treaty of peace, yet the old dispute over the meaning of its terms was as far from settlement as ever. At the close of the French and Indian War Great Britain came into possession of Canada, and, for purposes of government, marked out the Province of Quebec. As set forth in the King's proclamation of 1763, its limit on the south was the forty-fifth parallel from the St. Lawrence eastward to the highlands which separate the waters flowing into the St. Lawrence from those which fall into the sea; along the highlands and the north shore of Chaleur Bay and the coast of the Gulf of St. Lawrence to Cape Rozier, and thence across the St. Lawrence by the west end of Anticosti t, the mouth of the river St. John. Hitherto, Maine and Nova Scotia extended northward to the waters of the St. Lawrence. One effect of the proclamation of 1763 was, therefore, to move this boundary southward from the bank of the St. Lawrence to the sources of the rivers which flowed into it —the Chaudière, Ouelle, Greene, Metis, and the tributaries of Lake Memphremagog—and part them from the waters of the Connecticut, the Androscoggin, the Kennebec, Penobscot, Restigouche, and St. John.

East of Maine was the province of Nova Scotia, whose western limit, as described in the commissions of her governors, was a line from Cape Sable across the Bay of Fundy to the mouth of the river St. Croix, the river to its source, and a meridian to the south boundary of the Province of Quebec.

Long before the Revolution, therefore, the extent of Maine, both northward and eastward, had been defined with what seemed to be precision. But to describe it in proclamations and commissions was one thing, and to locate it on the ground was quite another, for nobody knew just which river was the St. Croix.

In the early days of discovery and exploration Pierre

du Guast, Sieur de Monts, Gentleman in Ordinary of the King's Chamber, obtained a patent to Acadie, a vast stretch of North America from the fortieth to the forty-sixth degree northern latitude. He was made lieutenant-general, was given viceroyal authority, a monopoly of the fur trade, and power to impress vagabonds and idlers as settlers for his colony. With such material and Champlain for pilot, De Monts sailed from Havre de Grace one April day in 1604, reached the southern coast of Nova Scotia, passed around Cape Sable, spent two weeks in St. Mary's Bay, discovered Annapolis river, explored the Bay of Fundy, named the St. John river, and finally dropped anchor in Passama-quoddy Bay.

While there, Champlain, in the course of his explorations, entered a river which he called Rivière des Etechemins, and not far from its mouth, found an island which he named St. Croix, and which De Monts decided to make the site of his colony. Landing with all speed, the emigrants, soldiers, sailors, artisans, and gentlemen went hard to work, and before the end of autumn had covered the north side of the island with buildings in the form of a square. With the first fall of snow all the horrors of a northern winter began. Great blocks of ice, swept in and out by the tide, cut off the colonists from the mainland and deprived them of wood and water. The scurvy raged, and ere spring opened thirty-five of the seventy-nine died. All thought of remaining at St. Croix was abandoned, and on the return of early summer De Monts and Champlain, with a party, explored the New England coast as far south as Cape Cod, and finding no better site, returned to St. Croix and moved the colony to Port Royal—or, as we know it, Annapolis—taking many of the buildings with them. The few left standing were demolished by Samuel Argall during his raid on the French in 1613, and the location of the place passed out of memory, while the name of the river remained. In time the St. Croix, wherever it might be, was made part of the line of demarcation between Nova Scotia and Maine, and at last, in 1755, a river called the St. Croix was placed, by John Mitchell, on a map of the British and French possessions in

North America, which was used by the commissioners at Paris when framing the treaty of peace in 1783.

As neither Quebec nor Nova Scotia sided with us in the war for independence, no right to demand their cession existed, and in the definitive treaty the western boundary of Nova Scotia and part of the south line of Quebec were made the limits of the United States on the northeast.

The language of the treaty seemed plain enough. The words are: " East, by a line to be drawn along the middle of the river St. Croix, from its mouth in the Bay of Fundy to its source, and from its source directly north to the aforesaid highlands, which divide the rivers that fall into the Atlantic Ocean from those which fall into the St. Lawrence."

But the definitive treaty had scarcely been framed, and had not yet been ratified and proclaimed, when complaint was made to the Continental Congress that the subjects of Great Britain were encroaching on the lands of the State of Massachusetts, and were planting a town and making settlements on the east bank of the Schoodic river. Congress referred the matter to the Governor of Massachusetts, who applied to the General Court, which promptly despatched Benjamin Lincoln and Henry Knox to see if encroachments had really been made, and, if so, to politely request the Governor of Nova Scotia to recall the intruders.

Repairing with all haste to Passamaquoddy Bay, the commissioners found that three rivers flowed into the bay; that the British considered the Schoodic, or most westerly of the three, to be the St. Croix; that all the lands to the eastward had been surveyed and granted to refugees who but a few months before had fled from the United States; that St. Andrews, on the eastern bank, was a town of three hundred houses; that at Schoodic, near the head of navigation, were a hundred more; and that other towns were already in process of forming. They examined the three rivers flowing into the bay—the Schoodic, the Copstock or Passamaquoddy, and the Magaguadavic—and gave it as their opinion that the latter was the St. Croix of the treaty, and that the British were encroaching on the territory of Massachusetts.

Governor John Hancock now requested the governor of

the newly formed province of New Brunswick to recall the intruders, and was informed in reply that the Schoodic was the St. Croix of the treaty, that it was the only river large enough to be a boundary, and that the loyal refugees settled on its eastern bank would not be disturbed. But Massachusetts also claimed to own Moose, Dudley, and Frederick Islands, all lying to the west of the mouth of the Magaguadavic, had sold land on them, and was exercising jurisdiction over the few settlers they contained.

To test this right the provincial sheriff of Charlotte County repaired to Moose Island, one day in 1785, and summoned the male inhabitants to send jurors to the county court. A justice of the peace holding a commission from Massachusetts, hearing of the visit of the British sheriff, sailed over to the island and warned the people not to heed the summons. A new complaint was now made to the Continental Congress, which sent the papers to Jay, who advised that Massachusetts, without noise or delay, garrison such places in her possession as were exposed to British attack. In this shape the matter stood when Washington was inaugurated.

Meantime, many acts of violence and of sovereignty were done by provincials on the disputed soil. On one occasion the Massachusetts deputy collector of imports and excises was arrested for debt and ordered to find bail or go to jail at St. Andrews. On another two vessels at anchor were seized by custom-house officers from New Brunswick. Yet neither Congress nor the President could do anything toward mending matters till John Jay went to London, in 1794, to frame the memorable treaty which still bears his name, when he was charged with the settlement of the long-disputed question— Which river is the St. Croix?

But it could not be settled offhand at London. The matter was therefore referred for final adjustment to a commission, which was to do three things: "Decide what river is the river St. Croix intended by the treaty," and "particularize the latitude and longitude of its mouth and of its source." To determine the river proved an easy matter, for in 1797, on an island in the river so long claimed by the British as the true St. Croix, were found the remains of the little settle-

65

49

C. Rosiers

C. Gaspe

48

alew

Miramichi Bay

47

N B R U N S W I C K

46

D Y

45

S C O T I A

A

44

C E A N

Cape Sable

65

L.L. POATES. ENGR. N.Y.

ment made by De Monts more than one hundred and ninety years before.* To "particularize the latitude and longitude " of the source of the St. Croix was not an easy matter. From this duty the commission was therefore relieved, by an explanatory article added to the treaty of 1798, and to-day the spot agreed on as the source is marked by a monument resembling those it used to be customary to erect in country churchyards.

And now a new difficulty arose. The treaty of 1783 set forth that the mouth of the St. Croix was in the Bay of Fundy. The commission fixed it in Passamaquoddy Bay,† and by so doing left the ownership of the group of islands—Dudley, Moose, and Frederick—to be settled some time in the future. Once, in 1803, and again in 1806 it seemed as if a settlement was about to be reached. But it was not till the great adjustment of old disputes in 1815 that a provision for a commission to decide who owned the islands was made part of a ratified treaty; and it was not till 1817 that, under the decision of the commission, Moose, Dudley, and Frederick were assigned to the United States, and all other islands in Passamaquoddy Bay and Grand Menan, in the Bay of Fundy, were awarded to Great Britain.‡

The river St. Croix once agreed on, and its source discovered and plainly marked, the location of the remainder of the eastern boundary seemed to present no difficulty. The line was to be a true meridian from the source of the St. Croix to the highlands separating the waters flowing into the St. Lawrence from those which made their way into the ocean. But the determination of these highlands, on which so much depended, proved far from a simple matter, delayed the settlement of the boundary nearly fifty years, provoked bad feeling between the contending parties, and more than once called forth from Maine and Massachusetts the assertion of a doctrine dangerous to the safety of the Union. The idea

---

* Details and Documents may be found in International Arbitrations, J. B. Moore, vol. i, pp. 1–43. For Benson's Report, see pp. 33–43.

† At Joe's Point, latitude 45° 5′ 5″ north, longitude 67° 12′ 30″ west from Greenwich.

‡ For all the details see International Arbitrations, Moore, vol. i, pp. 45–64.

that highlands meant mountains was early formed and held
to persistently. No such mountainous ridge appears on the
map used by the treaty makers in 1783. But it does on
later maps, and not till 1802 did the Government become
aware that nothing of the sort existed.

In that year the Governor of Massachusetts assured the
Secretary of State that commissioners had traversed the
country in vain to find the highlands designated in the
treaty; that south of the St. Lawrence there were no mountains; that the country was a great morass; that the rivers
rising in it flowed many miles apart in opposite directions,
some to the St. Lawrence and some to the Atlantic; and
that, in his opinion, a commission should be appointed to
ascertain and mark the northwest angle of Nova Scotia.

Influenced by this advice and information, Madison
promptly instructed Rufus King to begin negotiations for
the settlement of the Maine boundary, and bade him secure,
if possible, a commission similar to that of 1795 to determine
a point most proper to be substituted for that called in the
treaty of 1783 the northwest angle of Nova Scotia. Mr.
King did as commanded, and in the convention of 1803,
which the Senate amended and Great Britain never ratified,
was an article providing for the desired joint commission.
Like provision was again made in the treaty concluded by
Monroe and Pinkney in 1807. But this never reached the
Senate, and when the peace commissioners met at Ghent in
1814 the boundary of Maine, from the source of the St.
Croix to the head waters of the Connecticut, was still unde-
termined. Then, however, full provision was made, and in
the summer of 1817 the work of surveying began in earnest.
The country to be explored was a vast wilderness, uninhab-
ited save by a few Indians and in one place by a few Frenchmen. The survey proved much more difficult, slow, and costly than had been expected, so that May, 1821, came before
the board of commissioners met at New York to hear the arguments of the agents of the two contending governments.
Starting at the source of the St. Croix river, the meridian
as traced by the surveyors reached a high elevation at Mars
Hill, descended thence into the valley of the St. John river,

crossed that stream, rose again to the summit of a ridge parting waters flowing into the St. John from those which reached the Restigouche, and one hundred and forty-three miles from the point of beginning, met a ridge on the north slope of which are the head waters of the river Metis, which enters the St. Lawrence. Where the meridian crossed the crest of this ridge was, the Americans held, the long-sought northwest angle of Nova Scotia.

From this the British agent dissented, and gave two reasons. In the first place, the ridge, he said, was a mere watershed, and had neither such elevation nor such continuity as would justify him in accepting it as the highlands meant by the treaty. In the second place, it parted the Metis, which fell into the St. Lawrence river from the Restigouche, which entered the Bay of Chaleurs, and could not, therefore, be said to "divide those rivers which empty themselves into the river St. Lawrence from those which fall into the Atlantic Ocean," as the treaty required. The words of the treaty "north to the highlands" meant that the meridian should end at the first highlands which "in any part of their extent" divided waters falling into the St. Lawrence from those falling into the Atlantic, and such a highland was Mars Hill. The hill, in truth, parted no such waters; but he held to his view, and as the north boundary of Maine and New Hampshire drew a line from Mars Hill to what he claimed as the northwesternmost head of the Connecticut river. Here, again, he took issue with the American agent, whose line met the head of Hall's stream. From the point where the Connecticut river crossed the forty-fifth parallel of north latitude the boundary line ran due west to the St. Lawrence. But the astronomers, to their dismay, found that the parallel had been wrongly marked by the old-time surveyors; that just east of Lake Champlain the true line lay three fourths of a mile south of the false one; and that on the territory belonging to Great Britain the United States had built one great fort at Rouse's Point and near by was rapidly finishing another.

As the result of the long and costly survey, the commissioners were called on to settle three questions: Where is the northwest angle of Nova Scotia? Where is the north-westernmost head of the Connecticut river? Shall the parallel of forty-five degrees remain as marked, or shall the error be corrected? To agree on any one of these was hopeless; the commissioners accordingly gave up the attempt, filed their dissenting opinions, presented their reports, and in November, 1821, adjourned subject to the pleasure of their governments. Failure to agree now made it the duty of Great Britain and the United States, under the treaty of Ghent, to refer the reports of the two commissioners to " some friendly sovereign or state " as arbitrator. But one delay followed another, and nearly seven years slipped by before the King of the Netherlands was chosen as the arbitrator, and three more ere he made his decision.

The statement which the United States laid before the King began with a discussion of " the highlands " as used in the treaty of 1783. Definite words, such as mountains, hills, or other terms, it was said, which might be construed to apply to the peculiar character of the country, had been carefully excluded, and the general term highlands had been carefully inserted. It meant land more or less elevated, which at some point due north from the source of the St. Croix divided the waters falling into the St. Lawrence from those falling into the Atlantic, and which continued so to do eastwardly all along the north boundary of Nova Scotia, and westwardly all the way to the north-westernmost head of the Connecticut river. Now, there were but two places on the line due north from the source of the St. Croix where the land parted rivers flowing in different directions. One was ninety-seven miles north of the St. Croix, and separated the tributary streams of the river St. John, which entered the Bay of Fundy, from tributaries of the Restigouche, which found its way to the Bay of Chaleurs and so to the Gulf of St. Lawrence. The other was forty-seven miles farther north, and divided the waters of the Restigouche from those of the Metis, which joined the river St. Lawrence. Which of these was the point intended by the treaty depended, then, on what that instrument meant by " rivers that empty themselves into the river St. Lawrence "

and by " those which fall into the Atlantic Ocean." The first
expression was clear enough, for it embraced such, and such
only, as flowed into the particularly designated river. In
the second the words Atlantic Ocean meant that great sub-
division of the sea which, with its bays, gulfs, and inlets,
washed the shores of the east coast of North America. If
this were not so, then there was no river in Maine or Nova
Scotia which fell into the Atlantic Ocean. The Restigouche entered the Bay of Chaleurs and Gulf of St. Lawrence; the river St. John, the Bay of Fundy; the Magaguadavic and Schoodic, Passamaquoddy Bay and the Bay of
Fundy; the Penobscot, the bay of the same name; the Kennebec, the Sagadahock Bay. But the treaty makers, with
Mitchell's map before them, had very properly considered
that these rivers fell into the Atlantic, and had contrasted
them with those which emptied themselves into the St. Lawrence. The highlands of the treaty were therefore those
which separated the waters of the Restigouche, which fell
into the Atlantic, from the waters of the Metis, which entered the St. Lawrence, and where these highlands were met
by the due north line from the source of the St. Croix was
the northwest angle of Nova Scotia.

The British statement set forth, on the other hand, that
the northwest angle of Nova Scotia was at Mars Hill; that
the highlands of the treaty were those running thence to the
Connecticut river, and that the Penobscot, the Kennebec,
and the Androscoggin were the rivers which the treaty referred to as falling into the Atlantic and which were to be
separated from those entering the St. Lawrence. Waters
falling into the Atlantic Ocean, not those falling into the
Gulf of St. Lawrence or the Bay of Fundy, were to be sopa-
rated from the tributaries of the St. Lawrence. The Bay
of Fundy was never intended by the treaty to be considered
as the Atlantic, nor the St. John as one of the rivers falling
into that ocean. The plain intent and purpose of the treaty
was to make the St. Croix part of the eastern boundary
of Maine, and so divide the country above it that all great
rivers discharging their waters within British territory
should be British from mouth to source, and all falling into

the ocean within American territory should be American throughout their entire course. The highlands must, therefore, lie to the south of the St. John river, and the northwest angle of Nova Scotia must be at or near Mars Hill.

This hill, said the American statement, does not fulfil any of the requirements of the treaty. It does not divide any waters; it is at least one hundred miles from the source of any stream falling into the St. Lawrence, and no highlands extend eastward from it in such wise as to form the northern boundary of Nova Scotia. The sole reason for mentioning the northwest angle of Nova Scotia was to identify the highlands of the treaty with those described in the proclamation of 1763 as forming the south boundary of the Province of Quebec, which in the commission of Montague Wilmot were also made the north boundary of Nova Scotia. It was clear, therefore, that Mars Hill was not on the highlands of the treaty.

From the surveys it appeared that, of the many streams which formed the head waters of the Connecticut, four— Hall's stream, Indian stream, Perry's stream, and the main Connecticut—rose in the highlands, and that all united their waters north of the true latitude of forty-five degrees. Great Britain claimed that head which, of all others, should be found to lie most to the northwest of the main stream. As the river was known as the Connecticut far above its junctions with Hall's stream and Indian stream, even to a body of water called Connecticut Lake, Great Britain held that the source of the most northwestern tributary of this lake was the northwesternmost head of the Connecticut. This, the American commissioner argued, was a branch of the northeasternmost head; the source contemplated by the treaty was that of the west branch of Indian stream.

Concerning the third point in controversy, the commissioner from the United States submitted that the treaty dealt with that part of the boundary only which had never been surveyed and marked; that the forty-fifth parallel had been run out and marked between 1771 and 1774, had ever since been the basis of land grants and jurisdiction, and should be suffered to remain as it was. The British commissioner insisted on the letter of the treaty—the true parallel, and no other.

On the tenth of January, 1831, the arbitrator made his award. Disregarding the arguments of the two parties as to the first point in dispute, the King drew a line due north from the source of the St. Croix to the middle of the St. John, up the St. John and the St. Francis to the source of its southwesternmost branch, and cut the disputed territory in twain. The northern piece he awarded to Great Britain, and the southern to the United States. The northwesternmost head of the Connecticut he declared to be the most northwestern of the streams which enter Connecticut Lake. The forty-fifth parallel he decided should be truly located without regard to former surveys, but the forts near Rouse's Point should remain with the United States.[*]

No sooner was the award announced than the Minister of the United States at The Hague, without waiting for instructions, protested. King William had drawn his own boundary because he did not believe it possible to execute the treaty of 1783. In doing so the King had, in the opinion of the American Minister, exceeded his powers, for the question where the boundary line should be drawn was one the United States would submit to no sovereign.[†] In Maine, when the award became known, indignation rose to fever heat. Some denounced the Government for its folly in submitting the interests of a republic to the decision of a crowned head. Others held that the Senate could not part with an inch of American soil, nor change the boundary claimed by a State without its consent. In a dispute of this kind the Government was merely the agent of Maine. In these views the Legislature shared, and in February, 1831, gave expression to them in no uncertain language. The Convention of 1827, said one resolution, tended to violate the Constitution of the United States and to impair the sovereign rights and powers of the State of Maine, and relieved her of all obligation to submit to any decision made

---

[*] International Arbitrations, J. B. Moore, vol. i, pp. 119–136.

[†] Senate Executive Documents, No. 3, First Session, Twenty-second Congress.

or to be made under the Convention. It is the opinion of the Legislature, said another, that the decision of the King of the Netherlands cannot and ought not to be considered as obligatory on the United States either on principles of honor, right, or justice. No decision, said the third, made by any umpire under any circumstances, if it dismembers a State, either has or can have any constitutional force or obligation on the State so dismembered unless the State sanction the decision, which Maine was far from doing.*

When Massachusetts consented to part with the district of Maine she reserved a share in the wild lands. As an interested party, her General Court now resolved that the adoption of the line drawn by the King of the Netherlands would deprive both Maine and Massachusetts of large tracts of territory; that the Government of the United States had no constitutional right to cede any portion of the territory of the States composing the Union to any foreign power, nor to deprive any State of land or property belonging to it; that any act purporting to have such an effect would be wholly null and void, and in no way obligatory upon the government or people of either of the States; that the General Court of Massachusetts solemnly protested against the adoption of the proposed line; that any act purporting to put it into effect would be performed without the consent of Massachusetts and in violation of her rights, and would be null and void and in no way binding on her government or people; and that she would cheerfully cooperate with Maine in any measures best calculated to prevent the adoption by the Government of the United States of the line recommended by the King of the Netherlands.†

That Maine was serious in her determination not to recede from her claims was made yet more manifest by two acts of the Legislature. One incorporated a new town, to be called Madawaska, within the bounds of which was some

---

* Resolves of the State of Maine, 1829–1835, pp. 242–246; Resolve of February 28, 1831.

† Resolves of the Commonwealth of Massachusetts, Resolve of February 15, 1832.

land to the south of the St. John and the disputed country beyond that river to the northward. The other authorized the inhabitants to elect a representative to the Legislature. They were intended to be a new assertion of the right of the State to jurisdiction over the region in dispute,* and not to be carried into effect immediately. But the inhabitants of the Madawaska settlements took matters into their own hands, met south of the river, organized their town government, and, a little later, gathered in town meeting and elected a representative.†

For these acts of sovereignty four citizens of Maine were seized by the New Brunswick authorities, carried by force out of the State, tried on a charge of attempting to subvert his Majesty's authority, found guilty, fined, and imprisoned. The Governor of Maine at once complained to the Department of State at Washington, urged that steps be taken to secure the immediate release of the Americans, and asked that the State be protected from invasion.

Livingston replied that an arrangement had been made with the British Minister to preserve the state of things then existing till a final decision was reached; that it was distinctly understood that no exercise of State authority should take place meanwhile in the country in dispute; that the President was most desirous to keep the agreement with the utmost good faith; and that the proceedings of the Madawaska people could not but be considered as a breach of the agreement. Nevertheless, the President did as requested, secured the release of the imprisoned citizens of Maine, and was assured by the British Minister that no violation of the agreement by the provincial authorities would be permitted. Maine thereupon resolved that the Constitution " does not invest the General Government with absolute powers, but confers only a special and modified sovereignty without authority to cede to a foreign power any portion of a territory belonging to a State without its consent; . . . that if there is an attribute of that sovereignty

* Message of Governor S. E. Smith, January 9, 1832.
† Resolves of the State of Maine, 1829–1835, pp. 473–496.

willing to concede to the United States a detached piece of country on the Pacific and the Strait of Juan de Fuca, stretching from Bullfinch Harbor to Hood's Canal.

Mr. Gallatin based the claims of the United States on the purchase of Louisiana in 1803, and the acquisition by this means of titles of France to the country; on the Spanish treaty of 1819 and the acquisition by this means of the titles of Spain above forty-two degrees; on the discovery of the mouth of the Columbia by Captain Gray in 1792; on the exploration of the region by Lewis and Clark; on the settlement at Astoria in 1811; on the virtual recognition of American title by Great Britain in the restoration of the Astoria fur in 1818; and on contiguity, a doctrine always maintained by Great Britain. If, said he, some trading factories on the shores of Hudson Bay offered her ground for asserting an exclusive right to occupancy as far as the Rocky Mountains, if the infant settlements on our Atlantic coast once justified her in claiming all the continent to the South Sea, and of enforcing it to the Mississippi, the presence of millions of American citizens already within reach of the Pacific cannot certainly be rejected.

To this the British negotiators replied, and the reply was sound and conclusive, that the province of Louisiana was the country drained by the Mississippi; that the region drained by the Columbia had never been a part of it; that it had never belonged to France; that, admitting it had been part of Louisiana, the cession of French territory west of the Mississippi to Spain in 1763 had merged all title in Spain, and, this being the case, Captain Gray had discovered a river and Lewis and Clark had explored and Astor planted a settlement in a country already belonging to Spain. It was only by acknowledging the region to be the property of no nation that the United States could derive titles from discovery and exploration and settlement. Having thus disposed of the French claims, the British plenipotentiaries declared that the claims of Spain because of discovery prior to 1790 were futile and visionary, and cut off by the Nootka Convention of that year between her and Great Britain; that the rights derived by the United States above forty-two degrees, under the Spanish treaty of 1819, were such as Spain possessed after the Nootka Convention, and none other; and that these were to trade and settle in that region and to navigate its waters in common with Great Britain.

The valid claim of our country to the Oregon region rested on discovery, exploration, and settlement.   To this Great Britain replied, in the first place, that Lieutenant Meares, of the Royal Navy, entered the Columbia four years before Captain Gray, but admitted that Gray was the first to discover that the bay formed by the discharge of the waters of the Columbia into the Pacific was the outlet of a great river; in the second place, that the exploration of Lewis and Clarke was of no consequence, because the country traversed by them fell within the provisions of the Nootka Convention of 1790; in the third place, that agents of the Northwest Fur Company had planted posts on the northwest branch of the Columbia, and were extending them down that river before Astoria existed.   Finally, it was stated that Great Britain did not claim exclusive possession of any part of the country, but merely the rights of trade, navigation, and settlement—rights which she conceded to the United States, as the successor of Spain, and no others.

To come to an agreement as to boundary was impossible. The attempt was therefore abandoned, and in 1827 a new convention was drawn, and joint occupation continued indefinitely, with the provision that either party might end it after one year's notice to the other.

The attention which in one way and another was thus drawn to the Oregon country in the course of four years now began to produce visible results.   Men in various parts of the United States became eager to throw off the restraints of life in the East, brave the hardships of a march across the plains, and begin a life of adventure on the Pacific coast. Three associations or companies of adventurers—one in Massachusetts, one in Ohio, and one in New Orleans—were readily formed, and when the Twentieth Congress began its second session, in December, 1828, a bill in their interests was reported by a committee.   As presented, it provided for the establishment of a territorial government over the whole

while above and beyond it the mountains rear their snowy and impassable tops, many hundreds of feet higher than the summits of the Council Bluffs. They stand like a Chinese wall, and must forever and effectually guard us from all attacks from that quarter. Should any foreign power ever be so senseless as to take possession of Oregon, she can never injure the United States on that side.

"But suppose it possible to settle such a country. The next step will be to organize it into a Territory, and then you will be called on to turn this Territory into a State. And what then? It can be but a few years before such a State must of its own weight fall off from this Confederacy. You have no practical means to connect such a State with the rest of the Republic. No delegate or representative can come thence to this House and return within a twelvemonth. Let his journey average twenty-five miles a day, and it will take him three hundred and sixty-eight days to come here and go back. His mileage will amount to nearly four thousand dollars, and be paid him for no other service than travelling. No, sir, let those restless spirits who cannot be content to cultivate their native soil, let such beings go to Oregon, but let them go at their own risk." *

Twenty years from the day on which this speech was made, a delegate from the Territory of Oregon was sitting in the House of Representatives.

There were, however, others more hopeful. "It is a mistake," said one, "to suppose that Oregon could never become a part of the Confederacy. I believe the Stony Mountains in time will be passed with as much ease as the Alleghanies now are. The improvements of the age remove the obstacles imposed by distance and Nature. Twenty years since, a man who predicted that a voyage from New Orleans to Louisville would be made in eight days, as it now is, would have been thought insane. Then a journey from the Atlantic to the Ohio river was a great and hazardous undertaking. Now it may be made over a comfortable

---

* Speech of Mr. Mitchell, of Tennessee, Register of Debates in Congress, vol. v, 1828–1829, pp. 134–137.

road in three days." Others declared Oregon was not the desert waste the opponents of the bill had represented, but a fertile and healthful region, well watered and wooded, and to make good their assertions, quoted at length from the writings of Vancouver, Lewis and Clark, Humboldt, Mr. Prevost, who received the surrender of Astoria, Major Brooks, who had often visited the coast, and Franchere, a French Canadian and a member of the first party sent out by Mr. Astor in 1810. But the belief that Oregon was of little importance, that it could not become a State in the Union, and that to organize it as a Territory or spread over it the laws of the United States would be a violation of the Convention of 1827, prevailed, and in the end the House refused to order the bill to a third reading, a vote which amounted to rejection.*

But there was yet another subject of dispute with Great Britain, and one that threatened to be serious—the West Indian Islands were again shut to vessels from the United States. Never since the colonies renounced allegiance to the Crown and founded the Republic had trade with Britain and her dependencies rested on fair and liberal principles. No sooner was the war for independence over than the colonial system just thrown off was applied in all its rigor to the West Indies, and during twelve years not a vessel carrying the flag of the United States could lawfully enter a British port in one of them. Now and then a governor of one or another of the colonies, when the needs of its inhabitants required, would open its ports to the products of the United States if they came in British vessels. But these relaxations were few in number and short in duration, and the exclusion of American ships and products was still a grievance when Jay went to London to negotiate a treaty in 1794. There was little in that instrument to commend it to any one; but the most objectionable article of all was the twelfth, which opened the ports of the British West Indies to American ships of seventy tons and under; which restricted their cargoes to such goods and merchandise grown,

* January 9, 1829.

manufactured, or produced in the United States, as could also be carried from our shores in British vessels of any tonnage; and which forbade an American ship to enter any port on the face of the earth (save our own) with molasses, sugar, coffee, cocoa, or cotton either from his Majesty's islands or from the United States. That a provision at once manifestly beneficial to British navigation and so hurtful to American trade, commerce, and shipping should have been inserted in any treaty to which we were a party so astonished the Senate that ratification was secured only on condition that the article regulating colonial trade should be suspended. To this Great Britain willingly agreed, and for twenty years went on imposing such arbitrary restrictions as she pleased. At the next great settling of accounts, in 1815, another effort was made to put colonial trade on the same footing as direct trade with the mother country. But again Great Britain refused, and in the Convention of 1815 is an express stipulation that "intercourse between the United States and his Britannic Majesty's possessions in the West Indies and on the continent of North America shall not be affected by any provisions of" the article regulating trade and commerce with British possessions in Europe.

Once more left to do as she would, Great Britain shut our ships from the islands, and laid duties that came near to being prohibitory on American provisions, even when brought in British bottoms.* Having led the way, Nova Scotia and New Brunswick followed, and in 1816 laid a duty of twenty shillings a ton on plaster of Paris if taken by an American coaster from any port in the provinces to any port in the United States east of Boston.† And now Congress struck back, and a commercial war began in earnest. By one act ‡ foreign vessels were forbidden to bring plaster of Paris, wherever produced, to the United States unless they came from ports from which American ships were equally free to bring it. The blow was effective;

---

* History of the People of the United States, vol. iv, pp. 346–348.
† Ibid., vol. iv, p. 347.
‡ Act of March 3, 1817, "to regulate the trade in plaster of Paris."

the provincial restrictions were repealed, and Congress followed up the attack by a " navigation act " * directed against the British West Indies. This provided, in the first place, that no ship owned wholly or in part by a subject of Great Britain could enter the United States if it came from a port in any part of his Majesty's dominions from which American-owned vessels were excluded; and, in the second place, that when a British ship laden with American products cleared from one of our ports she must give bond not to land her cargo at any British port closed by the first section of the act.

The effect was immediate. The General Assembly of the island of Jamaica voted a memorial to the Prince Regent setting forth " the dreadful evils they were threatened with," and praying for the adoption of measures to avert them.† The Governor of St. Lucia, where a drought destroyed the products of the earth, opened the port of Castries to lumber and provisions from the United States in " any vessel," even though such vessel had neither register, clearance, nor papers of any kind save a manifest of her cargo.‡ And the British Government,# by Orders in Council, turned Halifax, in Nova Scotia, and St. John, in New Brunswick, into free ports in which the products of the West Indies could be exchanged for flour, potatoes, tar, pitch, potash, beans, poultry, live stock, and lumber of every sort from the United States. Once more Congress struck back, and in 1820 shut the ports of the United States to British vessels from New Brunswick, from Nova Scotia, Lower Canada, Newfoundland, the island of Cape Breton, the Bahamas, Bermuda, Caicos and their dependencies, and from every port or place belonging to Great Britain in the West Indies or on the continent of America south of the United States, and required that all British West India goods must be imported direct from the place of production.‖ This cut

---

* Act of April 15, 1818.

† Niles's Weekly Register, October 31, 1818, vol. xv, p. 156.

‡ Ibid., September 26, 1818, vol. xv, p. 80.

Act of Parliament, May 8, 1818. Orders in Council, May 30, 1818.

‖ Act of Congress, May 15, 1820.

off all trade with the British Indies, opened the way for smuggling on a great scale, and forced from Parliament an act * which admitted American ships, laden with certain goods, into specified ports in Canada, Newfoundland, Nova Scotia, New Brunswick, and the West Indies, but taxed goods coming from the United States ten per cent more than like articles from the British North American colonies. Monroe, thereupon, by proclamation,† opened the ports of the United States to British West Indian products, subject to a like extra duty of ten per cent when brought in British vessels, on which was imposed a further duty of one dollar a ton. Congress at its next session reduced the tonnage duty to ninety-six cents, and limited British ships to a direct trade between the colonies and the United States.‡ Great Britain a few months later retaliated and met this with a duty of four shillings and sixpence a ton on American shipping trading in her West Indies.# No finer exhibition was ever made of the folly of retaliation when carried to an extreme. Again the purposes of statesmen were confounded by the acts of the people; illicit trade sprang up, smuggling flourished, the island authorities encouraged it, and thousands of dollars worth of goods called by names other than their own went through the custom-houses duty free. A senator from Connecticut, long engaged in the West Indian trade, used to narrate an incident which well illustrated the state to which colonial commerce was now brought. He shipped, on one occasion, a cargo of candles, the importation of which was prohibited, but the custom-house inspector declared they were herrings, and as such they passed without question.‖

When matters had gone on in this wise for two years Great Britain revised her policy. To nations with colonies she offered reciprocity, mother country against mother country, colonies against colonies.△ To nations without colonies she offered the same trade in her colonial ports that was given to her and her possessions in their ports, provided the proposition was accepted within a year. Neither act

---

* Act of June 24, 1822.
† August 24, 1822.
‡ Act of March 1, 1823.

\# Orders in Council, June 17, 1823.
‖ Memoirs of John Quincy Adams, vol. vii, p. 429
△ Acts of June 27 and July 5, 1825.

was ever officially made known to the United States, nor was their purpose, nor the construction to be placed on them, ever explained. Indeed, the colonial officers whose duty it was to enforce the acts could not agree as to their meaning. In one island they were interpreted to mean one thing, and in another something else. Nevertheless, the act of July fifth, though not officially known, was submitted to Congress, for the United States must accept before July, 1826, or take the penalty. But as Congress did nothing, Adams, the moment the session closed, despatched Albert Gallatin to London to reopen the long-suspended negotiation. Gallatin reached London in August, 1826, and before he had time to deliver his letter of credence was met with an Order of Council, dated July twenty-seventh, which decreed that on and after December first no vessel from the United States should enter a port of the British West Indies.* Expostulation was vain. Great Britain would not yield, and the loss of trade was made much of by the friends of Jackson in the campaign for the presidency then well under way.

---

* Message of Adams, December 5, 1826. See also Gallatin-Canning Correspondence, Niles's Register, vol. xxxi, pp. 268–277, and Report of Committee on Commerce made to the House of Representatives. Ibid., pp. 355 361.

CHAPTER LII.

THE PEOPLE IN CONTROL.

IN the previous chapters of this history an attempt has been made to describe that peaceful and happy revolution through which our country passed between the day when war was a second time ended with Great Britain and the day when a triumphant people sent Andrew Jackson to the White House. It has been my purpose to show how, with the fall of Napoleon and the return of peace, questions of foreign policy which for two-and-twenty years had divided Federalists and Republicans ceased to distract the people; how a period of good feeling, of political calm followed; how, during this time, there arose questions of a domestic kind, the regulation of the currency, the charter of a national bank, the protection of manufactures, the use of the public domain, the construction of roads and canals at Government expenses, the rights of the States and their status under the Constitution; how these questions fostered the growth of sectionalism, rent the once harmonious Republican party in pieces, brought about the contest of 1824, and made straight the way for the election of Andrew Jackson. An attempt has been made to describe the life of the people in the cities, in the towns and villages, on the frontier; their ideas on government, on banking, on labor, on education, on literature, on the social problems of the time, have been reviewed; the astonishing betterment in the conditions of life brought about by new inventions and discoveries, new means of locomotion, and the rise of new industries, and new ways of gaining a livelihood, have all been described, and it is now time to turn to the second phase of that political contest waged by the friends of Adams, Clay, and Jackson.

The defeat of Jackson in the House of Representatives was followed by an outburst of indignation from every journal controlled by his friends. "Expired at Washington," said one, " on the ninth of February, of poison administered by the assassin hands of John Quincy Adams, the usurper, and Henry Clay, the virtue, liberty, and independence of the United States." "The sale of the presidency to Mr. Adams," said another, " has disheartened many worthy persons and made them doubt the capacity of the people for self-government." "Five Western States," exclaimed a third, " bought and transferred to the usurper like so many live cattle or a drove of negroes! The people stand aghast and are lost in amazement." The people were indeed astonished, and more than one Western member of the House of Representatives found it necessary to explain to his constituents beyond the mountains just how the election of Adams came about. A Tennesseean assured his supporters, in a circular letter, that he could put aside his grief for the defeat of Jackson, and even forget how deep had been the affront to the pride of his much-injured State, if it were with the will of the people that these things were done. " But it is not Jackson that has been defeated, nor Tennessee that has been overlooked. It is the sovereign will of the people, the almighty voice of this great nation, that has been set at defiance. Is ours a government of the people? Is their will subject to no control but that which they themselves, not their servants, have placed over it? And have we in less than half a century come to this, that the first magistrate can be chosen not by the choice, but against the known, expressed, and solemn choice of at least seventeen of the twenty-four States, and, worse than all, by the votes of the six States falsely given by their representatives against the known will of their constituents? The fact is undeniable that the votes of seven States were given against General Jackson, of which six—those of Maryland, Ohio, Illinois, Kentucky, Missouri, and Louisiana—were cast for Mr. Adams, and that of North Carolina for Mr. Crawford.

What were the motives which directed this course, or the means by which the end was attained" need not be considered. "It is enough that the deed was done."

Said another Tennesseean to the voters of his district: "As our Government is in all respects a representative republic, where the voice of the people governs, there must be a manifest defect in the Constitution in relation to the election of President. One candidate was greatly preferred by the people of eleven out of twenty-four States. Yet, when the power passed from their hands to the House of Representatives the voice of the people was not regarded. The man clearly the choice of a majority of the people was not raised to that high place for which his talents so preeminently fitted him, and to which his public services so richly entitled him. This is a subject for serious consideration by the people, and it will be for them to say on some subsequent occasion whether their voice shall be heard and their rights respected, or whether they will tamely yield those inestimable rights to the unhallowed dictation of politicians."

"Your favorite candidate," said an Indiana member to the people of his district, "was not before Congress. Mr. Clay, not being one of the three highest supported by the people, was excluded by the Constitution. Agreeable to the principles avowed to you, I supported General Jackson, the next in your regard, as shown by the electoral returns of my district. My sincere hope is that the administration of Mr. Adams may be prosperous and happy. Yet I hope never again to see a President of the United States who is not the choice of the people, and trust soon to see the Constitution so amended as to preclude Congress from any sort of interference in the matter, leaving the decision where it ought to be—in the hands of the people."

"The qualifications of the candidates," said a Kentucky member, "were examined by us fully, fairly, and deliberately, and every view we took of them resulted in favor of Adams. That Adams is as much superior to Jackson in the necessary qualifications of a chief magistrate as Jackson is superior to Adams in fitness to command an army was admitted generally. It has always been held to be a settled principle of our elective system that the candidate best qualified should be preferred, and on this the old Republicans acted. The superior fitness of Adams for the presidency ought to justify our vote in the eyes of all sober-minded men."

That Mr. Kremer should be silent in this hour of personal explanation was impossible, and from him came another letter to the electors in his district. "Recurring to the specific charges in my letter, have I not redeemed my pledges," said he, "and made them good? I stated that Henry Clay had transferred his interests to John Quincy Adams. Has not time disclosed the reality? Can any human being acquainted with the circumstances doubt that it was by the agency of Mr. Clay, and by that alone, that the members of five Western States were induced, contrary to the wishes of their constituents, to vote for Mr. Adams? There is no part of the Union where the people maintain the right to instruct their representatives with more jealous inflexibility than in the Western States. Can it be believed, then, that some twenty or thirty of the representatives of such a people would have thought for one moment of voting for Mr. Adams, who was known to be odious to them, and against Jackson, who was known to be their decided choice, if it had not been for the influence of Henry Clay? No, fellow-citizens; Mr. Clay has to answer for the double sin of defeating the will of his constituents and of sacrificing his friends at the shrine of his own unchastened ambition.

"I said that as a consideration for this abandonment of duty to his constituents, it was said and believed, should this unholy coalition prevail, Mr. Clay was to be appointed Secretary of State. This time has verified to the very letter. He has been offered the appointment of Secretary of State, and has agreed to accept it. It would now be affected squeamishness in me were I to say, 'it is believed' that the appointment of Secretary of State is the consideration given for the support rendered by Mr. Clay to Mr. Adams. I entertain no doubt upon the subject." The address closed with an appeal to the voters to punish the perpetrators " of

with an object it was impossible to mistake. No man but himself could know the nature, extent, and variety of the means used to awe him. At last came a letter purporting to be written by a member of the House over which he pre- sided. When he saw it he felt that a crisis had come in his public career, that silence could no longer be kept, and he issued his card.

The address went on to narrate how Kremer came for- ward with a card acknowledging the authorship of the anony- mous letter; how and why Clay brought the matter before the House; how Kremer, standing in his place, declared he was ready and willing to make good every charge; how, a day later, he repented and assured one member " that he never intended to charge Mr. Clay with corruption or dis- honor in his intended vote for Mr. Adams "; how an ex- planation was put on paper and the Speaker asked if he would be satisfied if Kremer read it in his place; and how the House referred the matter to a committee, before which Kremer refused to come and make good the charges he had made.

Turning from Kremer, Clay next discussed the question, Ought the fact that a plurality has been given to one candi- date have any weight in determining an election by the House; has a Legislature any authority to instruct a mem- ber of the House of Representatives and to a long explana- tion of why he cast his vote for Adams? Coming next to Jackson's letter, Clay protested that he was at a loss to know what the general meant by stating that he held no secret conclaves, entered into no cabals, formed no plans to pros- trate the will of the people. No such charges had ever been made against the general. Why, then, this defence? Could it be that he intended to impute to Clay the miscon- duct described? Taking the whole context of the letter and coupling it with Mr. Kremer's address, others might think he did. If so, he must have based his belief on the infor- mation of others who deceived his credulity and were un- worthy of all credit. " I," said Clay, " entered into no cabals; I held no secret conclaves; I enticed no man to vio- late pledges given or instructions received; and how I prostrated the will of the people I am entirely at a loss to comprehend. The illusions of the general's imagination deceive him. The people of the United States never decided the election in his favor. If the people had willed his election he would have been elected. It was because they did not will his election nor that of any other candidate that the duty of making a choice devolved on the House of Representatives." *

Thus was the issue on the charge of corrupt bargain joined and made the platform for the election yet almost four years away. Jackson had received ninety-nine electoral votes. This was a plurality, therefore he was the choice of the people. As such the House was bound to elect him, and would have done so had it not been for the corrupt bargain between Adams and Clay. No such thing ever existed. But Jackson believed it did, and from this time forward lost no opportunity to give public expression to his opinion. The election over, he wound his way slowly back to Tennessee. Everywhere the people received him with demonstrations of delight. At Nashville a public reception awaited him, and there, in reply to the address of welcome, he reminded the crowd of listeners that it was without any agency on his part that the Legislature of Tennessee presented Andrew Jackson as a candidate for the presidency. He had always regarded that exalted place as a situation not to be sought by any man, however great his talents, however eminent his services. When brought before the people of the United States he had never in any way interfered in the canvass, nor did he, when the election passed to the House of Representatives, attempt in any way to influence its decision.

At Franklin, Tennessee, on the Fourth of July, in reply to another address, he declared that ours is " a government of the people "; that it belongs to them; that it must be kept pure; that the chief magistracy was a post of high distinction, yet the distinction disappeared whenever it was

---

* National Journal, March 28, 1825; Niles's Weekly Register, vol. xxviii, pp. 71–79.

and had received as reward the office of Secretary of State. As such it opened the campaign of 1828, and gave currency and authority to the bargain and corruption cry which followed Clay to the end of his career.

A leader, a platform, and a popular idea once provided, a newspaper was started at Washington, local committees of correspondence were organized all over the Union, a central committee was appointed in each State, able managers were found, office holders were set to work, and a party of opposition to the Administration came rapidly into existence, and grew in numbers and in violence with every act of the President or his advisers. No party name was yet assumed, but under the general designation of " Friends of General Jackson " were gathered all those who for any reason disliked Adams or hated Clay; all who opposed internal improvements at Federal expense; all who believed the tariff laws were exercises of a power not delegated to Congress, and were deliberate, palpable, and dangerous violations of the Constitution; all who believed the story of the bargain; and the great body of office holders the country over. No high principles of national policy as yet bound these elements together, but the lack of these was more than supplied by a savage personal opposition, by a determination to thwart the President at every turn, break down his Administration, and discredit him before the people. Scarcely had the nineteenth Congress been organized when this work of malevolent resistance began. Now it took the form of an amendment to the Constitution prohibiting the appointment of a member of Congress to office during the term for which he was elected; now of a call on Adams for a list of the names of the members of Congress appointed to offices of trust or profit under the authority of the United States by all Presidents since the adoption of the Constitution; now of a report and six bills to reduce the Executive patronage; and now of an amendment to the Constitution declaring the President ineligible to a second term. Adams, in his message, had dwelt at great length on the importance of internal improvements, and sketched with much fulness the course they should take. A call was therefore made for a committee to frame such an amendment to the Constitution as should define the powers of Congress over internal improvements, and so restrict them as to protect State sovereignty.   Adams, in his message on the Panama Congress, had stated that Ministers "will be commissioned."   Thereupon a resolution was promptly brought before the Senate setting forth that the Executive had no authority to appoint Ministers till he had first consulted the Senate, and that the Senate solemnly protested against such a usurpation of power.   The mover * assured the Senate that such a usurpation, such a palpable infraction of the spirit and the letter of the Constitution, isolated, unconnected with anything else, was enough to appall the friends of liberty.   But when "connected with the covert and insidious innovations which gave existence to and characterizes the conduct of the present Chief Magistrate," he was of the opinion that every friend of his country should be at his post.   "I will not say that he came into office in violation of the letter of the Constitution.   He came in under it.   He is our President.   And yet (it is unnecessary to disguise the fact) he came into office in opposition to three fourths of the American people, in opposition to seventeen or eighteen States out of twenty-four.   He came in by the prostration of our dearest principles.   He came in by a total disregard of the right of instruction, the basis of a republic.   He came in, sir, in opposition not only to the sovereign will of the people, but he overcame the most formidable of all difficulties.   He came in in opposition to the will of the representatives, too.   And what, Mr. President, is the policy of the present Administration?   The original debt of gratitude is to be paid at all hazards; the one fourth is to become the majority, if the creation of offices and the patronage of the Government can effect it.   Yes, sir, the first appointment made by the present Administration is conclusive on this point, and its subsequent course is in entire accord." †

---

* Senator Branch, of South Carolina, Register of Debates in Congress, March 30, 1826, vol. ii, part i, 1825–1826, p. 386.

† Senator Branch, Register of Debates in Congress, vol. ii. part i, 1825–1826, p. 388.

"This is the first Administration," said John Randolph, speaking on the resolution, "that has openly run the principle of patronage against that of patriotism; that has unblushingly avowed, aye, and executed its purposes of buying us up with our own money. Sir, there is honor among thieves—shall it be wanting among the chief captains of our Administration? Let Judas have his thirty pieces of silver, whatever disposition he may choose to make of them hereafter—whether they go to buy a Potter's field in which to inter this miserable Constitution of ours, crucified between two gentlemen suffering for conscience' sake under the burden of the two first offices of this Government, or whether he shall do that justice to himself which the finisher of the law is not, as yet, permitted to do for him, is quite immaterial." A little later in the same speech Randolph declared that he was "defeated, horse, foot, and dragoons—cut up, and clean broke down by the coalition of Blifil and Black George—by the combination, unheard of till then, of the Puritan with the Blackleg."

This was too much for Clay. A challenge followed; the two met, exchanged shots, shook hands, and, with honor quite satisfied, went back unharmed to their posts at Washington, while Randolph's words describing "the coalition of Blifil and Black George, the combination of the Puritan and the Blackleg," swept over the country.

During the debate on a resolution that the Constitution ought to be so amended as to prevent the choice of President devolving on the House and of Vice-President on the Senate, a representative from South Carolina spoke more plainly still.* "I assert it as a fact," said he, "that the present Chief Magistrate was elevated to the presidency against the known and undoubted will of a clear constitutional majority of the people of this Union. If the present Secretary of State had not persevered against all hope, and thereby distracted the vote of the Western States, General Jackson would certainly have received the electoral vote of Kentucky, Ohio,

---

* Mr. McDuffie, of South Carolina, February 15, 1826; Register of Debates in Congress, vol. ii, part ii, 1825–1826, pp. 1955–1958.

and Missouri, which, added to those actually received, would have swelled his number to one hundred and thirty-two—one more than a majority of the whole. In the first place, then, I say, in round terms, that Mr. Clay made the President, in opposition to the will of a decided majority of the State he represented and of the whole Union. He represented a State where an overwhelming majority of the people were in favor of General Jackson and opposed to Mr. Adams, and where the obligation of the representative to conform to the will of his constituents is regarded as a fundamental article of the true political creed. Yet, in direct opposition to the will of his constituents, of his State, and of the United States, he threw the whole weight of his influence in favor of a candidate whom he had habitually professed to despise as a man and detest as a politician. It is but too obvious, then, that Mr. Clay sacrificed his political animosities and his political principles, his duty to himself and his duty to his country, at the unhallowed shrine of ambition. Am I asked for proof? Hear it! He gives the vote of his own State in opposition to his own principles, against the will of the people of that State, and thereby makes the President; and then has the frontless, shameless audacity to set public opinion at defiance by instantly and openly receiving, as the reward of his treachery to the people, the highest office the President can confer upon him! "

The cry of bargain and corruption fabricated by Kremer, sanctioned by Jackson, and affirmed by senators and representatives in the halls of Congress, was next indorsed by political meetings under the guidance of party managers. In June the friends of General Jackson in Philadelphia declared that there was just cause to believe that the will of the American people was not treated by the present public agents with the profound acquiescence to which, in the spirit of American institutions, it was entitled; that efforts had been made and were making to defeat, intimidate, and suppress it by combinations as corrupt as they were disastrous; that they disapproved and condemned " the origin, character, and proceedings of the existing Administration "; and that they regarded the election of Jackson as essential to the revival of republican principles.* As yet, however, the people gave little heed to the outcry of the politicians. The election over, they accepted the result without question and without suspicion. They were too busy gathering their crops, selling their wares and merchandise, and enjoying the fruits of prosperity to believe that the charge of bargain and corruption was seriously made. Even the toasts to which the revellers drank on Independence Day show no widespread animosity toward Adams and Clay.

Many events have made that particular Fourth of July a memorable one in our annals, for it was the fiftieth anniversary of the adoption by the Continental Congress of the document we know as the Declaration of Independence, and it was the day on which, within a few hours of each other, died Thomas Jefferson and John Adams, the man who wrote the declaration and the man who, more than any other, persuaded a hesitating Congress to approve it. Each had been a member of the committee that drafted the declaration; each had signed it when approved; each had served his country on a foreign mission; each had been raised by his countrymen first to the vice-presidency and then to the presidency; each had become the leader of a party; and that each should pass away on the same day was, in the language of the time, a "singular coincidence." But that the day should be the fiftieth anniversary of that event in which each had borne so conspicuous a part was a triple occurrence without parallel in our history.

As the autumn of 1826 drew to a close the indifference of the people to the coming struggle for the presidency began to wear away. The agitation of the politicians was taking effect, and at meeting after meeting the candidacy of Jackson was heartily indorsed. With the new year came new charges against the Administration, new journals to aid in spreading them, and a searching of the opinions of every public man that he might be forced to side with the one candidate or the other.

First came a letter written by a member of Congress who

---

* Niles's Weekly Register, June 3, 1826, vol. xxx, p. 235.

pretended to have visited the White House on New Year's Day, and to have been greatly shocked at what he saw. He went, he said, to see the East Room, to furnish which twenty-five thousand dollars had been voted at the last session of Congress. "It was," said he, "truly a gorgeous sight to behold, but had too much the look of regal magnificence to be perfectly agreeable to my old republican feelings." The statement was wholly false. No attempt at decoration had been made, not a cent of the money had been drawn from the Treasury, and, save a few old chairs and a settee or two, the room was without furniture of any sort. Nevertheless, the story went the rounds of the press; convinced many a country voter that Adams was living in regal splendor, in undemocratic luxury; became serious enough to call forth a flat denial in the House of Representatives, and an explanation from the writer. He was not present himself, but had been informed by one who was, and who probably mistook some other gorgeously furnished apartment for the East Room in question. But campaign material, not truth, was wanted, and the denial and retraction went for naught.

Quite of a piece with this was the story of the billiard table and the chessmen. The committee on public buildings at the last session of Congress found it necessary to obtain an inventory of the furniture in the President's house bought with money previously appropriated, obtained the schedule from the private secretary, and, without examination, attached it to their report, which the House ordered printed. Most of the items were useless for campaign purposes, but among them were two which gave new proof of the extravagant and aristocratic tastes of John Quincy Adams. There was a billiard table, with cues and balls, valued at sixty-one dollars, and a set of chessmen said to have cost twenty-three dollars and a half. "There are items in the account rendered," said a Georgia member while the report was under discussion, "which I wish had been kept in the dark and never brought to light." "Is it possible, Mr. Chairman," exclaimed another, "to believe that it ever was intended by Congress that the public money should be applied to the purchase of gaming tables and gambling furniture? And if it is right to purchase billiard tables and chessmen, why not, also, faro banks, playing cards, race horses, and every other article necessary to complete a system of gambling at the President's palace, and let it be understood by the people that this is a most splendid gambling Administration? Such conduct in the Chief Magistrate of this nation is enough to shock and alarm the religious, the moral, and the reflecting part of the community." * There was, however, no occasion for any one to be shocked, for the billiard table had not been purchased. Indeed, no sooner did Adams see the printed report than he informed the chairman of the committee that the Secretary was mistaken, that the inventory was wrong, and that no part of the appropriation had or ever would be applied to the purchase of the chessmen or the table. But no member of the committee troubled himself to enter a denial,† and the charge went out to the public, to be dragged forth a year later as good material for the campaign.

Meantime, Jackson had twice reiterated the bargain and corruption charge. In declining an invitation to come to Kentucky to " counteract the intrigue and management of certain prominent individuals against him " he took occasion to say that when he " reflected on the management and intrigue which are operating abroad, the magnitude of the principles which they are endeavoring to supplant, and the many means which they can draw to their assistance from the patronage of the Government " he felt it " due to himself " and " to the American people to steer clear of every conduct " which might give color to the belief that he was seeking his own aggrandizement. " If it be true," said he, " that the Administration have gone into power contrary to the voice of the nation and are now expecting, by means of this power thus acquired, to mould the public will into an acquiescence with their authority, then is the issue fairly made out—Shall the Government or the people rule? " ‡

That the Administration had gone into power by such

---

* Register of Debates in Congress, 1825–1826, vol. ii, part ii, pp. 2655, 2656.

† The explanation of the chairman is in Niles's Weekly Register, April 26, 1827, vol. xxxii, pp. 149, 150.

‡ Niles's Weekly Register, October 14, 1826, vol. xxxi, p. 103.

means was by that time so evident to Jackson that he began to believe that overtures of a corrupt nature had been made to him by Clay, and one day in March a most extraordinary letter appeared in the Fayetteville Observer. The writer, Mr. Carter Beverley, declared that he had just returned from a visit to Jackson; that he found him surrounded by "a crowd of company," and that " before all his company " the general said that "Mr Clay's friends made a proposition to his friends that if they would promise for him not to put Mr. Adams into the seat of Secretary of State, Clay and his friends would, in one hour, make him (Jackson) the President." * This new piece of evidence, it may well be believed, spread far and wide, and in time was brought to Clay's attention, and denied emphatically. So false was the story, he was " unwilling to believe that General Jackson had made any such statement," but, no matter with whom it originated, it was " a gross fabrication." † The veracity of the writer having thus been called in question, Mr. Duff Green, then editing a Jackson newspaper at Washington, indorsed the letter, and declared that Jackson had made the same statement to him two years before.‡ " The general," said another journal, " now stands before the nation as the direct public accuser of Mr. Clay and his friends, and by inference of Mr. Adams also. The accusation has been deliberately denied. And if General Jackson should not sustain it by competent and credible proof the American people will not be restrained by the grateful respect which they have hitherto cherished for him from characterizing the charge, as in that event it will deserve to be considered." #

Thus called on for proof, Mr. Beverley fell back on Jackson, who replied in detail. " Early in January, 1825," he said, " a member of Congress of high respectability visited me one morning and observed that he had a communication he was desirous to make; that he had been informed by the

---

* Letter of Carter Beverley, March 8, 1827. Niles's Weekly Register, May 5, 1827, vol. xxxii, p. 162.

† Democratic Press, Washington, April 18, 1827.

‡ Washington Telegraph, April 26, 1827.

National Journal, April 28, 1827.

friends of Mr. Clay that the friends of Mr. Adams had made overtures to them, saying that if Mr. Clay and his friends would unite in aid of the election of Mr. Adams, Mr. Clay should be Secretary of State; that the friends of Mr. Clay stated the West did not wish to separate from the West, and if I would say, or permit any of my confidential friends to say, that in case I was elected President Mr. Adams should not be continued Secretary of State, by a complete union of Mr. Clay and his friends they would put an end to the presidential contest in an hour. To which, in substance, I replied that in politics, as in everything else, my guide was principle, and, contrary to the expressed and unbiassed will of the people or their constituted agents, I never would step into the presidential chair, and requested him to say to Mr. Clay and his friends that before I would reach the presidential chair by such means of bargain and corruption I would see the earth open and swallow both Mr. Clay and his friends, and myself with them. The second day after this communication and reply it was announced in the newspapers that Mr. Clay had come out openly and avowedly in favor of Mr. Adams." *

The letter had scarcely reached Mr. Beverley, at Wheeling, when Clay, on his way down the river to Lexington, reached the same town and found the contents of the note the one topic of conversation. While the captain detained the steamboat a copy was made, and once at Lexington, Clay gave to the public " a direct, unqualified, and indignant denial." † A fortnight later, at a dinner given him at Lexington, he spoke at great length, reviewed the letter word by word, and called on Jackson to name the congressman. " I rejoice again and again," said he, " that the contest has at last assumed its present practical form. Heretofore malignant whispers and dark surmises have been clandestinely circulated, or openly and unblushingly uttered by irresponsible agents. They were borne upon the winds, and, like them,

---

* Jackson to Mr. Carter Beverley, June 5, 1827. Niles's Weekly Register, July 7, 1827, vol. xxxii, p. 317.

† Clay's Letter " To the Public"; Kentucky Reporter, July 4, 1827; Niles's Weekly Register, July 21, 1827, vol. xxxii, p. 350.

were invisible and intangible. No responsible man stood forward to sustain them with his acknowledged authority. They have at last a local habitation and a name. General Jackson has thrown off the mask, and comes confessedly forth from behind his concealed batteries publicly to accuse and convict me. We stand confronted before the American people. Pronouncing the charges, as I do again, destitute of all foundation and gross aspersions, whether clandestinely or openly issued from the halls of the Capitol, the saloons of the Hermitage, or by press, by pen, or by tongue, and safely resting in my conscious integrity, I demand the witness, and await the event with fearless confidence." *

The challenge thus thrown down was promptly accepted, and Jackson, in a letter to the public, declared that the member of Congress who approached him was James Buchanan, of Pennsylvania.† The address to the public, for such it was, appeared in a Nashville newspaper, was copied all over the Union, was read by Buchanan in the columns of the Cincinnati Advertiser, and called forth from him an immediate and flat denial. He had, he stated, called on Jackson in the early part of January, 1825, had found him surrounded by friends, had remained till they left, and had then been invited to join him in a walk. As the two were strolling along the streets Buchanan remarked that a report was abroad that Jackson, if elected, intended to appoint Adams Secretary of State; that the rumor was likely to injure his chance of election; that unless he had so determined, the report ought to be contradicted, as there were several able and ambitious men, Mr. Clay among them, who aspired to the office. When Buchanan had finished, the general declared that he thought well of Mr. Adams; that he had never said or intimated that he would or would not appoint him Secretary of State; that he kept such matters to himself;

---

* The speech was delivered July 12, and is reported in Niles's Weekly Register, August 4, 1827, vol. xxxii, pp. 375–380.

† Jackson's letter to the public, dated July 18th, is in Niles's Weekly Register, August 11, 1827, vol. xxxii, pp. 399–400.

Jackson for twelve years past; and gave the whole to the public in pamphlet form.*

With the opening of the new year the Senate of New York, following the example of Tennessee, attacked the Administration in a set of resolutions with a long preamble. The Constitution of the United States, in the opinion of the Senate Committee, needed immediate amendment. The framers of that instrument supposed, and the writers of the Federalist had triumphantly pointed out, that the prescribed manner of choosing a Chief Magistrate was superior to every other known. But futile was the expectation. At the election of 1801 the electoral colleges were decoyed into giving their votes in such a manner that the choice devolved on the House of Representatives. "Even at this day no friend of his country can look back on that eventful period without a deep feeling of the awful consequences which might have ensued if fraud, chicanery, and unhallowed combinations had been successful in defeating the election of the great and good Jefferson. Thirty-five times was the fate of America suspended on a single ballot of a single member." An amendment of the Constitution followed; but the root of the evil was not reached—the House of Representatives was still left the arbiter, and again the expectations of the people were disappointed. It was with pain and grief that the committee alluded to the belief entertained by many that an unhallowed coalition was entered into between persons who had ever before been the most violent antagonists, and that improper means were used to defeat the will of the people. For the honor of the country they hoped the imputations were unfounded, but a reference to them was necessary to show the need of an immediate remedy. Nor was this the only evil. Experience had shown that it was unwise to permit a President to have more than one term. The conduct of Mr. Adams furnished good reason to believe that a second election had been kept steadily in view. Appointments of

* An Address of Henry Clay to the Public, containing Certain Testimony in Refutation of the Charges against him made by General Andrew Jackson touching the last Presidential Election. Washington, 1827, pp. 61.

worn-out men to most important stations; unnecessary, improper, and extravagant allowances to political friends sent abroad; useless and visionary missions to congresses that never met, were so many instances to prove that personal ambition might have been hitherto the chief care of the present Administration.

The resolutions set forth that the election of John Quincy Adams by the House of Representatives in defiance of the clear and undoubted sense of the American people, and in consequence of systematic efforts to prevent a choice by the electoral colleges, admonished the people to so amend the Constitution as to give the choice of President and Vice-President to the people; that the measures of the present Administration made necessary a further amendment declaring that no person once chosen President could ever again be eligible to that office; and that the New York delegation in Congress be instructed and requested to propose and support such amendments to the Constitution.*

The session of the Kentucky Legislature was drawing to a close when the mail brought to each member a copy of Clay's pamphlet franked by himself. His friends in the Senate, and they were in the majority, considered the defence and the documents so conclusive that they determined to give the bargain and corruption charge a flat denial officially as senators. Some resolutions were accordingly made ready, and, one day late in January, were moved as a substitute for a set relating to internal improvements then under consideration in Committee of the Whole. One of them declared that the Legislature, with deep concern and with feelings of just indignation, saw the efforts being made throughout the United States to blast the reputation of the members of Congress from Kentucky who voted for John Quincy Adams; that, after great deliberation and a full examination of all the evidence adduced, they had no hesitation in saying that the charges of bargain, sale, and corruption were utterly false and malicious, and were brought forward for party purposes and to elevate

---

* Niles's Weekly Register, January 19, 1828, vol. xxxiii, pp. 35–52.

system, we find the strongest reasons to oppose any change in the Executive.   In New Jersey, in Maryland, in Ohio, in Indiana, indeed in almost all the States, the electoral tickets of both parties were framed at conventions of delegates sent up by the people in the towns, counties, or congressional districts.   In Virginia the Jackson men held a mixed Convention, made up of members of the State Senate and House of Burgesses, and twenty-two special deputies from the counties and boroughs having no Jackson men in the Legislature. In North Carolina the Adams delegates were chosen in the fifteen electoral districts into which the State was parted. In Georgia two electoral tickets of Jackson men were put in the field by the " Clarkite " and " Troupite " factions. Of the four-and-twenty States in the Union, but two, Delaware and South Carolina, held to the old-time method and appointed the electors by legislative action.   Never before had the people so much to say in the choice of electors.   The overthrow of the congressional and legislative caucus, the want of party organization, the absence of the National Convention and the nominating machinery of later days, the almost universal adoption of the general ticket or the district system and the great extension of the suffrage, the outcry against the " dynasty of the secretaries," the demand for a President who was " a man of the people," and the belief that Jackson had really been cheated out of the presidency by bargain and corruption, left all matters of detail entirely in the hands of the people.

Never before, as a consequence, were such appeals made to the voter.   The mass of campaign literature surpasses anything of the kind that ever went before in quantity, scurrility, and falsehood.   Records, both public and private, were ransacked, the career of each candidate was passed in review, and no act of the least importance was suffered to go unquestioned.   Jackson was charged with marrying his wife before she was divorced from her first husband; with the murder of six deserters from the militia at Mobile in 1815; with being a party to Burr's conspiracy; with usurping the powers of Congress and making war on Spain by invading Florida; with defying and disobeying the orders of the President by capturing St. Marks and Pensacola; with executing Arbuthnot and Ambrister without trial; with banishing citizens of Pensacola on the charge of being spies in time of peace; with unlawfully and arbitrarily forcing Colonel Collaver to surrender archives and documents when Governor of Florida; with placing military above the civil power at New Orleans, and insolently defying a judge; with using profane language; and with hostility to the American system.

Adams, on the other hand, was denounced as a monarchist, as an aristocrat, as an old Federalist in disguise, as a man who had changed his party but not his principles, as a ruler above the law and blind to duty. He was charged with assuming power not granted by the Constitution in claiming the right to send Ministers to Panama against the will and without the consent of the Senate. He was charged with causing the loss of the British West Indian trade by mismanagement; with gross extravagance in the expenditure of public money; with having fed all his life at the public crib; with having received such great sums of public money as salaries, outfits, and allowances for the many offices he had held that the grand total was equal to sixteen dollars for every day of his life since he first drew breath. He was a Northern man from a free State, he had used Federal patronage to influence elections, had corrupted the civil service, had quarrelled with his father, was the friend of duellists, had written a scurrilous poem against Jefferson, was an enemy of the West, and while at St. Petersburg had surrendered a beautiful American servant girl to the Emperor of Russia.

The present contest, said one Jackson newspaper, is "a movement of the people," a revolt of democracy against aristocracy. Employed all his life in subordinate stations, it never was the intention of the people to put Adams at the head of the nation. He was born and bred among the aristocracy, and early imbibed those principles against which we fought in the days of the black cockade; he has denied the right of the people to instruct their representatives, authorized useless expenditures, lost us the British colonial

trade, hushed up insulted wrongs suffered from Brazil, and left us unrepresented at the Court of St. James. The people have determined on a change, and every good citizen should assist in the great work of reform. Andrew Jackson is of the people, is the candidate of the people, and by the people ought to be elected President of the United States.*
A Vermont newspaper, said another, describes the tariff of 1828 as " a Jackson tariff "; but in Georgia it is thought oppressive, and the people are called on to set up manufactures in self-defence. Where it is popular the Jacksonians proclaim it; where it is unpopular they denounce it.† But for the strong and energetic steps taken by the Jacksonians of the North, said a third, the tariff bill must have failed. To them and to them alone is the credit due of thwarting the combined efforts of the Adams men.‡ The party of the Administration, anxious to have a pretext to censure the Jackson majority, attempted to speak eternally on every subject that could be discussed, and had they not been stopped by the previous question, would have debated the bill till the end of the session, and thus abused the Jacksonians as enemies of the tariff.* Utterly at a loss to determine which side Jackson was on, the Senate of Indiana requested the Governor to ask him to state explicitly whether or not he favored internal improvements at Government expense and a tariff for the protection of American manufactures.|| His answer △ referred his questioner to a letter written on the very same subject to another inquirer four years before,◊ a letter purposely muddled, vague, and contradictory, which committed him to a " judicious " tariff and left the reader to determine what that was. In the West men believed he meant a tariff for protection,

* Ohio Monitor, April 26, 1828.

† New England Palladium, June 17, 1828.

‡ Quoted from a Saratoga newspaper by the New England Palladium, June 17, 1828.

* Ibid., June 20, 1828, quoted from a Kentucky newspaper.

|| Ohio Monitor, April 19, 1828.

△ Niles's Weekly Register, May 3, 1828, vol. xxxiv, p. 158.

◊ Ibid., vol. xxvi, p. 245, June 24, 1824. This was written to Dr. L. H. Coleman, of North Carolina, and appeared in the Raleigh Star.

but in the South they held it to be clear that he stood for a tariff for revenue, because no other was " judicious."

As the summer passed, unmistakable signs of what was to come were to be seen on every hand. At raisings, at musters of the militia, at the Court-House during court week, the one cry all over the South and West was " Jackson and Reform." East of the Alleghanies and north of the Potomac river, New York and Maryland were the only doubtful States. In New York, for the first time in her history, the people were to take part in the choice of presidential electors. Her electoral vote was thirty-six, but the number to be chosen by popular vote was thirty-four, and by this body, when assembled, two more were to be elected to represent the United States senators. What would be done in New York city and in the towns and villages of the Hudson river valley was well known. But a belt of New England settlers stretched across the State from Troy to Buffalo, and what they would do was far from certain, for the bitter struggle between the Masons and the Antimasons had greatly complicated the contest for the presidency.

The presidential election took place in seven instalments. On the thirty-first day of October Pennsylvania and Ohio chose electors, and both went to Jackson, the one by more than fifty thousand and the other by less than six thousand majority. On the third of November in nine other States, and on the third, fourth, and fifth in New York and in Louisiana, and on the fourth and fifth in New Jersey, the people voted for electors. Elsewhere, save in Delaware and South Carolina, elections were held on the tenth, eleventh, thirteenth, or thirteenth and fourteenth of November.

For a few days it seemed as if New York for the second time in her history would cast no vote for President. Thirty-four of her electors were chosen in districts. But when the first returns came in, seventeen were reported carried by Jackson and seventeen by Adams, and as this body was to choose two more electors it was feared that the college would either be unable to organize or unable to elect the two remaining members. In the end Jackson carried eighteen districts and Adams sixteen, and New York's weight in the

contest was four votes.* In Georgia, where the action of
the President in behalf of the Indians made him bitterly
hated, no Adams ticket was nominated and no votes for him
were cast. In all the vast stretch of country south of the
Potomac and west of Pennsylvania not one elector was
secured by Adams. More than eleven hundred and fifty-
five thousand voters went to the polls, and gave Jackson
a majority of one hundred and thirty-nine thousand votes.
It was indeed a great uprising of the people, a triumph of
democracy, another political revolution the like of which
the country had not seen since 1800, and no mere driving
from office of a man or class of men. To the popular mind
it was the downfall of a corrupt and aristocratic Administration that had encroached on the rights of the States and
the liberties of the people, and had used the Federal patronage to carry elections and the Federal treasury to reward

* STATES.	Mode.	No.	Time.	Jackson.	Adams.
Maine.............	Districts.	9	Nov. 3.	13,927	20,733†
New Hampshire....	General ticket.	8	Nov. 3.	20,922	24,134
Vermont.........	General ticket.	7	Nov. 11.	8,350	25,363
Massachusetts......	General ticket.	15	Nov. 3.	6,016	29,876
Rhode Island	General ticket.	4	Nov. 10.	821	2,754
Connecticut........	General ticket.	8	Nov. 3.	4,448	13,838
New York.........	Dist. & 2 by elec. col.	36	Nov. 3, 4, 5.	140,763	135,413
New Jersey........	General ticket.	8	Nov. 4, 5.	21,951	23,764
Pennsylvania.......	General ticket.	28	Oct. 31.	101,652	50,848
Delaware..........	Legislature.	3	Legislature.	......	......
Maryland..........	Districts.	11	Nov. 10.	24,565	25,527
Virginia...........	General ticket.	24	Nov. 3.	26,752	12,101
North Carolina.....	General ticket.	15	Nov. 13.	37,857	13,918
South Carolina.....	Legislature.	11	Legislature.	......	......
Georgia...........	General ticket.	9	Nov. 3.	19,363	No ticket.
Tennessee.........	Districts.	11	Nov. 13, 14.	44,293	2,240
Kentucky..........	General ticket.	14	Nov. 10.	39,397	31,460
Ohio..............	General ticket.	16	Oct. 31.	67,597	63,396
Indiana...........	General ticket.	5	Nov. 10.	22,257	17,052
Illinois...........	General ticket.	3	Nov. 3.	9,560	4,662
Missouri...........	General ticket.	3	Nov. 3.	8,273	3,400
Louisiana	General ticket.	5	Nov. 3, 4, 5.	4,683	4,076
Mississippi	General ticket.	3	Nov. 3.	6,772	1,581
Alabama...........	General ticket.	5	Nov. 10.	17,138	1,938
Totals	....	261	....	647,276	508,064

† Scattering, 94.
The effect of a restricted franchise is well shown in Rhode Island, where, with
a population of 97,000, but 3,575 votes were cast.

its followers. As such the victory was hailed with the wildest joy. The people have rallied in their strength, said one journal, and put down the wealth and power of an overbearing aristocracy, the only stay of a corrupt coalition, and restored the administration of the Government to its pristine purity. The same States that voted for Jefferson in 1800 have voted for Jackson in 1828. Those which supported Adams the elder have befriended Adams the younger, with the same result. He may now retire from the strife of parties, and nib his pen for a memoir of his own time, while Mr. Clay broods over his treasonable practices against the will of the people and contrives artifices to rise from his own ruin. Jackson is the President of the people, and as such they will hail him everywhere, not as a god, but as an instrument taken to avenge their wrongs.

As the day drew near when he must set out for Washington, towns and cities vied with one another to do him honor. Nashville, Lynchburg, Philadelphia, sought visits from him. The people of Pittsburg tendered a steamboat to carry " the old hero " up the Ohio from Cincinnati. The Legislature of Pennsylvania invited him to Harrisburg, and great preparations were making all over the South and West to celebrate the eighth of January, when the death of Mrs. Jackson changed joy to mourning. The journey of the President-elect from the Hermitage to the Capitol was therefore quiet and uneventful. He reached there while the two Houses were witnessing the count of the electoral vote, and just in time to hear the booming of the guns that announced to the people that he had been declared duly elected President of the United States, and took up his residence at Gadsby's Hotel. There a host of office seekers, office holders, and admirers beset him from morn to eve. The people acted, said one who witnessed the scene, as if the country had been rescued from some great danger,* and came by thousands from every quarter to behold the triumph of their deliverer. The dress, the language, the behavior of the crowd gave vis-

---

* Life of Webster. George Tichnor Curtis, vol. i, p. 340.

ible evidence of the revolution that had taken place. Never before had so many of the plain people been seen at any one time in Washington. Ere the end of February, the keepers of hotels, taverns, boarding-houses, lodgings, were turning applicants away, or finding accommodations for them on the floors of tap-rooms and hallways.*

To the mass of men thus herded in Washington and waiting with impatience for the fourth of March, the question of the hour was, To whom will Jackson give seats in the Cabinet? To Van Buren, lately inaugurated Governor of New York, was assigned by common rumor the Secretaryship of State; to S. D. Ingham, of Pennsylvania, the Treasury; to John H. Eaton, of Kentucky, the War Department; to John Branch, of North Carolina, the Navy; to John Mc-Pherson Berrien, of Georgia, the Attorney-Generalship; and to John McLean, of Ohio, the Post-Office, which he

No. of elec-tors.	* STATES.	PRESIDENT.		VICE-PRESIDENT.		
		Andrew Jackson, Tenn.	John Quin-cy Adams, Mass.	John C. Calhoun, S. C.	Richard Rush, Pa.	William Smith, S. C.
9	Maine................	1	8	1	8	..
8	New Hampshire..........	..	8	..	8	..
15	Massachusetts...........	..	15	..	15	..
4	Rhode Island..........	..	4	..	4	..
8	Connecticut..............	..	8	..	8	..
7	Vermont.................	..	7	..	7	..
36	New York..............	20	16	20	16	..
8	New Jersey.............	..	8	..	8	..
28	Pennsylvania	28	..	28	..	..
3	Delaware..............	..	3	..	3	..
11	Maryland................	5	6	5	6	..
24	Virginia.................	24	..	24	..	..
15	North Carolina...........	15	..	15	..	..
11	South Carolina...........	11	..	11	..	..
9	Georgia.................	9	..	2	..	7
14	Kentucky	14	..	14	..	..
11	Tennessee................	11	..	11	..	..
16	Ohio....................	16	..	16	..	..
5	Louisiana................	5	..	5	..	..
5	Indiana.................	5	..	5	..	..
3	Illinois.................	3	..	3	..	..
5	Alabama................	5	..	5	..	..
3	Mississippi..............	3	..	3	..	..
3	Missouri.................	3	..	3	..	..
261	....	178	83	171	83	7

Register of Debates in Congress, vol. v, 1828–'29, p. 350.

then held and administered with signal success.* When objection was made that such a Cabinet would be weak, that, save Van Buren, there was not a strong man in it, those close to Jackson answered that he did not intend to be advised by his secretaries, that he would pursue an independent course, and that he would have a privy council composed of Van Buren, Calhoun, and McLean. When this assurance failed to satisfy the malcontents, another rumor was set afloat, and McLean was said to have been selected for Secretary of War,† in order that he might become a member of the Cabinet, which up to that time no Postmaster-General had been, and add strength to a body no political leader respected. That such a change was really considered may well be believed, for, when the list of secretaries was made public in the Telegraph,‡ the official Jackson newspaper of Washington, it was found to agree in every respect with that announced before, save that McLean was made a member of the Cabinet, a dignity which every succeeding Postmaster-General has since held.

With the announcement of the names of the Cabinet officers the scramble for office grew fiercer and fiercer. For the first time since 1801 a great political revolution had taken place, a real change in the Administration had come about, and certain reforms long promised and demanded must be carried out. But, as Jefferson had stated a generation before, when the will of the nation called for a change in the Administration, there must be a change of administrators, and never before had the will of the nation in this respect been so clearly and emphatically expressed. At the head of the Cabinet, moreover, and in high favor with Jackson, was a man whose whole political training had been gained in the corrupt school of New York, a man who had raised himself from the humblest to the highest office in that State by a steady adherence to the maxim that the laborer is worthy of his hire, that political office is the just

* United States Gazette, February 23, 1829.

† Ibid., February 27, 1829.

‡ The Telegraph, February 26, 1829; United States Gazette, February 29, 1829.

reward for political service, and that service must be not only partisan but personal. It would be the height of injustice, however, to attribute to Jackson, or Van Buren, or any other one man the widespread proscription which now began. The people, not the leaders, were to blame. They were proud of their country, their form of government, their political institutions. They believed firmly and sincerely that these institutions were in danger; that the election of Adams had been secured, in open defiance of their wishes, by a corrupt bargain, and that the men in power were hostile to the great principle that in our country the people shall rule. After four years of ceaseless agitation the people had triumphed; their day had come, and it is folly to suppose that they would be content to see power remain in the hands of men who had worked for the leaders they had overthrown, or had remained passive spectators of a struggle they had so earnestly carried on. He who was not with them was against them, and had Jackson been as resolutely bent on non-partisan administration as was John Quincy Adams, they would have swept him aside as they did his predecessor. In the course of events the time had come for a departure from old-time methods, and, whatever may be thought of the character of that change, it had to be made. No leader in our country can debase the people. He is exactly what the will of the people enable him to be, and the moment he ceases to execute that will he ceases to be a leader. As we look back on those days the wonder is, not that so many were turned out of office, but that so many were suffered to remain.

The first indication of what was to come was given by the Senate, which from the day the election of Jackson was assured held back the confirmation of every nomination to office made by Adams.* The next was the work of

---

* "After General Jackson was known to be elected, and before his term of office began, many important offices became vacant by the usual causes of death and resignation. Mr. Adams, of course, nominated persons to fill these vacant offices. But a majority of the Senate was composed of the friends of General Jackson, and instead of acting on these nominations, and filling the various offices with ordinary promptitude, the nominations were postponed to a day beyond the

the House and Senate when each took away the public printing from Gales and Seaton, proprietors of the National Intelligencer, and gave it to Duff Green, proprietor of the Telegraph. The Intelligencer was accused of having published the scandalous libel on Mrs. Jackson, and its owners were now, in the eyes of the people, justly punished. The charge was false,* but it mattered not, for the place was wanted as a reward for political service. Nor was this without precedent, for we are informed by Adams that when he took his seat in the United States Senate in 1803 he was visited by Mr. Samuel Allyne Otis, who had been the secretary of that body since 1789; that he was told that Otis had been notified that if he wished to remain secretary he must give the Senate printing to William Duane, editor of the Aurora, and that he was asked what was best to do. The advice given is not stated, but Otis held his office, and Duane printed the Senate documents for many years.

Well knowing what was to come, the seekers of office looked forward with high hopes to the fourth of March. The ceremonies which attended the inauguration were of the simplest kind. No parade, no music, none of the pomp and show of a military chieftain, it was proudly said, marred the day. At ten the officers and soldiers, having assembled at Brown's, marched to Gadsby's and delivered an address. At half-past eleven the President-elect, on foot, uncovered, preceded by the Central Committee of the District of Columbia, surrounded on the right hand and the left by gigs, wood wagons, vehicles of every sort crowded with women eager to be near the chief, and followed by the officers of his suite, worthies of the Revolution, and hundreds of strangers without distinction of rank, " and influenced by no other order than that which their own feelings dictated," walked to the Capitol, made his way to the Senate chamber, and at noon and on the east portico, in the presence of an immense assemblage of his fellow-citizens,

---

4th of March for the purpose, openly avowed, of giving the patronage of the appointments to the President who was then coming into office." **Works of Daniel Webster, vol. i, p. 359.**

* National Intelligencer, February 16 and 23, 1829.

same sort to the Secretary of the Treasury brought a reply which well illustrates the hunger for office everywhere prevailing. If there were an enemy threatening the good city of New York with destruction there might be some reason for excitement, the Secretary wrote. But that so many wise men should go into hysterics because an appointee of Mr. Adams continued to collect the duties for a few days or weeks longer was surprising. Yet it was the same everywhere. One of Jackson's best friends in Baltimore left Washington two days after the inauguration, filling the air with imprecations because he had not been given an office not then vacant, and because all the late Administration inspectors had not been removed. But he had since come to his senses. The inspectors were removed, and throngs were "getting right there." Boston, too, where the friends of Jackson were so strong that they could afford to split into two parties, was in a ferment. Providence, where seventy-two votes were given to Jackson, also had the fever, and Egg Harbor, New Jersey, where five democratic votes were cast, was in the same condition. " I should hope there was soberness enough among you to resist the impotence of expectants until their vain hopes shall yield to reason and common sense." There was an immense mass of public business to be transacted. This could not be postponed; the appointments could and must. Only at intervals few and far between could time be found to consider them.* When at last time was found and the removals began, discontent was greater than ever. " Two of the very best offices in the gift of the Government," exclaimed a partisan, " given to personal friends and without even consulting his Cabinet. If the President pursues this course the party is ruined, and the sooner we begin to build up a new the better." † Another, shocked at the number of newspaper editors placed in office, declared to one of them that the appointment of personal friends and editorial partisans had aroused such feeling as he never ex-

---

* Secretary S. D. Ingham to Jesse Hoyt, April 14, 1829. Mackenzie, Life of Van Buren, pp. 216, 217.

† J. I. Coddington to Jesse Hoyt, March 29, 1829. Ibid., pp. 213, 214.

pected to witness. The dignity of the press was injured, and its lofty independence brought down * by the touch of Executive power. When the editor replied that if gentlemen of his cloth were kept poor there was danger of the press becoming dependent, he was answered that dependence on a party or on the people was one thing, and dependence on the Administration quite another; that in the case of ordinary offices there should be no connection between the press and the President; that editors and congressmen should be put under the same rules and the same exceptions; that independence of the press and freedom of elections were the safeguards of our liberties; and that both were laid at the feet of the President when editors and members of Congress took office.†

The distress caused by such acts was terrible. A clerk in the Auditor's office, from mere fear of removal, cut his throat from ear to ear.‡ Another, in the Department of State, went raving crazy. A third found on his desk one morning an official letter. Opening it, he read with dismay that the Secretary would have no further use for his services after the end of the current month, and that he might leave at once or serve out the allotted time, as pleased him best. A fourth, in a controversy with Van Buren, described a scene he beheld when a dismissed clerk broke the news to his wife and children. At Boston an official in the Custom-House, on whom a mother and sisters depended for their daily bread, never heard of his removal till the new incumbent came to take his place. Some received the news that, in the language of the day, they had been " turned out to graze," that their " walking papers were ready," from the columns of the newspapers.* One day in April eleven inspectors were turned out at the Baltimore Custom-House,|| and soon after eleven more were removed from office at

---

* Thomas Ritchie to Mordecai Noah, of the New York Enquirer, March 25, 1829.

† Thomas Ritchie to Mordecai Noah, April 11, 1829.

‡ National Intelligencer, May 9, 1829.

Baltimore Patriot. National Intelligencer, May 1, 1829.

|| American Daily Advertiser, April 16, 1829.

Philadelphia.* By the first of June it was estimated that three hundred postmasters, in as many cities, towns, and villages, had been deprived of their places, and that the clerks, when there were any, had been ejected by the new incumbents. Some took loss of office as a matter of course. " The reader will observe," said one of them, " that the editor of this paper has been removed from the post-office at Circleville. In October last he voted for the Adams ticket, and for this heretical act his official services have been cut short with just as little ceremony as were the lives of Arbuthnot and Ambrister. The long and the short of the matter is just this: The editor did not wish that General Jackson should be President; so General Jackson did not choose that the editor should be postmaster. The general succeeded in his wishes and the editor did not, and the account is closed." Others appealed to the Postmaster-General. The course of still others was taken up by their fellow-townsmen and made the matter of public resolutions. But all to no avail.

To the people at large it made little difference who were clerks in the departments, collectors of the customs, registers of the land offices, Ministers, or consuls abroad. But when the sweep of the post-offices began, when it became known that by the first of July three hundred postmasters, in as many cities, towns, and villages, had been turned out because they had dared to cast a vote for the Adams electors, a large part of the community became deeply interested. To remove an official with whom not one citizen in a thousand ever had occasion to transact business was a small matter, but to eject the postmasters who for five, ten, in some cases twenty years, had faithfully served their little community and were personally known to everybody in the towns, was quite another thing, and the Jackson press soon found it necessary to explain. Wait a bit, it was said, and all will be explained; do not judge too harshly; such a mass of evidence will be laid before Congress as will satisfy the most prejudiced; these men have interfered with elections, or

* National Intelligencer, April 27, 1829.

are unfit to discharge the duties of their offices, or have abused their trust; the voice of the people calls for their removal.

As we look back to the opening of Jackson's Administration, the volume of business transacted by the Post-Office Department each year seems small indeed. Nevertheless, the growth of it since revolutionary days to the men of 1829 was astonishing. When Washington was inaugurated at New York there were in the United States but seventy-five post-offices. When Jackson was inaugurated, forty years later, there were seventy-six hundred. In 1789 letters could with difficulty, in the best of weather, be carried fifty miles between sun and sun. In 1829 on many routes the mail was conveyed one hundred miles each twenty-four hours, and that every day in the year. Now there are one thousand times as many post-offices as in 1789, and ten times as many as in 1829, in which, despite the great reduction in the rates of postage, there is gathered fifteen hundred times as much revenue as in 1789, and seventy times as much as in 1829.

On a single letter, and that was one sheet of paper, no matter how large or how small, the postage in Jackson's time might be six, ten, twelve and a half, eighteen, or twenty-five cents, according to the distance it was carried. Double, triple, quadruple letters were charged two, three, and four times these rates. Every packet of four or more bits of paper, or one or more other articles, and weighing one ounce avoirdupois, paid quadruple rates, and in that proportion up to three pounds, which was the limit.* Postage marked on every letter and charged in the post bill accompanying it was lawful postage and must be paid, unless the letter was opened in the presence of the postmaster or his clerk and overrating proved before them. This provision of the law had never been rigidly enforced, but the Postmaster-General had not been long at his desk when a circular went forth

* If a newspaper did not go out of the State in which it was printed, the postage was one cent for any distance. If it left the State, the rate was one cent for distances less than a hundred miles and one cent and a half beyond that limit. An editor might send one copy of his paper to every other editor in the United States free of postage. Law of March 3, 1825.

charging the new officials to be diligent in the execution of the law, and explaining its intent and meaning. The franking privilege was greatly abused by men high in station and by the postmasters themselves. Many persons seemed to be of the opinion that printed sheets of paper were not chargeable with letter postage. This was erroneous. Everything that went by mail must pay letter postage, except newspapers, pamphlets, and legislative journals. Printed circulars, special advertisements, handbills, and proposals for publications were to be rated as letters.* More care must be used in rating letters. To determine the proper rate was often a hard matter, but when a letter seemed to be double or triple it should be so marked, and if the receiver questioned the correctness he might open it in the presence of the postmaster and have the error, if any, corrected.†

With the prospect of instant removal before them, the postmasters, both old and new, at once began to enforce the law most strictly. No risks were taken, and in a few weeks the merchants were crying out that the post-office was grossly defrauding them. A letter was double, triple, or quadruple whenever it contained one, two, or three pieces of paper of any size. A merchant writing to his correspondent, or a depositor to a bank, or a subscriber to the editor of a journal and inclosing one bank-note, by so doing made his letter subject to double postage. Should he send three bank-bills the packet would cost him as much as four huge sheets of paper covered with writing. Under the best of conditions, as weight had nothing to do with postage, it was often a hard matter for a postmaster to determine whether a letter should be rated as single, double, or triple. As post rates were almost invariably paid by the receiver, it was customary for him when overcharged to report to the postmaster, who, taking the complainant at his word, would correct the error. Now all was changed. The new officials, it was claimed, were showing their zeal and seeking to impress their superiors with their fidelity by deliberately overrating let-

---

* Four folio, eight quarto, sixteen octavo, twenty-four duodecimo pages were rated as one sheet or a single letter.

† Circular to Postmasters, May 18, 1829.

ters, and, when asked for a rebate, refusing to make it unless
the packets were opened in their presence or before their
clerks.   This, it was said, might do in country towns and
faraway places, at cross-roads, and frontier hamlets, but
was impossible in great cities without a waste of time, a
squeeze in the crowd, and a delay in the whole business of
the office out of all proportion to the amount involved.
Imagine a great merchant at New York standing before the
window in the post-office opening letter after letter to see
that none were overrated, while a clerk looks idly on, and
a long line of busy men to whom time is money chafe at
the delay!   Thousands of persons have their letters delivered to them, but under the new order of things they must in
future be present when the carrier arrives, detain him until
their packets are examined, and send back such as are overcharged, or tamely submit to imposition.*   A New York
merchant was said to have paid fifteen dollars excessive postage in two months.†   Another, who complained to the Postmaster-General, was told that the law was simply being
enforced, and that the evil was as broad as it was long.
When a double letter was rated single the recipient did
not send to the post-office to pay the deficiency, and the
Government lost; but if a single letter was rated double he promptly demanded repayment of the excess.
This he could have, provided the letter was opened in the
presence of the postmaster or a clerk, and not otherwise.‡
The new postmaster at Portsmouth, New Hampshire,
having applied for " positive instructions " as to the return of excess postage, received an answer to the same
effect.#

Complaints proving unavailing, those who used the mails
sought relief in such wise as best pleased them.   One editor,
and he was but a type of many, gave up his box at the post-
office, closed his account, and declared he would call for
his mail in person, hold his place at the window, and open
every letter in the presence of a clerk, no matter how incon-

---

* Niles's Weekly Register, July 11, 1829, vol. xxxvi, pp. 313–315.
† Ibid., p. 315.
‡ Ibid., p. 315.   # Ibid., August 15, 1829, p. 393.

venient it might be to himself or the public.   Others sought
private conveyances, and for a time it was proposed to establish a line of carriers between Baltimore and Boston, who
should travel faster than the mails and deliver letters in
their charge at less cost than did the post-office.

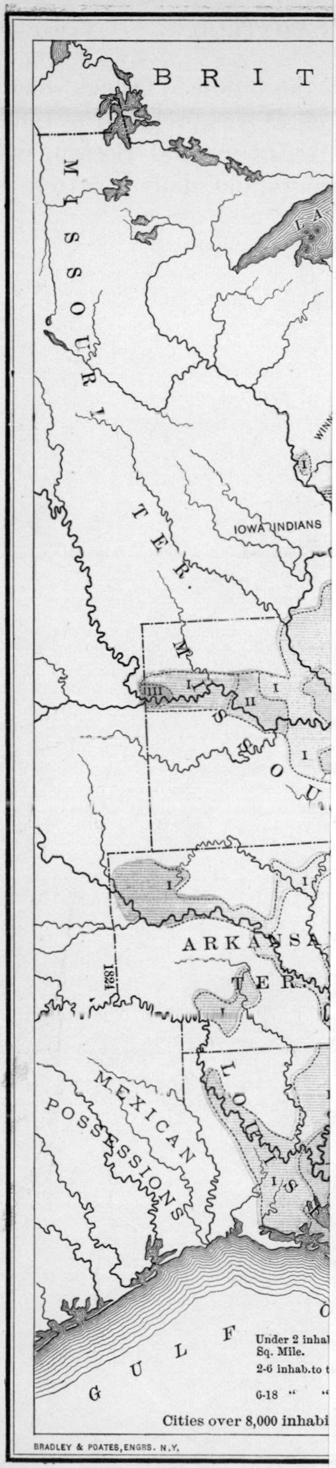
BRIT
MISSOURI TER.
IOWA INDIANS
MISSOU
ARKANSA
TER.
1824
MEXICAN POSSESSIONS
GULF
Under 2 inhab
Sq. Mile.
2-6 inhab.to t
6-18 " "
Cities over 8,000 inhabi
BRADLEY & POATES, ENGRS. N.Y.

CHAPTER LIII.

ISSUES OF THE DAY.

THE policy of proscription having thus been adopted and the work of reform well begun, the new President and his secretaries began to define the position to be taken by the party on the question and issues of the day. None called for more prompt consideration than the long-standing quarrel between Georgia and the Indian within her bounds. The extension of her laws over the Cherokee lands in 1827 had been followed in the last days of Adams's term by the arrival at Washington of a delegation from the Cherokee nation, and an appeal to the outgoing President, through the Secretary of War. But it came too late for him to act, and was not answered till Eaton had been a month in office. The Indians complained that Georgia, in defiance of the laws of the United States and of solemn treaties duly made with them, had spread her jurisdiction over their lands; had decreed that all laws and usages made and in force in the Indian country should be null and void after June first, 1830; and that no Indian or descendant of an Indian should be a competent witness or concerned in any suit to which a white man was a party unless he lived with the Indian tribes; and asserted that, as their nation had no voice in the formation of the Union and had never been subject to the laws of any State, the recent act of Georgia was a wanton usurpation of power granted to no State either by the common law of the land or by the law of nations.

To this, said the Secretary, there is but one answer. During the War for Independence your nation was the friend and ally of Great Britain, who claimed absolute sovereignty over the thirteen States. By the treaty of 1783 this sovereignty passed to the original States, including North Carolina and Georgia, within whose limits your nation was then living. If you have since been suffered to dwell there, enjoying the use of the soil and the privileges to hunt, it has been because of compacts with your people, and affords no ground for a denial of the right of those States to exercise their original sovereignty. One of these compacts was made in 1785, and another in 1791. By them no right whatever was secured to you, save a mere possessory one; the soil and the use of it were conceded to you while the sovereignty abided, just as it did before, with the States within whose limits you resided. Later still, in 1802, when Georgia assumed her present limits and ceded all her western territory, the United States bound herself to extinguish your title to all lands within the bounds of Georgia as soon as it could be done peaceably and on reasonable terms. She did not ask that the military force of the Union be employed to drive you away, but that the soil be acquired by peaceable means. The course you have taken of establishing an independent government within her boundary, against her will and without her consent, has put an end to forbearance, and forced her as a sovereign, free, and independent State to extend her laws over your country, which she has a right to do without the authority of the General Government.

But suppose that Georgia ought not to exercise such power. What then? You ask that the Government step forward and stop the operation of constitutional acts of an independent State within her limits. Should this be done, and Georgia persist in the maintenance of her rights, an appeal might be made to the sword. But this can never be done. The President will not beguile you with such an expectation. The arms of this country can never be used to stay any State of this Union in the exercise of those powers which belong to her as a sovereign. Such interference is not within the range of powers granted by the State to the General Government, and cannot be undertaken.

There was, the Secretary continued, but one remedy: remove beyond the Mississippi river. So long, said he, as you remain where you are the President can promise you nothing but interruption and disquiet. But once across the Great River there will be no conflicting interests. The United States, uncontrolled by the high authority of State jurisdiction, will be able to say to you, in the language of your own people, the soil shall be yours while the trees grow or the streams run. There is, then, but one alternative: yield to the laws Georgia has a right to extend throughout her own limit, or remove, and, joining your brothers beyond the Mississippi, become again a nation ·enjoying the protection the Government will then have power to afford.*

Much the same advice was given to the Creeks in a " talk " read to their chiefs by order of the President. " Friends and brothers," said he, " listen: Where you now are, you and my white children are too near to each other to live in harmony and peace. Your game is gone, and many of your people will not work and till the earth. Beyond the great river Mississippi, where a part of your nation has gone, your father has provided a country large enough for all of you, and he advises you to remove to it. There your white brothers will not trouble you; they will have no claim to the land, and you can live upon it, and all your children, as long as the grass grows or the water runs, in peace and plenty. The land beyond the Mississippi belongs to the President and to none else, and he will give it to you forever.

" My children, listen: My white children in Alabama have extended their law over your country. If you remain in it you must be subject to that law. If you remove across the Mississippi you will be subject to your own laws and the care of your father the President." †

The meaning of these communications was plain. The policy of the Administration was removal of the Indians

---

* Niles's Weekly Register, June 13, 1829, vol. xxxvi, pp. 258, 259. Secretary of War to the Cherokee Delegation, April 18, 1829.

† Jackson to the Creek Indians, March 23, 1829. Niles's Weekly Register, June 13, 1829, vol. xxxvi, pp. 257, 258.

opened a correspondence with the authorities at Havana, and in July a Spanish army four thousand five hundred strong sailed from Havana under the command of Isidore Barradas. A landing near Tampico de Tamaulipas was easily effected, but no re-enforcements came, and six weeks later Barradas and his men were prisoners of war. That now, if ever, Mexico might be persuaded to part with Texas seemed likely. At all events, the attempt was worth making, and in August Poinsett was bidden to open negotiations for the purchase of as much of Texas as he could get, for any one of four pieces would be acceptable. The present boundary, Van Buren said, was far from satisfactory. The Sabine was too petty a stream to be a highway of commerce, but, from the character of the country to the eastward, was well fitted to encourage extensive smuggling. So long as the river remained the line of separation the frontier must continue to be what it was and had been—the home of outlaws and smugglers. The presence of such people near the boundary was well calculated to lead to incessant broils and difficulties, to which our neighbors across the line were only too much inclined. The want of attachment between Mexico and the Texans giving rise to four revolts in five years, the presence on her soil of the warlike Shawnee, Cherokee, and Kickapoo Indians, invited there to defend the Mexicans against the Comanches, and now announcing their determination to stay; the removal to that neighborhood of the great body of our own Indians; the comparatively small value to Mexico of the territory in question; its remote and disconnected situation; the unsettled condition of her affairs; the ruinous condition of her finances, and the threatening attitude of Spain—all combine to point out the wisdom of parting with Texas.*

For so much as lies east of a line starting at a point on the shore of the Gulf midway on the great plain between the Nueces and the Rio Grande, and thence running westward and northward along the middle of the plain

---

* Van Buren to Poinsett, August 25, 1829. Register of Debates in Congress, vol. xiv, part ii; Appendix, pp. 127–130.

to the mountains separating the waters of the Rio Grande from those flowing eastward to the Gulf, and along the mountains to the forty-second degree of north latitude, Mr. Poinsett might offer five million dollars. Should Mexico refuse to part with so much territory, he was to propose the west bank of the Rio de la Baca from mouth to source, a due north line to the Colorado, the west bank of the Colorado to its source, and a line around the head waters of the Arkansas and the Red rivers to the parallel of forty-two degrees. In lieu of this he might offer a third line along the west bank of the Colorado from its mouth to the source of its largest tributary, and thence around the head waters of the Arkansas and the Red rivers as before. Finally, could nothing else be had, he might accept the west bank of the Rio Brassos de Dios from its mouth to the source of its most westerly branch, and then to the parallel of forty-two degrees. The amount to be paid in each case should be proportionate to the area ceded, taking five millions as the maximum.

The plan to buy Texas, or a part of it, having thus been started, the next step was to prepare the people for the cession, should one be made. With this in view, essays on the subject appeared suddenly and simultaneously in the leading Jackson newspapers in different parts of the country. Some writers were content with a single article. Others, as Benton, supplied a series.* One of the earliest of these papers, and it may be taken as a sample of the many, began with a long description of the physical geography, climate, soil, and productions of Texas; drew a parallel between that country and Louisiana. told of the mines, the river system, the wild animals, the population, and boldly declared that a land so highly favored ought to belong to the United States: First, because the Mexican Government was financially embarrassed, her navy gone, her army diminished, her people so ripe for revolution that she would now be more likely to listen to a proposition to part with Texas than in better times; and, in the second place, because the safety

---

* Americanus in the St. Louis Beacon and in the Richmond Enquirer.

Administration will embrace the present favorable occasion for regaining an extensive and fertile region within the natural limits of the United States.* Some of its best soil is washed by rivers that flow into the Mississippi. There is no hill, mountain, or desert between us and Texas to form a good natural barrier.† Repeated revolutions in Mexico make good order and stable government in Texas out of the question, and has already turned that province into a place of refuge for unclean birds of every sort—runaway slaves, fugitives from justice, debtors fleeing from their creditors, and men who respect no government and know no law. Texas is like an abandoned ship at sea—the prize of any captor, and the captors are ready.‡ Spain has begun anew her attempts at reconquest. Great Britain is by no means a disinterested spectator. Mexico owes her a great debt. She bears us no good will, and would gladly set bounds to us on the southwest by acquiring Texas. Already wild stories are afloat to arouse her people. They are told that, excited by the invasion of Mexico by Spain, we are to loan the Republic fifty million dollars, and take Texas and California as security for a term of years. Should the money not then be paid, both provinces will be ours forever; # that it is against the welfare of Great Britain to allow this to come about; that while she checks the power of Russia she must not forget to stop the aggrandizement of the United States.‖ With the Rio Grande as our boundary—and Heaven seems to rule it shall be—the whole valley of the noblest of rivers would be ours, and a vast stream, with a desert as barren as the sands of Sahara a hundred miles wide on each side of it, would separate us from Mexico.ᐃ

The Custom-House of New Orleans has paid the purchase money of Louisiana. If there is any man in the Union who has felt himself straitened in his private affairs in consequence of this payment, let him proclaim his name, and he shall have redress—but there is not one. The customs of

---

* Edgefield Carolinian.   # London Gazette, August 18, 1829.
† Nashville Banner.   ‖ John Bull.
‡ New York Courier and Enquirer. ᐃ National Intelligencer, October 1, 1829.

Texas would do the same thing. The Mexicans, steeped to the lips in poverty, threatened with a powerful invasion by the mother country, will part with this property or anything else for the sake of money. Now is the time and this is the hour to strike for our country's weal. Commercial men, every way qualified to form an estimate and give an opinion, have said that Texas, in the hands of the British, would be of as much importance to them as the island of Jamaica. Let us for a moment imagine this delightful region in the hands of that proud and overbearing nation, flinging bones of discord to the two sister Republics, and then imagine, if you can, the deep-toned imprecations that would pervade this nation from Maine to the Sabine, from the sources of the Missouri to the mouth of the Chesapeake!

To all this the opponents of expansion replied: Our country is large enough; beware lest it become so bulky that it fall to pieces of its own weight.* In a Republic such as ours all the members should be firmly united, but each extension of territory tends to destroy this union and weaken the administration of government. Monarchs and despots may rule widely spread countries, but not presidents. The Northern States must preserve what little influence they still have in the affairs of the country. But expansion in the South will surely utterly destroy the weight of the North. Even now the South believes her interests are opposed to those of the Eastern and Middle States, and because it cannot rule the nation threatens secession.† The great and unjust preponderance of the slave States in our union may well cause the people of the free States to pause and consider the effects of the addition of half a dozen more slave-holding States bound together by one common bond of peril, profit, and power.‡ We cannot longer disguise the fact that the advocates of slavery are determined to get Texas for the sole purpose of adding five or six more slave States to this Union.#

---

* Virginia Free Press; also Newark Sentinel.
† Rhode Island Journal.
‡ New York American.
# Genius of Universal Emancipation, September 16, 1829.

It is now time for the people of the United States who are opposed to the further extension of this horrible evil to arouse from their lethargy and nip the monstrous attempt in the bud. It must be borne in mind that the system of slavery has been abolished in Texas by the Mexican Government. It is now a free State. But the avowed design of Senator Benton and others of his political clan is to change this state of things and again introduce the slave system, with all its barbarities. Should the territory be added to the Union, on condition that it should remain free, a great number of the colored people in our States might be induced to remove thither. But a greater curse could scarcely befall our country than the annexation of that immense region, with slavery re-established.*

The statement that slavery did not exist in Texas was wrong. It did exist, and how little it was in danger of abolition was well set forth by an incident which happened just at this time.

The Constitution of 1827, which joined Texas to Coahuila and made of them one State, forbade the further importation of slaves, and gave freedom to all children thereafter born within its jurisdiction. But now, by a decree of September fifteenth, Guerrero took one more step forward, finished the good work of emancipation, and set all slaves free.† To this the Americans in Texas gave not the smallest heed, and had the Republic attempted to carry out her decree they would have risen in revolt, declared their independence, and sought annexation to the United States at once. So great was the danger that the Mexican commandant on the Texan frontier hastened to declare

---

* Genius of Universal Emancipation, September 23, 1829.

† Be it known: That in the year 1829, being desirous of signalizing the anniversary of Independence by an act of national justice and beneficence . . . . I have thought proper to decree—

1. That slavery is exterminated in the Republic.

2. Consequently those are free who up to this day have been looked upon as slaves.

3. Whenever the condition of the public Treasury will permit, the owners of slaves shall be compensated in such manner as shall be provided by law.

Decree of September 15, 1829.

that, by order of Guerrero, the decree was not to apply to Texas.*

But what, meantime, was the conduct of Mexico toward the United States, and how was the proposition to sell Texas received? The part taken by Mr. Poinsett in establishing the York lodges and the success of the Yorkinos brought down on him the wrath of a great part of the Mexican people, and began sensibly to affect the relations between the Governments of the two Republics. He was openly accused of meddling in the affairs of Mexico, was abused without stint, and his position made so uncomfortable and the discharge of his official duties so impossible that in the summer of 1829 he asked leave to return. Permission was granted; but the letter containing it had not been sent when the Mexican *chargé d'affaires* made a formal demand in the name of his Government for Mr. Poinsett's recall. In a postscript, therefore, permission to return or stay, as might seem best, was revoked, instructions to take leave as soon as possible were given, and the usual official letter of recall was inclosed for delivery to President Guerrero.†

Mr. Anthony Butler was next commissioned *chargé d'affaires*, and in writing his instructions Van Buren took occasion to review at great length the relations between the two countries. He described the behavior of Mexico as unfriendly, as undeserved by us, and charged her, most truly, with ingratitude. He recalled how, from the earliest dawn of the Mexican struggle for independence, the people of the United States displayed a sympathy so warm that it attracted the notice of the Mexicans and drew from the mother country charges of partiality; how nothing but the immutable principles of non-interference in the domestic concerns of other nations and strict neutrality toward all belligerents prevented them from extending a helping hand to the young Republic; how, the moment, consistent with this rule of conduct and the principles of public law, we could consider

---

* Executive Documents, Twenty-fifth Congress, Second Session, vol. xii, No. 351, p. 315.

† Executive Documents, Twenty-fifth Congress, Second Session, vol. xii, No. 351, pp. 37–40.

Spain and Mexico as two distinct nations, we declared the freedom of America, invited Mexico to take her place among the nations of the earth, and asked the good offices of three great powers to persuade Spain to end the war; and how, in a spirit of good will, we had opened negotiations for treaties and conventions intended to cement the bonds of peace and friendship, but, unhappily, had opened them in vain. Our first proposals for a treaty of commerce were met first by indifference and then by propositions of countervailing restrictions and exclusive privileges to other American States, whose sole title to them was community of language. A whole year passed before a treaty on any terms was concluded, and when at last the document was signed it was so burdened with illiberal conditions and so hampered by a narrow policy that the Senate of the United States was forced to give its consent to ratification under certain conditions. Sent back in this modified form to Mexico, the Executive waited two months before submitting it to the Chamber of Deputies, where it still lay six months after the expiration of the date named for exchange of ratifications. Proceedings so unusual gave just cause for complaint. But allowance was made for the embarrassed state of Mexican affairs, and, after a delay of eight months, a new conference was opened, and the negotiators assembled only to be told that Mexico would do nothing till a treaty had been concluded defining the boundaries between her and the United States. Unwilling to put any obstacles in the way, the United States Minister yielded, framed the treaty of limits, and transmitted it to Washington, where, twelve days after its receipt by the Department of State, it was ratified by the Senate. But when the representative of Mexico was informed that the Secretary was ready to exchange ratifications he replied that he was without instructions; when they came, the time within which the exchange of ratifications must be made had elapsed, and the Senate was not in session.

To the misconduct of the Government might be added that of the several states. The manifesto of the Legislature of the state of Vera Cruz, denouncing our accredited agent in open violation of the sacred rights of ambassadors and of the laws of nations, was a document without example in the annals of diplomacy. Had it come from some misguided faction, the spirit of enmity toward the United States which it employed would have been a matter of no concern; but, emanating as it did with the representatives of a sovereign state, it bore on its face a character of nationality which wanted but the seal of Federal sanction to be resented as an insult to the honor of the United States. Other legislative bodies in the Mexican Confederation had gone further yet, and had attempted to dictate to the Executive the expulsion of our Minister from Mexico. One of these, the Legislature of Tlalpam, had gone so far as to attempt to justify its conduct by publishing to the world a violent attack on the national character of the United States, and on the public and private character of its accredited agent.

It was indeed true that these were not the acts of the Federal Government of Mexico. Had they been, satisfaction would long ago have been demanded and obtained. Yet it was incumbent on that authority, when a false impression was abroad respecting the conduct of a friendly power, to check the evil by furnishing correct information as to the real intent and wishes of the nation wrongfully assailed. A single denial by President Guerrero of the charges against Mr. Poinsett would have convinced the Legislatures of the State of the falsity of the accusations. This he did not make, and, what was more, the correspondence between Mexico and the United States left no room to doubt that even he was under the influence of the general prejudice.*

While such was the conduct and such the feeling of the rulers and the people of Mexico toward the United States, it was idle to expect a cession of Texas, and this Mr. Butler soon discovered. Indeed, his letter of credence had been presented when a newspaper of prominence boldly declared that the purpose of his mission was to bring about a sale of Texas; that he was to offer five million dollars, and that a proposition so degrading to the Republic would never be lis-

---

* Van Buren to Mr. Butler, October 16, 1829. Executive Documents, Twenty-fifth Congress, Second Session, vol. xii, No. 351, pp. 40-53.

tened to by the Administration nor subscribed to by any Minister,* and he had not been long at his post when he received from the Secretary of State copies of a report made in secret to the Mexican Congress,† in which sentiments of the same kind found expression in yet more vigorous language.

For fifty years past, Mr. Alaman declared, the United States had slowly but surely been acquiring every piece of foreign soil that touched her own. No armies had been raised, no battles fought, no conquests made; but means had been used which, slow, ineffectual, absurd as they seemed when considered separately, had, when united, proved certain and irresistible. We generally began by introducing settlers into the region coveted, under pretence of trade or the establishment of colonies. Once on the soil, the colonies would grow rapidly in size, increase in number, become the dominant party in the population, and then assert rights too preposterous to be seriously discussed and bring forward pretensions founded on historical tales admitted by nobody —such as La Salle's voyages, which everybody knew had never been made. This done, men would be sent in to excite movements which disturbed the political condition, weakened the authority of government, fomented insurrections and disputes well calculated to wear out the patience of the legitimate owner. Sometimes more direct means were used, and, taking advantage of the enfeebled state or the domestic troubles of the possessor of the soil, we would, on an extraordinary pretext, make ourselves masters of the country, as we did in the case of the Floridas, and defy the owner to put us out.

Now, said he, this is just what has long been going on in Texas. A majority of the population is composed of natives of the United States. They have come in from all directions, have settled on the best lands in utter disregard of the laws and in open violation of contracts, and hold the best sites on the seacoast and occupy the mouths of all the rivers, and settled on the frontiers from which they are expressly excluded

---

* From the Sun, January 9, 1830.   Ibid., p. 310.   † Ibid., pp. 311–322.

by law. The order of 1826, forbidding colonization by adjoining nations; the order of 1827, restricting families in the new settlements to the number authorized in the contracts; that of 1828, providing that in colonies formed on territory along the boundary line of the United States and Mexico there must be no families from the United States—have all been disregarded. Not a slave has been set free as required by law; not one colonist in Texas is a Roman Catholic, as required by the contracts; and the importation of slaves has not stopped.

Not only were these North American colonies in Texas formed under pretext of colonization, but others of considerable extent established without any authority. Such a one was Aires, five leagues beyond Nacogdoches, which, with the adjoining settlements at Atoyac and Sabinas, formed a population of two thousand souls, not one of them a Mexican. They all came from the United States, and were the people who showed such unmistakable signs of insurrection against the decree abolishing slavery that the commandant general was forced to declare it did not apply to Texas.

Having gone so far, the United States, the Secretary continued, was about to complete her policy by a bold attempt to acquire Texas. Government newspapers were already discussing the rights of the North Americans to that country as far as the Rio Grande; handbills had been printed on the subject and thrown into circulation; the matter was soon to be taken up at Washington; a fifty-gun frigate, the Brandywine, was to be sent to the Texan coast; and it was well known the new *chargé d'affaires* was specially empowered to offer five million dollars for the territory. If not accepted, the United States would probably propose to appoint an arbitrator, as in the Maine boundary dispute. This done, Texas would be lost to Mexico unless measures were promptly taken to prevent it.

These measures, the Secretary said, were five in number: Increase the Mexican population by sending men condemned to the galleys to certain places in Texas where, under the eye of the army, they might become farmers; colonize Texas with people whose language, customs, manners, and interests were different from those of the people of the United States; bring Texas into closer relations with other states of the Republic by encouraging the coastwise trade; suspend the colonization law of 1824, and make Texas dependent on the General Government in matters of colonization, and send an agent to the colonized territory to see that all contracts are truly executed. A firm attitude such as would give the United States to understand that Mexico would preserve her territory inviolate and would not suffer it to be dismembered was most important.

The advice of Alaman was not taken in all its fulness. Had it been, the revolution he so much feared would surely have broken out, and Texas, as was said, would have come into our hands without the cost of a dollar.* Yet it was not wholly neglected, and in April a law passed the Mexican Congress forbidding citizens of the United States to settle in Texas.†

Despite the display of anti-American feeling, the hostility toward Poinsett, the bitter attacks in the newspapers, the report of Alaman, and the exclusion in future of our citizens from Texas, Butler for awhile continued to believe that the territory in question might be acquired.‡ But a little experience in Mexico convinced him of his error, and for the third time the attempt was abandoned.# "No hopes need therefore be entertained," said the Arkansas Gazette, "of our acquiring Texas till some other party more friendly to the United States than the present shall predominate in Mexico, and perhaps not until the people of Texas shall throw off the yoke of allegiance to that Government, which they

---

* Butler to Van Buren, March 9, 1830.

† "ARTICLE IX. On the northern frontier the entrance of foreigners shall be prohibited, under all pretexts whatever, unless they be furnished with passports, signed by the agents of the Republic, at the places whence they proceed.

"ARTICLE XI. In the use of the power reserved by the general Congress, in the Seventh Article of the law of August 18, 1824, it is prohibited to neighboring nations to settle in those States and Territories of the federation which border on their nations. Consequently, contracts which have not been executed, and are opposed to that law, shall be superseded." Law of April 6, 1830.

‡ Butler to Van Buren, April 15, 1830.

Ibid., May 19, 1830.

will no doubt as soon as they have a reasonable pretext for so doing."

While the opposition press and the antislavery men were thus attacking the policy of the Administration in attempting to buy Texas, another incident happened which led the followers of Clay to believe that Jackson was bent on destroying the American system.   Mr. Louis McLane, of Delaware, had been appointed Minister to Great Britain, and when about to start for London a statement went the rounds of the press that he was to negotiate a treaty doing away with the objectionable features of the tariff.   Great Britain was to relax her corn laws in favor of the United States, and in return her manufactures were to be admitted on the payment of a moderate duty.   The purpose of General Jackson, it was said, is to rid the country of the many hateful provisions of the tariff, and especially of those which have caused so much dissatisfaction at the South, without the interposition of the House of Representatives.   With this end in view, a treaty of commercial reciprocity, stipulating that neither power shall tax the produce or manufactures of the other above twenty per cent *ad valorem,* has been in agitation, and it is understood that the British Minister at Washington has expressed the belief that his Government will come into the agreement.   A few of the opposition journals scouted the story as too improbable to believe and, even if true, declared the scheme could not be executed.   The British Ministry might have power to set aside an act of Parliament, but it could not for a moment be pretended that the treaty-making power of the President and Senate could do away with an act of Congress.   Some of the Administration papers flatly denied the tale, but there were others which were not quite so sure, and were much disposed to encourage the attempt.

If, it was argued, in the course of negotiations intended to reopen the colonial trade, lost by the incapacity of the late President, the interests of our commerce, our navigation, our agriculture, could be furthered without injury to our manufactures, the plain duty of the Administration is to do so by the lasting obligations of a treaty.   We do not expect to see those barriers which, in the language of our adversaries, protect the industries of both countries broken down, but we do hope to see justice done to all branches of industry at home and in Great Britain, and, to avoid the evil of encouraging one at the cost of the others, some stipulation ought to be made to abolish prohibitory duties on each side. We trust, therefore, that some such treaty will be made, and when it is, we will refer the question of right to the decision of the grain- and cotton-growing sections of the country.

As to the right to do this the argument was: the President, says the Constitution, shall have power, by and with the consent of the Senate, to make all treaties, provided two thirds of the senators present concur; and all treaties made, or which shall be made, under the authority of the United States shall be the supreme law of the land. So far as foreign nations are concerned, the President therefore may, by treaty, set aside an act of Congress, provided two thirds of the Senate consent. True it is that Congress has power to lay taxes, duties, imposts, and excises, but a treaty is the supreme law of the land and must be obeyed by Congress as well as by the people. True it is that all bills for raising revenue must originate in the House of Representatives, and that the House might retaliate by withholding supplies. This would bring the Government to a stand, or, in the case of a treaty requiring an appropriation, prevent its full execution. But important commercial privileges may be and often are given to nations without the payment of money. True it is that the House might impeach the President, but, as the Senate tries impeachments, such a proceeding would be useless.

Discussion, having drifted from the question of fact to that of constitutional right, gradually died away, but the belief that the new President and his followers were planning an attack on the tariff in the interest of the South remained unshaken, and received yet further confirmation from the steadily growing excitement in the cotton States.

INDEX TO VOL. V.

(15)

END OF VOLUME V.